The Rule of Metaphor

Multi-disciplinary studies
of the creation of meaning
in language

PAUL RICOEUR

Translated by

ROBERT CZERNY
with Kathleen McLaughlin
and John Costello, SJ

ROUTLEDGE

London

First published in 1978
and first published as a paperback in 1986 by
Routledge & Kegan Paul plc
11 New Fetter Lane, London EC4P 4EE

Reprinted 1994 by
Routledge
11 New Fetter Lane, London EC4P 4EE

Translated from La métaphore vive
French edition © Éditions du Seuil, 1975
English translation © University of Toronto Press 1977

Printed in Great Britain by
TJ Press (Padstow) Ltd, Padstow, Cornwall

British Library Cataloguing in Publication Data

Ricoeur, Paul
   The rule of metaphor.
   1. Metaphor
   I. Title   II. Czerny, Rober   III. McLaughlin,
   Kathleen   IV. Costello, John
   808   PN228.M4

ISBN 0–415–10933–7

Contents

Translator's introduction vii

Introduction 3

STUDY 1 / BETWEEN RHETORIC AND POETICS: ARISTOTLE 9

1 Rhetoric and poetics 9
2 The intersection of the *Poetics* and the *Rhetoric*:
   '*Epiphora* of the name' 13
3 An enigma: metaphor and simile (*eikôn*) 24
4 The place of *lexis* in rhetoric 27
5 The place of *lexis* in poetics 35

STUDY 2 / THE DECLINE OF RHETORIC: TROPOLOGY 44

1 The rhetorical 'model' of tropology 44
2 Fontanier: the primacy of idea and of word 48
3 Trope and figure 52
4 Metonymy, synecdoche, metaphor 55
5 The family of metaphor 59
6 Forced metaphor and newly invented metaphor 62

STUDY 3 / METAPHOR AND THE SEMANTICS OF DISCOURSE 65

1 The debate between semantics and semiotics 66
2 Semantics and rhetoric of metaphor 76
3 Logical grammar and semantics 83
4 Literary criticism and semantics 90

STUDY 4 / METAPHOR AND THE SEMANTICS OF THE WORD 101

1 Monism of the sign and primacy of the word 101
2 Logic and linguistics of denomination 104

3 Metaphor as 'change of meaning' 110
4 Metaphor and the Saussurean postulates 120
5 Between sentence and word: the interplay of meaning 125

STUDY 5 / METAPHOR AND THE NEW RHETORIC 134

1 Deviation and rhetoric degree zero 138
2 The space of the figure 143
3 Deviation and reduction of deviation 149
4 The functioning of figures: 'semic' analysis 157

STUDY 6 / THE WORK OF RESEMBLANCE 173

1 Substitution and resemblance 173
2 The 'iconic' moment of metaphor 187
3 The case against resemblance 191
4 In defence of resemblance 193
5 Psycholingustics of metaphor 200
6 Icon and image 207

STUDY 7 / METAPHOR AND REFERENCE 216

1 The postulates of reference 216
2 The case against reference 221
3 A generalized theory of denotation 229
4 Model and metaphor 239
5 Towards the concept of 'metaphorical truth' 247

STUDY 8 / METAPHOR AND PHILOSOPHICAL DISCOURSE 257

1 Metaphor and the equivocalness of being: Aristotle 259
2 Metaphor and *analogia entis*: onto-theology 272
3 Meta-phor and meta-physics 280
4 The intersection of spheres of discourse 295
5 Ontological clarification of the postulate of reference 303

Appendix 315

Notes 323

Works cited 369

Index of authors 381

Translator's introduction

This translation was done from the author's manuscript. It diverges at several points from the first edition of La Métaphore vive (Éditions du Seuil, Paris 1975), where errors have been found in that edition, and where Professor Ricoeur has undertaken revisions.

In general, I have attempted to translate as literally as possible, in order not to obscure precise points of interpretation, but on the contrary to facilitate the interdisciplinary communication that Paul Ricoeur promotes. So too, to assist further study by readers restricted to English, I have used readily available translations of works originally in other languages wherever I could.

There are, of course, several exceptions to the pattern of literal translation. One exception is the title of the book. Uncomfortable with the more literal translations of La Métaphore vive that came to mind, I have offered The Rule of Metaphor because of its metaphorical suggestiveness. The primary reference is to Aristotle's assertion, quoted often by Ricoeur,[1] that 'the greatest thing by far is to be a master of metaphor. It is the one thing that cannot be learnt from others; and it is also a sign of genius, since a good metaphor implies an intuitive perception of the similarity in dissimilars.' And besides rule as mastery of metaphor, the reader will encounter the language rules that impinge on metaphor, and the domains of discourse in which metaphor holds sway. Perhaps this phrase will disclose other meanings as well.

Since many readers of The Rule of Metaphor may be unfamiliar with the development of Ricoeur's work, a broader overview than the author's own introduction is reprinted below as an appendix (pages 315-22). Although this address was given in May 1971, it is still relevant as a general introduction to Ricoeur's current work.[2] Nevertheless, it should be read with a few pointers in mind. First, etiquette demands that the many other authors to whom Ricoeur has turned appreciative and critical attention be assured that his list of citations was shortened and focused by the nature of the address and its locale, the University of Chicago. Second, Ricoeur might well present his orientations and projects differently now from six years ago. Third, Ricoeur does not allude here to his interests in the social sciences and political philosophy, and in many social issues.[3]

When first discussing this project with me, Professor Ricoeur requested that the final product read more like his own work than like that of someone else. If that and any other worthwhile standards have been met, it is due to his own great co-operation in checking the translation and answering specific queries; to Kathleen McLaughlin, who assisted in this checking and undertook the first draft of the translation of Study 8; and to John Costello, SJ, who corrected the entire translation. Many friends helped on particular sections; Michael Czerny, SJ, Geoffrey Williams, SJ, and Peter McCormick deserve special mention.

This book has been published with the help of a grant from the Humanities Research Council of Canada, using funds provided by the Canada Council, and with the help of the Publications Fund of the Universir of Toronto Press. The University of Toronto Research Fund supported the translation. The assistance of these institutions is gratefully acknowledged.

Besides the philosophical education it provided, I am thankful for the contribution of this experience to a coincident maturation over the past three years of my aesthetic and personal perspectives. The far greater debt, in all of this, is owed to my wife, Katharina.

Robert Czerny
Ottawa

THE RULE OF METAPHOR

Introduction

These eight Studies on metaphor grew out of a seminar course given at the University of Toronto in Autumn 1971, under the auspices of the Department of Comparative Literature. In this connection, I wish to express my very sincere thanks to Professor Cyrus Hamlin, who invited me to Toronto. These explorations progressed further during courses given subsequently at the University of Louvain, then at the University of Paris-X, within the framework of my Phenomenological Research Seminar, and finally at the University of Chicago, under the auspices of the John Nuveen professorship.

Each of these Studies develops one specific point of view and constitutes a complete whole. At the same time, each forms part of a unique path, which begins with classical rhetoric, passes through semiotics and semantics, and finally reaches hermeneutics. The progression from one discipline to the other corresponds to changes of the linguistic entity chosen for consideration: the word, the sentence, and then discourse.

The rhetoric of metaphor takes the *word* as its unit of reference. Metaphor, therefore, is classed among the single-word figures of speech and is defined as a trope of resemblance. As figure, metaphor constitutes a displacement and an extension of the meaning of words; its explanation is grounded in a theory of substitution.

The first two Studies correspond to this initial level. Study 1, 'Between Rhetoric and Poetics,' is devoted to Aristotle. It is he who actually defined metaphor for the entire subsequent history of Western thought, on the basis of a semantics that takes the word or the name as its basic unit. Furthermore, his analysis is situated at the crossroads of two disciplines – rhetoric and poetics – with distinct goals: 'persuasion' in oral discourse and the *mimêsis* of human action in tragic poetry. The meaning of this distinction is not developed until Study 7, where the heuristic function of poetic discourse is defined.

Study 2, 'The Decline of Rhetoric: Tropology,' is devoted to the last works on rhetoric in Europe, particularly in France. The work of Pierre Fontanier, *Les Figures du discours*, serves as the basis for discussion. Two principal points are to be demonstrated here. I wish to show, first of all, that rhetoric terminates in classification and taxonomy, to the extent that it focuses on the figures of *deviation*, or tropes, in which the meaning of a word departs from its lexically codified usage. Secondly, I wish to show that while a taxonomic viewpoint is adequate for a static account of figures, it fails to explain the production of meaning as such, of which deviation at the level of the word is only the effect.

The semantic and the rhetorical viewpoints do not begin to be differentiated until metaphor is transferred into the framework of the *sentence* and is treated not as a case of *deviant denomination*, but as a case of *impertinent predication*. The next three Studies belong to this second level of consideration.

Study 3, 'Metaphor and the Semantics of Discourse,' contains the decisive step of the analysis; it can, therefore, be considered the 'key' Study. Here a theory of the statement-metaphor and a theory of the word-metaphor are set provisionally in radical opposition. The confrontation is prepared by distinguishing (in the manner of the French linguist Émile Benveniste) between a semantics, where the sentence is the carrier of the minimum complete meaning, and a semiotics, where the word is treated as a sign in the lexical code. Corresponding to this distinction between semantics and semiotics I propose a parallel opposition between a tension theory and a substitution theory. The former theory applies to the production of metaphor within the sentence taken as a whole, the latter concerns the meaning effect at the level of the isolated word. The important contributions of three English-language authors – I.A. Richards, Max Black, and Monroe Beardsley – are discussed within this framework. I try first to show that the seemingly disparate points of view represented by each of them ('philosophy of rhetoric,' 'logical grammar,' 'aesthetics') can be arrayed together under the aegis of the semantics of the sentence introduced at the beginning of the Study. I then endeavour to delimit the problem that these authors leave unsolved: that of the creation of meaning, for which newly invented metaphors are the evidence. This question of semantic innovation will animate Studies 6 and 7.

Measured against the question that emerges at the end of Study 3, the fourth and fifth Studies may appear to move backwards. But their essential aim is to integrate the semantics of the word, which the preceding Study seemed to have eliminated, with the semantics of the sentence. The definition of metaphor as transposition of the name is actually not wrong.

It allows metaphor to be identified and to be classed among the tropes. Above all. the traditional rhetorical definition cannot be eliminated because the word remains the carrier of the effect of metaphorical meaning. It should be remembered in this connection that, in discourse, it is the word that assumes the function of semantic identity: and it is this identity that metaphor modifies. What is vital, then, is to show how metaphor, which is produced at the level of the statement as a whole, 'focuses' on the word.

This demonstration is limited in Study 4, 'Metaphor and Semantics of the Word,' to works in the tradition of Saussurean linguistics, especially those of Stephen Ullmann. By stopping at the threshold of structuralism properly speaking, I show that a linguistics that does not distinguish between semantics of the word and semantics of the sentence cannot but assign the phenomena of meaning-change to the history of word usage.

The fifth Study, 'Metaphor and the New Rhetoric,' carries this same demonstration into the framework of French structuralism. This deserves a separate analysis inasmuch as it has produced a 'new rhetoric' that applies the rules of segmentation, identification, and combination to figures of speech, rules that already have been applied with success to phonological and lexical entities. The discussion is introduced by a detailed examination of the notions of 'deviation' and 'rhetoric degree zero,' by a comparison of the notions of 'figure' and 'deviation,' and then by an analysis of the concept of 'reduction of deviation.' This extended preparation prefaces the examination of neo-rhetoric properly speaking, where extremely careful consideration is given to its effort at reconstructing the set of figures systematically on the basis of the operations that govern the atoms of meaning at the infra-linguistic level. The essential aim of the demonstration is to establish that the undeniable subtlety of the new rhetoric is completely exhausted in a theoretical framework that overlooks the specificity of the statement-metaphor and limits itself to confirming the primacy of the word-metaphor. Nevertheless, I try to show that the new rhetoric hints from within its limits at a theory of statement-metaphor, which it cannot elaborate given the resources of its system of thought.

The transition from the semantic level to the hermeneutical level is provided by Study 6, 'The Work of Resemblance,' which takes up the problem left unresolved at the end of the third Study, that of semantic innovation or creation of a new semantic pertinence. The notion of resemblance is itself reintroduced for further examination in order to solve this problem.

The first step is to refute the view (which Roman Jakobson still holds) that the fate of resemblance is linked indissolubly to that of a substitution theory. I try to show that resemblance is no less required in a tension theory, for the semantic innovation through which a previously unnoticed 'proximity' of two ideas is perceived despite their logical distance must in fact be related to the work of resemblance. 'To metaphorize well,' said Aristotle, 'implies an intuitive perception of the similarity in dissimilars.' Thus, resemblance itself must be understood as a tension between identity and difference in the predicative operation set in motion by semantic innovation. This analysis of the work of resemblance suggests in turn that the notions of 'productive imagination' and 'iconic function' must be reinterpreted. Indeed, imagination must cease being seen as a function of the image, in the quasi-sensorial sense of the word; it consists rather in 'seeing as ...' according to a Wittgensteinian expression – a power that is an aspect of the properly semantic operation consisting in seeing the similar in the dissimilar.

The passage to the *hermeneutic* point of view corresponds to the change of level that moves from the sentence to discourse properly speaking (poem, narrative, essay, etc.). A new problematic emerges in connection with this point of view: the issue is no longer the *form* of metaphor as a word-focused figure of speech, nor even just the *sense* of metaphor as a founding of a new semantic pertinence, but the *reference* of the metaphorical statement as the power to 'redescribe' reality. The most fundamental support of this transition from semantics to hermeneutics is to be found in the connection in all discourse between sense, which is its internal organization, and reference, which is its power to refer to a reality outside of language. Accordingly, metaphor presents itself as a strategy of discourse that, while preserving and developing the creative power of language, preserves and develops the *heuristic* power wielded by *fiction*.

But the possibility that metaphorical discourse says something about reality collides with the apparent constitution of poetic discourse, which seems to be essentially non-referential and centred on itself. To this non-referential conception of poetic discourse I oppose the idea that the suspension of literal reference is the condition for the release of a power of second-degree reference, which is properly poetic reference. Thus, to use an expression borrowed from Jakobson, one must not speak only of split sense but of 'split reference' as well.

This theory of metaphoric reference is supported by a generalized theory of denotation close to that of Nelson Goodman in *Language of Art*; and I justify the concept of 'fictional redescription' by means of the kinship established by Max Black, in *Models and Metaphors*, between the functioning of metaphor in the arts and that of models in the sciences. This relationship on the heuristic level constitutes the principal argument of this hermeneutics of metaphor.

This brings the work to its most important theme, namely, that metaphor is the rhetorical process by which discourse unleashes the power that
certain fictions have to redescribe reality. By linking fiction and redescription in this way, we restore the full depth of meaning to Aristotle's discovery in the *Poetics*, which was that the *poiêsis* of language arises out of the
connection between *muthos* and *mimêsis*.

From this conjunction of fiction and redescription I conclude that the
'place' of metaphor, its most intimate and ultimate abode, is neither the
name, nor the sentence, nor even discourse, but the copula of the verb *to
be*. The metaphorical 'is' at once signifies both 'is not' and 'is like.' If this
is really so, we are allowed to speak of metaphorical truth, but in an
equally 'tensive' sense of the word 'truth.'

This incursion into the problematic of reality and truth demands that
the philosophy implicit in the theory of metaphorical reference be eluci-
dated. The eighth and last Study, 'Metaphor and Philosophical Discourse,'
is a response to that demand.

This Study is essentially a plea for the plurality of modes of discourse
and for the independence of philosophical discourse in relation to the propositions of sense and reference of poetic discourse. No philosophy proceeds directly from poetry: this is shown through what appears to be the
most difficult case, that of Aristotelian and medieval analogy. Nor does
any philosophy proceed indirectly from poetry, even under cover of the
'dead' metaphor in which the collusion between meta-physical and metaphorical, denounced by Heidegger, could take place. The discourse that
attempts to *recover* the ontology implicit in the metaphorical statement is
a different discourse. In this sense, to *ground* what was called metaphorical
truth is also to *limit* poetic discourse. Poetic discourse is justified in this
manner within its own circumscription.

This, then, is how the work unfolds. It does not seek to replace rhetoric
with semantics and the latter with hermeneutics, and thus have one refute
the other, but rather seeks to justify each approach within the limits of the
corresponding discipline and to demonstrate the systmatic continuity of
viewpoints by following the progression from word to sentence and from
sentence to discourse.

The book is relatively long because it takes pains to examine the metho-
dologies proper to each point of view, to set out the detailed analyses belonging to each, and always to relate the limits of a theory to that of the
corresponding point of view. In this connection, it will be noted that the
book sets out and criticizes only those theories that at one and the same
time carry a viewpoint to its highest degree of expression and contribute
to the progress of the overall argument. Blistering refutations, then, will

not be found here – at most, a demonstration of the unilateral character of doctrines that proclaim themselves to be exclusive. With respect to their origins, some of the decisive doctrines are taken from English-language literature and some from the French. This is an expression of the double allegiance of my research as well as my teaching in recent years; and I hope by this to help reduce the mutual ignorance that persists among specialists in these two linguistic and cultural worlds. I propose to rectify the injustice this seems to do to German-language authors in another book on which I am working currently, which takes up the problem of hermeneutics in its full scope.

These Studies are dedicated to several of those with whom I sense a philosophical affinity, or who have welcomed me in the universities where the Studies took shape: Vianney Décarie, université de Montréal; Gérard Genette, École pratique des hautes études à Paris; Cyrus Hamlin, University of Toronto; Émile Benveniste, Collège de France; A.-J. Greimas, École pratique des hautes études à Paris; Mikel Dufrenne, université de Paris; Mircea Eliade, University of Chicago; and Jean Ladrière, université de Louvain.

Between rhetoric and poetics: Aristotle

For Vianney Décarie

1 / RHETORIC AND POETICS

The historical paradox of the problem of metaphor is that it reaches us via a discipline that died towards the middle of the nineteenth century, when it ceased to be part of the collegial *cursus studiorum*. This link between metaphor and a dead discipline is a source of great perplexity: does not the return of contemporary thinkers to the problem of metaphor commit them to the hopeless project of resurrecting rhetoric from its ashes?

Assuming for the present that such an undertaking is not entirely in vain, it seems appropriate to begin with Aristotle, since he is the one who first conceptualized the field of rhetoric.

A reading of Aristotle tells us that we must begin cautiously. First of all, a simple examination of the table of contents of Aristotle's *Rhetoric* shows that we have received the theory of figures of speech from a discipline that is not merely defunct but amputated as well. For Aristotle, rhetoric covers three areas. A theory of argumentation (*inventio*, the 'invention' of arguments and proofs) constitutes the principal axis of rhetoric and at the same time provides the decisive link between rhetoric and demonstrative logic and therefore with philosophy (this theory of argumentation by itself takes up two thirds of the treatise). Rhetoric also encompasses a theory of style (*elocutio*) and, finally, a theory of composition (*compositio*).

Compared to this, what the latest treatises on rhetoric offer us is, in G. Genette's fitting words, a 'restricted rhetoric,'[1] restricted first to a theory of style and then to the theory of tropes. The history of rhetoric is an ironic tale of diminishing returns.* This is one of the causes of the death

---

* 'L'histoire de la rhétorique, c'est l'histoire de la peau de chagrin.' Ricoeur is referring to the leather talisman in Balzac's *La Peau de chagrin*, which shrank each time it granted its possessor's wish. (Trans.)

of rhetoric: in reducing itself thus to one of its parts, rhetoric simultaneously lost the nexus that bound it through dialectic to philosophy; and once this link was lost, rhetoric became an erratic and futile discipline. Rhetoric died when the penchant for classifying figures of speech completely supplanted the philosophical sensibility that animated the vast empire of rhetoric, held its parts together, and tied the whole to the *organon* and to first philosophy.

This sense of irremediable loss increases all the more if we remember that the broad Aristotelian program itself represented the rationalization (if not reduction) of a discipline that in Syracuse, its birthplace, endeavoured to regulate all facets of public speech.[2] Because there was oratory [*éloquence*], public oratory, there was rhetoric. This remark implies a great deal. Originally, speech was a weapon, intended to influence people before the tribunal, in public assembly, or by eulogy and panegyric; a weapon called upon to gain victory in battles where the decision hung on the spoken word. Thus Nietzsche writes: 'Oratory is republican.' The old Sicilian definition 'Rhetoric is the master of persuasion' (*peithous dêmiurgos*)[3] reminds us that rhetoric was added to natural eloquence as a 'technique,' but that this technique is rooted in a spontaneous creativity. Throughout all the didactic treatises written in Sicily, then in Greece after Gorgias established himself in Athens, rhetoric was this *technê* that made discourse conscious of itself and made persuasion a distinct goal to be achieved by means of a specific strategy.

Thus, before taxonomy of figures of speech, there was Aristotle's far more embracing rhetoric; but even before the latter, there was undisciplined common speech [*l'usage sauvage de la parole*] and the wish to harness its dangerous power by means of a special technique. Aristotle's rhetoric is already a domesticated discipline, solidly bound to philosophy by the theory of argumentation, from which rhetoric, in its decline, severed itself.

Greek rhetoric did not just have a singularly larger program than modern rhetoric; from its relation to philosophy, it derived all the ambiguities of its position. The properly dramatic character of rhetorical activity is explained well by the 'savage' roots of rhetoric. The Aristotelian corpus presents us with just one possible equilibrium between such extreme tensions, an equilibrium that corresponds to the situation of a discipline that is no longer simply a weapon in the public arena but is not yet a mere botany of figures of speech.

Rhetoric is without doubt as old as philosophy; it is said that Empedocles 'invented' it.[4] Thus, rhetoric is philosophy's oldest enemy and its oldest ally. 'Its oldest enemy' because it is always possible for the art of 'saying it well' to lay aside all concern for 'speaking the truth.' The technique founded on knowledge of the factors that help to effect persuasion puts formidable power in the hands of anyone who masters it perfectly – the power to manipulate words apart from things, and to manipulate men by manipulating words. Perhaps we must recognize that the possibility of this split parallels the entire history of human discourse. Before becoming futile, rhetoric was dangerous. This is why Plato condemned it.[5] For him, rhetoric is to justice, the political virtue *par excellence*, what sophistry is to legislation; and these are, for the soul, what cooking in relation to medicine and cosmetics in relation to gymnastics are for the body – that is, arts of illusion and deception.[6] We must not lose sight of this condemnation of rhetoric, which sees it as belonging to the world of the lie, of the 'pseudo.' Metaphor will also have its enemies, who, giving it what one might call a 'cosmetic' as well as a 'culinary' interpretation, will look upon metaphor merely as simple decoration and as pure delectation. Every condemnation of metaphor as sophism shares in the condemnation of sophistry itself.

But philosophy was never in a position either to destroy rhetoric or to absorb it. Philosophy did not create the arenas – tribunal, political assembly, public contest – in which oratory holds sway, nor can philosophy undertake to suppress them. Philosophical discourse is itself just one discourse among others, and its claim to truth excludes it from the sphere of power. Thus, if it uses just the means that are properly its own, philosophy cannot break the ties between discourse and power.

One possibility remained open: to delimit the legitimate uses of forceful speech, to draw the line between use and abuse, and to establish philosophically the connections between the sphere of validity of rhetoric and that of philosophy. Aristotle's rhetoric constitutes the most brilliant of these attempts to institutionalize rhetoric from the point of view of philosophy.

The question that sets this project in motion is the following: what does it mean to persuade? What distinguishes persuasion from flattery, from seduction, from threat – that is to say, from the subtlest forms of violence? What does it mean, 'to influence through discourse'? To pose these questions is to decide that one cannot transform the arts of discourse into techniques without submitting them to a radical philosophical reflection outlining the concept of 'that which is persuasive' (*to pithanon*).[7]

A helpful solution was offered at this point by logic, one which, moreover, took up one of rhetoric's oldest intuitions. Since its beginnings, rhetoric had recognized in the term *to eikos*[8] ('the probable') a title to which the public use of speech could lay claim. The kind of proof appropriate to oratory is not the necessary but the probable, because the human affairs over which tribunals and assemblies deliberate and decide are not subject to the sort of necessity, of intellectual constraint, that geometry and first philosophy demand. So, rather than denounce *doxa* ('opinion') as inferior to *épistêmê* ('science'), philosophy can consider elaborating a theory of the probable, which would arm rhetoric against its characteristic abuses while separating it from sophistry and eristics. The great merit of Aristotle was in developing this link between the rhetorical concept of persuasion and the logical concept of the probable, and in constructing the whole edifice of a philosophy of rhetoric on this relationship.[9]

Thus, what we now read under the title of *Rhetoric* is the treatise containing the equilibrium between two opposed movements, one that inclines rhetoric to break away from philosophy, if not to replace it, and one that disposes philosophy to reinvent rhetoric as a system of second-order proofs. It is at this point, where the dangerous power of eloquence and the logic of probability meet, that we find a rhetoric that stands under the watchful eye of philosophy. It is this deep-seated conflict between reason and violence that the history of rhetoric has plunged into oblivion; emptied of its dynamism and drama, rhetoric is given over to playing with distinctions and classifications. The genius for taxonomy occupies the space deserted by the philosophy of rhetoric.

Hence, Greek rhetoric had not only a much broader program, but also a problematic decidedly more dramatic than the modern theory of figures of speech. It did not, however, cover all the usages of speech. The technique of 'saying it well' remained a partial discipline, bounded not only from above by philosophy, but laterally by other domains of discourse. One of the fields that remained outside rhetoric is poetics. This split between rhetoric and poetics is of particular interest to us, since for Aristotle metaphor belongs to both domains.

The duality of rhetoric and poetics reflects a duality in the use of speech as well as in the situations of speaking. We said that rhetoric originally was oratorical technique; its aim and that of oratory are identical, to know how to persuade. Now this function, however far-reaching, does not cover all the uses of speech. Poetics – the art of composing poems, principally tragic poems – as far as its function and its situation of speaking are concerned, does not depend on rhetoric, the art of defence, of deliberation, of blame, and of praise. Poetry is not oratory. Persuasion is not its aim; rather, it purges the feelings of pity and fear. Thus, poetry and oratory mark out two distinct universes of discourse. Metaphor, however, has a foot in each domain. With respect to structure, it can really consist in just one unique operation, the transfer of the meanings of words; but with respect to function, it follows the divergent destinies of oratory and tragedy. Metaphor will therefore have a unique *structure* but two *functions*: a rhetorical function and a poetic function.

This duality of function, which expresses the difference between the political world of eloquence and the poetic world of tragedy, represents a still more fundamental difference at the level of intention. This opposition has been concealed to a great extent for us, because rhetoric as we know it from the last modern treatises is amputated from its major part, the treatise on argumentation. Aristotle defines it as the art of inventing or finding proofs. Now poetry does not seek to prove anything at all: its project is mimetic; its aim (as will be elaborated later) is to compose an essential representation of human actions; its appropriate method is to speak the truth by means of fiction, fable, and tragic *muthos*. The triad of *poiêsis-mimêsis-catharsis*, which cannot possibly be confused with the triad *rhetoric-proof-persuasion*, characterizes the world of poetry in an exclusive manner.

Hence, it will be necessary to set the unique structure of metaphor first against the background of the mimetic arts, and then against that of the arts of persuasive proof. This duality of function and of intention is more radical than any distinction between poetry and prose; it constitutes the ultimate justification of this distinction.

2 / THE INTERSECTION OF THE *POETICS* AND THE *RHETORIC*: '*EPIPHORA* OF THE NAME'

We will bracket provisionally the problems posed by the double insertion of metaphor in the *Poetics* and the *Rhetoric*. To do so is justified by the fact that the *Rhetoric* – whether it was composed or only revised after the *Poetics* was written[10] – adopts, pure and simple, the well-known definition of metaphor given in the *Poetics*:[11] 'Metaphor consists in giving the thing a name that belongs to something else; the transference being either from genus to species, or from species to genus, or from species to species, or on grounds of analogy' (*Poetics* 1457 b 6-9).[12] Furthermore, in both works metaphor is placed under the same rubric of *lexis*, a word difficult to translate for reasons which will appear later;[13] for the present, I will say simply that the word has to do with the whole field of language-expression. In fact, the difference between the two treatises turns on the poetic function of *lexis* on the one hand, and on its rhetorical function on the other, not on the position of metaphor among the elements of *lexis*. Thus, in each case *lexis* is the means by which metaphor is inserted, albeit in different ways, into the two treatises under consideration.

What is the nature of the link between metaphor and *lexis* in the *Poetics*? Aristotle begins by rejecting an analysis of *lexis* that would be organized according to 'modes of speech [*élocution*]' (*ta skhêmata tês lexeôs*) and would link up with notions such as command, prayer, simple statement, threat, question, answer, etc. (1456 b 10). Hardly has this line of analysis been alluded to when it is interrupted by the remark: 'Let us pass over this, then, as appertaining to another art, and not to that of poetry' (1456 b 19). This other 'art' can only be rhetoric. Then another analysis of *lexis* is introduced, one that no longer has to do with *skhêmata* but with *mérê* ('parts,' 'constituants') of diction: 'Diction viewed as a whole is made up of the following parts: the Letter ... the Syllable, the Conjunction, the Article, the Noun, the Verb, the Case, and the Speech [*logos*]' (1456 b 20-1).

The difference between these two analyses is important for our purposes. The 'modes' of *élocution* are obviously facts of speech; in Austin's terminology, these are the illocutionary forms of speech. On the other hand, the 'parts of diction' arise from a segmentation of discourse into units smaller than or as long as the sentence, divisions that today would arise from a properly linguistic analysis.

What is the result, for a theory of metaphor, of this change of level? Essentially, it is that the term common to the enumeration of parts of speech and to the definition of metaphor is the *name* or *noun* (*onoma*). Thus the destiny of metaphor is sealed for centuries to come: henceforth it is connected to poetry and rhetoric, not at the level of discourse, but at the level of a segment of discourse, the name or noun. It remains to be seen whether, because of examples used, a latent theory of metaphor at the level of discourse might not cause the breakdown of the explicit theory of metaphor at the level of the noun.

Let us look more closely, therefore, at how the noun functions in these two contexts – in the enumeration of the parts of speech and in the definition of metaphor.

If one considers first the analysis of speech into 'parts,' it is clear that the name or noun is the pivot of the enumeration. It is defined as 'a composite significant sound not involving the idea of time, with parts which have no significance by themselves in it' (1457 a 10-11). Accordingly, it is the first of the entities enumerated to be endowed with signification; in modern parlance, it is the semantic unit. The four preceding parts of *lexis* are situated below the semantic level and are presupposed by the definition of the noun. In fact, the noun is first of all a complex sound, so one must first define the 'indivisible sound.' This is the first part of speech, the 'letter' (today we would say 'phoneme'); it belongs to 'metrics' (which now would be phonetics, or better, phonology). This pattern is repeated with the second part of speech, the syllable, which is first defined negatively in relation to the noun – 'A syllable is a nonsignificant composite sound [*asêmos*]' – then positively in relation to the letter – it is 'made up of a mute and a Letter having a sound' (1456 b 34-5). So, too, the conjunction and the article are 'non-significant sounds.' Thus, it is in opposition to the 'indivisible' sound (letter) and the 'semantically meaningless [*asémique*]' sound (syllable, article, conjunction) that the noun is defined as a 'composite significant sound.' Onto this semantic stem of diction the definition of metaphor as a transfer of the meanings of nouns or names will presently be grafted. This is why the key position of the noun in the theory of diction is of such decisive importance.

The definition of the 'parts' of speech following the noun confirms this position. This point deserves attentive examination, because these are the parts of speech that connect the noun to discourse and subsequently could displace the centre of gravity of the theory of metaphor from the noun to the sentence or discourse. The sixth part of *lexis* is the verb; it differs from the noun only in its relation to time (Aristotle's doctrine here agrees completely with that of his treatise *On Interpretation*).[14] The definitions of noun and verb have one part in common – 'composite significant sound' – and one part different – 'not involving the idea of time' and 'involving the idea of time.' Whereas the noun 'does not imply *when*,' the verb implies 'time present or time past' (1457 a 14-18). Would their definition in relation to time, negatively as regards the noun and positively for the verb, imply that the verb has priority over the noun, and thus the sentence over the word (since *onoma* signifies both noun in opposition to verb and word in opposition to sentence)? Not at all; the eighth and last part of *lexis* – the 'phrase [*locution*]' (*logos*)[15] – takes its definition from the 'composite significant sound,' which, as we have seen, defines the noun; to this is added 'some of the parts of which have a certain significance by themselves' (1457 a 23-4). So it is not only a composite sound but also a composite meaning. Two species are thus included: the *sentence*, which is a compound of noun and verb, according to the definition of the treatise *On Interpretation*;[16] and the *definition*, which is a combination of nouns.[17] Therefore, one cannot translate *logos* as *sentence* or *statement*, but only as *locution*, in order to cover the two domains of sentence and definition. Consequently, the sentence has no special status whatsoever in semantic theory. The word, as noun and as verb, remains the essential unit of *lexis*.

However, I have two reservations with respect to this rather harsh conclusion. In the first place, the *logos* itself comprises a unity that does not appear to be derived from that of the word – witness 'A Speech [sentence or phrase, *locution*] is said to be one in two ways, either as signifying one thing, or as a union of several speeches made into one by conjunction' (1457 a 28-9). The remark is interesting on two counts. On the one hand, the unity of meaning referred to as *logos* could serve as the basis of a theory of metaphor that would be less dependent on the noun; on the other hand, it is a combination of phrases that constitutes the unity of a work, for example the *Iliad*. Hence, one should add a theory of discourse to a theory of the word. But it must be admitted that this double consequence is not to be taken explicitly from the remark on the unity of signification provided by *logos*.

My second reservation is this: can one not take the expression 'composite significant sound' as descriptive of a semantic unit common to the noun, the verb, and the locution, and consequently deny that this expression captures the definitional core of the noun alone? By means of this expression, Aristotle would then have designated, beyond the difference between noun, verb, sentence, and definition, the carrier of the semantic function as such – let us say, the 'semantic kernel.' The modern reader certainly has the right to isolate this 'semantic kernel' and, by the same token, to initiate a purely internal critique of the privileged status of the noun. It is important for the theory of metaphor that its link to the noun can be cut in this way. As we shall see, some examples of metaphor, even Aristotle's examples, follow this direction. However, even in the broadest of interpretations, the 'composite significant sound' would at the most designate the word and not the sentence. This kernel, common to the noun and to other things besides the noun, cannot really designate specifically the unity of meaning of statements, since *logos* covers composites of nouns as well as verb-noun composites, i.e. definitions as well as sentences. Accordingly, it is wiser to leave in abeyance the question of that element, common to noun, verb, and *logos*, called 'composite significant sound.' Finally, by its analysis into 'parts,' the explicit theory of *lexis* aims at isolating, not the kernel of meaningfulness (which eventually proves to be common to many of these parts), but the parts themselves, and one among them in particular. The noun is the pivot.

As a matter of fact, the noun is spoken of immediately after the analysis of *lexis* into parts and just before the definition of metaphor: 'A Noun must always be either (1) the ordinary word for the thing (*kurion*), or (2) a strange word, or (3) a metaphor, or (4) an ornamental word, or (5) a coined word, or (6) a word lengthened out, or (7) curtailed, or (8) altered in form' (1457 b 1-3). This textual bridge explicitly joins the theory of metaphor to that of *lexis* by means of the noun.

Let us turn now to the definition of metaphor cited above. I will draw particular attention to the following features:

The first characteristic is that *metaphor is something that happens to the noun*. As has been repeated since the introduction, in connecting metaphor to noun or word and not to discourse Aristotle establishes the orientation of the history of metaphor vis-à-vis poetics and rhetoric for several centuries. Aristotle's definition contains *in nuce* the theory of tropes, or figures of speech that focus on the word. Certainly, confining metaphor among *word-focused figures of speech* will give rise to an extreme refinement in taxonomy. It will, however, carry a high price: it becomes impossible to recognize a certain homogeneous functioning that (as Roman Jakobson will show) ignores the difference between word and discourse and operates at all the strategic levels of language – words, sentences, discourse, texts, styles.[18]

The second characteristic is that *metaphor is defined in terms of movement*. The *epiphora* of a word is described as a sort of displacement, a movement 'from ... to ...' This notion of *epiphora* enlightens at the same time as it puzzles us. It tells us that, far from designating just one figure of speech among others such as synecdoche and metonymy (this is how we find metaphor taxonomized in the later rhetoric), for Aristotle the word *metaphor* applies to every transposition of terms.[19] Indeed, its analysis paves the way for a global reflection concerning *the figure as such*. In the interests of a clearer glossary one might regret that the same term sometimes designates the genus (the phenomenon of transposition, that is, the *figure as such*) and sometimes a species (what later we will call the *trope of resemblance*). This equivocation is interesting in itself. Within it is hidden an interest distinct from the one that governs the taxonomies and culminates in the genius for classification, eventually becoming bogged down in the disaggregation of discourse. It is an interest in the transpositional movement as such, in processes more than in classes. We can formulate this interest as follows: what does it mean to transpose the meaning of words? This question could be set into the semantic interpretation proposed above. Indeed, to the extent that the notion of 'composite significant sound' simultaneously covers the domains of noun, of verb, and of locution (thus of the sentence), one could say that *epiphora* is a process that concerns the semantic kernel, not just of the noun and verb but of all meaningful linguistic entities, and that this process designates change of meaning as such. Let us keep in mind this extension of the theory of metaphor, supported by the homogeneous character of *epiphora*, beyond the limits imposed by the noun.

The counterpart of its indivisibility of meaning is the perplexity caused by *epiphora*. To explain metaphor, Aristotle creates a metaphor, one borrowed from the realm of movement; *phora*, as we know, is a kind of change, namely change with respect to location.[20] But we are anticipating the subsequent theory in saying that the word *metaphor* itself is metaphorical because it is borrowed from an order other than that of language. With the later theory, we are supposing: (1) that metaphor is a borrowing; (2) that the borrowed meaning is opposed to the proper meaning, that is, to the meaning that 'really belongs' to a word by virtue of being its original meaning; (3) that one resorts to metaphor to fill a semantic void; and (4) that the borrowed word takes the place of the absent proper word where such exists. What follows will show that none of these diverse interpretations is implied by *epiphora* as it appears in Aristotle himself. At least, though, the vagueness of this metaphor about metaphor gives free scope to such interpretations.

Any wish to avoid prejudging the theory of metaphor by calling metaphor an *epiphora* would be shattered quickly by the realization that it is impossible to talk about metaphor non-metaphorically (in the sense implied by borrowing); in short, that the definition of metaphor returns on itself. Naturally, this warning applies to the subsequent pretension of rhetoric to the mastery and control of metaphor and of figures in general by means of classification – the word *figure* is itself obviously metaphorical. It takes in as well every philosophy that might wish to rid itself of metaphor in favour of non-metaphorical concepts. There is no non-metaphorical standpoint from which one could look upon metaphor, and all the other figures for that matter, as if they were a game played before one's eyes. In many respects, the continuation of this study will be a prolonged battle with this paradox.[21]

The third characteristic is that *metaphor is the transposition of a name* that Aristotle calls 'alien' (*allotrios*), that is, 'a name that belongs to something else' (1457 b 7), 'the alien name' (1457 b 31). This term is opposed to 'ordinary,' 'current' (*kurion*), which is defined by Aristotle as 'used by everybody,' 'in general use in a country' (1457 b 3). Metaphor accordingly is defined in terms of deviation (*para to kurion*, 1458 a 23; *para to eiôthos*, 1458 b 3); thus, as the enumeration quoted above indicates, the use of metaphor is close to the use of strange, ornamental, coined, lengthened, and shortened terms. In these characteristics of opposition or deviation and kinship are the seeds of important developments regarding rhetoric and metaphor:

(1) First, the choice of ordinary usage as point of reference foreshadows a general theory of 'deviations,' which becomes the criterion of stylistics for certain contemporary authors.[22] This character of deviation is emphasized by other synonyms given by Aristotle for *allotrios*: 'The perfection of Diction is for it to be at once clear and not mean. The clearest indeed is that made up of the ordinary words for things, but it is mean ... Diction becomes distinguished and non-prosaic by the use of unfamiliar terms [*xenikon*], i.e. strange words, metaphors, lengthened forms, and everything that deviates from the ordinary modes of speech [*para to kurion*]' (1458 a 18-23). In the same sense of deviation we have 'escapes banality' (*exallatousa to idiôtikon*, 1458 a 21). Hence all the other usages (rare words, neologisms, etc.) that metaphor approximates are themselves also deviations in relation to ordinary usage.

(2) Besides the negative idea of deviation, the word *allotrios* implies a positive idea, that of a *borrowing*. Herein lies the specific difference between metaphor and all the other *deviating* usages. This particular meaning of *allotrios* derives not only from its opposition to *kurios*, but also from its ties with *epiphora*. Thus, Ross translates, 'Metaphor consists in giving the thing a name that belongs to something else' (1457 b 7). The displaced meaning comes from somewhere else; it is always possible to specify the metaphor's place of origin, or of borrowing.

(3) Must one say that ordinary usage has to be 'proper,' in the sense of primitive, original, native,[23] in order for there to be deviation and borrowing? It is but one step from the idea of ordinary usage to that of proper meaning, a step that leads to the eventually customary opposition between *figurative* and *proper*. Later rhetoric takes this step, but there is no evidence that Aristotle took it.[24] That a name belongs properly, that is to say essentially, to an idea is not implied necessarily by the idea of current meaning; this is perfectly compatible with a conventionalism like that of Nelson Goodman, which we will talk about in due course.[25] The synonymy (referred to above) of 'current' (*kurion*) and 'usual' (*to eiôthos*), as also the proximity between 'clarity' and 'ordinary words' (1458 a 19), preserves the possibility of disconnecting the notion of ordinary usage from that of proper meaning.

(4) Another, contingent development of the notion of 'alien' usage is represented by the idea of *substitution*. We will see later that an *interaction* theory is readily contrasted with the *substitution* theory by English-language authors.[26] Now, the fact that the metaphorical term is borrowed from an alien domain does not imply that it substitutes for an ordinary word which one could have found in the same place. Nevertheless, it seems that Aristotle himself was confused on this point and thus provided grounds for the modern critiques of the rhetorical theory of metaphor. The metaphorical word takes the place of a non-metaphorical word that one could have used (on condition that it exists); so it is doubly alien, as a present but borrowed word and as substitute for an absent word. Although distinct, these two significations appear in constant association in rhetorical theory and in Aristotle himself. Thus, examples of the displacement of meaning quite often are treated as examples of substitution: Homer says of Ulysses that he performed '"ten thousand good deeds" ... *in place of* [*anti*] ... "a large number"' (1457 b 12) [emphasis added] ; similarly, if the cup is to Dionysus what the shield is to Ares, one could use the fourth term 'in place of' (*anti*) the second, and vice versa (1457 b 18). Does Aristotle mean that the presence of a borrowed metaphorical word is always linked to substitution for an absent, non-metaphorical word? If so, the deviation involved would always be one of substitution, and metaphor would dwell under the sign of poetic licence.[27]

Thus, the idea of substitution appears to be bound up firmly with that of borrowing; but the former does not proceed from the latter by necessity, since it admits of exceptions. On one occasion Aristotle cites the case in which no current word exists that could substitute for the metaphorical word. So, for example, the expression 'sowing around a god-created flame' is analysed according to the rules of metaphor of proportion (B is to A what D is to C) – the action of the sun is to its light what sowing is to grain (1457 b 25-30). But there is no name for the B term (at least in Greek; French has *darder*).* In this manner Aristotle points to one of metaphor's functions, which is to fill a semantic lacuna. This function supplements that of ornamentation in the later tradition. So, if Aristotle does not dwell on this point,[28] it is because he is interested here only in the analogy itself, and the absence of a word for one of the terms of the analogy, which could be supposed to jeopardize the analogy, he finds in fact does not prevent the analogy from functioning: 'It may be that some of the terms thus related have no special name of their own, but for all that they will be metaphorically described in just the same way' (1457 b 25-6). Nevertheless, we can keep this exception in mind in anticipation of a modern critique of the idea of substitution.

In conclusion, the Aristotelian idea of *allotrios* tends to assimilate three distinct ideas: the idea of a *deviation* from ordinary usage; the idea of *borrowing* from an original domain; and the idea of *substitution* for an absent but available ordinary word. By contrast, the opposition between figurative and proper meaning, omnipresent in the later tradition, is not implied here. It is the idea of substitution that appears to bear the greatest consequences: for if the metaphorical term is really a substituted term, it carries no new information, since the absent term (if one exists) can be brought back in; and if there is no information conveyed, then metaphor has only an ornamental, decorative value. These two consequences of a purely substitutive theory characterize the treatment of metaphor in classical rhetoric. Rejection of these consequences will follow rejection of the concept of substitution; and this is itself tied up with a rejection of displacement or movement of names.

The fourth feature of this definition of metaphor is this: at the same time as the idea of *epiphora*, preserving the unity of metaphor's meaning, counterbalances the classificatory tendency that predominates in the later taxonomies, *a typology of metaphor is outlined in the continuation of the definition*. We are told that the transfer goes from genus to species, from species to genus, from species to species, or is made by analogy (or propor-

---

*   And English the verb *beam* (Trans.)

tion). The outcome in subsequent rhetoric of the dismembering and count-
ing out of *epiphora*'s domain as sketched here is that metaphor becomes
nothing more than a figure related to the fourth type in Aristotle's list.
It alone refers explicitly to resemblance – the fourth term in analogy is related to the third in the same way (*omoiôs ekhei*, 1457 b 20) as the second
is related to the first; old age is related to life *as* evening is related to the
day. We will reserve for later the question whether the idea of an identity
or a similarity between the relationships exhausts the idea of resemblance,
and whether the transfer from genus to species, etc. is not also grounded
on resemblance.[29] What interests us now is the relationship between this
embryonic classification and the concept of transposition, which constitutes the unity of meaning of the genus 'metaphor.'

Two facts should be noted. First, transposition operates between logical
poles. Metaphor occurs in an order already constituted in terms of genus
and species, and in a game whose relation-rules – subordination, co-ordination, proportionality or equality of relationships – are already given. Second, metaphor consists in a violation of this order and this game. In giving
to a genus the name of a species, to the fourth term of the proportional relationship the name of the second term, and vice versa, one simultaneously
recognizes and transgresses the logical structure of language (1457 b
12-20). The *anti*, discussed earlier, applies not just to the substitution of
one word for another, but also to the jumbling of classification in cases
that do not have to do only with making up for lexical poverty. Aristotle
himself did not exploit this idea of a categorial transgression, which some
modern authors compare to Gilbert Ryle's concept of 'category mistake.'[30]
Doubtless this was because he was more interested, within the perspective
of his *Poetics*, in the semantic gain attached to the transference of names
than in the logical cost of the operation. The reverse side of the process,
however, is at least as interesting to describe as the obverse. If pursued, the
idea of categorial transgression holds not a few surprises in store.

I propose three interpretative hypotheses. First, in all metaphor one
might consider not only *the* word alone or *the* name alone, whose meaning
is displaced, but *the pair* of terms or relationships between which the
transposition operates – *from* genus *to* species, *from* species *to* genus, *from*
species *to* species, *from* the second *to* the fourth term (and vice versa) of a
proportional relationship. This has far-reaching implications. As the English-language authors put it, it always takes two ideas to make a metaphor.
If metaphor always involves a kind of mistake, if it involves taking one
thing for another by a sort of calculated error, then metaphor is essentially
a discursive phenomenon. To affect just one word, the metaphor has to
disturb a whole network by means of an aberrant attribution. At the same
time, the idea of categorial transgression allows us to fill out that of devia-

tion, which seemed to be implied in the transposition process. 'Deviation' appeared to belong to a purely lexical order, but now it is linked to a kind of deviance that threatens classification itself. What remains to be puzzled out is the relationship between the two sides of the phenomenon, between logical deviation and the production of meaning that Aristotle calls *epiphora*. This problem will be solved in a satisfactory manner only when the statement-character of metaphor is fully recognized. The name-related aspects of metaphor can then become fully attached to a discursive structure.[31] As we shall see later, Aristotle himself invites us to take this path when, in the *Rhetoric*, he takes up the obviously discursive metaphor of comparison (*eikôn*), or simile.

A second line of reflection seems to be suggested by the idea of categorical transgression, understood as a deviation in relation to a pre-existing logical order, as a dis-ordering in a scheme of classification. This transgression is interesting only because it creates meaning; as it is put in the *Rhetoric*, metaphor 'conveys learning and knowledge through the medium of the *genus*' (1410 b 13). What is being suggested, then, is this: should we not say that metaphor destroys an order only to invent a new one; and that the category-mistake is nothing but the complement of a logic of discovery? Max Black's integration of model and metaphor,[32] in other words of an epistemological concept and a poetic concept, allows us to exploit thoroughly this idea, which is completely opposed to any reduction of metaphor to a mere 'ornament.' Pushing this thought to the limit, one must say that metaphor bears information because it 'redescribes' reality. Thus, the category-mistake is the de-constructive intermediary phase between description and redescription. The seventh Study will be devoted to this heuristic function of metaphor. However, this cannot be brought to light without prior recognition not only of the statement-character of metaphor, but also of its place within the orders of discourse and of the work.

A third, more venturesome hypothesis arises on the fringe of the second. If metaphor belongs to an heuristic of thought, could we not imagine that the process that disturbs and displaces a certain logical order, a certain conceptual hierarchy, a certain classification scheme, is the same as that from which all classification proceeds? Certainly, the only functioning of language we are aware of operates within an already constituted order; metaphor does not produce a new order except by creating rifts in an old order. Nevertheless, could we not imagine that the order itself is born in the same way that it changes? Is there not, in Gadamer's terms,[33] a 'metaphoric' at work at the origin of logical thought, at the root of all classification? This is a more far-reaching hypothesis than the others, which presuppose an already constituted language within which metaphor operates. Not only is the notion of deviation linked to this presupposition, but also the opposition between 'ordinary' language and 'strange' or 'rare' language, which Aristotle himself introduced, as well as, most definitely, the opposition introduced later between 'proper' and 'figurative.' The idea of an initial metaphorical impulse destroys these oppositions between proper and figurative, ordinary and strange, order and transgression. It suggests the idea that order itself proceeds from the metaphorical constitution of semantic fields, which themselves give rise to genus and species.

Does this hypothesis go beyond the boundaries of Aristotle's analysis? Yes, if one focuses on the explicit definition of metaphor as the *epiphora* of the name and if one's criterion of *epiphora* is the obvious opposition between ordinary usage and unusual usage. No, if one takes into account all that appears in Aristotle's own analysis outside of this explicit definition and this explicit criterion. One of Aristotle's observations (held in reserve until now) seems to justify the boldness of this rather extreme hypothesis: 'It is a great thing, indeed, to make a proper use of the poetical forms, as also of compounds and strange words. But the greatest thing by far is to be a master of metaphor [literally: to be metaphorical, *to metaphorikon einai*]. It is the one thing that cannot be learnt from others; and it is also a sign of genius [*euphuias*], since a good metaphor [literally: to metaphorize well, *eu metapherein*] implies an intuitive perception of the similarity [*to to homoion theôrein*] in dissimilars' (*Poetics* 1459 a 3-8; see also *Rhetoric* 1412 a 10).

Several things are notable in this text. (a) Metaphor becomes a verb, 'metaphorize'; this brings to light the problem of usage (*khrêsthai*, 1459 a 5) – process prevails over result. (b) Next, the problem of use brings up that of 'appropriate' use (*prepontôs khrêsthai*). It is a question of 'metaphorizing well,' of 'using in an appropriate way' the processes of *lexis*. The same strokes depict the user of this usage: he is the one called to this 'greatest thing,' to 'be metaphorical'; he alone, unaided, can learn it or not learn it. (c) For – and this is precisely the point – to metaphorize well cannot be taught; it is a gift of genius, of nature (*euphuias to sêmeion estin*). Are we not now back at the level of finding or inventing, of that heuristic that we said violates an order only to create another, that dismantles only to redescribe? All of modern creativity theory confirms that there are no rules for invention, no recipes for the concoction of good hypotheses, only rules for the validation of hypotheses.[34] (d) But still, why can we not learn to 'be metaphorical'? Because to 'metaphorize well' is to 'see *resemblance*.' This phrasing may seem surprising. Up to this point resemblance has not been mentioned, except indirectly through the particular nature of the fourth sort of metaphor, that by analogy, which, as we have seen, is analysed as an identity or similarity of two relations. But are we not forced to suppose resemblance at work in all four kinds of metaphor, as the positive principle of which 'categorial transgression' is the negative side? Is it not necessary that genus and species be brought together in terms of similarity, for the name of either to be given to the other? Metaphor – or, better, to metaphorize, that is, the dynamic of metaphor – would rest, therefore, on the perception of resemblance. This brings us very close to our most extreme hypothesis, that the 'metaphoric' that transgresses the categorial order also begets it. But that the finding or discovering peculiar to this fundamental metaphoric is that of resemblance calls for its own particular proof, which cannot be presented until much later.[35]

3 / AN ENIGMA: METAPHOR AND SIMILE (*EIKÓN*)

The *Rhetoric* presents an enigma of minor proportions. The *Poetics* contains nothing about simile or comparison; why then does *Rhetoric* 3·4 introduce a parallel between metaphor and comparison (*eikôn*),[36] when it claims to add nothing to the definition of metaphor given in the *Poetics*? This is a minor problem if one is dealing only with purely historical questions of priority and dependence within the Aristotelian *corpus*. On the other hand, it is extremely instructive for a study like this one, which is at pains to assemble all indications of an interpretation of metaphor in terms of discourse as against its explicit definition in terms of names and naming. Indeed, the essential feature of comparison is its discursive character. 'Achilles sprang up like a lion.' To make a comparison, one needs two terms that are both equally present in the discourse – 'like a lion' is not a comparison by itself. Let us say (anticipating the terminology of I.A. Richards) that one needs a *tenor* (Achilles springs up) and a *vehicle* (like a lion).[37] We can discern the implicit presence of this discursive moment in the notion of *epiphora* (the transposition from one pole to another). It is as present in the categorial transference (giving the name of a species to the genus, etc.) as in the transfer by analogy (replacing the fourth term of a proportion with the second). The modern authors who say that to make a metaphor is to see two things in one[38] are faithful to this feature, which simile brings to light and which the definition of metaphor as *epiphora* of the name could conceal. While it is true in a formal sense that metaphor is a deviation in relation to the ordinary use of words, from the dynamic point of view it proceeds from the encounter between the thing to be named and that foreign entity from which the name is borrowed. Simile makes explicit this mutual approach that underlies borrowing and deviation.

It may be objected that Aristotle's express purpose here is not to explain metaphor by means of simile, but simile by metaphor. And, true enough, in six spots Aristotle subordinates simile to metaphor.[39] The fact that later rhetorical tradition does not follow Aristotle here makes this point all the more remarkable.[40]

Several converging lines of argument serve to subordinate simile to metaphor. First, the realm of phenomena that come under simile is split up. One part, called *parabolê*, is connected to the theory of 'proof,' to which book 1 of the *Rhetoric* is devoted. This consists in illustration through example, which can be historical or fictitious.[41] The other part, under the title *eikôn*, is attached to the theory of *lexis* and falls into the special domain of metaphor.

Let us further note that it is the special kinship between simile and the proportional metaphor that guarantees its place within the field of metaphor: 'Successful similes also, as has been said above, are in a sense metaphors, since they always involve two relations [literally: they are said or made on the basis of two] like the proportional metaphor. Thus: a shield, we say, is the "drinking-bowl of Ares," and a bow is the "chordless lyre" (1412 b 34-1413 a 2). Indeed, the proportional metaphor comes to give the name of the second term to the fourth by elision from the complex comparison that holds not between the things themselves but between the relations of the two pairs of things. In this sense, the proportional metaphor is not as simple as might appear when, for example, we call Achilles a lion. Therefore, the simplicity of simile, when contrasted with a proportion between four terms, is not the simplicity of a word but that of a relation between two terms[42] – that very relation, in fact, that proportional metaphor results in: 'The shield is the drinking-bowl of Ares.' In this manner, the metaphor by analogy tends to become identified with the *eikôn*; so the supremacy of metaphor over the *eikôn*, if not reversed, is in any case 'modified' (ibid.). But it is because *eikôn* 'always involves two relations'[43] – like metaphor by analogy – that the relation can be inverted so easily.

Lastly, the grammatical analysis of simile confirms its dependent status with regard to metaphor in general. They differ only by the presence or absence of a specific term of comparison: the particle *like* or *as* (*bôs*) in all the quotations in *Rhetoric* 3:4; in the example from Homer (whom Aristotle misquotes, incidentally), the verb (he compares) or adjective (similar) of comparison, etc.[44] In Aristotle's eyes, the absence of some term of comparison in metaphor does not imply that metaphor is an abbreviated simile, as was claimed from Quintilian onwards. Rather, simile is a metaphor developed further; the simile says 'this is *like* that,' whereas the metaphor says 'this *is* that.' Hence, to the extent that simile is a developed metaphor, all metaphor, not just proportional metaphor, is implicit comparison or simile.

Accordingly, the explicit subordination of simile to metaphor is possible only because the metaphor presents the polarity of the terms compared in an abridged form. 'When the poet says of Achilles that he "Leapt on the foe as a lion," this is a simile; when he says of him "the lion leapt," it is a metaphor – here, since both are courageous, [Homer] has transferred to Achilles the name of "lion"' (1406 b 20–3). Perhaps the best way to put it is that the element common to metaphor and simile is the assimilation that serves as foundation for the transfer of names. In other words, it is the apprehension of an identity within the difference between two terms. This apprehension of the genus by means of resemblance makes metaphor truly instructive: 'When the poet calls old age "a withered stalk," he conveys a new idea [literally: he has produced a knowledge] [*epoiêse mathêsin kai gnôsin*], a new fact, to us by means of the general notion [*dia tou genous*] of "lost bloom" ... ' (1410 b 13-15). And herein lies metaphor's superiority over simile, that it is more elegant (*asteïa*) (we will return later to metaphor's 'virtue' of urbanity, of brilliance): 'The simile, as has been said before, is a metaphor, differing from it only in the way it is put [*prothesei*]; and just because it is longer, it is less attractive. Besides, it does not say outright that "this" *is* "that," and therefore the hearer is less interested [*dzeteï*] in the idea. We see, then, that both speech and reasoning are lively in proportion as they make us seize a new idea promptly' (1410 b 17-21). Thus the chance to instruct and to provoke inquiry, contained in the abrupt subject-predicate confrontation, is lost by a too explicit comparison, which somehow dissipates that dynamism of comparison by including the comparative term. Beardsley's controversion theory[45] epitomizes the modern attempt to take the fullest possible advantage of this idea of semantic collision. And Aristotle saw that, underlying the *epiphora* of the alien name, a strange attribution operates: 'this is that' – an attribution whose grounds simile makes clear only by displaying them *in deliberate comparison*.

Herein lies the interest of the confrontation between metaphor and simile. At the very moment that Aristotle subordinates simile to metaphor, he sees within metaphor this paradoxical attribution. In the same vein, consider a suggestion made in passing in the *Poetics* and then abandoned: 'But a whole statement in such terms [deviations from ordinary modes of speech] will be either a riddle or a barbarism, a riddle, if made up of metaphors, a barbarism, if made up of strange words. The very nature indeed of a riddle is this, to describe a fact in an impossible combination of words (which cannot be done with the real names for things, but can be with their metaphorical substitutes)' (*Poetics* 1458 a 23-33). On the whole, then, this text tends to dissociate metaphor and enigma. But the problem would not even arise if they did not have a common feature, the common constitution that the *Rhetoric* always emphasizes under the heading of the 'virtue' of elegance, brilliance, urbanity: 'Liveliness is especially conveyed by metaphor, and by the further power of surprising the hearer; because the hearer expected something different, his acquisition of the new idea impresses him all the more ... Well-constructed riddles are attractive for the same reason; a new idea is conveyed, and there is metaphorical expression' (1412 a 18-24). We note once more the instructive and informative functions linked to a bringing-together of terms that first surprises, then bewilders, and finally uncovers a relationship hidden beneath the paradox.

But is not the proximity between enigma and metaphor founded completely on the odd name-giving, 'this (is) that,' that simile develops and depletes at the same time but that metaphor preserves by the brevity of its expression?[46] Deviation in the use of names proceeds from deviation in attribution itself – from what the Greeks call *para-doxa*, that is, a divergence from pre-existing *doxa* (1412 a 26).[47] All this is a very clear lesson for the theoretician, but it remains an enigma to the historian.[48]

In conclusion, this close juxtaposition of metaphor and simile allows the question of *epiphora* to be taken up again. First, as simile, the transfer takes place between two terms; it is a fact of discourse before being a fact of name-giving. One could say of *epiphora*, too, that it is something involving two things or terms. Furthermore, the transfer rests on a perceived resemblance that simile makes explicit by means of its characteristic terms of comparison. The closeness of metaphor to simile brings to language the relationship that operates in metaphor without being articulated, and confirms that the inspired art of metaphor always consists in the apprehension of resemblances. We shall say that simile explicitly displays the moment of resemblance that operates implicitly in metaphor. The poet, as we read in the *Poetics*, is one who 'perceives similarity' (1459 a 8). 'In philosophy also,' adds the *Rhetoric*, 'an acute mind will perceive resemblances in things far apart. Thus Archytas said that an arbitrator and an altar were the same, since the injured fly to both for refuge. Or you might say that an anchor and an overhead hook were the same, since both are in a way the same, only the one secures things from below and the other from above' (1412 a 10-15). To apprehend or perceive, to contemplate, to see similarity – such is metaphor's genius-stroke, which marks the poet, naturally enough, but also the philosopher. And this is what remains to be discussed in a theory of metaphor that will conjoin poetics and ontology.[49]

4 / THE PLACE OF *LEXIS* IN RHETORIC

The definition of metaphor common to the *Poetics* and the *Rhetoric* and the very important variant introduced by the latter work have been established. The principal remaining task is to appreciate the difference in function that results from the different ways in which *lexis* is inserted in the *Rhetoric* and in the *Poetics*.

We begin with the *Rhetoric*, whose place in the Aristotelian *corpus* is easier to determine. As was noted at the beginning of this study, Greek rhetoric had an impressively larger scope and a conspicuously more articulated internal organization than rhetoric in its dying days. As the art of persuasion, the aim of which was the mastery of public speech, rhetoric covered the three fields of argumentation, composition, and style. The reduction of all of these to the third part, and of that to a simple taxonomy of figures of speech, doubtless explains why rhetoric lost its link to logic and to philosophy itself, and why it became the erratic and futile discipline that died during the last century. With Aristotle we see rhetoric in its better days; it constitutes a distinct sphere of philosophy, in that the order of the 'persuasive' as such remains the object of a specific *techné*. Yet it is solidly bound to logic through the correlation between the concept of persuasion and that of the probable. In this way a philosophical rhetoric – that is, a rhetoric grounded in and watched over by philosophy itself – is constituted. Our subsequent task will be to display the intermediary links between the rhetorical theory of metaphor and such an enterprise.

Rhetoric's status as a distinct *techné* poses no great difficulties. Aristotle was careful to define what he calls *techné* in a classical text of his *Ethics*.[50] There are as many *technai* as there are creative activities. A *techné* is something more refined than a routine or an empirical practice and in spite of its focus on production, it contains a speculative element, namely a theoretical enquiry into the means applied to production. It is a method; and this feature brings it closer to theoretical knowledge than to routine. The idea that there is a technique for producing discourse can lead to the sort of taxonomical project that we will consider in the next Study. Now, is not such a project the ultimate stage of the technicization of discourse? Without doubt this is so; however, in Aristotle, the autonomy of *techné* is less important than its linkage with other disciplines of discourse, especially that of proof.

This linkage is assured by the connection between rhetoric and dialectic. With undeniable genius, Aristotle makes a statement right at the beginning of his work that keeps rhetoric under the sway of logic and, through logic, of philosophy as a whole: 'Rhetoric is the counterpart [*antistrophos*] of Dialectic' (1354 a 1). Dialectic here refers to the general theory of argumentation as regards that which is probable.[51] So we now have the problem of rhetoric posed in terms of logic. Aristotle, we know, is proud to have invented that demonstrative argument or proof called the 'syllogism.' Now, to this corresponds the probable argument in dialectic called 'enthymeme.' Rhetoric is thus a technique of proof: 'Only proofs have this character of technique' (1354 a 12). And because enthymemes are 'the substance of rhetorical persuasion' (ibid.), rhetoric as a whole must be centred on the persuasive power attached to this kind of proof. A rhetoric dealing only with those methods likely to sway the judge's passions would not really be a rhetoric at all: 'About the orator's proper modes of persuasion they have nothing to tell us; nothing, that is, about how to gain skill in enthymemes'; and a bit further, 'Rhetorical study [*techne*] is concerned with the modes of persuasion. Persuasion is clearly a sort of demonstration ... The orator's demonstration is an enthymeme ... The enthymeme is a sort of syllogism' (1354 b 21-2; 1355 a 4-8).

This does not mean that there is no distinction between rhetoric and dialectic. Certainly rhetoric resembles dialectic in a number of ways: it deals with 'popular truths,' the accepted opinions of the majority of people;[52] it does not require special training, since anyone can discuss an argument, accuse another, and defend himself (*Rhetoric* 1:1. par. 1). But in other ways they are different. First, rhetoric comes into play in concrete situations – the deliberations of a political assembly, judgment by a tribunal, public orations that praise and censure. These three sorts of situations that discourse takes place in define the three genres of rhetoric – deliberative, judicial, and epidichtic. Whereas ancient rhetoric before Aristotle concentrated on the second (there the ways to influence a judge stand out), a rhetoric based on the art of argumentative proof will pay attention to all situations in which it is necessary to arrive at a judgment (*krisis, Rhetoric* 1:1. 12). This leads to a second point of divergence: such an art has to do with judgments regarding individual situations.

In addition, rhetoric cannot become absorbed in a purely 'argumentative' or logical discipline, because it is directed to 'the hearer' (1404 a 4). It cannot avoid taking into account the speaker's character and the mood of his audience. In short, rhetoric is a phenomenon of the intersubjective and dialogical dimension of the public use of speech. As a result, the consideration of emotions, of passions, of habits, and of beliefs is still within the competence of rhetoric, even if it must not infringe upon the priority of argument based on probability. So an argument that can properly be called rhetorical takes into account both the degree to which the matter under discussion seems to be true and the persuasive effectiveness it has, which depends on the quality of the speaker and listener.

This feature brings us to a final point. Rhetoric cannot become an empty and formal technique, because it is linked to what is contained in the most highly probable opinions, that is, what is admitted or endorsed by the majority of people. Now with this connection between rhetoric and non-critical subject matter goes the risk of turning rhetoric into a sort of popular science. This collusion with *accepted ideas* throws rhetoric into a scattered and dissipating pursuit of argument-motifs or 'positions,' which amount to so many recipes to protect the speaker from being taken by surprise in debate[53] – a collusion, then, between *Rhetoric* and *Topics*, which was doubtless one of the causes of the former's death. Perhaps rhetoric finally died of an excess of formalism in the nineteenth century; paraodoxically, however, it was already doomed by its overburdening content – witness book 2 of the *Rhetoric*, which abounds in what Kant would have called 'popular' psychology, 'popular' morality, 'popular' politics. This tendency of rhetoric to identify with a sub-science of man poses a formidable question that could reflect back on rhetoric itself: does not the solidarity between rhetoric and topics, and beyond this, between rhetoric and a sub-science of man, imply that the inclination to speak in parables, comparisons, proverbs, and metaphors arises from this same complex of rhetoric and the commonplace? We must keep this question in mind. But before heralding the death of rhetoric, this alliance at least assures it a cultural content. Rhetoric does not develop in some empty space of pure thought, but in the give and take of common opinion. So metaphors and proverbs also draw from the storehouse of popular wisdom – at least, those of them that are 'established.' This qualification is important, because it is this topology of discourse that gives the rhetorical treatment of *lexis* and metaphor a background and an aftertaste different from those of the *Poetics*.

All these distinctive features are reflected in the Aristotelian definition of rhetoric – 'the faculty of observing in any given case the available means of persuasion' (1355 b 25, 1356 a 19-20). It is a theoretical discipline, but without determinate theme. Its measure is the (neutral) criterion of *pithanon*, of *'the persuasive as such.'* This adjective transformed into a noun remains faithful to the primordial intention of rhetoric, namely persuasion, but it expresses rhetoric's movement towards a technique of arguments or proof. In this regard the relationship (lost in French and English) between *pithanon* and *pisteis* is very instructive. In Greek, *pisteis* (in the plural), i.e. 'proofs,' marks the priority of objective argument over the intersubjective aims of the project of persuasion. And yet the initial notion of persuasion is not abolished; it is merely set aright. In particular, the orientation of argument to a listener – evidence that all discourse is addressed to someone – and its adherence to contents defined by the *topics*, keep 'the persuasive as such' from turning into a logic of probability. Thus, rhetoric will remain at most the *antistrophos* ('counterpart') of dialectic, but will not dissolve into it.

It is now possible to sketch a truly rhetorical theory of *lexis*, and consequently of metaphor, since metaphor is one of its elements.

Let us note right away that the rhetorical and poetic functions of metaphor do not coincide: 'The language [*lexis*] of prose is distinct from that of poetry' (1404 a 28).[54] Unfortunately, notes Aristotle, the theory of *lexis* is further ahead in poetry than in the field of public discourse.[55] He has to close the gap, if not fill a void. The task is not easy. We noted earlier that *argumentation, style,* and *composition* are the three parts of rhetoric. But since rhetoric really cannot be identified at all with the theory of style, which is just one of its parts, we might ask ourselves whether rhetoric does not have a privileged relationship with the 'discovery' (*eurêsis*) of arguments by the orator, i.e. with the first part (of rhetoric). Was it not claimed that everything that does not concern proof is 'merely accessory' (1354 a 14, 1354 b 17)? And does not book 3 confirm this privileged position in saying that 'we ought in fairness to fight our case with no help beyond the bare facts: nothing, therefore, should matter except the proof of those facts' (1404 a 4-6)? So, it seems, it is only because of the 'defects of our hearers' that we need to linger over these external considerations (1404 a 8).

No one denies that the link is weak between *lexis* and the rest of the Treatise, which is centred on argumentation. Nevertheless, we must not turn what is possibly just an accident in the composition of the Treatise into an absence of logical connection between *pisteis* and *lexis*. 'For it is not enough,' says Aristotle, 'to know *what* we ought to say; we must also say it *as* we ought; much help is thus afforded towards producing the right impression of a speech' (1403 b 15-18). It is the link between the way discourse *appears* and discourse itself that we must examine here, for in it germinates the future course of the idea of figure of speech.[56] The 'how' of discourse is distinct from the 'what.' Taking the same distinction up again later, Aristotle opposes 'how ... these facts [are] set out in language' to 'the facts themselves' (*ta pragmata*) (1403 b 18-20). Now this 'appearance' is not external to discourse in the same way as is simple 'delivery' (*hupokrisis*, 1403 b 21-35), which has to do only with the way the voice is used, as in tragic plays (in the same way the *Poetics* distinguishes *lexis* from mere staging). Rather, one must search in the area of an 'appearance' more intimately connected to the dynamics of persuasion and to argument, which was said to be 'the stuff of proof.' In this case, *lexis* would rather be one kind of manifestation of thinking, linked to any kind of instruction (*didaskalia*): 'The way in which a thing is said does affect its intelligibility [*pros to dêlôsai*]' (1404 a 9-10). When the proof itself is the only thing of importance, we do not bother about *lexis*; but as soon as the relationship to our hearer comes to the foreground, it is through our *lexis* that we teach.

So the theory of *lexis* seems bound to the thematic mainstream of the *Rhetoric* quite loosely, although not in as loose a manner as to that of the *Poetics*, which, as we shall see later, sums it up neatly as one 'part of tragedy,' i.e. of the poem. Now one might hypothesize that in poetry, the form or 'figure' and the meaning of a message are integrated to form a unity similar to that of a sculpture.[57] But in oratorical delivery, the manner in which something is said retains an extrinsic and variable character. One might even venture to say that eloquence, or the public use of speech, involves precisely this tendency, to dissociate style from proof. By the same token, the lack of consistency in the link between a treatise on argumentation and a treatise on style reveals something of the instability of rhetoric itself, torn apart by the internal contradiction within the very project of persuasion. Set between two limits exterior to it – logic and violence – rhetoric oscillates between its two constitutive poles – proof and persuasion. When persuasion frees itself from the concern for proof, it is carried away by the desire to seduce and to please; and style itself ceases to be the 'face [figure],' that expresses and reveals the body, and becomes an ornament, in the 'cosmetic' sense the word. But this possibility was written into the origins of the rhetorical project, and moved within the very heart of Aristotle's treatise. To the degree that style is the external manifestation of discourse, it tends to separate the concern to 'please' from that of 'arguing.' It is doubtless because writing constitutes a second degree of exteriorization that the separation is particularly dangerous in this case: 'Speeches of the written or literary kind owe more of their effect to their diction [lexis] than to their thought' (1404 a 18-19).

What, now, is the present status of the properly rhetorical features of metaphor? Do they throw any light on this manifestational function of lexis? Reversing the question, does lexis reflect in any way the internal contradictions of public speech?

Since rhetoric remains the art of 'saying things well,' its special features are those of good usage and are related to those of public discourse in general; and these last constitute what Aristotle calls the 'virtues' (the merits or 'excellences') of lexis. They guide what one might call the strategy of persuasion in public discourse. This idea of 'virtues of lexis' is so important that it provides the guiding thread for the analysis in book 3 of the Rhetoric. Among these virtues, those that concern metaphor most directly are 'clarity' (chapter 2), 'warmth' (opposed to 'coldness,' chapter 3), 'facility' (chapter 6), 'appropriateness' (chapter 7), and, above all, 'urbanity or elegance' (chapter 10).[58]

Clarity is obviously a touchstone for the use of metaphor. The expression that 'points out' (dêloi) something is clear. Now, it is the use of words in their ordinary fashion (ta kuria) that makes for clarity of style. In deviating[59] from ordinary usage, metaphor, together with all the other unusual expressions, also abandons clarity and makes 'the language appear more stately' (1404 b 9). In the eyes of ordinary citizens, it is as if they were confronted with a foreign (xenen) language (1404 b 10), for these variations and turns in language give discourse an out-of-the-ordinary air: 'People like what strikes them, and are struck by what is out of the way' (1404 b 12). Actually, these remarks are more appropriate to poetry than to prose, where nobility and dignity befit only the more extraordinary subjects and personalities: 'In prose passages they [effects that give an unfamiliar air] are far less often fitting because the subject-matter is less exalted' (1404 b 14-15). Therefore, the ways in which poetic and rhetorical language operate are the same, but the latter is more subdued. Keeping this caveat in mind, one can say that 'the chief merit of rhetorical discourse' is to give discourse an 'unfamiliar' air, while not doing so in an obvious manner. Thus, rhetorical style combines clarity, embellishment, and the unusual, all in due proportion.

The interplay between distance and close kinship, to which I alluded earlier in connection with relationships of type in metaphorical transposition, contributes to this air of the 'unusual,' which finds itself set against the demand for clarity. It also gives rise to the enigmatic character of good metaphors (1405 b 3-5).[60]

The second quality or 'virtue' is treated negatively.[61] *Rhetoric* 3:3 deals with stylistic 'frigidity.' Among its causes it notes the inappropriate, even ludicrous, use of poetic metaphors in prose – style too grandiose or tragic, metaphors too far-fetched and thus obscure (as when Gorgias talks of 'events that are green and full of sap') (1406 b 9-10). Prose must not be 'too much like poetry' (ibid.). What, then, shall be our criterion? Aristotle does not hesitate: 'All these expressions fail ... to carry the hearer with them' (*apithana*) (1406 b 14).[62]

The quality of 'appropriateness' (chapter 7) is another occasion for underlining the difference between prose and poetry. It is significant that this characteristic of the 'appropriateness' of style to its subject-matter is called 'proportion' (*to analagon*) by Aristotle. That which is appropriate for prose is not appropriate for poetry, because 'poetry ... is an inspired thing [*entheon*]' (1408 b 18).

But the most interesting remarks on the rhetorical use of metaphor are occasioned by reflections on the elegance and liveliness of expression (literally: urbane style, *asteion*, as opposed to popular or vulgar speech) (*Rhetoric* 3:10).[63] And it is in this context that Aristotle first speaks of the *instructive* value of metaphor. This quality really concerns the pleasure of understanding that follows surprise. For this is the function of metaphor, to instruct by suddenly combining elements that have not been put together before: 'We all naturally find it agreeable to get hold of new ideas easily: words express ideas, and therefore those words are the most agreeable that enable us to get hold of new ideas. Now strange words simply puzzle us; ordinary words convey only what we know already; it is from metaphor that we can best get hold of something fresh. When the poet calls old age "a withered stalk," he conveys a new idea, a new fact, to us by means of the general notion (*genous*) of "lost bloom" ...' (1410 b 10-15). Furthermore, Aristotle attributes the superiority of metaphor over simile to this same virtue of elegance. More concentrated and shorter than simile, metaphor astonishes and instructs rapidly. Here surprise, in conjunction with hiddenness, plays the decisive role.

To this same characteristic Aristotle attributes another feature of metaphor that has not appeared before, and that seems somewhat disconcerting at first glance. Metaphor, he says, 'sets the scene before our eyes' (1410 b 33). In other words, it gives that concrete colouration – imagistic style, figurative style it is called now – to our grasp of genus, of underlying similarity. It is true that Aristotle does not use the word *eikôn* at all in the sense in which, since Charles Sanders Peirce, we speak of the iconic aspect of metaphor. But the idea that metaphor depicts the abstract in concrete terms is already present. How does Aristotle connect this power of 'placing things before our eyes' to the feature of spiritedness, elegance, urbanity? By appealing to the characteristic of all metaphor, which is to point out or show, to 'make visible.' And this feature brings us to the heart of the problem of *lexis*, whose function, we said, is to 'make discourse appear to the senses.' 'To place things before the eyes,' then, is not an accessory function of metaphor, but the proper function of the figure of speech. Thus, the same metaphor can carry both the logical moment of proportionality and the sensible moment of figurativity. Aristotle enjoys combining these two seemingly contrasting moments: 'Liveliness is got by using the proportional type of metaphor and by being graphic [literally: making your hearers *see* things]' (1411 b 21). This is true of all the examples listed in 3:10 (1411 a 25-b 10). But, pre-eminently among all the others, the metaphor that displays the inanimate by means of the animate has this power of making relationships visible. Following Heidegger and Derrida,[64] one might be tempted to detect here some shameful traces of Platonism. Does not the invisible appear to us through the visible in virtue of the supposed resemblance of one to the other? Whatever the verdict on Platonism may be, if metaphysics is joined here to metaphor, it is truly Aristotle's metaphysics and not Plato's: 'By "making them see things" I mean using expressions that represent things as in a state of activity [*hosa energounta sêmainei*]' (1411 b 24-5). Showing inanimate things as animate is indeed not relating them to something invisible, but showing these things themselves *as if* in act.[65] Taking some remarkable expressions from Homer, Aristotle comments: 'In all these examples the things have the effect of being active [*energounta phainetai*] because they are made into living beings' (1412 a 3). Now in all these examples the power of making things

visible, alive, actual is inseparable from either a logical relation of proportion or a comparison (but as we already know, the backbone of simile with
its two terms is the same as that of the four-termed analogy). Thus one
and the same strategy of discourse puts into play the logical force of analogy and of comparison – the power to set things before the eyes, the
power to speak of the inanimate as if alive, ultimately the capacity to signify active reality.

The objection might arise now that the frontier between prose and
poetry has been erased. Is not Homer the author most frequently cited?
And is it not said of Homer that 'he represents everything as moving and
living; and activity is movement' (1412 a 8)? Might metaphor not be a
poetical process extended to prose?

This objection cannot be dealt with completely without returning to
Aristotle's *Poetics*.[66] Let us say provisionally that the difference lies not in
the process but in the end that is envisaged. That is why figure-filled and
enlivened presentation is treated in the same context as brevity, surprise,
hiddenness, enigma, antithesis. Liveliness of speech serves the same purpose as all of these: persuasion of one's hearers. This purpose remains the
distinguishing characteristic of rhetoric.

5 / THE PLACE OF *LEXIS* IN POETICS

Let us take up the other side of the problem of the inclusion of metaphor
in both rhetoric and poetry via the medium of *lexis*. What is poetic *lexis*?
In the course of my reply, I will connect the definition of metaphor, common to both treatises, with the distinct function that the project of the
Poetics gives it.

The definition of metaphor led us into a descent from *lexis* towards its
elements, and among these, to the *noun* or name, which is transposed by
metaphor. An inquiry into the function of metaphor now demands that
we rise above the level of *lexis* towards its conditions or terms.

The most immediate term is the poem itself – here Aristotle considers
the tragic poem specifically, or tragedy – seen as a whole: 'There are six
parts [*merê*] consequently of every tragedy, as a whole [that is] of such or
such quality, viz. a Fable or Plot (*muthos*), Characters (*êthê*), Diction
(*lexis*), Thought (*dianoia*), Spectacle (*opsis*) and Melody (*mélopoia*)' (1450
a 7-9). The plot is 'the combination [*sustasis*] of the incidents of the story'
(1450 a 15). The character is what confers coherence upon action, by a
sort of unique 'purpose' underlying the action (1450 b 7-9). The *lexis* is
'the composition of the verses' (1449 b 39). The thought is what a character says in arguing or justifying his actions (1450 a 7); thought is to action
what rhetoric and politics are to discourse (1450 b 5-6). Hence the thought

is the properly rhetorical aspect of the tragic poem (1456 a 34-6). Spectacle refers to the externally visible configuration (*cosmos*) (1449 b 33). Finally, melody is the 'greatest of the pleasurable accessories of tragedy' 1450 b 17).

In the same way, then, as the word was called a 'part' of *lexis*, in its turn *lexis* is a 'part' of tragedy. Once the poem itself is being considered, the strategic level changes. Though something that happens to words, metaphor, mediated by *lexis*, is attached to tragedy, or, as is said from the first lines on, to the 'poetry [*poiêsis*]of the tragic play' (1447 a 13).

Tragedy too is defined by one of its traits, 'the imitation of human action' (1448 a 1, 29). This will furnish a second-level condition for *lexis*. A later discussion will be devoted to the Aristotelian concept of *mimêsis*, which performs the same sort of guiding-concept function for poetry as *persuasion* does for prose in the public arena.

Staying now with the enumeration of the constituents of tragic poetry, we must, in order to understand the role of *lexis*, grasp how the relationships among all these elements are articulated. They form a network, as it were, in which everything centres on one dominant factor: the fable, the plot, the *muthos*. In fact, three factors together play an instrumental role: spectacle, melody, and *lexis* ('for these are, truly, the means used for imitation' [1449 b 33-4]). Two others, thought and character, are called the 'natural causes' of action (1450 a 1). Character gives action the coherence of purpose or valuation; and thought makes action coherent by arguing that its reasons are such-and-such. Everything links up within the factor called *muthos*, fable, plot. And here the sort of transposition of actions that Aristotle calls the *imitation of nobler actions* is achieved: 'Now the action [that which was done] is represented in the play by the Fable or Plot' (1450 a 3). So there is no longer just a means-end or natural cause-effect relationship between *muthos* and tragedy, but a link at the level of essence. This is why, from the first lines of the Treatise on, this inquiry is addressed to 'ways of composing plots' (1447 a 8). Thus, it is important for our purpose to have a keen sense of the proximity between the *muthos* of the tragic poem and the *lexis* of which metaphor is part.

The fundamental trait of *muthos* is its character of order, of organization, of arranging or grouping. This characteristic of order, in turn, enters into all the other factors: the arrangement of the spectacle, coherence of character, sequence of thoughts, and finally the ordering of the verses. Thus *muthos* is echoed in the discursive nature of action, character, and thought. Now it is essential that *lexis* also share in these traits of coherence – but how? Only once does Aristotle say that it originates *dia tês onomasias hermêneian* (1450 b 15), which I should like to translate as *language-istic interpretation* [*l'interprétation langagière*], and which Bywater renders as 'the expression of their thoughts in words.'[67] Here there is no issue of prose versus poetry; this interpretation or expression, says Aristotle, 'is practically the same thing with verse as with prose' (ibid. 16).

This *hermêneia* or interpretation is by no means exhausted in what Aristotle has just termed *dianoia*; this latter, nevertheless, already contains all the rhetorical features that add to plot and character – and consequently it already belongs to the order of language (it is rhetorical like 'everything [that is] to be effected [*paraskeuasthênai*] by ... language,' [1456 a 37]). What this ordering *in* language still lacks is the coming *into* language, the fact of having been made manifest, of *appearing* in spoken words: 'What, indeed, would be the good of the speaker, if things appeared in the required light even apart from anything he says?' (1456 b 8).[68] Drawing these three traits together – arrangement of the verses, interpretation by words, manifestation in language – we see the function of *lexis* taking shape as that which exteriorizes and makes explicit the internal order of *muthos*. We might even say that there is a relationship between the *muthos* of tragedy and its *lexis* like that between interior and exterior form. This, then, is how, within the tragic poem, *lexis* (of which metaphor is one part) is bonded to *muthos* and becomes, in turn, 'one part' of tragedy.

Our investigation turns now to the relationship between the *muthos* of the tragic poem and the function of *mimêsis*. One must admit that very few modern critiques speak favourably about the definition in terms of imitation that Aristotle gives for tragic and (secondarily) epic poetry. Most of them see in this concept the original sin of Aristotelian aesthetics, perhaps of all Greek aesthetics. Richard McKeon and, more recently, Leon Golden and O.B. Hardison have tried to clear up the misunderstandings obscuring the interpretation of the Aristotelian concept.[69] But perhaps our translators were hasty in choosing as the equivalent of the Greek *mimêsis* a term that we think we understand better than we really do. They chose 'imitation,' which turns out to be easily accused of a naturalistic tendency. It is only since the exclusively modern opposition between figurative and non-figurative art that, ineluctably, we are really approaching the Greek *mimêsis*.[70] Furthermore, this development should not be mistaken for some desperate project of mustering those characteristics of *mimêsis* that distinguish it from a simple copy of nature.[71]

Let us note, to begin with, that the concept of *mimêsis* is narrowed down remarkably in passing from Plato to Aristotle.[72] Its extension with Plato is boundless; it applies to all the arts, to realms of discourse, to institutions, to natural entities which are imitations of ideal models, and thus to the very principles of things. The dialectical method, understood in the broad sense as the procedure of dialogue, assigns determinations to the meaning of the word that are contextual for the most part, confronting the semanticist with a discouraging plethora of meanings. The only reliable guideline is the very general relationship between something that *is* and something that *resembles*, where the resemblance can be good or bad, real or apparent. The reference to ideal models merely allows the construction of a scale of resemblance, marking the degree to which this or that appearance approximates being. Thus, a painting could be described as 'imitation of imitation.'

Aristotle will have none of this. First of all, definition occurs at the beginning of scientific discourse, not as the outcome of dialectical usage. Words may have more than one meaning, but their use in science permits just one. And it is the division of the sciences that defines this normative usage. Consequently, one and only one literal meaning of *mimêsis* is allowed, that which delimits its use in the framework of the *poetical* sciences, as distinct from theoretical and practical sciences.[73] There is *mimêsis* only where there is a 'making [*faire*].' So there could not be imitation *in* nature since, as opposed to making, the principle of its motion is internal. Moreover, there could not be imitation of ideas, since making is always production of an individual thing; speaking of *muthos* and its unity of composition, Aristotle remarks that 'one imitation is always of one thing' (1451 a 30-5).

A possible objection is that the *Poetics* 'uses' the concept of imitation but does not 'define' it. This would be true if the only canonical definition were by means of *genus* and *differentia*. Now the *Poetics* defines imitation in a perfectly rigorous manner by enumerating its species (epic poetry, tragedy, comedy, dithyrambic poetry, compositions for flute and lyre), and then by relating this division into species to the division according to the 'means,' 'objects,' and 'modalities' of imitation. If one notes further that the 'function' of imitation is to afford pleasure (we still have to learn what sort), one may hazard the interpretation[74] that imitation is defined in full by just this structure, which corresponds, point by point, to the distinction between material, formal, efficient, and final cause.

This non-generic definition provides a fourfold structure so strong[75] that, in fact, it determines the distribution of the six 'parts' of tragedy. That is, three of them have to do with the object of imitation (*muthos, êthos, dianoia*), two others concern the means (*melos, lexis*), and the last the manner (*opsis*). What is more, *katharsis*, although not a 'part' as such, can be linked to the fourth dimension of imitation, the 'function,' as the tragic variant of the pleasure associated with imitation. Accordingly, *katharsis* would be less dependent on the spectator's psychology than on the intelligible composition of the tragedy.[76] Imitation is thus a 'process,' the process of 'forming each of the six parts of the tragedy,'[77] from plot through to spectacle.

We will concentrate, within this logical structure of imitation, on the two traits likely to interest our philosophy of the metaphor. The first of these traits really belongs to the role of *muthos* in poetic creation. As I said above, this is what *mimêsis* is. More precisely, it is the 'structure' of plot that constitutes *mimêsis*. Now this is quite a strange brand of imitation, which composes and constructs the very thing it imitates! Everything said about the 'whole and entire' character of myth, of the ordering of beginning, middle, and end, and in general of the unity and order of action (1451 a 28, b 23), helps distinguish imitation from all duplication of reality. We have also noted that, in various degrees, all the other constitutive elements of the tragic poem display the same character of composition, order, and unity. So, in different ways, they are all factors of *mimêsis*.

It is this function of ordering that allows us to say that poetry is 'more philosophic ... than history' (1451 b 5-6). History recounts what has happened, poetry what could have happened. History is based on the particular, poetry rises towards the universal: 'By a universal statement I mean one as to what such or such a kind of man will probably or necessarily say or do' (1451 b 9). And through this universal 'kind' of man, the spectator 'believes in the possible' (ibid. 16).[78] In this manner a tension is revealed at the very heart of *mimêsis*, between the submission to reality – to human action – and the creative action which is poetry as such: 'It is evident from the above that the poet must be more the poet of his stories or plots than of his verses, inasmuch as he is a poet by virtue of the imitative element in his work, and it is actions that he imitates' (1451 b 27-9).

Further, it is this ordering function that explains why the pleasure that imitation gives us would be a variety of the pleasure that man finds in learning. What pleases us in the poem is the sort of clarification, of total transparency, that the tragic composition achieves.[79]

Therefore, it is only through a grave misinterpretation that the Aristotelian *mimêsis* can be confused with imitation in the sense of copy. If *mimêsis* involves an initial reference to reality, this reference signifies nothing other than the very rule of nature over all production. But the creative dimension is inseparable from this referential movement. *Mimêsis* is *poiêsis*, and *poiêsis* is *mimêsis*. A dominant theme in the present research,[80] this paradox is of the utmost import; and it was anticipated by Aristotle's *mimêsis*, which holds together this closeness to human reality and the far-ranging flight of fable-making. This paradox cannot but concern the theory of metaphor. First, though, let us finish describing the concept of *mimêsis*.

The second trait of interest to this investigation is expressed in the following manner: in tragedy, as opposed to comedy, the imitation of human action is an imitation that magnifies, ennobles. This trait, even more than the preceding one, is the key to understanding the function of metaphor. Of comedy and tragedy Aristotle says that 'the one would make its personages worse [*kheirous*], and the other better [*beltiones*], than the men of the present day' (1448 a 17-18). (This theme is repeated several times, cf. 1448 b 24-7; 1449 a 31-3; 1449 b 9.) Thus, *muthos* is not just a rearrangement of human action into a more coherent form, but a structuring that elevates this action; so *mimêsis* preserves and represents that which is human, not just in its essential features, but in a way that makes it greater and nobler. There is thus a double tension proper to *mimêsis*: on the one hand, the imitation is at once a portrayal of human reality *and* an original creation; on the other, it is faithful to things as they are *and* it depicts them as higher and greater than they are. With these two traits combined, we return to metaphor.

Relocated on the foundations provided by *mimêsis*, metaphor ceases to be arbitrary and trivial. If considered simply as a fact or element of language, it could be taken for a mere deviation in relation to ordinary usage, alongside the rare word, the newly coined, the lengthened, abbreviated, and altered. But the subordination of *lexis* to *muthos* already puts metaphor at the service of 'saying,' of 'poetizing,' which takes place no longer at the level of the word but at the level of the poem as a whole. Then the subordination of *muthos* to *mimêsis* gives the stylistic process a global aim, comparable to rhetoric's intention to persuade. Considered formally, metaphor as a deviation represents nothing but a difference in meaning. Related to the imitation of our actions at their best, it takes part in the double tension that characterizes this imitation: submission to reality *and* fabulous invention, unaltering representation *and* ennobling elevation. This double tension constitutes the referential function of metaphor in poetry. Abstracted from this referential function, metaphor plays itself out in substitution and dissipates itself in ornamentation; allowed to run free, it loses itself in language games.

Let us go further. Within the bounds of this second trait of *mimêsis*, is it not possible to apply a still more closely fitting relationship between the elevation of meaning proper to tragic imitation and operating in the poem taken as a whole, and the displacement of meaning proper to metaphor and taking place on the level of the word? Aristotle has a few remarks on the proper use of metaphor in poetry,[81] which are an exact counterpart of the expressions we assembled under the title of 'virtues' of metaphor in rhetoric. They tend towards a de-ontology of poetic language, which is not unlike the teleology of *mimêsis* itself.

What does Aristotle say on this point? 'The perfection [virtue, *aretê*] of *lexis* is for it to be at once clear and not mean' (1458 a 18). What is meant here by clarity and meanness? A poetic composition that is at once clear and base is precisely one that employs only the most familiar vocabulary in its most common usage. Here, then, is the right place for deviation. Two strands meet here, the strange and the noble (*semnê*); and we cannot avoid pushing this connection further. If the 'strange' and the 'noble' meet in the 'good metaphor,' is it not because the nobility of such language befits the grandeur of the actions being depicted? Now I readily admit that this interpretation goes beyond Aristotle's intentions, but it is permissible in terms of his text and arose from my reading of it. In any case, if this interpretation is valid, we are forced to ask whether the secret of metaphor, as a displacement of meaning at the level of words, does not rest in the elevation of meaning at the level of *muthos*. And if this proposal is acceptable, then metaphor would not only be a deviation in relation to ordinary usage, but also, by means of this deviation, the privileged instrument in that upward motion of meaning promoted by *mimêsis*.

In this way we can discover a parallel between the elevation of meaning accomplished by *muthos* at the level of the poem, and the elevation of meaning by metaphor at the level of the word – a parallelism that really should be extended to *katharsis*, which one could consider an elevation of feeling like that of action and of language. Considered from a functional point of view, imitation constitutes a unitary whole in which mythic elevation, displacement of language by metaphor, and the purging of feelings of fear and pity work side by side.

It will be objected, however, that no exegesis of *mimêsis* based on its connection to *muthos* can suppress the important fact that *mimêsis* is *mimêsis phuseôs*. For it is untrue that *mimêsis* is the final concept attained in the climb towards the primary concepts of the *Poetics*. It would appear that the expression *imitation of nature* takes us out of the domain of the *Poetics* and into the *Metaphysics*.[82] Is the entire preceding analysis not subverted by restoring the connection between discursive creation and natural production? In the last analysis, does not linking the fullness of meaning to natural abundance render the deviation of metaphor useless and impossible?[83]

We will have to return, then, to the reference to nature, such a scandalous stumbling-block in an aesthetics that nevertheless wishes to make room for *muthos* and metaphor.

If it is true that imitation functions in the Aristotelian system as the differentiating characteristic that distinguishes the fine and the useful arts from nature, it follows that the function of the expression *imitation of nature* is as much to distinguish human making from natural production as to align them. The proposition that 'Art imitates nature' (*Physics* 2:2. 194 a 21-2; *Meteorology* 4:3. 381 b 6) introduces a discriminant as well as a connective element.[84] The precise meaning given by this thematic usage of the words cannot be outweighed by any simply operative usage, like that put into play by the different occurrences of the word *nature* or its cognates in the text of the *Poetics*.

It is because the aim of the expression *imitation of nature* is to distinguish the poetic from the natural that the reference to nature does not appear at all as a restriction on the composition of the poem. The poem imitates human actions 'either as they were or are, or as they are said or thought to be or to have been, or as they ought to be' (1460 b 7-11). An enormous range of possibilities is thus kept in play. On this basis one can understand how the same philosopher could have written '[The poet] is a poet by virtue of the imitative element in his work' (1451 b 28-9, 1447 b 1-5) *and* 'The action [that which is done] is represented in the play by the Fable or Plot' (1450 a 4). It is also because nature leaves space for the 'making' of imitation that human actions can be depicted as 'better' or 'worse,' according to whether the work is tragedy or comedy. Reality remains a reference, without ever becoming a restriction. Therefore, the work of art can be judged on purely intrinsic criteria, without any interference (*contra* Plato) from moral or political considerations, and above all, without the burdensome ontological concern for *fitting the appearance to the real*. In renouncing that Platonic use of *mimêsis* that allowed even the things of nature to be taken as imitations of eternal models and allowed a painting to be called imitation of imitation, Aristotle undertakes not to use the concept of imitation of nature except within the limits of a science of poetic composition that has won its full autonomy. It is in the composition of the fable or plot that the reference to human action, which is in this case the nature being imitated, must become apparent.

In ending, I would like to venture a last argument that goes beyond the resources of a semantics applied to the words of a philosopher of the past, an argument that puts into play his meaning reactivated in a contemporary context and therefore arises from a hermeneutic. The argument concerns this very term *phusis*, the ultimate reference of *mimêsis*.

We believe that we understand *phusis* when we translate it by *nature*. But is not the word *nature* as far off the mark with respect to *phusis* as is the word *imitation* concerning *mimêsis*? Certainly Greek man was far less quick than we are to identify *phusis* with some inert 'given.' Perhaps it is because, for him, nature is itself living that *mimêsis* can be not enslaving and that compositional and creative imitation of nature can be possible. Is this not what the most enigmatic passage of the *Rhetoric* suggests? Metaphor, it relates, makes one *see things* because it 'represents things as in a state of activity' (1411 b 24-5). The *Poetics* echoes that one may 'speak in narrative' or present 'personages as acting [*hôs prattontas*] and doing [*energountas*]' 1448 a 22, 28). Might there not be an underlying relationship between 'signifying active reality' and speaking out *phusis*?

If this hypothesis is valid, it can be understood why no *Poetics* can truly ever have done either with *mimêsis* or with *phusis*. In the last analysis, the concept of *mimêsis* serves as an index of the discourse situation; it reminds us that no discourse ever suspends our belonging to a world. All *mimêsis*, even creative – nay, *especially* creative – *mimêsis*, takes place within the horizons of a being-in-the-world which it makes present to the precise extent that the *mimêsis* raises it to the level of *muthos*. The truth of imagination, poetry's power to make contact with being as such – this is what I personally see in Aristotle's *mimêsis*. *Lexis* is rooted in *mimêsis*, and through *mimêsis* metaphor's deviations from normal *lexis* belong to the great enterprise of 'saying what is.'

But *mimêsis* does not signify only that all discourse *is* of the world; it does not embody just the *referential* function of poetic discourse. Being *mimêsis phuseôs*, it connects this referential function to the revelation of the Real as Act. This is the function of the concept of *phusis* in the expression *mimêsis phuseôs*, to serve as an *index* for that dimension of reality that does not receive due account in the simple description of that-thing-over-there. To present men '*as acting*' and all things '*as in act*' – such could well be the *ontological* function of metaphorical discourse, in which every dormant potentiality of existence appears *as* blossoming forth, every latent capacity for action *as* actualized.[85]

Lively expression is that which expresses existence as *alive*.

The decline of rhetoric: tropology

For Gérard Genette

The guiding thread of this work passes from rhetoric to semantics and from semantics to hermeneutics. The present Study deals with the passage from the first to the second. We hypothesized in the introduction, and will now try to prove, that a purely rhetorical treatment of metaphor is the result of the excessive and damaging emphasis put initially on the word, or, more specifically, on the noun or name, and on naming, in the theory of meaning; whereas a properly semantic treatment of metaphor proceeds from the recognition of the sentence as the primary unit of meaning. The first orientation makes metaphor a trope, that is, a change or deviation affecting the meaning of a word. In the second case, it is a phenomenon of predication, an unusual attribution precisely at the sentence-level of discourse (we will see whether, and to what extent, one can still speak of deviation at this level of analysis).

This change of approach could be accomplished by means of a direct analysis, which, bypassing the rhetoric of tropes, would be applied straight away on the level of propositional logic; in fact, this is the usual tactic of English-language authors since I.A. Richards. Instead, we have chosen the longer route of an indirect proof that argues basically from the failure of rhetoric on the wane. This gives us, in effect, a proof *a contrario* of the need to back up the theory of metaphor with that of discourse as sentence. We will pursue this path by examining one of the last treatises of rhetoric, *Les Figures du discours* by Pierre Fontanier.

1 / THE RHETORICAL 'MODEL' OF TROPOLOGY

Our hypothesis leads us to give an explanation of the decline of rhetoric which is palpably different from the one given by certain new-rhetoric theorists of structuralistic bent. They[1] give as its cause the progressive reduction of the domain of rhetoric, which we described above.[2] Indeed, since the Greeks, rhetoric diminished bit by bit to a theory of *style* by cutting itself off from the two parts that generated it, the theories of *argumentation* and of *composition*. Then, in turn, the theory of style shrank to a classification of figures of speech, and this to a theory of tropes. Tropology itself now paid attention only to the complex made up of metaphor and metonymy, at the price of reducing the first to resemblance and the second to contiguity.

This explanation, which is also a critique, aims at clearing the way for a new rhetoric, which would first reopen the rhetorical regions that had been progressively closed. Such a project would be opposed to the dictatorial position of metaphor. Nevertheless, it would not be any the less faithful to the taxonomical ideals of classical rhetoric; it would only pay greater attention to the multiplicity of figures. Its slogan could be 'Yes, figures of speech – but all of them!'

As I see it, the reduction of the domain of rhetoric is not the decisive factor. This is not to deny that an extremely significant cultural phenomenon is involved, and that we are warned thereby against overrating metaphor. But even this warning cannot be put to good use, unless one lays bare a deeper root that the neo-rhetoricians might not be prepared to recognize. The problem is not to restore the original domain of rhetoric – in any case, this may be beyond doing, for ineluctable cultural reasons – rather, it is to understand in a new way the very workings of tropes, and, based on this, eventually to restate in new terms the question of the aim and purpose of rhetoric.

The decline of rhetoric results from an error that affects the theory of tropes directly, independently of the place given to it within the field of rhetoric. This initial error has to do with the tyranny of the word in the theory of meaning. We now glimpse only the most distant effects of this error: the reduction of metaphor to a mere ornament. A whole series of postulates is at work between the point of departure – the primacy of the word – and the final outcome – metaphor as ornament. Step by step, they bring together the initial theory of meaning, whose axis is naming, and a purely ornamental theory of tropes, which finally proclaims the futility of a discipline that Plato had long before placed among the 'cosmetic arts.'

This series of postulates can be made explicit as follows; taken together, they constitute the implicit model of tropology.

(a) Certain names belong properly to certain kinds (genera and species) of things; the meaning of these terms can be called 'proper meaning.' By contrast, metaphor and the other tropes are improper or figurative meanings. This is the postulate of 'the proper versus the improper or figurative.'

(b) Certain sorts of things are called by an improper term, instead of the applicable proper word being used. This absence of the proper word in actual discourse may result from a stylistic choice or from some real lack. In either case, recourse to an improper term has as its purpose the filling of a semantic or, better, a lexical lacuna, in the actual message or in the code. Thus, the postulate of 'semantic lacuna.'

(c) The lexical lacuna is filled by borrowing an alien term – the postulate of 'borrowing.'

(d) The price paid for applying the borrowed term to the sort of thing being considered is the divergence between the improper or figurative meaning of the borrowed word and its proper meaning – the postulate of 'deviation.'

(e) The borrowed term, taken in its figurative sense, is substituted for an absent word (which is lacking, or which one does not wish to use) that, in its proper meaning, could be used in that place. This substitution is a matter of preference; one is not forced into it, when the proper word exists. In that case we speak of trope in its strict sense. When the substitution corresponds to a real gap in vocabulary, when it is forced, one speaks of catachresis. This gives us the 'axiom of substitution.'

(f) Between the figurative sense of the borrowed word and the proper meaning of the absent word, there exists a relationship that can be called the 'reason' (in the sense of rationale or basis) for the transposition. This reason constitutes a paradigm for the substitution of terms. In the case of metaphor, the paradigmatic structure is that of resemblance. This is the postulate of 'the paradigmatic character of the trope.'[3]

(g) To explain (or understand) a trope is to be guided by the trope's 'reason,' that is, the paradigm of substitution, in finding the absent proper word; thus, it is to restore the proper term for which an improper term had been substituted. In principle the restitutive paraphrase is exhaustive, so the algebraic sum of substitution and subsequent restitution is zero. Here we have the postulate of 'exhaustive paraphrase.'

Two last postulates, which characterize the properly rhetorical treatment of metaphor and of tropes in general, result from this chain of presuppositions:

(h) The figurative use of words does not provide any new information. This postulate is part and parcel of the preceding one: if restitution annuls the substitution, if an exhaustive paraphrase of the metaphor (and of tropes in general) can be given, then the metaphor says nothing new. Thus, the postulate of 'no new information.'

(i) The trope, teaching us nothing, has a merely decorative function. Its fate is to please by serving as the ornament of language, in giving 'colour' to discourse, in 'clothing' the naked expression of thought.

Such is the chain of presuppositions implicit in the purely rhetorical treatment of metaphor. There is no break between the point of departure, which makes metaphor an accident in naming, and the conclusion, which gives metaphor a simply ornamental function and confines rhetoric as a whole to the art of pleasing. These two assertions, that metaphor teaches or says nothing new and serves only to ornament language, proceed step by step from the initial decision to treat metaphor as an unusual way of naming things.

Aristotle's analysis viewed in this light seems to anticipate this model. Now this is not to say that Aristotle can be accused of having reduced the fuller scope of rhetoric to a theory of style, much less to a theory of figures of speech, nor that the vitality of his analysis is dissipated in purely taxonomical exercises. The four species that he distinguished are still species of metaphor, and metaphor itself has no counterpart, is opposed to no other figure. As for the distinction between metaphor and simile, his analysis is completely reductive, and the reduction is finally in metaphor's favour. If, then, Aristotle is the father of this model, it is not at all because of his definition of the field of rhetoric, and thus of the place of *lexis* in it, but solely because of the central position accorded the noun in the enumeration of the parts of *lexis* and the reference to noun in the definition of metaphor. This is why the Aristotelian theory of metaphor abounds in allusions that apply more or less directly to this or that postulate in our sequence above: the opposition between the 'ordinary' word and the 'strange' word, and the deviating character of the second when compared with the first; the transfer of the meaning of the 'borrowed' word to the thing to be named; the 'substitution' of one word for another that could have been used in the same place; the possibility of 'restoring' this other word; the ornate character of metaphorical style; and the pleasure one takes in this style.

It is true that there are other features of Aristotle's description which resist reduction to the model under consideration. But these features in no way recall, at the heart of the theory of *lexis*, the original extension of rhetoric; they point more towards a discursive, and no longer to a nominalistic, theory of metaphor. Let us recall some of these traits: first, the close connection between metaphor and simile – in which metaphor is the more important of the two only because it contains, in summary form, the attribution (Achilles is a lion) that simile spells out as if in a logical argument (Achilles is like a lion). The difference between metaphor and comparison or simile, therefore, is the difference between two forms of predication: 'to be' and 'to be like.' This is why metaphor is the more powerful: the direct attribution causes surprise, whereas simile dissipates this surprise. At the same time, the operation that consists in giving one thing's name to another reveals how closely related it is to the predicative operation. It is not just the proportional metaphor that is so akin to simile, but all the species of metaphor, by virtue of the polarity between two terms that the other three kinds of metaphor also presuppose. How, indeed, is one to give the name of the species to the genus, if the metaphor does not 'say' two things, the thing that lends its name and the thing that receives it? Accordingly, the *epiphora* of metaphor does not seem to exhaust its meaning in the notions of borrowing, of deviation, and of substitution. To the extent that it seems enigmatic, metaphor invokes a 'tension' theory more than a theory of substitution. This is certainly why Aristotle claims in addition that metaphor 'teaches through the genus'; this declaration undercuts the last two postulates that round out the rhetorical model.

Thus, even while being the originator of the model that will hold sway in the last days of rhetoric, Aristotle also provides some of the arguments that will put it in check. However, this is not because his rhetoric covers a greater area than a theory of diction, but because *lexis*, whose explicit centre is the noun, rests implicitly on a predicative operation.

2 / FONTANIER: THE PRIMACY OF IDEA AND OF WORD

Pierre Fontanier's treatise *Les Figures du discours* (1830) comes as close as any to the rhetorical model that we sketched systematically. It affirms unambiguously the pre-eminence of the word. This primacy is assured by the analytical method (related to the method of ideology, if not borrowed from it) which, before being applied to figures, is applied to 'the basic elements of thought and of expression: ideas and words' ('Preliminary Notions' 39). This is the place to begin, because the definition of trope is constructed on that of the idea-word pair: 'Tropes are *certain meanings more or less different from the primitive meaning, which words, when applied to new ideas, evince in the course of the expression of thought*' (ibid.). At the heart of the coupled terms 'idea-word,' idea is in the governing position: 'Thought is made up of ideas, and the expression of thought by speech is made up of words. Let us see, then, what ideas are in themselves ...' (41). So it is the primacy of idea that guarantees that of the word. Thus, rhetoric depends upon some extra-linguistic theory, an 'ideology' in the proper sense of the term [i.e., 'idea-logy'], that secures the passage from idea to word.[4]

Let us review the elements of this 'ideology,' thus set as a foundation beneath the theory of word and, by extension, the theory of tropes. Ideas are 'the objects which our mind sees' (41). All the distinctions between ideas are formed in relation to this direct vision: complex, simple ('none are truly simple except those that resist analysis' [42]), concrete, individual, and general ideas. This is also true of the way in which they 'link up, one to the other, and form chains in our minds, in a manner to form groupings there on the basis of association, by collection, or in other diverse ways' (43). The distinction between principal and secondary or accessory ideas is founded on these 'chains.' The principle of a grammar is contained here: before introducing the 'substantive,' one can define by itself the substantive idea (or idea of a substance); that is, 'If an idea relates immediately to such a given particular object that exists as a substance, it is an *individual* idea' (42). Before speaking of adjectives, one can likewise define the concrete idea, that is, the idea that 'points out some quality, action, or passion in the object of a complex idea' (ibid.). Finally, one must look among the accessory ideas for the ideas of relationship or circumstance that 'we can make known only through words, which are their signs' (44).

It follows that everything that can be said concerning words is the result of their 'correspondence with ideas' (44). To talk about ideas and about words is to talk twice about ideas: once about 'ideas in themselves,' and the second time about ideas as 'represented by words' (41).

The list of species of words, therefore, will reflect that of the kinds of ideas. Two broad classes of words are distinguished: signs for ideas of objects, and signs for ideas of relationship. Noun, adjective, participle, article, and pronoun belong to the first class. Nouns correspond to ideas of substances; and they are divided further into the proper noun, corresponding to an individual idea, and the common noun, which corresponds to general ideas. Adjectives correspond to concrete ideas of quality, and participles to concrete ideas of action, of passion, or of state of being. Articles define the extension of nouns, while pronouns take the place of nouns.

The second class is made up of the verb, preposition, adverb, and conjunction. Here, *verb* means just the verb *to be*; actual verbs are formed by combining the verb *to be* with a participle (I read, I am reading). The verb *to be* points to the coexistence of some idea of substance and a concrete idea, corresponding to a participle or an adjective. By dealing with the verb in this fashion, under the heading of 'ideas of relationship.' Fontanier not only brings the verb into the idea-word theory, that is, a theory of the elements of thought and of expression; he also makes it subject to the primacy of the first species of words, the noun. Considering the six species that can vary according to gender, number, person, time, and mood, Fontanier notes: 'But it is easy to see that they all converge more or less directly on the idea of substance, which subjects them to itself either by itself or through accessory ideas that it carries along with it' (46). Converge, subject, carry along: so many and so insistent are the ways in which the noun's position of pre-eminence – already assured by that of the idea of substance – is reinforced.

True, its rule is not undivided; a second point of departure is proposed, which is not the idea any more but thought itself. Thought was mentioned from the start, at the same time as the word: 'Thought is made up of ideas, and the expression of thought by speech is made up of words' (41). This was implied in the definition of trope as well: 'Tropes are certain meanings more or less different from the primitive meaning, which words, when applied to new ideas, evince in the course of the expression of thought' (39). Hence thought and word appear to be equally fundamental. Moreover, a specific theory of thought and its expression is prepared for by the distinction between the idea of an object and the idea of a relationship. While the verb is the sign of the coexistence of a substantive idea and a concrete idea, this coexistence can be affirmed or denied; for thought is nothing but 'the reunion of these two ideas, via the inner act of our mind that sets one inside the other or sets one outside the other' (49). Here, then, we have rhetoric established upon a dual-focus analysis, an analysis in terms of idea and judgment; correspondingly, from the point of view of expression, we have the duality of word and proposition, the latter being nothing but 'judgment projected outside our mind, as if *set before us*, as if *set in front of* the minds of others' (49).

Accordingly, it is possible to transcribe all the distinctions between kinds of words in terms of the function of their role in the proposition. Considered in judgment, the substantive idea becomes the propositional subject, the concrete idea becomes the so-called attribute, and the relationship of coexistence expressed by the verb *to be* is now called the copula.

The definition of the notions of meaning and of signification supports the view that word and proposition constitute two distinct poles of the expression of thought. Meaning is defined first of all in relation to the word: 'Relative to a word, *meaning* is what this word makes us understand, think, *feel* by means of its *signification*; and its *signification* is what it signifies, that is to say, that of which it is a sign, when it acts as a sign' (55). But 'the word *meaning* can also be used of a whole sentence, sometimes even of a whole discourse' (ibid.). Furthermore, 'a *proposition* is a *sentence* only when, because of a certain construction, it presents a complete and finished meaning' (52-3). And it is with reference to the proposition in its entirety that objective, literal, and spiritual or intellectual meaning can be distinguished. Objective meaning is not opposed to the two others; it is the basic meaning of the proposition: 'that which it has relative to the object to which it applies' (56). The broad categories subsumed under objective meaning are precisely the ones provided by the theory of ideas – substantive or adjectival meaning, active or passive meaning, etc. More important for our purposes is the distinction between literal meaning and spiritual or intellectual meaning; unlike objective meaning, these form a pair. Both of these meanings belong to the proposition, but they differ because of a trait that is peculiar to words: 'The literal meaning is that which is borne by words taken to the letter, by words understood according to the way they are accepted in common usage. Consequently, it is the meaning that suggests itself immediately to those who understand the language' (57). 'The spiritual meaning, the diverted or figurative meaning of a group of words, is that which the literal meaning causes to be born in the spirit by means of the circumstances of the discourse, by tone of voice, or by means of expressed connections with unarticulated relationships' (58-9).

It is most significant for us that the theory of the word prevails ultimately over the theory of the proposition. Indeed, the theory of tropes will be organized finally with reference to the word and not the proposition. The notion of tropological meaning is related immediately to that of literal meaning, but with the express restriction on literal that it is the literal meaning of a word in isolation that is meant: 'The literal meaning that belongs only to the isolated word is either primitive, natural and proper, or "derived" (if one must speak in this way) and tropological' (57). The notion of figure is itself placed in the same context, not primarily as the genus of which the trope would be the species, but as one of the two ways in which tropes take place: 'by choice and figuratively' versus 'as required and by extension' (ibid.). This second case, that of tropological meaning by extension, is one of 'stepping into the breach when the language lacks a word for a certain idea' (ibid.). The first case, figurative tropological meaning, involves 'presenting ideas through images that are more lively and more striking than their proper signs' (ibid.).

The hegemony of the word, which a theory of the proposition could have balanced, thus is reaffirmed even in the distinction between literal and spiritual meaning – just when the notion of meaning seemed to be assumed by the sentence in its entirety rather than by the word.

The distinction between one-word tropes, or 'tropes properly speaking,' and tropes consisting of several words is made on the same basis. And yet the very distinction between letter and spirit would seem to demand that the accent be on the other pole. For is the 'spiritual sense' not always to some degree the meaning 'of a collection of words,' and consequently linked to the more extended tropes? And is it not 'through the circumstances of the discourse, by the tone of voice or because of the ties between those ideas that are expressed and those that are not' – that is, by means of those traits that affect thought at the level of propositions – that the literal meaning gives rise to spiritual meaning in our minds? And does the very expression of spiritual meaning not remind us that it is 'spirit that forms it'? Surely the internal act in our mind is judgment, is it not?

As we see, the primacy of the word does not abolish entirely the bipolar organization of thought and its expression. But every time the examples seem to put discourse above the word, idea re-establishes the reign of the word.

3 / TROPE AND FIGURE

Even while calling in various places for a return to the polarity of idea and judgment, reflected in that of word and sentence – which alone presents a 'complete and finished meaning' (53) – the entire theory of tropes and figures is based upon this primacy of the word.

It might seem, however, that the foundation-stone of the taxonomical enterprise would not be the trope, whose dependence on word we have begun to see, but the figure, which refers equally to word, to statement, to discourse. For Gérard Genette, in his remarkable introduction to the 1968 reissue of Fontanier's treatise, the work's principal interest lies in the reunion of tropes and non-tropes under the notion of *figure*. To choose figure – which is neither word nor statement – as the basic unit is to take an intermediate course between that of Aristotle, who still took in the whole of the field of rhetoric (that is, argumentation, composition, style), and that of Dumarsais, who reduced rhetoric to grammar, the function of the latter being 'to make one understand the true signification of words and in what sense they are used in discourse' (cited by Genette 8). Fontanier's basic unit could not be discourse, nor yet the word, 'the unit for grammar more than for rhetoric' (ibid.). His intermediate course is expressed well by the maxim 'only the figures, but all the figures' (ibid.). The advantage of this third course is that it establishes rhetoric upon an entity that can sustain that ambition for complete enumeration and systematic classification that makes of Fontanier's work a 'chef-d'oeuvre of taxonomic intelligence' (Genette 13).[5] The figure can take on this architectonic role because it is coextensive with discourse in general: 'What are figures of discourse in general? They are these more or less remarkable forms, features or turns, varyingly successful, through which discourse, as expression of ideas, thoughts, or feelings, makes itself more or less different from what would have been the simple and common expression' (Fontanier 64, 179). Thus, figure can apply equally to word, to sentence, or to the traits of discourse that express the workings of feelings and passion.

But what is to be said of figure as such? It must be admitted that figure, like Aristotle's *epiphora*, is itself spoken of only metaphorically. Figures are to discourse what contours, characteristics, and exterior form are to the body: 'Even though it is not a body but an act of mind, discourse ... has, nevertheless, in its different ways of signifying and expressing, something analogous to the differences of forms and characteristics that are found in real bodies' (63).

We are reminded again of Aristotle's distinguishing the 'how' of discourse from its 'what,' and assimilating the 'how' to an 'appearing' of discourse.[6] (Perhaps the same metaphor exists germinally in the notion of expression.)

Fontanier does not appear to be bothered by this incipient circle (metaphor is a figure and the word *figure* is metaphorical).[7] He prefers to go directly to two traits of figure. The first is what the new rhetoric will call 'deviation' and what Fontanier uses in saying that 'discourse, as expression of ideas, thoughts or feelings, departs more or less from what would have been the simple and common expression' (64). It is true that to depart, deviate, or turn away from are still, like Aristotle's *epiphora*, metaphors of movement. However – and this is the essential point – at least the notion of deviation applies equally well no matter how extended the expression is, be it word, sentence, or discourse. Thus one of the basic postulates of our model, that of deviation, stands out from the rest.

The second trait brings with it a restriction; it has to do with application rather than with extension. The use of figure must remain free, even if it becomes habitual; a deviation that is imposed by the language, forced usage, no longer deserves the name of figure. Accordingly catachresis, the forced extension of the meaning of words, is excluded from the field of figures (213-19). The present trait calls to mind two other postulates of our model. First of all, free and unconstrained use implies that expressions are being diverted from their proper meaning, that is, taken 'in a sense that one gives them for the moment and that is merely borrowed' (66). Then too, free use supposes that the proper expression is available and that another is substituted for it as a result of free choice. To write 'flame' for 'love' is to form a figure; 'the figure exists,' comments Genette, 'only to the extent that one can oppose to it a literal expression ... the criterion of figure is the substitution of one expression (word, phrase, sentence, and even group of sentences) for another, which the rhetorician must be able to restore mentally in order to have the right to speak of figure ... So, with Fontanier, we see a clear and forthright affirmation of the essence of figure as *substitution*' (Genette, 10-12). Genette goes on to link this 'substitutive obsession' to a 'piercing and very precious awareness of the paradigmatic dimension of the units (small or large) of discourse' (12). This paradigmatic character is extended step by step from word to sentence and to discourse – that is, to ever larger syntagmatic units.[8]

Thus, the essence of the rhetorical model with which we began this chapter is to be found in Fontanier, at least at the level of the program as a whole. The only exception might be the primacy of the word, which we had believed was the fundamental postulate. Is it reasonable to suggest, then, that Fontanier was trying to found a rhetoric of figures that is not reducible to a tropology, to a theory of deviations in the significations of words?

This was beyond doubt Fontanier's aim. And it is also true that his ambition is partially realized in his treatise *Les Figures du discours*. His 'division' of figures[9] is truly imposing – in Genette's words, it establishes Fontanier as the 'Linnaeus of rhetoric' (13). Ancient tropology consists of just one class of figures among others: the figures of signification, or tropes properly speaking, that is single-word tropes. The rest of the field is divided up into five other classes: figures of expression, of construction, of elocution, of style, and of thought.

It is difficult to say as much for the detailed development of this work. One point certainly puts us on guard: the theory of metaphor is completely unaffected by the choice of figure as the characteristic unit of rhetoric. Metaphor remains classed among the single-word tropes, the tropes properly speaking. And the theory of tropes itself constitutes an autonomous whole; the notion of figure is superimposed on it pure and simple. In this way the rhetorical model, whose network of postulates we reconstructed, continues to function at the level of trope, oblivious to the addition of other classes of figures and to the superimposition of the concept of figure itself, which is more general than that of trope. As to the other figures, they are simply added to the trope-figures. More important, among all classes of figures, the trope is 'marked' for special duty. The treatise is composed so as to begin with 'tropes properly speaking,' which are single-word figures of signification. It then adds the 'tropes improperly speaking' or the longer figures of expression, and it ends with all the other figures which throughout are called 'non-trope figures.'[10] The key unit remains the trope because the foundation remains the word. This is what makes the treatise seem rather odd: the trope is at once both one class among others and the paradigm of all figures.[11]

Fontanier's treatise thus appears as if constructed according to two blueprints: one establishes figure as the basic unit; the other guarantees a key position to idea, therefore to word, and hence to the trope. While it is true that the first scheme is the floor-plan for the treatise as general taxonomy of the figures of discourse, the second determines the division of figures between tropes and non-tropes. The first would prevail over the second were discourse to have supplanted the word in the theory of 'first foundations' (39). But, in the spirit of ideology, this latter remains a theory of 'elements' (ibid.). This is why the key unit remains the simple idea, which alone can be called 'a simple element of thought' (453).

In spite of the theory of figures, then, the theory of tropes, and especially that of metaphor, verifies our model. Only the second signification of the notion of figure – the opposition to catachresis – is retained. Hence, this notion can be treated no longer as the higher genus, but as the specific difference: 'The tropological meaning is either *figurative* or purely an *extension*, according to whether the new signification of concern was given freely and as if playfully to the word, or whether it had become a forced, habitual signification, almost as *proper* as the primitive signification' (75). Hence the paradoxical consequence that the theory of tropes envelopes the distinction between figure and catachresis ('But, whether *figure* or *catachresis*, in how many different ways do single-word tropes occur?' [77]).

True, Fontanier sustains the possibility that propositions, like words, might offer 'a sort of tropological sense' (77). This possibility is written right into the definition of primitive and tropological meaning, which, as we recall, was applied from the start to the various meanings that the proposition can have. However, to be precise, this is only 'one sort' of tropological meaning, presented by 'figures of expression' that are only tropes 'improperly speaking' (109).

4 / METONYMY, SYNECDOCHE, METAPHOR

Systematically and exhaustively, Fontanier constructs the list of possible kinds of tropes within the limits so set out, and based on the relationship through which tropes 'occur' (77).[12]

This last expression is notable: tropes are indeed events, since the figures of signification 'occur through a new signification of the word' (ibid.). The opposition between free and forced usage, essential to the figurative character of the trope, makes of the trope a semantic innovation that exists only 'for the moment' (66). Therefore, the trope is not the relationship itself; it is based on the relationship, which is recognizable as what, in the fifth postulate, we called the 'reason' of the substitution. But relationship between what and what? The relationship through which tropes take place is one between ideas. More specifically, it is a relationship between two ideas: on the one hand, 'the primary idea attached to the word,' that is, the primitive signification of the borrowed word; and on the other, 'the new idea given to it' (77), or the tropological meaning substituted for some other proper word that one did not wish to use in this particular situation.

Except for a few points of divergence, this relationship between a primary and a new idea corresponds to the Aristotelian *epiphora*. Let us look at these differences for a moment. The first is that Fontanier's definition does not appear to point explicitly to the movement of transference. Now while this is true enough, the *'static' of relationships* provides the foundation for the *'dynamic' of transferences*, as the listing of the types of tropes will show. Next, Aristotle treats metaphor as a genus, not as a species. Aristotle's metaphor is a trope for Fontanier; and Fontanier's metaphor corresponds approximately to the fourth species of metaphor in Aristotle's scheme. This difference seems more serious than the preceding one; however, it can be treated, up to a certain point, as just a difference of glossary. Another seeming difference is that, for Fontanier, relationship affects 'ideas' before it links words or names; but, as we saw, idea is the element of thought that underlies words (or names in the case of the 'substantive' ideas). With these few reservations, Fontanier's trope and Aristotle's *epiphora* mirror each other fairly well.

We are now able to say of the relationship through which the trope occurs what we said earlier of *epiphora*: the trope truly does consist *of* one word; however, if one may speak in this manner, it occurs *between* two ideas, by a transfer from one to the other. Hence, in a sense that will have to be clarified, the trope, like *epiphora* before it, occurs 'based upon a duality' (see above, page 25).

Next, while *epiphora* and trope correspond to a high degree, this cannot be said for Aristotle's four species of metaphor and Fontanier's three kinds of relationships. Herein lies Fontanier's profound originality compared to all his predecessors and also, as we shall see, in relation to his successors. Fontanier prides himself on having given an exhaustive theory of the relationships between ideas by distinguishing between *relations of correlation* or *correspondence, relations of connection*, and *relations by resemblance*. The three species of tropes – metonymies, synecdoches, and metaphors – 'take place' through these three kinds of relationships respectively.

What is remarkable in this system of paradigms is the breadth and fullness that Fontanier gives to each of these three relationships. By correspondence he understands something quite different from the contiguity to which his successors reduce the functioning of metonymy; he sees in it a relationship that brings together two objects each of which constitutes 'an absolutely separate whole' (79). This is why metonymy divides up in turn according to the variety of relationships that satisfy the general condition of correspondance: relationship of cause to effect, instrument to purpose, container to content, thing to its location, sign to signification, physical to moral, model to thing.

In the relationship of connection, two objects '*form an ensemble, a physical or metaphysical whole, the existence or idea of one being included in the existence or idea of the other*' (87). It follows that this relationship will also have many species: relations of part to whole, of material to thing, of one to many, of species to genus, of abstract to concrete, of species to individual. The inclusiveness of all these relationships varies, some being greater and some narrower, but according to a wider range than just numerical relation or even a simple generic extension.

Correspondence and connection thus designate two relationships as distinct as exclusion ('absolutely separate whole') and inclusion ('included in ...'). Furthermore, we should note that these two initial relationships connect objects prior to connecting ideas, so that alteration in the designating reference of names follows the objective relationship. (There is, however, a slight difference to be noted. In the relationship of connection, objects are said to belong to the same whole if the existence or idea of one object is contained in the existence or the idea of another.) From this arises the almost total symmetry between the definitions of metonymy and synecdoche. In both cases, one object is designated by the name of another; and in both cases, it is the objects (or, in the exception just noted, the ideas) that enter into a relationship of exclusion or inclusion.

It is in the play of resemblances that this symmetry is broken and metaphor is set somewhat apart. In the first place, its definition does not refer directly to a changing of the designations of things by names or nouns; it mentions only the relationship between ideas. This is not a chance omission; for while metaphor lacks species, as opposed to the other two tropes, 'it takes in far greater territory' than they, 'since not only the noun or name, but also the adjective, participle, verb, and actually all the species of words belong to its domain' (99). Now why does metaphor allude to every type of word, whereas metonymy and synecdoche affect only the designation of things by nouns? There is a strong suggestion here of an extremely important shift that will be recognized only by a properly predicative theory of metaphor. We can follow this up by considering the examples. What is the metaphorical use of a noun? To 'make a tiger of an angry man,' 'of a great writer a swan': is this not already something other than designating a thing by a new name? Is it not 'naming' in the sense of characterizing, of qualifying? And is this operation, which consists in 'carrying the name outside its species,' not a sort of attribution, which requires the whole sentence? The adjective, the participle (which is similar to it when acting as an epithet), the verb (which is analysed into participle and copula), and the adverb (which modifies the verb) lend themselves most readily to metaphorical usage. Is this not because they function only within a sentence that relates not just two ideas but also two words, namely one term taken non-metaphorically, which acts as a support, and the other taken metaphorically, which fulfils the function of characterization? This remark brings us close to the distinction made by I.A. Richards between *tenor* and *vehicle*.[13] Fontanier's examples already lean in this direction. When one says 'the *Swan* of Cambrai,' '*consuming* remorse,' 'courage *craving* for peril and praise,' 'his *seething* spirit,' and so on, these metaphors do not name, but characterize what has already been named.

This quasi-predicative character of metaphor is confirmed by another trait. Not only does the definition of metaphor make no direct reference to the noun or name, it does not even refer to objects. It consists '*in presenting one idea under the sign of another that is more striking or better known*' (99). Analogy operates between ideas; and idea itself is to be understood not 'from the point of view of the objects seen by the spirit' but 'from the point of view of the spirit that sees' (41). For it is in this sense only that an idea can be called 'more striking or better known'; even if one discovers objective relationships supporting the analogy (when one calls a man a tiger), 'the name is not transferred from one member of a species to another but from one species to another' (100). But it is important that the 'common opinion' recognizes such resemblance (ibid.). Hence, connection and correspondence are primarily relationships between objects, while resemblance is principally a relationship between ideas, between generally held beliefs. This is why the second trait confirms the first: characterization, as distinct from naming, is formed through comparisons of opinions, that is, within the realm of judgment.

Fontanier evidently was prevented from seeing these consequences by the preoccupation that dominates the conclusion of his analysis of metaphor. Perhaps to re-establish symmetry between metaphor and the two other figures, and despite his initial declaration that 'ordinarily we do not divide *metaphor* into species as we do *metonymy* and *synecdoche*' (99), he does attempt to divide metaphor into species. He finds his principle of classification in the nature of objects as they define either the domain from which they are borrowed or the place of their application. Did he not say, however, that metaphor takes place between ideas? But even when considered from the point of view of the spirit that sees, ideas remain images of the objects seen by the spirit (41). So it is always possible to invoke the ideas behind the words and the things beyond the ideas. Furthermore, since the resemblance has to do with the character that things are believed to have, it is possible to pass from this character to the realm of the things that possess it; Fontanier says that the 'transfer' (101) takes place between the things as characterized. But how are the regions of borrowing and application to be classified? After remarking that metaphors can be taken from everything that surrounds us, from all of the real and the imagined, from intellectual or moral as well as physical entities, and that they can be applied to all the objects of thought, no matter what they are, Fontanier somewhat arbitrarily chooses the dividing line to be between the animate and the inanimate. This is how he comes to preserve an old classification that saves him from the difficulty of infinite divisions. His five species of metaphor – 'transfer of something that belongs to an animate thing to some other animate thing,' 'of something inanimate but physical to something inanimate and usually purely moral or abstract,' 'from an inanimate thing to an animate,' 'physical metaphor going from the animate to the inanimate,' and 'moral metaphor going from the animate to the inanimate' – can be reduced ultimately to the pair made up of 'the physical metaphor, that is, one in which two physical objects (whether animate or inanimate) are compared'; and 'the moral metaphor, in which

something abstract and metaphysical, something from t[...]
compared with something physical, the meanings of bo[...]
whether the transfer is from the second to the first or fr[...]
second' (103).

The opportunity will arise later to report on the comp[...]
this principle of classification and the completely 'metaphysical' distinction between the physical and the moral.[14]

It seems reasonable to agree that this classification is more a concession
to the past than a necessary implication of the definition of metaphor by
resemblance. The division into species does not in any way proceed from a
diversification of the resemblance relationship, as in the case of metonymy
and synecdoche; it remains completely extrinsic to the definition. So we
must return to this definition: nowhere is the distinction between animate
and inanimate implied in *'presenting one idea under the sign of another*
that is more striking or better known' (99). Far from having to reconstruct
the interplay of resemblances beginning in the *real* domains of the borrowing and application, one would have to derive the domains from familiar
and striking characteristics and these latter from popular opinion. Nelson
Goodman will do this in treating the notion of 'realm' as a collection of
'labels' and defining metaphor as a redescription involving the transposition of labels.[15] Something of this theory is prefigured in Fontanier's initial formula, 'presenting one idea under the sign of another that is more
striking or better known'; but the notion of the one-word trope kept him
from seeing all that is implied in this notion of second-degree signification.

5 / THE FAMILY OF METAPHOR

The notion of trope taken as a single word not only snuffs out the potential meaning contained in the admirable initial definition of metaphor; it
also breaks up the unity of the problematic of the analogy between ideas,
which is thereby dispersed among all the classes of figures.

Among the 'tropes improperly speaking,' namely the *'figures of expres-*
sion' that 'concern the proposition's particular manner of expression'
(109), *poetic fancy* (what Fontanier calls *fiction*) has a striking resemblance to metaphor. To give one thought 'the features or colours of another, in order to make it more tangible or more pleasant' (ibid.) – is this
not the same as presenting one idea under the sign of another which is
more striking and better known? Personification (the first sub-species of
this poetic fancy) in turning an inanimate, non-sentient, abstract, or ideal
entity into a living and feeling being, into a person, reminds us of the metaphorical transfer from the inanimate to the animate. It is true that personification does not take place only through metaphor but also by metonymy

nd synecdoche. But what distinguishes personification by means of metaphor and metaphor properly speaking, except the extension of the verbal entity?

It is tempting to say the same of *allegory* which also '*presents one thought in the image of another that is better suited to making it more tangible or more striking than if it were presented directly and without any sort of disguise*' (114). But another trait besides its connection to the proposition distinguishes allegory from metaphor. According to Fontanier, metaphor – even the extended metaphor that he calls 'allegorism' – has only one true meaning, the figurative meaning; whereas allegory 'consists *in a proposition with a double meaning, having a literal and a spiritual meaning together*' (114).[16] Is this to say that double meaning happens only with the figures of expression and cannot appear in figures of signification? It seems so, although the reason is far from clear. Perhaps to hold together the two meanings an act of spirit is necessary, thus a judgment, and thus a proposition. One wonders whether it was with an eye to this analysis of allegory that the notions of literal and spiritual meaning were defined in the context not of the word but of the proposition.

Poetic fancy bears an additional interest for our discussion. It highlights repeatedly a trait of the notion of figure that perhaps was already suggested in the definition of metaphor that has been referred to several times. To present an idea under the sign of another implies that the two ideas differ not only as to the species of the objects involved, but also in the vivacity and familiarity of the ideas. Now this difference is not studied as such by Fontanier; nevertheless, it implies a nuance in the meaning of the notion of figure that poetic fancy and allegory help isolate, namely, the presentation of a thought in a sensible or tangible form. This trait is very often called 'image.' Fontanier himself uses this term in saying that allegory 'presents one thought in the image of another that is better suited to making it more tangible or more striking' (114). Thus he says that Marmontel, 'comparing his spirit to a shrub, depicts the advantageous influences that he has drawn from his acquaintance with Voltaire and Vauvernagues, whom he presents in the image of two rivers' (116). So figure, picture, and image go hand in hand. A bit later, again, speaking of imagination as 'one of the causes that generate tropes' (161-2), Fontanier judges it to be at work 'in all the tropes that offer some image or some picture to the spirit' (162). And if there is 'something enchanting, something magical' (173, 179) in poetic language, it must be because a poet like Racine is 'so *figurative*; everything in him is, so to speak, in images, wherever this is appropriate to the subject and the genre' (173). Is this not the effect of all the tropes; not satisfied with just transmitting ideas and thoughts, 'they depict them in a more or less lively fashion, they clothe them in richer or duller colours; like so many mirrors, they reflect the different faces of objects and show them off in their most advantageous light; they adorn the ideas and thoughts, setting them into relief or giving them a new grace; they trail, as if before our eyes, a train of images and scenes, whose nature we long to know, as this nature presents itself with entrancing novelty' (174). As this indicates, it is truly the figure that confers outward appearance on discourse by giving it contours, characteristics and exterior form, similar to the traits of physical bodies (63). It must be said that all the tropes are, 'like poetry, the children of fictive fancy' (180). For poetry, less mindful of truth than of resemblance, gives itself over to 'creating figures, to colouring its language, to putting it into images and scenes, to turning it into a living and speaking picture' (181). This is not to say that the tropes that take after metaphor all present 'a sensible or tangible image, one that could be formed by the eye and by the hand of a painter' (185). Fontanier protests that this would be giving too much over to sight. His reservation here anticipates a distinction exploited by Wittgenstein and Hester, that between 'seeing' and 'seeing as.'[17] So we will say that *to figure* is always *to see as*, but not always *to see* or *to make visible*.

We should still take our investigation beyond the tropes improperly speaking, in order to see how analogy works within the 'figures of construction,' the 'figures of elocution,' and the 'figures of style.' Imitation is brought up in this context, first in the 'figures of construction' (288) and later in the 'figures of style' (390). The 'figures of thought' themselves, although they 'have to do with thought alone,' come close to metaphor and analogy; thus the 'figures of thought' by imagination (*prosopopée*) and by development exhibit the general character of figure that we have just explained, namely that of providing thought with a stage-setting. Indeed, one can say of 'description,' which in general covers the field of 'figures of development,' 'that it consists in setting an object before our eyes and in making it known by presenting the detail of all its most interesting aspects ... it gives rise to *hypotyoposis*, when the exposition is so lively and emphatic that an *image*, a tableau, appears in the style' (420). This notion of description is particularly interesting; it covers topography and chronography (descriptions having to do with space or place and time), prosopography, ethopy, and portrait (physical and moral personification of living beings and their combination), and parallelism and tableau, which combine the foregoing (422-33).

This vast domain of analogy could not be restructured except by a refusal to confine metaphor within the tropes of a single word and by pursuing to its conclusion the action that detaches it from the linguistic activity of naming in order to attach it to the central act of discourse, namely, predication.

6 / FORCED METAPHOR AND NEWLY INVENTED METAPHOR

I will end this analysis with a trait which, more than all the others, takes us in this direction. It concerns the distinction between the figurative and the catachretic character of each trope. Fontanier finds this distinction so important that he even claims that these 'principles concerning catachresis constitute a foundation for our entire tropological system' (213).

The difference has to do first with a fact of language, namely that certain ideas *lack* signs: '*In general, catachresis refers to a situation in which a sign, already assigned to a first idea, is assigned also to a new idea, this latter idea having no sign at all or no other proper sign within the language.* Consequently, every trope whose use is forced and necessitated, every trope that results in a pure *extension* of *meaning*, is a case of catachresis. This is a proper meaning of secondary origin, something between *primitive proper meaning* and *figurative meaning* but closer by nature to the first than the second, even though in principle it could itself have been used *figuratively*' (213). Thus one cannot call forced metaphors figures, be they nouns ('light' for spiritual clarity, 'blindness' for confusion and obscurity in understanding), adjectives (a 'ringing' voice), verbs ('grasp' in the sense of 'understand'), prepositions ('to' in connection with both destination and purpose), etc. This purely extensional trope, giving rise to a proper meaning of second degree, presents (or intends to present) one idea only; and it presents this idea 'completely naked and undisguised, as opposed utterly to *figurative tropes*, which always present two ideas, present them intentionally, and present one under the image of the other or beside the other' (219).

Hence, the thing that should draw our attention in the figure-trope is its characteristic of being *free*. This alone – its freely presenting one idea under the image of another – seems to indicate that the trope properly speaking, even though it takes place in one word, has the features of what Benveniste will call 'the instance of discourse.'[18]

What Fontanier says about newly invented metaphors (504) confirms the close relationship between the trope and the living event of actual speech. As the free-forced distinction applies to usage, all usage tends to become habitual, and metaphor tends to resemble catachresis. The metaphor still remains a figure, for its purpose is not to fill a gap in signs. However, it appears in a more and more fixed and standardized fashion, and, in this sense, can be said 'to be part of the foundation of language' (104) – that is, it begins to act like a literal meaning. This is why the conditions necessary for a good metaphor – realism, clarity, nobility, naturalness, coherence – 'apply only to the *newly invented metaphors* that one intends as figures and that have not yet received the sanction of general use' (104).

This point leads us to set up an internal distinction with regard to figure, parallel to that between figure and catachresis; this is a distinction between initial use and the eventual usage that can become 'forced in present-day speech' (213).

It is really this ordinary usage that rhetoric reflects. If we observe, with Boileau and Dumarsais, that 'there are more tropes used in the marketplace in a single day than in the entire *Aeneid*, or in several consecutive sessions of the Academy' (157), we must admit that most of these are examples of standardized tropes. One can be said to 'know them through regular use, like one's mother tongue, without being able to say when or how one learned them' (157). This is also why we can turn around and say that 'they are an essential part of spoken language' (157) and 'part of the very foundation of language' (164). To put it differently, standardized tropes are midway between the tropes of invention and catachresis. The boundary between forced tropes and catachresis tends to fade away all the more as the phenomenon of erosion, just as the tropes themselves, seems to go back to the beginnings of language. The reason for catachresis is found in the origin of tropes themselves, namely 'the failure of proper words, and the need, the necessity to supplement their deficiency and failure' (158). This is a deficiency and lack for which we should be grateful, for if we had as many words as ideas, 'what memory would be sufficient to learn so many words, and to retain them and reproduce them?' (158). In the same way that von Humboldt defines discourse as an infinite use of finite means, Fontanier attributes to memory 'a fairly restricted number of words [which] furnish the means to express an infinite number of ideas' (158). In this manner, at least at its origins, the figure-trope has the same extended function as the catachresis-trope. For this reason they tend to blend into one another in the course of normal use.

But besides being needed in view of the deficiency of vocabulary, the figure trope is occasioned by another cause, that is, pleasure. 'The chosen, the stylistic tropes, the *figure-tropes*, are also brought about by the delight and pleasure that, as if by a sort of instinct, we first anticipate and then experience in them' (160). So this pleasing quality acts as an incentive to invention, as opposed to just being necessary.

This invention forces us to distinguish between the occasional causes of tropes (necessity and also pleasure), and the properly generative causes: imagination, spirit, passion. To give colour, to astonish and surprise through new and unexpected combinations, to breathe force and energy into discourse – so many impulses express themselves only in the figure-tropes, which must be called 'writer's tropes' since they are the 'special creation of poets' (165). While the metaphor 'burdened with age' is obviously a standard part of the language, 'who before Corneille ever said *consume* a kingdom [*dévorer un règne*]?' (ibid.).

However, the consideration of tropes 'as to their use in discourse' (499) is not along the same lines. This use (which Fontanier investigates in the third section of the theory of tropes), though not constitutive for the trope as founded on a specific relationship, is at least constitutive for its character as figure. If the indirect meaning is one 'lent for the moment' (66) to the word, the most authentic tropes are the tropes of invention alone. Therefore, we must shift our focus from the word to discourse, because only the conditions proper to discourse can distinguish between the figure-trope and the catachresis-trope, and within the figure-trope, between constrained and free usage.

Metaphor and the semantics of discourse

For Cyrus Hamlin

In our first two Studies, the change of meaning constituting the trope and continually referred to as metaphor in ancient and classical rhetoric found its locus in the *word*. This allowed us to adopt, as an initial approximation, a definition of metaphor that identifies it with giving an unaccustomed name to some other thing, which thereby is not being given its proper name. But the investigation of the interrelationships of meaning that give rise to this transposition of the name also relentlessly forces open the frame of reference determined by the word, and *a fortiori* that determined by the name or noun, and imposes the *statement* as the sole contextual milieu within which the transposition of meaning takes place. The present Study is devoted to a direct examination of the role of the statement, as the carrier of 'complete and finished meaning' (according to Fontanier's own expression), in the production of metaphorical meaning. Hence, we will speak from now on of the *metaphorical statement*.

Does this mean that the definition of metaphor as transposition of the name is wrong? I prefer to say that it is nominal only and not real, using these terms as Leibniz does. The nominal definition allows us to identify something; the real definition shows how it is brought about. The definitions that Aristotle and Fontanier gave are nominal, in that they specify which tropes are metaphors. Restricting themselves to identifying metaphor, however, they also restrict themselves to classifying it. In this sense, the sort of taxonomy belonging to tropology cannot rise above the level of nominal definition. But as soon as rhetoric looks into generative causes, it is already considering discourse and not just the word. Thus, a theory of the metaphorical statement will be a theory of the production of metaphorical meaning.

Consequently, the nominal definition should not be abolished by the real definition. This Study may, however, seem to sanction such a choice, for we shall continually contrast a discursive theory of metaphor with a reduction of metaphor to an accident of naming. Several authors go somewhat further than this and take an *interaction* theory, which is intimately connected to a discursive conception of metaphor, to be incompatible with a *substitution* theory, where substitution, as we have seen, is inseparable from the definition of metaphor as a deviation in naming.

Foreshadowing an analysis to be undertaken in the fifth Study, let us establish now that the real definition of metaphor in terms of statement cannot obliterate its nominal definition in terms of word or name, because the word remains the locus of the effect of metaphorical meaning. It is the word that is said to take a metaphorical meaning. This is why Aristotle's definition is not abolished by a theory that no longer deals with the place of metaphor in discourse but with the metaphorical process itself. Using Max Black's terminology (which will be justified later), the word remains the 'focus' even while it requires the 'frame' of the sentence. And the reason why the word remains the locus of the effect of metaphorical meaning is that the function of the word within discourse is to embody the semantic identity. It is this identity that metaphor affects. But nothing is more difficult to appreciate than the function of the word, which at first sight seems to be divided between a semiotics of lexical entities and a semantics of the sentence. We must thus postpone any attempt to co-ordinate a theory of substitution and a theory of interaction, which are both valid though at different levels, until the end of our reflection on the function of the word as mediator in semiotics and in semantics.

In this Study, accordingly, we will adopt a provisionally disjunctive conception of the relationships between semiotics and semantics. First we will outline this conception. Then we will connect it to the interaction theory which is summoned to replace a purely substitutive theory of metaphor. Thus we will derive all the consequences of the opposition between the nominal definition and the genetic definition of metaphor.

1 / THE DEBATE BETWEEN SEMANTICS AND SEMIOTICS

The working hypothesis underlying the notion of metaphorical statement is that the semantics of discourse is not reducible to the semiotics of lexical entities. (A discussion of the word as such will occur in the fifth Study.)

In the theories of metaphor that arise more or less within the English-language tradition of linguistic analysis, the theory of discourse itself is not developed by linguists but by logicians and epistemologists, who occasionally pay some attention to literary criticism but more rarely to the linguistics that linguists themselves engage in. The advantage of a direct attack on the phenomenon of discourse, omitting the linguistic stage, is that the traits proper to discourse are recognized in themselves without any need to contrast them with anything else. But with the contributions that the linguistic study of language has made to the humanities, one cannot any longer simply disregard the relationship between discourse and language. Nowadays, whoever wants his research to be up-to-date in the good sense must take the indirect route of the contrast between the unity of discourse and the unity of language. The results that English-language philosophical semantics reaches directly and with greater elegance must be attained more laboriously by a semantics influenced by linguistics, via the indirect path of a confrontation with the linguistics of language. We will take this route here. Our guide will be the distinction between semiotics and semantics in the work of Émile Benveniste,[1] with which the results of English-language linguistic analysis will be compared.

Benveniste's choice of the word *discourse* is itself significant. To the extent that it is above all a *linguistics* of language, linguistics tends to turn speech into a mere residue of its analyses. Benveniste chooses the term *discourse [discours]*, preferring it to *speech [parole]*, in order to point out the consistency of the object of his study. In considering the different levels in the architecture of language, this great French Sanskritist introduces the distinction between the fundamental units of language and of discourse: the signs and the sentence respectively. The notion of level is itself integral, not external, to the analysis; it is incorporated into the analysis as an 'operator' (104). This is meant to indicate that any linguistic unit whatsoever can be accepted as such only if one can identify it within some higher-level unit – the phoneme in the word, the word in the sentence. In this way the word occurs in 'an intermediary functional position that arises from its double nature. On the one hand it breaks down into phonemic units, which are from the lower level; on the other, as a unit of meaning and together with other units of meaning, it enters into a unit of the level above' (104). We will return to this claim in the fifth Study.

And what of this higher-level unit? The reply is quite definite: 'This unit is not a longer or more complex word – it belongs to another class of notions; it is a sentence. The sentence is realized in words, but the words are not simply segments of it. A sentence constitutes a whole which is not reducible to the sum of its parts; the meaning inherent in this whole is distributed over the ensemble of the constituents' (105). Thus, not only does the sentence not derive from the word understood as lexeme, that is, the isolated word as it exists in the lexical code; but the word as meaning is itself a constituent of the sentence – 'a syntagmatic element, a constituent of empirical utterances' (105). Rather than there being a linear progression from one unit to the other, then, new properties appear, which derive from this specific relationship between units of different levels. Whereas distributional relationships hold between units of the same level, the elements of different levels are governed by integrative relationships.

The distinction between these two sorts of relationships governs that between form and meaning. Distributional analysis within one level exposes the formal segments, the 'constituents.' On the other hand, decomposition into units of a lower level results in 'integrators,' which have a meaning-relationship with those of the higher level: 'This is the point: the analysis discloses the formal constituents; the integration discloses meaningful units ... The *form* of a linguistic unit is defined as its capacity for being broken down into constituents of a lower level. The *meaning* of a linguistic unit is defined as its capacity to integrate a unit of a higher level' (107).

If we apply these distinctions to the passage from lexeme to discourse, we find, as we suspected, that 'with the sentence a boundary is crossed and we enter into a new domain' (108). Benveniste puts 'being a *predicate*' (109) at the forefront of the characteristics that belong to this level. It is, in his eyes, 'distinctive beyond all others and inherent in the sentence' (ibid.). The presence of even a grammatical subject is optional; a single sign suffices to constitute a predicate.

Now this unit is not defined in opposition to other units, as was the case with phonemes and lexemes (which is why the principle of phonematic analysis could be extended to lexematic analysis). There is no range of kinds of predication. One cannot set up contrasts between 'categoremes' (*categorema = predicatum*) or between 'phrasemes' (sentential units), as is done with lexemes and phonemes: 'It is thus necessary to recognize that the categoremic level contains only one specific form of linguistic utterance, the proposition, which does not constitute a class of distinctive units' (109). As a consequence, there is no unit of an order higher than the proposition, in relation to which the proposition would constitute a class of distinctive units. Propositions can be set one after the other in a consecutive relationship, but they cannot be integrated. Another consequence is that the proposition, though containing signs, is not itself a sign. A final consequence is that, as opposed to phonemes and morphemes, which have a distribution at their own levels and a use at higher levels, 'sentences have neither distribution nor use (as integrated in some higher level)' (110). Benveniste concludes: 'The sentence is the unit of discourse'; again; 'The sentence, an undefined creation of limitless variety, is the very life of human speech in action' (110).

This has considerable methodological implications. Two different kinds of linguistics refer respectively to the sign and to the sentence, to language and to discourse. They proceed in opposite directions, and their paths cross. Taking the smallest units that can be differentiated as its point of departure, the linguistics of language sees in the sentence its highest possible level. But the process it follows presupposes the inverse analysis, which is closer to the speaker's awareness. Starting with the infinite variety of messages, it works downward to that limited number of units that it uses and encounters, the signs. It is this procedure that the linguistics of discourse takes for its own. Its guiding conviction is: 'It is in discourse, realized in sentences, that language is formed and takes shape. There language begins. One could say, in imitation of a classical formula: nihil est in *lingua* quod non prius fuerit in *oratione*' (111).

A few years later,[2] Benveniste gave these two forms of linguistics the names 'semiotics' and 'semantics.' The sign is the unit of semiotics while the sentence is the unit of semantics. As these units belong to different orders, semiotics and semantics hold sway over different arenas and take on restricted meanings. To say with de Saussure that language is a system of signs is to characterize language in just one of its aspects and not in its total reality.

The consequences are considerable for the extension of the well-known distinction between the signifier and the signified. This analysis of the sign holds only in the semiotic, and not the semantic, order. For semiology, says Benveniste, what the sign signifies does not have to be defined. It is necessary and sufficient for a sign to exist that it be accepted. (Does 'sun' exist? Yes. 'Zun'? No.) The question of the signified calls only for a yes-or-no answer: does it signify or not? But if the signified does not call for an intrinsic definition, it is defined extrinsically by the other signs that delimit its position within the language: 'Proper to every sign is that which distinguishes it from other signs. To be distinctive and to be meaningful are the same thing' ('La forme' 35). Circumscribed in this manner, the order of the sign leaves out the order of discourse.

The fruitfulness of this distinction between the semiotic and semantic orders is seen in its capacity to support and lead to numerous other distinctions. Some of these were made by Benveniste himself; others crop up here and there in the linguistic analysis of English-language writers, whose disregard for linguistics was noted above. This conjunction of philosophical semantics and linguistics is particularly valuable.

I wish to synthesize these divergent descriptions; their respective, often disparate origins will be mentioned only in passing. Specifically, I offer the following enumeration of the distinctive traits of discourse. These traits readily permit a presentation in pairs, which gives discourse a pronounced dialectical character; and it emphasizes the need for a methodology different from that which applies to the operations of segmentation and of distribution appropriate to a purely taxonomic conception of language.

First pair: discourse always occurs as an event, but is to be understood as meaning.

To point out the event character of discourse, Benveniste creates the expression 'instance of discourse,'[3] which is meant to encompass 'the discrete and always unique acts by which the language is actualized in speech by a speaker' (217). The contrast between discourse and language finds sharp focus in this trait. A linguistic system, precisely because it is synchronic, has only a virtual existence within the passage of time. Language really exists only when a speaker takes it in his possession and actualizes it. But at the same time as the event of discourse is fleeting and transitory, it can be identified and reidentified as 'the same'; thus, meaning is introduced, in its broadest sense, at the same time as the possibility of identifying a given unit of discourse. There is meaning because there is sameness of meaning. As P.F. Strawson shows in *Individuals*, it is true to say of every individual entity that what can be identified can also be reidentified. Such, then, is the 'instance of discourse': an event which is eminently repeatable. This is why this trait can be mistaken for an element of language; but what we have here is the repeatability of an event, not of an element of a system.

To this first pair one can add the distinction introduced by Paul Grice, whose theory of meaning differentiates between utterance meaning, meaning of the uttering, and utterer's meaning.[4] It belongs to the very essence of discourse to allow these distinctions. Their foundation is to be found in Benveniste's analysis, in his speaking on the one hand of the instance of discourse (as we have just seen), and on the other hand, of the 'intended' of discourse. This is something completely different from the meaning of an isolated sign. Ferdinand de Saussure said quite rightly that this meaning, the signified, is only the counterpart of the signifier, a simple difference within the language system; whereas the intention or the intended is 'what the speaker wants to say' ('La forme' 36). The signified meaning belongs to the semiotic order, the intention to the semantic; Grice deals with the latter in his analysis.

A second pair distinguishes between identifying function and predicative function.

This familiar polarity has a long history. In the *Cratylus, Theaetetus,* and *Sophist,* Plato designates it as *logos* itself and pictures it as the 'interlacing' (*sumplokē*) of the noun and the verb;[5] and this recourse to articulated *logos* lets him escape the impasse to which the question of the 'correctness' of words led him. Indeed, at the level of word, there is no solution: 'conventionalism' is just as good as 'naturalism'; only the interlacing of discourse '*has to do with something.*'[6] Correctness and error belong to discourse alone. The stalemate reached in the *Cratylus,* which is the stalemate of a theory of naming (and which demands the creation of a theory of predication), finds an echo in the stalemate of a theory of metaphor that also dwells within the limits of a reflection on the designative property of names.

The pair of identification and predication has been described meticulously by P.F. Strawson.[7] By reduction after reduction, every proposition bears upon an individual (Peter, London, the Seine, this man, that table, the man who saw the man who saw the bear). *Individual* here means 'logically proper subject.' Language is constructed so as to permit singular identification. Among the means employed for this, four stand out: the proper noun; the demonstrative; the pronouns; and especially the most frequently used means – what since Russell is called 'definite description'[8] – the such-and-such (the definite article followed by a determinant). To specify one thing and one alone – such is the function of identifying expressions, to which the logical subjects are ultimately reducible. Associated with the predicate are the adjectives of quality (great, good) and their substantival counterparts (greatness, goodness); the classes to which individuals belong (minerals, animals); relations (X is beside Y); and actions (Brutus killed Caesar). What qualities, classes, relations and actions have in common is that they are universalizable (for example, running, as a type of action, can be said of both Achilles and the tortoise). This produces the fundamental polarity of language, which on the one hand is rooted in named individuals, and on the other hand predicates qualities, classes, relations, and actions that in principle are universal. Language works on the basis of this dissymmetry between two functions. The identifying function always designates entities that exist (or whose existence is neutralized, as in fiction);[9] when I speak of something, in principle I speak of something that exists. The notion of existence is linked to the singularizing function of language. Proper logical subjects are potentially existents. This is the point at which language 'sticks,' where it adheres to things. By contrast, in having the universal in view, the predicative function concerns the nonexistent. The unfortunate dispute over universals in the Middle Ages was possible only because of confusion between the singularizing and predicative functions: for it makes no sense to ask whether goodness exists, only whether some thing, which is good, exists. The dissymmetry of the two functions thus also implies the ontological dissymmetry of subject and predicate.

Benveniste remarks that the predicate is sufficient in itself to be the criterion of units of discourse, and it is tempting to oppose this to Strawson's analysis: 'The presence of a "subject" alongside the predicate is not indispensable; the predicative term of the statement is sufficient unto itself since it is in reality the determiner of the "subject"' (*Problems* 109). Perhaps this apparent disagreement is the result of the difference between the logician's point of view and that of the linguist. The latter can point out predicates without a subject; whereas the former can argue that the determination of a subject – which is the task of the predicate – is always the counterpart of a singularizing identification. The Strawsonian distinction actually has an equivalent, if not even a justification, in the distinction between semiotics and semantics. In effect, semiotics has the generic or universal function and semantics the view to the singular: 'The sign's value is always and only generic and conceptual. Therefore, it has nothing to do with any particular or contingent signified, and anything individual is excluded; circumstantial factors are to be regarded as irrelevant' ('La Forme' 35). This characteristic proceeds from the very notion of 'instance of discourse'; it is language, as used and in action, which can take circumstances into account and have particular applications. Benveniste goes further: 'The sentence, the expression that belongs to semantics, is only concerned with the particular' (ibid. 36). Thus we are brought back to Strawson's analysis, for only within discourse does a generic term take on a singularizing function. This was already established convincingly by Russell's theory of definite descriptions. Now, the predicate, which in itself has a universalizing function, only has this circumstantial character to the extent that it determines a proper logical subject.

An important difference does remain between Strawson's analysis and that of Benveniste if it is proposed that the predicate by itself characterizes the sentence. For in Strawson's analysis, predicates have a generic value in that they designate a class, a property, a relation, or a category of action. To resolve this remaining contradiction, it is necessary to make two points more precise. First, it is the sentence taken as a whole, that which is intended by discourse, that carries with it a particular application, even when the predicate is generic: 'A sentence is always embedded in the here and now ... Every verbal formation without exception, no matter what the idiom may be, is always linked to a particular present, thus to an always unique combination of circumstances, to which the language refers by means of a specific morphology' (ibid. 37). Second, as we shall see later, this sentence-as-a-whole itself has a sense and a reference. 'The king of France is bald' has a sense apart from any circumstances, and a reference that, in given circumstances, makes it sometimes true, sometimes false.[10] Here, linguistic analysis is more precise than the semantics of the linguists, who seem too dependent on the opposition between semiotics and semantics and hence pay too much attention to the sole trait that guarantees the difference between these two orders.

A third pair of traits has to do with the structure of acts of discourse.

Every such act can be considered with regard to its *locution* aspect and its *illocution* aspect (in addition, it has a *perlocution* aspect, which is not relevant in the context of the present discussion). It is easy to relocate this distinction, introduced by J.L. Austin,[11] in a further development of Benveniste's theory of the instance of discourse. What is one doing, in effect, when one speaks? One is doing several things at several levels. There is, first of all, the act of saying or the locutionary act. This is what we are doing when we bring the predicative and identifying functions together. But the same act of combining the action of 'closing' with the subject 'door' can be accomplished as a statement, command or wish, with regret, etc. These diverse modalities of the same propositional content have nothing to do with the propositional act itself, but with its 'force,' namely, what one does *in* saying (hence the prefix of *il*locution). *In* saying, I make a promise, or give an order, or submit a statement. The roots of this distinction are, in fact, quite old; the Sophists, with Protagoras, had already distinguished several forms of discourse – question and answer, prayer, order.[12]

What first interested Austin, the originator of this sort of analysis, is another difference (which later seemed to him to be a particular case of the one we are considering), namely, the difference between the constatives and the performatives, the model of the latter being the promise. In promising I *do* the very thing which is *said* in the promise: by saying, I commit myself, I place myself under the obligation of doing.[13] The performatives are first person singular statements in the present indicative, and they concern those actions that depend on the one who commits himself. The theory of speech acts progressed further when it was noted that the performative is not unique in *doing* something. In the constative, I commit myself in a way that is different from promising. I believe what I say. If I say, 'The cat is on the mat, but I do not believe it,' the contradiction exists not at the propositional level, but between the self-engagement implicit in the first proposition and the explicit denial that follows it. Accordingly, it is not just the performatives that present the complex structure of acts of discourse. It will be noted that the locutionary act allows one to anchor elements in language that are considered to be psychological – belief, desire, feelings, and in general, a corresponding 'mental act.'[14] This remark is important because it refers to the locutionary agent, the speaking subject, whom we will discuss later on.

Émile Benveniste did not find it difficult to integrate the speech act theory into his own views of the instance of discourse, as we see in his report of 'Analytical Philosophy and Language.'[15]

Our fourth pair concerns sense and reference.

These terms were introduced into contemporary philosophy by Gottlob Frege in 'Über Sinn und Bedeutung.'[16] It too, as we will see, finds a place in the concept of semantics according to Benveniste. It is really only the sentence that makes this distinction possible. Only at the level of the sentence, taken as a whole, can what is said be distinguished from that of which one speaks. This difference is implied already in the simple equational definition, A = B, where A and B have different meanings. But if one says that the one equals the other, one says at the same time that they refer to the same thing. One can expose the difference between sense and reference by looking at cases in which there are obviously two senses for one reference (Alexander's instructor and Plato's pupil), or cases in which no referent can be assigned empirically (the farthest thing from earth).

The distinction between sense and reference is a necessary and pervasive characteristic of discourse, and collides head-on with the axiom of the immanence of language. There is no reference problem in language: signs refer to other signs *within* the same system. In the phenomenon of the sentence, language passes outside itself; reference is the mark of the self-transcendence of language.

This trait, more than others perhaps, marks the fundamental difference between semantics and semiotics. Semiotics is aware only of intra-linguistic relationships, whereas semantics takes up the relationship between the sign and the things denoted – that is, ultimately, the relationship between language and world. Therefore, the definition of sign by the signifier-signified relationship and its definition by the relation to thing are not opposed to one another. The substitution of the first definition for the second simply means that semiotics is being taken as semiotics. But this does not abolish the second definition; it continues to be valid for language in use and in action, whenever language is taken in its mediatory function between man and man, between man and world, and so integrating man into society and assuring the correspondence between language and world.

It is also possible to link up the problem of reference with the notion of the intended, which was distinguished earlier from the notion of the signified. It is the intended, not the signified, whose reach goes outside language: 'In the sign we have reached the intrinsic reality of language, while with the sentence we connect up with things outside language; and whereas the constitutive counterpart of the sign is the signified, which is inherent to the sign, the sense of the sentence implies reference to the discourse situation and the speaker's attitude' ('La forme' 36). Leaving this last remark aside for the time being, it is clear that the transcendence-function of the intended captures perfectly the meaning of the Fregean concept of reference. At the same time, Husserl's phenomenological analysis based on the concept of intentionality is completely justified: language is intentional par excellence; it aims beyond itself.[17]

A fifth pair differentiates reference to reality from reference to the speaker.

Reference is itself a dialectical phenomenon. To the extent that discourse refers to a situation, to an experience, to reality, to the world, in sum to the extra-linguistic, it also refers to its own speaker by means of procedures that belong essentially to discourse and not to language.[18] On the first level of these procedures we find the personal pronouns, which are truly 'asemic': the word *I* has no signification in itself, but is an indicator of the reference of discourse to the one who is speaking. *I* means the one who can apply I to himself in a sentence, as being the one who is speaking. Thus the personal pronoun is the function of discourse essentially, and takes on meaning only when someone speaks and designates himself by saying 'I.' To personal pronouns can be added the tenses of verbs. These constitute very different grammatical systems, but they are anchored in the present. For the present, like the personal pronoun, is auto-designative. The present is the very moment at which the discourse is being uttered. This is the present of discourse. By means of the present, discourse itself qualifies itself temporally. The same is to be said of many adverbs (here, now, etc.), all of them connected to the instance of discourse. So too with the demonstratives, 'this one' and 'that one' [*ceci, cela*], whose oppositions are determined in relation to the speaker. In so far as it is auto-referential, discourse establishes an absolute this-here-now.

This auto-referential character is clearly implied in the very notion of instance of discourse. And it can also be linked up to the theory of speech acts. Indeed, 'the modalities of which the sentence is capable' (*Problems* 110) (that is, assertive, interrogative and imperative proposition), even though they are alike in their dependence on predication, express diverse ways in which the speaker is engaged in his discourse: 'Now these three modalities do nothing but reflect the three fundamental behaviours of man speaking and acting through discourse upon his interlocutor: he wishes to impart a piece of knowledge to him or to obtain some information from him or to give an order to him' (ibid.). Now what we have here are corollaries of the communication function, which itself depends on the auto-referential function of discourse. Indeed, 'these are the three inter-human functions of discourse that are implied in the three modalities of the sentence-unit, each one corresponding to an attitude of the speaker' (ibid.). Thus we find a good match established between the speech-act theory and the auto-referential character of discourse, itself implied in the notion of instance of discourse.

A last pair, very important for our study of metaphor, concerns the redistribution of the spheres of the paradigmatic and the syntagmatic, which the distinction between semiology and semantics brings along with it.

Paradigmatic relations (principally inflections, derivation, etc.) concern the signs in the system, and so belong to the semiotic order. The 'binary' law, cherished by Jakobson and the structuralists,[19] holds true for them. On the other hand, 'syntagma' is the name given to the specific formation in which the meaning of the sentence is achieved. The reason why this trait is so important for our investigation is that, if the paradigm is semiotic and the syntagma semantic, then substitution, a paradigmatic law, belongs on the side of semiology. Consequently, it will be necessary to say that metaphor as treated in discourse – the metaphorical statement – is a sort of syntagma. It follows that the metaphorical process can no longer be put on the paradigmatic side and the metonymic process on the syntagmatic side. As I shall show in Study 5, this does not prohibit the classification of metaphor, taken as a meaning phenomenon affecting words, among the substitutions; but, in return, this semiotic classification does not debar a properly semantic investigation into the form of discourse (therefore of syntagma) that is realized by metaphor. Indeed, it is as syntagma that the metaphorical statement must be considered if it is true that the meaning-effect results from a certain interaction of the words within the sentence. The place reserved for metaphor can be seen in this account by Benveniste: 'It is a consequence of their being set together, that words take on qualities they did not possess in themselves, which even contradict those they possess otherwise' ('La forme' 38).

2 / SEMANTICS AND RHETORIC OF METAPHOR

The pioneering job done by I.A. Richards' *The Philosophy of Rhetoric* cannot be overestimated. The theory of metaphor that we find in the fifth and sixth chapters of his book is connected to a new definition of rhetoric, and not initially to a semantics of the sentence. But it is not difficult to demonstrate that his idea of rhetoric[20] derives from a semantic conception close to the one that has just been articulated. Furthermore, he is aware that his is an attempt 'to revive an old subject' (3) on the basis of a new analysis of language.

Richards borrows his definition of rhetoric from one of the last great English treatises of the eighteenth century, that of Archbishop Whateley. Rhetoric, proclaims Whateley, is 'a philosophic discipline aiming at a mastery of the fundamental laws of the use of language' (7). It can be seen that the amplitude of Greek rhetoric is restored in each of the elements of this definition. By putting the accent on the use of language, the author situates rhetoric on the properly verbal plane of understanding and of communication; rhetoric is thus the theory of discourse, of thought as discourse. By seeking the laws of this usage, furthermore, he submits the rules of competence to a disciplined reflection. By proposing that the goal of rhetoric is the mastery of these laws, he sets the study of misunderstanding on the same level as the study of understanding. (Following him, Richards calls rhetoric 'a study of verbal understanding and misunderstanding' [23].) Finally, the philosophical character of this discipline is assured in that its major concern is to remedy 'losses in communication' (3) rather than to assign to rhetoric the office of persuading, of influencing, and lastly, of pleasing – an office that in the past cut rhetoric off progressively from philosophy. And so, rhetoric will be called 'a study of misunderstanding and its remedies' (3).

In addition to its aims, the frankly anti-taxonomical bent of this rhetoric distinguishes it from its decadent relations. Not a single attempt at classifying figures is to be found in this short work. Metaphor holds sway here without a single allusion to features that might oppose it to metonymy or to synecdoche, oppositions that were already explored in Aristotle's *Poetics*. But it does not have this negative trait just by chance. Deviations are what one classifies; further, deviations exist in relation to fixed significations. And what elements of discourse are fundamentally the carriers of fixed signification, if not nouns or names? Now Richards mobilizes his whole rhetorical enterprise with the aim of re-establishing the rights of discourse at the expense of the rights of the word. From the start he attacks the cardinal distinction in classical rhetoric between proper meaning and figurative meaning, a distinction for which he blames 'the Proper Meaning Superstition' (11). Words have no proper meaning, because no meaning can be said to 'belong' to them; and they do not possess any meaning in themselves, because it is discourse, taken as a whole, that carries the meaning, itself an undivided whole. Hence, in the name of an undisguisedly contextual theory of meaning – a theory summed up in 'the context theorem of meaning' (40) – the author denounces the notion of proper meaning.

Richards constructs his contextual law on the following considerations. First of all, it is the fact of change that makes the context primary: 'We are things peculiarly responsive to other things' (29). The context of discourse, therefore, is itself one part of a larger context, which is constituted by the question and answer. Furthermore, in any segment of discourse, the words owe their meaning only to a phenomenon of *'delegated efficacy'* (32). This phenomenon is the key to the notion of context, which is the 'name for a whole cluster of events that recur together – including the required conditions as well as whatever we may pick out as cause or effect' (34). Consequently, words have meaning only through the abridgment of the context: 'What a word means is the missing parts of the contexts from which it draws its delegated efficacy' (35). So it remains true that the word 'holds true for,' 'stands for' – but not for a thing or an idea. The belief that words possess a meaning that would be proper to them is a leftover from sorcery, the residue of 'the magical theory of names' (71). Words are not at all the names of ideas present to the mind; they are not constituted by any fixed association with data, whatever that data might be. All they do is refer back to the missing parts of the context. Consequently, constancy of meaning is never anything but the constancy of contexts. And this constancy is not a self-evident phenomenon; stability is itself something to be explained. (Something more likely to be self-evident would be a law of process and of growth, like that which Whitehead postulated as the principle of reality.)

Consequently, nothing prevents a word from signifying more than one thing. Since it refers back to 'contextually missing parts,' these parts can belong to opposed contexts. By their 'overdetermination,' therefore, words express the 'large scale rivalries between contexts' (40). This critique of the superstition concerning the single, true meaning quite obviously paves the way for a positive appreciation of the role of metaphor. However, this observation holds true for all forms of double meaning that can be linked to intentions, mental reservations, and conventions conveyed by the missing parts of the context.

The relationship of priority between word and sentence is thus entirely reversed. We might recall the coincidence between idea and proposition in Fontanier, and the ultimate privileged position of the idea in *Les Figures du discours*.[21] With Richards, hesitation is no longer possible. The meaning of the sentence is not the result of the meaning of the words; rather, the latter meaning proceeds from breaking down the sentence and isolating one of its parts. The route taken by the *Theaetetus* prevails over that of the *Cratylus*. In a chapter significantly titled 'The Interanimation of Words' (47), Richards sets down his theory of the interpenetration of parts of discourse, upon which the theory of the interaction proper to metaphor will be built.

The modalities of this interpenetration are themselves the function of the degree of stability of the meanings of words, that is, of the contexts that have been abridged. According to this perspective, technical language and poetic language constitute the two ends of a single scale. One end is occupied by univocal meanings anchored in definitions. At the other end, no meaning stabilizes outside the '*movement* among meanings' (48). Certainly, the work of good authors tends to give words fixed values of usage – which is, without doubt, the origin of the false belief that words have a meaning, that they possess their meaning. So too, the theory of usage did not overthrow, but finally strengthened, the preconception of the proper meaning of words. But, as opposed to the usage that fixes their meanings, the literary use of words consists precisely in restoring 'the interplay of the interpretative possibilities of the whole utterance' (55). This is why the meaning of words has to be 'guessed' (53) every time; one can never build upon an acquired stability. The experience of translation is parallel to this. It shows that the sentence is not a mosaic, but an organism. To translate is to invent an identical constellation, in which each word is influenced by all the others and, bit by bit, profits from its relation to the whole language.

We said that Richards broke with the theory of word conceived as the name of the idea. It must be added that he goes further than Benveniste regarding the primacy of the instance of discourse over the word. Benveniste certainly subordinated the actual meaning of the word to the entirely circumstantial meaning of the sentence, but he did not dissolve the one into the other. The fact is that, with him, semantics remains in tension with a semiology that assures the identity of signs by means of their differences and oppositions. We will return in Study 5 to this conflict between a semiology founded on differential laws and thus allowing the establishment of a taxonomy, and a semantics that recognizes only one sort of operation, that of the predicate, and allows at most one enumeration (perhaps endless, as Wittgenstein suggests)[22] of 'acts of discourse.' With Richards we enter into a semantics of the metaphor that ignores the duality of a theory of signs and a theory of the instance of discourse, and that builds directly on the thesis of the interanimation of words in the living utterance.

This theory is a rhetoric, in that it teaches the mastery of contextual interplay by means of a knowledge of criteria of understanding other than those of simple univocity upon which logic is built. Such attention to criteria is a descendant of the ancient reflection on 'virtues of *lexis*'[23]; but those older criteria – precision, liveliness, expressiveness, clarity, beauty – remain locked in to the superstition concerning proper meaning. If rhetoric is 'a study of misunderstanding and its remedies' (3), the remedy is the 'command'[24] of the shifts of meaning that assure the effectiveness of language in communication. Ordinary conversation consists in following these shifts, and rhetoric should teach their mastery. A 'systematic' study (73) of the recurrent forms of ambiguity and transference, therefore, is the most urgent task of the new rhetoric. It is doubtful, however, whether such a study could be systematic in the sense treasured by the taxonomic spirit. It is more a question of 'a clarification ... a translation of our skills into comprehension' (73), in a spirit close to the linguistic analysis of English-language authors.

And, indeed, the two lectures devoted to metaphor (lectures 5 and 6) undertake just such a clarification. We learn, first of all, that the functioning of metaphor is to be detected within ordinary usage; for, contrary to Aristotle's well-known saying that the mastery of metaphor is a gift of genius and cannot be taught, language is 'vitally metaphorical,' as Shelley saw very well.[25] If to 'metaphorize well' is to possess mastery of resemblances, then without this power we would be unable to grasp any hitherto unknown relations between things. Therefore, far from being a divergence from the ordinary operation of language, it is 'the omnipresent principle of all its free action' (90). It does not represent some additional power, but the constitutive form of language. By restricting itself to the description of the ornaments of language, rhetoric condemned itself to treating nothing but superficial problems – whereas metaphor penetrates to the very depths of verbal interaction.

This pervading presence of metaphor results from the 'context theorem of meaning.' If the word substitutes for a combination of aspects that are themselves the missing parts of their diverse contexts, the principle of metaphor derives from this constitution of words. According to one elementary formulation, metaphor holds two thoughts of different things together in simultaneous performance upon the stage of a word or a simple expression, whose meaning is the result of their interaction. Or, to bring this description and the theorem of meaning into accord, we can say that the metaphor holds together within one simple meaning two different missing parts of different contexts of this meaning. Thus, we are not dealing any longer with a simple transfer of words, but with a commerce between thoughts, that is, a transaction between contexts. If metaphor is a competence, a talent, then it is a talent of thinking. Rhetoric is just the reflection and the translation of this talent into a distinct body of knowledge.

At this stage of the description, the danger would be in fact the inverse of that to which the excessive minutiae of tropology was exposed. Would not every pair of thoughts condensed in a single expression constitute a metaphor? Here Richards introduces a distinctive factor that plays the role of specific difference in relation to the generic concept of 'transaction between contexts.' The two thoughts in metaphor are somehow disrupted, in this sense, that we describe one through the features of the other. Fontanier perceived something of this in his definition of metaphor, 'to present one idea under the sign of the other'[26]; but without an adequate theory of discourse, he was unable to draw out all its consequences. Richards suggests that we call the underlying idea the 'tenor' and that 'vehicle' be the name of the idea under whose sign the first idea is apprehended.[27] It is very important to note, however, that the metaphor is not the vehicle alone, but the whole made up of the two halves.

No doubt this terminology is less familiar than another. Why not say 'the original idea' and 'the borrowed idea'? Or 'what is really being thought or said' and 'what it is compared to'? Or 'the principal subject' and 'what it resembles'? Or, better, 'the idea' and 'its image'? No: the advantage of this esoteric terminology is precisely that it combats every allusion to a proper meaning, every return to a non-contextual theory of idea, but also and above all, anything borrowed from the notion of mental image. (Richards' principal adversaries here are the eighteenth-century English rhetoricians, against whom he quotes the insightful Coleridge.)[28] Nothing is more misleading in this regard than the confusion between figure of style and image, if image is understood as the copy of a sensible perception. Tenor and vehicle are neutral terms with regard to all these confusions. But above all, they prevent one from talking about tenor apart from the figure, and from treating the vehicle as an added ornament. The simultaneous presence of the tenor and vehicle and their interaction engender the metaphor; consequently, the tenor does not remain unaltered, as if the vehicle were nothing but wrapping and decoration. (We shall see presently the use Max Black makes of this remark.)

What can we say now about 'The Command of Metaphor' (lecture 6) as a conscious reflection on the spontaneous talent at work in metaphor? We are in great danger of letting our theories, necessarily 'oversimplifying' and 'fallacious,' usurp the place of our talent, which in many respects is 'prodigious and inexplicable' (116). Perhaps every renewal of rhetoric must risk making this mistake, which William James called 'the Psychologist's Fallacy' (116): 'Very likely a new attempt must again lead into artificialities and arbitrariness' (115). (Perhaps this warning applies to the explorations that we will examine in Study 5.)

A first, critical problem that a reflective rhetoric cannot elucidate is the outcome of the distinction between literal and metaphorical meaning. As we saw, the tenor-vehicle pair completely ignores this distinction. But even though it was not the point of departure, we might still end up there. The sole criterion of metaphor, in effect, is that the word presents two ideas at once,[29] that it comprises at once both tenor and vehicle in interaction. By contrast, this criterion can serve to define literal meaning: a word in which tenor and vehicle cannot be distinguished can be taken provisionally to be literal. So this distinction is not wholly lost; however, it does not arise from a characteristic indigenous to words, but from the manner in which interaction functions, on the basis of the contextual meaning theorem. But then literal meaning has no connection any longer with proper meaning. Moreover, literal language becomes quite rare outside of the technical language of the sciences.

Reflective lucidity applied to metaphorical talent consists in good part in locating the 'ground' of the metaphor (117), its underlying 'rationale.' Whether the metaphor concerned be dead (the leg of the chair) or living (an author's metaphor), our procedure is the same: we look for its ground in some shared characteristic. But this characteristic does not necessarily lie in a direct resemblance between tenor and vehicle; it can result from a common attitude taken to them both (118). And a vast range of intermediary cases fans out between these two extremes.

This brings up another critical problem: does the relationship between tenor and vehicle belong necessarily to the order of comparison? And what is comparison? To compare can be to hold two things together in order to let them act together; it can also mean perceiving their resemblance; or, again, it can mean apprehending certain aspects of one thing through the co-presence of the other. Resemblance, then, on which the last examples of classical rhetoric based their definition of metaphor, is just one particular form of the approximation [rapprochement] through which we describe one thing in terms of another. The vehicle has many techniques for influencing the way in which the tenor is apprehended. But if we adopt a thesis that is the exact counter-position of the strict definition of metaphor as resemblance – replacing comparison, as does André Breton, by the juxtaposition of two dissimilar ideas 'in an abrupt and gripping manner'[30] – then all the good we do is to produce a negative image of classical rhetoric. To compare, maintains Richards, is always to connect things, and 'The mind is a connecting organ, it works only by connecting and it can connect any two things in an indefinitely large number of different ways' (125). Evidently, however hostile this 'philosophy of rhetoric' may be to proper meanings, it does not advocate calculated anarchy. The bow may be stretched to the limit, but the arrow keeps its aim. There is no language, then, that does not bestow meaning on that which first created tension in the mind. Sometimes a whole poem is needed for the mind to invent or find a meaning; but always the mind makes connections.

Thus, one and the same tensive theory gives equal status to dissimilarity and to resemblance. Perhaps the modification imparted by the vehicle to the tenor is even greater because of their dissimilarity than because of their resemblance.[31]

The last critical problem concerns the *ontological* bearing of metaphorical language. This problem is first alluded to in connection with spontaneous competence. In effect, according to the contextual meaning theorem, the context lets us understand the missing parts of discourse implied in the meaning of the words, and also the situations represented by these missing terms. Therefore, we readily assent to speaking of a metaphorical grasp of reality itself: 'Our world,' says Richards, 'is a projected world, shot through with characters lent to it from our own life ... the exchanges between the meanings of words which we study in explicit verbal metaphors are superimposed upon a perceived world which itself is a product of earlier or unwitting metaphor ...' (108-9). This is all written into the general theorem of meaning. But Richards' analysis lacks the orientation towards the problem of the relationships between metaphor and reality that we will consider later in Study 7 with the work of Philip Wheelwright. Indeed, we have to set this problem aside as we are unable at this stage of our research to differentiate between sense and reference.

A reflective rhetoric cannot settle this problem either. It can, at best, clarify it by tying it up with the problem of belief. Must we believe what an utterance says in order to understand it fully? Must we accept as true what the Bible or the *Divine Comedy* says metaphorically? A critical response involves discerning four possible modes of interpretation and thus also of belief: 'We can extract the tenor and believe that as a statement; or extract the vehicle; or, taking the tenor and vehicle together, contemplate for acceptance or rejection some statement about their relations, or we can accept or refuse the direction which together they would give to our living' (135). This last possibility of understanding a metaphorical statement seems really to increase, but in a critical way, the spontaneous action (cited above) of a metaphorical grasp of the world. (We will return to this mode of comprehension as the paradigm of a hermeneutical conception of metaphor.)[32] Then, as Richards himself suggests, the 'command of metaphor' will be 'the control of the world that we make for ourselves to live in' (135). But he goes no further in this direction; he is content to remind us of the case of psychoanalysis, where 'transference' – a precise synonym for metaphor – does not reduce to a verbal interplay, but operates between our 'modes of regarding, of loving, of acting' (135). Indeed, it is within the very density of living relationships that we decifer new situations in terms of figures – for example, the parental image – that play the role of 'vehicle' with respect to these new situations considered as 'tenor' (135-6). Thus, the process of interpretation takes place at the level of modes of existing. The example of psychoanalysis, although dealt with briefly, gives us a glimpse of the horizon of the rhetorical problem: if metaphor consists in talking about one thing in terms of another, does it not consist also in perceiving, thinking, or sensing one thing in terms of another?

3 / LOGICAL GRAMMAR AND SEMANTICS

Max Black's article entitled 'Metaphor' and published in *Models and Metaphor*[33] has become a classic in its field on the west side of the Atlantic. And justly so: in a somewhat nuclear fashion, he condenses the essential theses of a semantic analysis of metaphor at the level of the statement as a whole in order to account for a change in meaning that is centred in the word. Nevertheless, this brief essay does not eclipse Richards' work, despite the tentativeness and a certain lack of technical development in the latter. For Richards made the breakthrough; after him, Max Black and others occupy and organize the terrain.

At first sight, Black's purpose seems quite different from that of Richards. He is not at all concerned with the restoration of the old rhetoric. His aim is rather to work out a 'logical grammar' of metaphor, by which he understands the set of convincing answers to questions of the following sort: What features let one recognize an instance of metaphor? Are there criteria for the detection of metaphor? Is metaphor to be seen as a mere ornament, added to the pure and simple meaning? What are the relationships between metaphor and simile? What effect does the use of metaphor attempt to achieve? Evidently the task of clarification raised by these questions hardly differs at all from what Richards calls rhetoric, since for Richards acquiring the command of metaphor demands that one understand its workings and those of the whole of language. Reflective mastery and clarification are closely related. Moreover, the two authors share a conviction about the presuppositions of their work of clarification: for Richards, technical competence in the use of metaphor is presupposed; for Black, spontaneous agreement on a preliminary list of obvious metaphors. In the same way, then, that it is impossible to begin to bring off well-formed expressions without a foundation in the grammatical consciousness that speakers have, spontaneous usage guides the first steps of logical grammar. Hence, it covers the same territory as the reflective rhetoric of Richards, to which it adds more highly technical precision, thanks to Black's skills as a logician and epistemologist.

Black's work marks decisive progress in clarifying the field in at least three ways. The first concerns the very structure of the metaphorical statement, which Richards expressed through the tenor-vehicle relationship. Before being able to introduce this distinction and criticize it, one must begin with this point: an entire statement constitutes the metaphor, yet attention focuses on a particular word, the presence of which constitutes the grounds for considering the statement metaphorical. This balance of meaning between the statement and the word is the condition of its principal feature, the contrast within a single statement between one word that is taken metaphorically and another that is not. In 'The chairman *plowed* through the discussion,' the word *plowed* is taken metaphorically, the others not. We shall say then that metaphor is 'a sentence or another expression in which *some* words are used metaphorically while the remainder are used non-metaphorically' (27). This trait provides us with a criterion that distinguishes metaphor from the proverb, allegory, and riddle, in which all the words are used metaphorically. For the same reason, Kafka's symbolism in *The Castle* is not a case of metaphor.

This attempt at greater precision, besides allowing us to circumscribe the phenomenon, lets us correct the distinction between tenor and vehicle. The problem with these words is that they bear on 'ideas' or 'thoughts,' which are said to be 'active together,' and above all that the meaning of each of them is too ambiguous (47, note 23). The definition above allows us to isolate the metaphorical word from the rest of the sentence. The word *focus*, then, will designate this word, and *frame* will designate the rest of the sentence. The advantage of this terminology is that it directly expresses the phenomenon of focusing on a word, yet without returning to the illusion that words have meanings in themselves. Indeed, the metaphorical use of *focus* results from the relationship between *focus* and *frame*. Now Richards saw this perfectly well; metaphor, he said, arises from the joint action of the tenor and the vehicle. Black's more precise vocabulary allows us to get closer to the interaction that takes place between the undivided meaning of the statement and the focused meaning of the word.

The second decisive advance occurs at this point. A distinct boundary is set up between the interaction theory, which comes from the above analysis, and the classical theory, which Black divides into two groups: a substitution and a comparison conception of metaphor. He leads the interpretation in this connection to a clear alternative, which will provide the point of departure for our own inquiries in Studies 4 and 5; but first we must work our way through the alternative that Black institutes.

What Black calls the substitutive theory very exactly matches the model that we set up at the beginning of Study 2, to act as a touchstone for the classical rhetorical conception. Black concentrates his attack on what we called the fifth postulate: instead of using a given literal expression, the speaker chooses to replace it with an expression taken in a sense that is different from its proper, normal meaning. To this postulate Black adds (as we did earlier) the two others that conclude the model. If the metaphor is an expression substituted for an absent, literal expression, then these two expressions are equivalent, and the metaphor can then be translated by means of an exhaustive paraphrase. Consequently, the metaphor introduces no new information. And if the metaphor teaches nothing, then its justification must be sought elsewhere than in its cognitive function; perhaps, like the catachresis of which it is just a species anyway, it fills a gap in our vocabulary. But then it functions like a literal expression and disappears as metaphor; or rather, it is merely an ornament for discourse, giving the hearer the joy of surprise, of disguise, or of imagistic expression.

But Black does not stop at contrasting an interaction theory with a substitution theory. To the latter he joins a theory of comparison, which he sees as a particular case of substitution. However, it is not introduced in that fashion, but through a general reflection on the notion of 'figurative' language. Every figure implies a displacement, a transformation, a change of semantic order, which makes the figurative expression a function 'in the algebraic sense' of a prior literal expression. This prompts the question: what characterizes the transformative function that metaphor puts in play? The reply: the grounds of metaphor are analogy or similarity (the first holding between relationships, the second between things or ideas). Richards, it will be remembered, adopted an argument of this sort in the framework of his reflective rhetoric. But, for Black, the comparison theory is just a particular case of the substitution theory; to spell out the grounds of an analogy is in effect to produce a literal comparison, which is held to be equivalent to the metaphorical statement and could therefore be substituted for it.

One may doubt, however, whether the similarity at work in metaphor is simply spelt out, 'literalized' if one can use such a word, in the comparison. Our study of Aristotle demonstrated the complexity of the relationship between metaphor and comparison or simile; the idea that metaphor is a condensed, abbreviated, or elliptical simile is not self-evident. Besides, there is nothing that says that a simile, restored by the explication of its comparative term (as, like, etc.), constitutes a literal expression that can be treated as equivalent to the metaphorical statement substituted for it. Briefly, a theory in which similarity plays a role need not be a theory in which comparison or simile constitutes the paraphrase of metaphor. We will return to this in Study 6.

In addition, Black confronts the comparison theory with a series of objections that have nothing to do with its dependence on the substitution theory. It is well that he does so, since the comparison theory has a logic of its own, and is connected to the preceding theory only by its consequences. Actually, Black does not return to the notion of figure and figurative language, although it calls for a separate discussion (as is shown by Aristotle's remarks on 'setting before the eyes' and Fontanier's concerning the kinship between figurative and imagistic language). Black's attack centres on the explication of the metaphorical figure by similarity or by analogy. Similarity, he declares, is a vague notion, if not an empty one. Besides admitting of degrees and thus of indeterminate extremes, it owes more to subjective appreciation than to objective observation. Finally, in the cases where it is legitimate to invoke similarity, it is more enlightening to say that the metaphor creates the similarity than that the metaphor gives verbal form to some pre-existent similarity. We will return at length to these objections in Study 6. In the meantime, we will say that it has been established only that the fates of similarity and formal comparison or simile are linked, and not that the latter constitutes a case of interpretation by substitution.

No doubt the destruction of the primacy of analogy or of similarity has the most far-reaching consequences, for this also eliminates the entire tropological theory and the theory of transformative functions that constitute it and of which analogy is one kind. Turning his back on all taxonomy, Black accepts that all sorts of 'grounds' allow for changes of meaning according to context and indeed even the absence of any true ground (43): 'There is, in general, no simple "ground" for the necessary shifts of meaning – no blanket reason why some metaphors work and others fail' (45). It is claimed that this argument is formally incompatible with the comparison thesis.

Starting with Study 4, we will reconsider the legitimacy of such an entrenched opposition between a substitution theory and an interaction theory. Underlying this opposition is the dichotomy between semiology and semantics. We have adopted it as a working hypothesis in the present Study, but it will have to be reviewed at some suitable moment. Let us first emphasize the benefits of this entrenched opposition between the interaction theory and its rivals. The decisive point is that, since substitution for an interaction metaphor is impossible, it also cannot be translated without 'loss of *cognitive* content' (46). Being untranslatable, it carries new information; briefly, it tells us something.

Black's third major contribution concerns the very functioning of interaction. How does the 'frame,' the context, act on the focal term so as to give rise in it to a new meaning, irreducible at once to literal usage and to exhaustive paraphrase? This is the problem faced by Richards. But his solution either takes us into a comparison theory by invoking a common character, or sinks into confusion by speaking of the simultaneous activity of two thoughts. Nevertheless, he is on the right track with his suggestion that the reader is forced to 'connect two ideas.' But how?

Let our metaphor be 'Man is a wolf.' The focus, 'wolf,' operates not on the basis of its current lexical meaning, but by virtue of the 'system of associated commonplaces' (40) – that is, by virtue of the opinions and preconceptions to which a reader in a linguistic community, by the very fact that he speaks, finds himself committed. This system of commonplaces, added to the literal uses of the word, which are governed by syntactic and semantic rules, forms a system of implications that lends itself to more or less easy and free invocation. To call a man a wolf is to evoke the lupine system of associated commonplaces. One speaks then of the man in 'wolf-language.' Acting as a filter (39) or screen (41), 'The wolf-metaphor suppresses some details, emphasizes others – in short, *organizes* our view of man' (41).

In this way metaphor confers an 'insight.' Organizing a principal subject by applying a subsidiary subject to it constitutes, in effect, an irreducible intellectual operation, which informs and clarifies in a way that is beyond the scope of any paraphrase. (An adequate account of this could be drawn from Black's juxtaposition, in another essay,[34] of model and metaphor, which would also reveal very decisively the contribution that metaphor makes to a logic of invention. We will follow this line of thinking in Study 7, once the referential function of metaphor has been distinguished clearly from the properly significative function.) The present Study, taking only immanent elements of discourse into account – a principal subject and a subsidiary subject – cannot do justice to the *redescriptive* power that belongs to the model and, by reflection, the metaphor. Nevertheless, within the limits of the present Study it is possible to speak of the 'cognitive content of metaphor' in contrast to the non-informative nature of metaphor according to the substitution theory.

Black's theory, then, has great merits. Nevertheless, there are questions that remain unanswered. We have already spoken of some reservations concerning the elimination of the substitution theory and especially of the comparison theory. And the explication of interaction by reference to the system of associated commonplaces warrants particular attention.

The major difficulty (which, by the way, Black himself recognizes, 43-4) is that to return to a system of associated commonplaces is to address oneself to connotations that are already established. In one stroke, the explication is limited to trivial metaphors. (In this connection, it is significant that the 'man is a wolf' example is surreptitiously substituted for the richer examples in the initial list.) Now, is it not the role of poetry, and sometimes of stately prose, to establish new configurations of implications? This must be admitted: 'Metaphors can be supported by specially constructed systems of implications, as well as by accepted commonplaces' (43). This is a sizeable adjustment: it nearly ruins the very foundation of the explication. In his final resumé, given as a set of theses, Black maintains: 'These implications usually consist of "commonplaces" about the subsidiary subject, but may, in suitable cases, consist of deviant implications established *ad hoc* by the writer' (44). But how are we to think of these implications that are created on the spot?

This same question arises again in connection with the following, different perspective. The author acknowledges that the system of implications does not remain unchanged by the action of the metaphorical utterance. To apply the system is to contribute at the same time to its determination – the wolf appears more human at the same moment that by calling the man a wolf one places the man in a special light. But then the creation of meaning, which belongs to what Fontanier called newly invented metaphors, is dispersed and attributed to all metaphorical statements, and the analogy of the filter or the screen no longer amounts to very much. The emergence of metaphorical meaning remains just as enigmatic as before.

This question of the emergence of meaning is posed still more directly by what Black calls the *application* of the metaphorical predicate. This application is plainly something unusual and, in the proper sense of the word, paradoxical; 'The metaphor selects, emphasizes, suppresses, and organizes features of the principal subject by implying statements about it that normally apply to the subsidiary subject' (44-5). There is in this a sort of misapprehension, already suggested in Aristotle's saying that one gives the name of the species to the genus, of the genus to the species, and so on. (As we will see later, Turbayne[35] puts great emphasis on this trait, likening it to Gilbert Ryle's category-mistake.) Now this paradox, in which the very notion of *epiphora* is mired, is blurred by a theory that puts more weight on the implications of the focal term than on their application as such.

As far as the epistemological status of the present description is concerned, one can ask whether Black has kept his promise to write a 'logical grammar' of metaphor. He proposes 'semantics' as an equivalent term, opposing it on one hand to 'syntax' and on the other to *'physical* inquiry' into language (28). Now, the fact of translation – the same metaphor appearing in different languages – makes metaphor independent of its phonetic configuration and its grammatical form. Its analysis would be purely semantic if the rules of our language by themselves, independently of utterance-circumstances on the one hand and of the thoughts, actions, feelings, and intentions of speakers on the other, would permit us to say whether a predicate expression has metaphoric value. But it is rare, the author agrees (29), for the 'recognition and interpretation of a metaphor' to authorize this double abstraction. What is called the 'weight' or the 'emphasis' (29) attached to a particular use of an expression depends largely on the intention of the one who uses it. For instance, to what degree does a thinker speaking of 'logical forms' have containers and contours in mind, and how much would he want to insist on this relationship (30)? It must be admitted, then, that metaphor owes as much to 'pragmatics' as to 'semantics' (30).

This question with its methodological flavour rejoins our previous inquiry concerning the status of the 'system of associated commonplaces.' It is hard to call semantic such an explication by means of the non-lexical implications of words. No doubt it will be claimed that there is nothing psychological about this explication, since the implications are still governed by rules to which the speaking subjects of a linguistic community are 'committed.' But it is also emphasized that 'the important thing for the metaphor's effectiveness is not that the commonplaces shall be true, but that they should be readily and freely evoked' (40). Now this evocation of a system of associations seems truly to constitute a creative activity that is spoken of here only in psychological terms.

From every angle, consequently, the explication in terms of 'logical grammar' or of 'semantics' borders on an enigma that eludes it, the enigma of novel meaning beyond the bounds of all previously established rules.

4 / LITERARY CRITICISM AND SEMANTICS

On what discipline does the explication of metaphor depend? We have heard two replies – rhetoric and logical grammar. Now, with Monroe Beardsley's *Aesthetics*, we have the reply of literary criticism. How is it rooted in the common ground of the semantics of the sentence? What distinct path does it take? What benefit does the theory of metaphor derive from this change of axis?

I have turned to the *Aesthetics* of Beardsley for two reasons. First, Beardsley offers an explanation of metaphor that focuses again on the questions left unanswered by the analysis of Max Black. Secondly, the literary criticism within which his explanation takes place is based on a semantics similar to the one I presented at the beginning of this Study.

Before constituting its own level of distinct organization, the literary work is, in effect, a linguistic entity homogeneous with the sentence, which is itself 'the smallest complete unit of discourse' (Beardsley 115). It is at this level, therefore, that the principal technical concepts to which criticism will have recourse must be elaborated. A purely semantic definition of literature will take shape in terms of these concepts.

The aim of these concepts is to demarcate the phenomenon of signification, in sentences and in words, as brought to light by literature. Centring on this, the author stays far away from any emotivist definition of literature. For the distinction between cognitive and emotive language (which comes out of logical positivism), Beardsley substitutes a distinction internal to signification, one between primary and secondary signification. The first is what the sentence 'states,' the second is what it 'suggests.'

This distinction does not coincide with Austin's 'constative' and 'performative.' This is because an assertive statement can establish one thing and at the same time suggest something else, both these things being capable of being true or false. Consider the example from Frege: 'Napoleon, who recognized the danger to his right flank, himself led his guards against the enemy position.' The complex sentence 'states' that Napoleon recognized ... and led ... but it 'suggests' that the manœuvre took place *after* danger was recognized and *because of* this recognition, that is, that this was Napoleon's reason for deciding on the manœuvre. It could be established that the suggestion is wrong, for example if it is discovered that such was not the sequence of decisions. Hence, what a sentence 'suggests' is what we can infer concerning what the speaker probably believes, based on what it 'states.' The nature of suggestion includes the possibility of leading astray. It can be called 'secondary signification' because it is not experienced as being as central or fundamental as the primary signification; nevertheless, it is part of the signification. Let us reiterate that it is implicit and not explicit. To varying degrees, every sentence thus has an implicit, suggested, secondary signification.

Now we may transfer this distinction from the sentence to the word. The word has a meaning all by itself, and yet it remains a part of the sentence, a part which one cannot define and understand except in relation to real or possible sentences (115). The explicit signification or meaning of a word is its denotation, what it points to or designates; the implicit meaning, its connotation. In ordinary language, any particular context never brings a whole 'range of connotations' into play, but only one chosen part – the 'contextual connotation' of the word (125). In certain contexts, the other words eliminate the undesirable connotations of a given word; such is the case with respect to technical and scientific language, where everything is explicit. But 'in other contexts, [the] connotations are liberated; these are most notably the contexts in which language becomes figurative, and especially metaphorical' (ibid.). Such discourse can be said to involve a primary level and a secondary level of meaning at the same time. Its meaning is multiple; play on words, implication, metaphor, and irony are some particular cases of this polysemy. It is important here to say multiple meaning rather than ambiguity, because, properly speaking, we are confronted with ambiguity only when one meaning alone of two possible meanings is required, and the context does not provide us grounds for deciding between them. But literature precisely does confront us with discourse where several things are meant at the same time, without the reader being required to choose between them. Thus, a semantic definition of literature – that is, a definition in terms of meaning – can be deduced from the degree to which a discourse involves implicit or suggested secondary meanings. Be it fiction, essay, or poem, 'a literary work is a discourse in which an important part of the meaning is implicit' (126).

But the literary work is not only a linguistic entity homogeneous to the sentence, differing from it just with respect to length. It is a whole, organized at a level proper to the drawing of distinctions between several classes of works, between poems, essays, and prose fiction (we take it that these are the principal classes; between them they include all literary works).[36] This is why the work poses a specific problem of reconstruction, which Beardsley calls 'explication.' However, before getting into the 'logic of explication,' a most important refinement can be introduced concerning the notion of meaning. Unlike the preceding distinction between the implicit and the explicit, this can be seen only at the level of the work taken as a whole, even though its foundation lies in the semantics of the sentence; for it is the work, taken as a work, that reveals 'in retrospect' this property of discourse. There are two different senses in which 'the meaning of a work' can be understood. On the one hand, one can understand this to mean *the world of the work*. What story does it tell? What characters does it display? What feelings and attitudes? What, overall, is brought to light? These are questions that occur spontaneously to the reader; they concern what in the seventh Study I will call the *reference*, in the sense of the ontological import of a work. In this sense, meaning is the projection of a possible and inhabitable world. It is what Aistotle has in mind when he combines the *muthos* of tragedy with the *mimêsis* of human actions.[37]

On the other hand, the question that preoccupies literary criticism when it asks what a work is concerns only the verbal design, or discourse as an intelligible string of words (115). The decisive point is that this question proceeds from the suspension and adjournment of the preceding one (which Beardsley relegates to book 5, section 15 of his *Aesthetics*). In the language of Aristotle, criticism gives rise to this second acceptation of 'meaning' in dissociating *muthos* from *mimêsis* and reducing *poiêsis* to the construction of *muthos*. This duality in the notion of meaning is the work of literary criticism; in any case, its possibility rests on a constitution of discourse whose foundation lies in the semantics of the sentence that was laid out at the beginning of this chapter. We have acknowledged with Benveniste that what discourse intends, as opposed to what is signified at the semiotic level, relates to things, to a world. However, following Frege, we have claimed with equal force that it is possible, with respect to every statement, to distinguish its purely immanent sense from its reference, that is, from its transcending motion towards an extra-linguistic 'outside.' In spontaneous discourse, understanding does not stop at the sense, but passes by sense towards reference. This is Frege's principal argument in his article 'On Sense and Reference': in understanding the sense, we proceed to the reference.

Literary criticism takes an opposing position, by suspending this spontaneous motion, stopping at the sense, and taking the problem of reference up again only in light of the explication of sense: 'Since [the world of the work] exists as what is meant, or projected, by the words, the words are the things to consider first' (115). The program of literary criticism is expressed well by this statement. We see how a purely semantic definition of the literary work proceeds from splitting sense from reference and from reversing the priority between these two planes of meaning. An issue to be resolved is whether this split and this reversal are written into the nature of the work as a literary work, and whether criticism is here merely obeying the behest of literature as such. We will return to this question in the seventh Study. Whatever the answer, nevertheless, and however far one may be able to go in negating reference (at least for certain forms of literary work), what must never be lost sight of is that the question of sense is separated in advance from that of reference; and that the sort of purely verbal intelligibility that can be granted metaphor within the limits of this abstraction proceeds from suppressing, and perhaps from forgetting, another question that no longer concerns structure but reference – namely, the power of metaphor to project and to reveal a world.

Beardsley himself is not guilty of such forgetfulness: 'The essential thing that the literary creator does is to invent or discover an object – it can be a material object or a person, or a thought, or a state of affairs, or an event – around which he collects a set of relations that can be perceived as connected through their intersection in that object' (128). Thus, the creative writer indulges in multivocal discourse only because he bestows the characteristics brought into play by the secondary meanings of his discourse on the objects to which he refers. So literary criticism is really rebounding, it takes a second step, when it returns from these diversely robed objects to the purely verbal phenomenon of multiple meaning.

Such is the benefit of an approach through literary criticism rather than via logical grammar. In making the work the level of consideration, literary criticism brings into view a conflict, which was invisible at the level of the sentence alone, between two modes of understanding: the first (which becomes the ultimate) having to do with the world of the work, the second (and most immediate) concerning the work as discourse, i.e. as a configuration of words. The difference of outlook between literary criticism and the rhetoric of I.A. Richards is faint by comparison. Perhaps it is even just a purely formal difference, rhetoric being defined in terms of processes of discourse (thus of transpositions of meaning, among them the tropes of ancient rhetoric) and literary criticism being defined in relation to works (poems, essays, prose fiction).

It is within a field with boundaries marked off in this manner that the question of a purely semantic definition of literature, and of metaphor with it, is raised.

But why pose the problem of metaphor now where the viewpoint is not that of rhetoric? And why pose the problem if the level of consideration proper to literary criticism is the literary work taken as a whole – poem, essay, prose fiction? The somewhat oblique manner in which Beardsley introduces the problem of metaphor is in itself very interesting. The explication of metaphor is to serve as a test-case (134) for a larger problem, that of the method of explication that is to be applied to the work itself, taken as a whole. To put it in another way, the metaphor is taken as a *poem in miniature*. The proposed working hypothesis is that if a satisfactory account can be given of what is implied in this kernel of poetic meaning, it must be possible equally to extend the same explication to larger entities, such as the entire poem.

Before proceeding, though, let us point out what is at stake. The very choice of the word *explication* indicates a steadfast intention to combat relativism in literary criticism. Indeed, relativism finds some solid support in the theory of meaning. If it is true that 'to point out a meaning in a poem is to *explicate* the poem' (129), and if it is true that the meaning of the poem reveals a great depth, an inexhaustible reserve, then the very idea of stating the meaning of a poem seems to be condemned in advance. How is the truth of the explication to be spoken of, if all meanings are contextual? And how could there be a method for identifying a meaning that exists only for the moment, a meaning which may well be called 'emergent meaning' (131)? Even supposing that one could take the 'range of connotations' to constitute an objective part of verbal meanings, on the grounds that the way they are delimited corresponds to the way things appear in human experience, the major difficulty still would remain of deciding which of these connotations is brought into play in any given poem. Lacking the power to summon up the intention of the writer, is it not the reader's preference that ultimately makes the decision?

Hence, it is in order to solve a problem similar to that of E.D. Hirsch in *Validity in Interpretation*[38] that Beardsley turns to metaphor as a distilled model of the formidable difficulty delineated by relativistic criticism. How is one 'to produce a nonrelativistic logic of explication' (Beardsley 134)? To put it more precisely, how do we know which potential meanings should be attributed to a poem and which others should be disclaimed?

We will not delay over the polemical aspects of the theory of metaphor. Beardsley's adversaries are more or less those of Max Black. He fights with equal vigour against the reduction of metaphor to simile. Such a reduction is assimilated into a 'literalist' theory; in effect, once the grounds of a simile are known, the enigma of the metaphor is dissipated and all problems of explication vanish.[39]

Beardsley's contribution (138-47) differs appreciably from that of Max Black, as regards the positive role assigned to logical absurdity at the level of primary meaning, functioning as a means of liberating the secondary meaning. Metaphor is just one tactic within a general strategy, which is to suggest something other than what is stated. Another such tactic is irony, in which you suggest the contrary of what you say by withdrawing your statement at the very moment that you make it. In all the tactics within this strategy, the trick consists in giving indicators that point towards the second level of meaning; and 'in poetry the chief tactic for obtaining this result is that of *logical absurdity*' (138).

Thus, the point of departure is the same for Richards, Black, and Beardsley. Metaphor is a kind of attribution,' requiring a 'subject' and a 'modifier' – an obviously analogous pair to those others, 'tenor-vehicle' and 'focus-frame.' What is new here is the stress put on the notion of 'logically empty attributions' and – especially among all the possible forms of such attributions – on incompatibility, that is, on 'self-contradictory attribution,' attribution which cancels itself out (139-40). Among the logically empty attributions, one must place (besides self-contradiction) redundancies, which are self-implicative attributions in expressions shorter than the sentence (two-legged biped); and tautologies, that is, self-implicative attributions that are sentences (bipeds are two-legged beings) (139).

In the case of incompatibility, the modifier, by means of its primary meanings, points to characteristics incompatible with the corresponding characteristics designated by the subject at the level of its primary meanings. Accordingly, incompatibility is a conflict between designations at the primary level of meaning, which forces the reader to extract from the complete context of connotations the secondary meanings capable of making a 'meaningful self-contradictory attribution' from a self-contradictory statement. Oxymoron is the simplest sort of meaningful self-contradiction (to live a living death). Within the domain of what is normally called metaphor, contradiction is more indirect: in calling the streets 'metaphysical,' the poet invites us to draw various applicable connotations from the attribute *metaphysical*, despite the manifestly physical character of streets. Let us say, then, that 'whenever an attribution is indirectly self-contradictory, and the modifier has connotations that could be attributed to the subject, the attribution is a *metaphorical attribution*, or metaphor' (141). So oxymoron is just an extreme case of direct contradiction; it bears in most cases on the joint presuppositions of the ordinary designations.

The important point to be underlined in the subsequent discussion concerns what I will call the production of meaning [*le travail du sens*]. It is the reader, in effect, who works out the connotations of the modifier that are likely to be meaningful. A significant trait of living language, in this connection, is the power always to push the frontier of non-sense further back. There are probably no words so incompatible that some poet could not build a bridge between them; the power to create new contextual meanings seems to be truly limitless. Attributions that appear to be 'non-sensical' can make sense in some unexpected context. No speaker ever completely exhausts the connotative possibilities of his words.[40]

We now see in what sense 'the explication of a metaphor is a model of all explication' (144). An entire logic of explication is put into play in the activity of constructing meaning. Two principles regulating this logic can now be transposed from the microcosm to the macrocosm, from the metaphor to the poem. The first is a principle of 'fittingness,' of congruence: it has to do with 'deciding which of the modifier's connotations can *fit* the subject' (ibid.).

This first principle is, as it were, one of *selection*. As we read a poetic sentence, we progressively restrict the breadth of the range of connotations, until we are left with just those secondary meanings capable of surviving in the total context. The second principle counterbalances the first, being a principle of *plenitude*. All the connotations that can 'go with' the rest of the context must be attributed to the poem, which 'means all it *can* mean' (144). This principle is a corrective to the first in the sense that poetic reading, as opposed to that involved with scientific or technical discourse, is not obliged to choose between two meanings that are equally admissible in the context; what would be ambiguity in the one is honoured as the plenitude of the other.

Are these two principles sufficient to exorcise the demon of relativism? If reading is compared to playing a musical score, then one could say that the logic of explication shows one how to give the poem a *correct* performance, even though every performance is *individual* and stands alone. If it is kept in mind that the principle of plenitude complements the principle of congruence and that complexity counterbalances coherence, it becomes clear that the principle of economy that rules over this logic does not just eliminate impossibilities. It also tends towards 'maximizing' the meaning, that is, towards getting as much meaning out of the poem as possible. The only thing this logic must do is maintain a division between getting meaning out of the poem and reading (i.e. forcing) meaning into the poem (147).

Beardsley's theory partially resolves some of the difficulties left unresolved by Max Black. Giving logical absurdity such a decisive role accentuates the inventive and innovative character of the metaphorical statement. And this has two advantages. First of all, it gives the old opposition between figurative and proper meaning an entirely new foundation. 'Proper meaning' can be the name of that meaning of a statement that reflects only the catalogued, lexical meanings of a word, those that constitute its designation. 'Figurative meaning' is then not a deviant meaning of words, but that meaning of a statement as a whole that arises from the attribution of connotative values of the modifier to the principal subject. Consequently, if a 'figurative meaning of words' is still to be spoken of, it can only concern meanings that are wholly contextual, 'emergent meaning' that exists only here and now.

Secondly, the semantic collision that forces designation to give way to connotation gives the metaphorical attribution not only a singular but also a made-up character. The dictionary contains no metaphors; they exist only in discourse. For this reason, metaphorical attribution is superior to every other use of language in showing what 'living speech' really is; it is an 'instance of discourse' *par excellence.* Accordingly, Beardsley's theory is directly applicable to newly invented metaphor.

The revision of the controversion theory that Beardsley proposes in 'The Metaphorical Twist' attempts in fact to highlight the 'constructed' character of metaphorical meaning. The notion of 'potential range of connotations' is open to the same objections as the notion of 'system of associated commonplaces' in Max Black. Are not newly invented metaphors just those metaphors that add to this storehouse of commonplaces, this range of connotations? It is really not good enough to say that the properties of a word at a given moment in its history have perhaps not yet all been used, and that there are unrecognized connotations of words. We ought to say that there may be connotations that 'wait, so to speak, lurking in the nature of things, for actualization – wait to be captured by the word ... as part of its meaning in some future context' (300). If, indeed, one's intention is to draw a line within the domain of metaphor between the class of familiar metaphors and the class of new metaphors, one should say that the first time that a metaphor is made up, the modifier receives a connotation that it never had until then. Similarly, Max Black was forced to speak of 'specially constructed systems,' and to admit that in metaphorical attribution, the subsidiary subject is modified just as much as the principal subject to which it is being applied. To do justice to the way the use of metaphor disrupts the very order of connotations, Beardsley comes to claim that 'the metaphor transforms a *property* (actual or attributed) into a *sense*' (302). In other words, metaphor 'would not only actualize a potential connotation, but establish it as a staple one' (302).

This modification is very important. Beardsley is here expounding a 'Verbal-opposition Theory' of metaphor, which, as against the 'Object-comparison Theory,' foreswears all resources except those of language itself. Here we find 'properties' spoken of as seeking to be designated, 'properties' receiving, through the metaphorical attribution itself, new status as moments of verbal meaning. When a poet writes for the first time that 'virginity is a life of angels, the enamel of the soul,'[41] something develops in the language. There accrue to the language various properties of enamel that until then had never been clearly established as recognized connotations of the word: 'Thus this metaphor does not merely thrust latent connotations into the foreground of meaning, but brings into play some properties that were not previously meant by it' (303). And so, as the author recognizes, the object-comparison theory does have a role to play: it establishes that some 'properties are eligible to become part of the intention' of the word; 'what was previously only a property is made, at least temporarily, into a *meaning*' (ibid. my emphasis).

Thus, Beardsley's theory of metaphor takes us a step further in the investigation of the new metaphor. But it too in turn is caught short by the question that asks where the secondary meanings in metaphorical attribution come from. Perhaps the question itself ('From where do we get ...?') is wrong-headed. In this connection, the 'potential range of connotations' says nothing more than the 'system of associated commonplaces.' Of course, we enlarge the notion of meaning by including secondary meanings as connotations within the perimeter of the entire meaning; but we have not stopped relating the creative process of metaphor to a non-creative aspect of language. Is it sufficient to add the range of properties that are not yet part of the range of connotations of our language to this potential range of connotations, as Beardsley does in his 'revised theory of controversion'? At first glance this addition improves the theory; but to speak of still unsignified properties of things or objects is to admit that the new, emerging meaning is not taken from anywhere, at least not from anywhere within language (since 'property' belongs to the sphere of things, not of words). To say that a new metaphor is not taken from anywhere is to recognize it for what it is, namely, a creation of language that comes to be at that moment, a *semantic innovation* without status in the language as something already established with respect to either designation or connotation.

Now this statement is hard to accept. Indeed, one could ask how we can speak here of *semantic innovation*, or *semantic event*, as something that can be identified and reidentified. And was this not the first criterion of discourse, according to the model laid out at the beginning of this Study? Only one line of defence remains open: one must adopt the point of view of the hearer or reader and treat the novelty of an emerging meaning as his work within the very act of hearing or reading. If we do not take this route, we do not really get rid of the theory of substitution. Instead of substituting (as does classical rhetoric) a literal meaning, restored by paraphrase, for the metaphorical expression, we would be substituting (with Black and Beardsley) the systems of connotations and commonplaces. I would rather say that metaphorical attribution is essentially the construction of the network of interactions that causes a certain context to be one that is real and unique. Accordingly, metaphor is a semantic event that takes place at the point where several semantic fields intersect. It is because of this construction that all the words, taken together, make sense.

Then, and only then, the metaphorical *twist* is at once an event *and* a meaning, an event that means or signifies, an emergent meaning created by language.

Only a truly semantic theory that pushes the analysis of Richards, Black, and Beardsley to their limits satisfies the principal features of discourse noted at the beginning of this Study. Let us return once more to the first contrasting pair, event and meaning. In the metaphorical statement (we will not speak any longer of metaphor as word, but of metaphor as statement), the contextual action creates a new meaning, which truly has the status of event since it exists only in the present context. At the same time, however, it can be reidentified as the same, since its construction can be repeated. In this way, the innovation of an emergent meaning can be taken as a linguistic creation. And if it is adopted by a significant part of the linguistic community, it in turn can become a common meaning and add to the polysemy of lexical entities, thus contributing to the history of the language as code or system. But at this final stage, where the meaning-effect we call metaphor has become this shift of meaning that increases polysemy, the metaphor is then no longer living, but a dead metaphor. Only authentic metaphors, that is, living metaphors, are at once meaning and event.

In the same way, contextual action calls for our second polarity, between singular identification and general predication. A metaphor distinguishes some principal subject and, as modifier of this subject, operates like a sort of attribution. All the theories to which I referred earlier rest on this predicative structure, whether they oppose 'vehicle' to 'tenor,' 'focus' to 'frame,' or 'modifier' to 'principal subject.'

We began to spell out the necessity of the sense-reference polarity for metaphor in presenting the theory of Monroe Beardsley; yet we deliberately attended to a theory of meaning where the question of reference is bracketed. But this abstraction is only provisional. What use would we have for a language that satisfies the two principles of congruence and plenitude, if metaphor did not enable us 'to describe, to fix and preserve, the subleties of experience and change ... while words in their standard dictionary designations can only cope with

> The weight of primary noon,
> The ABC of being,
> The ruddy temper, the hammer
> Of red and blue ...'

according to Wallace Stevens' magnificent expression in his poem 'The Motive for Metaphor.'[42]

But the question of the reference of poetic discourse would take us from semantics into hermeneutics, which will be the theme of the seventh Study. We are not yet finished with the duality of rhetoric and semantics.

Metaphor and the semantics of the word

For Émile Benveniste

This Study has two objectives. One purpose is to portray the theoretical and empirical background that forms the point of departure for those works which the next Study groups under the name of New Rhetoric. The other purpose is to set in perspective – and eventually to set aside – certain concepts and certain descriptions of the semantics of the word that are not integrated entirely into the later works, which have a more deliberately formalistic character. On the other hand, they are more compatible with the concepts and descriptions of the semantics of the sentence set out in the third Study than is the conceptual apparatus of the New Rhetoric. This second project will come into its own only gradually, and will be clarified only in the last section, which will try to put to effective use the connection between semantics of the word and semantics of the sentence.

1 / MONISM OF THE SIGN AND PRIMACY OF THE WORD

What motivates this retrospective glance over more than a century's history of semantics is the astonishment we experience when we compare the most recent works on metaphor coming out of the semantics of the linguists – especially those in French, which will be discussed in Study 5 – with the works, principally English ones, explored in the preceding Study. In the former one finds highly technical analyses, and this sets them apart; but their fundamental hypothesis is exactly the same as that of classical rhetoric, namely, that metaphor is a figure of one word only. This is why the science of deviations and their reductions creates no shock in the rhetorical tradition comparable to that produced by the theory of metaphor presented above. It just makes the theory of metaphor as substitution one degree more scientific, and above all, what is more important, it strives to enclose this theory within a general science of deviations and the reductions of deviations. But here metaphor remains what it was, a one-word trope. Substitution, its distinguishing characteristic, has become just a particular case of a more general concept, that of deviation and reduction of deviation.

This permanence of the thesis of the word-metaphor and this fidelity of neo-rhetoric to the theory of substitution are less astonishing once one considers the difference in historical contexts. The analysis typical of English-language authors owes so much less to linguistics as practised by linguists – which it imperially ignores often enough – than to logic or, more precisely, to propositional logic, which focuses immediately on the sentence as the point of interest, and spontaneously suggests that metaphor be considered within the framework of predication. In opposition to this, the new rhetoric grows out of the groundwork of a linguistics that tended in several ways to reinforce the link between metaphor and word and (as a corollary) to consolidate the substitution thesis.

The new rhetoric inherits a conception of language that gradually became more entrenched during the course of half a century, due principally to the influence of the *Cours de linguistique générale* by Ferdinand de Saussure. According to this work, the fundamental units that characterize various levels of organization in language are homogeneous, and they all come under a single science, the science of signs or semiotics. This fundamental orientation towards a semiotic monism is the most decisive reason for the divergence in the explanation of metaphor. We observed that the most important analyses of metaphor in the English-language school show a strong kinship with a theory of language like that of Émile Benveniste, who sees language as resting on *two* kinds of units – those of discourse or 'sentences,' and 'signs,' the units of language [*langue*]. Structural semantics, on the other hand, developed progressively on the postulate of the homogeneity of all the units of language, in so far as they are 'signs.' This difference at the level of basic postulates becomes a divorce at the level of metaphor-theories. Furthermore, the examination of ancient and classical rhetoric had already demonstrated the link between the substitution theory of metaphor and a conception of language whose fundamental unit is the word. This primacy of the word, however, was not based upon an explicit science of signs, but on the correlation between word and idea. Since de Saussure, modern semantics is in a position to provide a new foundation for the same description of tropes, because it has at its disposal a new concept of the fundamental linguistic entity, the sign. Godel's publication of the manuscripts of the *Cours de lingistique générale* shows this truly to have been the overriding preoccupation of the master of modern semantics: to identify, to define, to demarcate the fundamental linguistic unit, the sign.[1]

With de Saussure, semiotic monism still had its limits and various challengers. After him, it continually became more radical.

This explains why the opposition at the level of metaphor, between a substitution theory and an interaction theory, reflects the deeper opposition at the level of basic linguistic postulates between a semiotic monism (which rules the semantics of the word and of the sentence) and a dualism of semiotics and semantics, where the semantics of the sentence is built on principles distinct from all operations with respect to signs.

Now, whereas this general orientation became explicit and exclusive only in the most recent phase of the development of structural linguistics, a second motivation must be mentioned, which was in full force right from the beginning of the history of semantics. Since the beginning – in fact, since the time of Bréal and Darmesteter – semantics understands itself to be the science of the meaning [*signification*] of words and of changes in the meaning of words.[2] The pact between semantics and the word is so strong that no one would dream of placing metaphor in any framework other than that of changes of meaning applied to words.

I call this a second motivation because later the theory of the sign will absorb that of the word. But this is a distinct motivation in that it precedes the Saussurean definition of the sign and even, to a great extent, governs it; indeed, the Saussurean sign is *par excellence* a word. For de Saussure, phonetics is as yet nothing but an accessory science, and its distinctive units do not yet have the dignity of the sign. A dominating, extremely rigid framework, which very sharply delimits a thematic field, is thus set in place. It forces metaphor to be placed within the conceptual network that the Swedish linguist Gustaf Stern characterizes very well with his title *Meaning and Change of Meaning*. The semantic fields theory of Josef Trier[3] confirms that the Saussurean conception of a synchronic and structural linguistics, for which all the elements of language are independent and take their meaning from the entire system considered as a whole, finds its application principally in the study of vocabulary.

If we bring together these two major tendencies – monism of the sign, primacy of the word – it appears that the *Cours de linguistique générale* constitutes not just a rupture but also a stage within a discipline whose contours had already been sketched before de Saussure, and whose fundamentally lexical preoccupations it reinforces. As we will discuss at greater length later, de Saussure introduces a methodological crisis into a discipline whose definition precedes and survives him. This crisis takes place within the context of the word. The great dichotomies that dominate the *Cours* focus exclusively on the word: dichotomies of signifier and signified, synchronic and diachronic, form and substance. Not that it ignores the sentence: the very first dichotomy, between language and speech, involves the message, which can only be a sentence. But this is the last mention of speech, and linguistics becomes a linguistics of language, that is, of its lexical system.[4] This is why the *Cours* tends ultimately to identify general semantics with lexical semantics. This identification is so strong that for most authors influenced by de Saussure the very expression 'lexical semantics' is a pleonasm.

The level of the word is not just the intermediary level between those of the phoneme and syntagma; it is the connecting layer. From one side the first-level distinctive units presuppose the significant units of the lexical level: the test of commutation cannot be used if a phonematic change does not lead to a change in the meaning of a word, even if the question has to do only with whether this word exists or not, and not with what it signifies. In this sense phonology is semantically conditioned. But the situation is the same with the syntagma: the relational units on which it rests presuppose as terms the signifying units of the mediating level.

Such is the primacy of the word in the structure of language units for a semantics of Saussurean inspiration. Strictly speaking, it is true that semantics and lexicology do not coincide. For one thing, the word responds to two disciplines, for its form and for meaning (so lexical semantics contrasts with a lexical morphology – composition, derivation, fusion, suffixation, etc.). At the same time, syntax itself also presents a morphology and a semantics (the study of functions corresponding to syntactic forms, as far as meaning is concerned).[5] All the more astonishing, then, is the decision that the adjective-turned-substantive, '*the* semantics,' should be called on to designate, through abbreviation, lexical semantics alone, that is, the theory of the meaning of words. As for metaphor, it remains classed among the changes of meaning. It will be recalled that this was the place assigned it by Aristotle when he defined metaphor as *epiphora of the name*. Thus the most explicit aspect of the Aristotelian definition is taken up by the 'semantics of the word.'

2 / LOGIC AND LINGUISTICS OF DENOMINATION

Before considering the theories of metaphor that base the primacy of the word-metaphor on a purely *linguistic* analysis of the notions of signification and change of meaning, I would like to dwell on a French-language work which 'for more than twenty years,' according to a recent author, 'has justly been considered to be the best on the subject,'[6] namely, the study of metaphor by Hedwig Konrad.[7] Her description of metaphor considered as a modality of denomination is based on logico-linguistic considerations – this is Le Guern's expression, not the author's – rather than on linguistics properly speaking. Besides the considerable attraction of its many detailed analyses,[8] the work interests us because of the reinforcement that logic gives linguistics towards consolidating the primacy of the word and containing the theory of metaphor within the boundaries of denomination. This suggests a question for later: whether a componential analysis coming from the work of Pottier and Greimas (and serving as the foundation for works that we will study further on)[9] will succeed in freeing itself entirely from a logical theory and in clearly distinguishing the semic composition of words from the conceptual structure of their referents. In this sense, although it predates the current technical apparatus, this work has not aged at all. In fact, it anticipates real difficulties in contemporary semic analysis. But it is examined at this stage of our investigation not because of these factors, but in view of the primacy of denomination in its treatment of metaphor.

The author attaches her conception of the word and of metaphorical denomination to a theory of the concept and of the relationship between *linguistic* signification and the *logical* concept. This theory of concepts, which sees itself as a development of Cassirer and Bühler, is very original in many respects; and this originality extends to the explication of metaphor.

The author begins with a polemic against every conception that would oppose the vagueness of significations to the precision of the concept. Such conceptions sweep away the whole foundation of the difference between proper and figurative meaning and (as we will see later) of the difference that affects the operation of abstraction in both these cases. With a daring akin to Husserl's in the *Logical Investigations*, Konrad maintains that 'the normal value of the signification is equal to that of the concept' (49). But the concept does not have to be taken as a generality whose function would be to gather in a class (and thus to classify) some sensible objects; its function is to distinguish, to delimit, by assigning an order, a structure, to the object of reference. The prime function of the concept is to recognize the individual nature of the object, not to constitute general attributes.[10] This function is particularly suited to grounding the use of the substantive in language, prior to qualities or actions being brought to it by means of adjectives and verbs. It is of utmost importance to the theory of metaphor that the detection of structure by comparison with the context of objects precede the enumeration of species and the search for extension. The problems of classification are thus neatly subordinated to problems of structure. It is no less important that the role of the dominant trait or of the principal attribute itself be subordinated to the act of delimitation and systematic ordering of traits. The concept is thus nothing but the symbol at this fundamental level, that is, a system of relationships that relate the elements of a particular object.

A definition of *conceptual* abstraction (to which *metaphorical* abstraction will be opposed) can thus be given: conceptual abstraction is nothing but the illumination or setting-out of this complex of elements that the concept symbolizes. Partly because of the contrast with metaphorical abstraction, it is important to add that this conceptual abstraction does not consist in forgetting, ignoring, or eliminating the secondary attributes; it is a rule for completing and for differentiating structure (thus the concept of metal contains the representation of various possible colours).

These are the broad outlines of the theory of concept that underlies that of denomination. It has great advantages to offer for a *logico-linguistic* theory of metaphor.

First of all, a distinctive criterion of change of meaning is provided: metaphor 'does not take part in the normal use of the word' (80). But the price of this first advantage is high: it can be asked whether the specific problems of lexical semantics, especially that of polysemy, have not indeed been dismissed in favour of a logical theory of concept. This is something that Cassirer did not do, even if he teleologically related 'language' (the topic of the first volume of his *Philosophy of Symbolic Forms*) to conceptual thought (the subject of volume 3). What with Cassirer was still just teleological subordination of signification to concept becomes identification of the two.[11]

The second benefit, which will also have its negative side, is that the problem of metaphor is attached to that of the *delimitation* of objects. Both Bühler and Cassirer, and Geoffrey de Vinsauf[12] before them, saw that the problem of abstraction is indeed the central problem of metaphorical denomination.

Thus, changes of metaphorical meaning are not banished to psychology and sociology, as in the works of Wundt and Winkler, which place metaphor among individual transpositions of meaning, which, consequently, are willed and arbitrary transpositions. Rather, changes of metaphorical meaning are treated linguistically, which here means logico-linguistically. That these changes are involuntary and unconscious confirms that they obey universal laws of structure and proceed from a 'tendency' in language itself. In this regard, we are indebted to the author for her energetic and extensive subordination of other tendencies (irony, euphemism, ennoblement, disparagement) and other psycho-social factors (association, cultural influence) to the 'tendencies of denomination' (116) that come under the jurisdiction of the logico-linguistic method.

Metaphorical denomination (which is here called 'linguistic metaphor' to distinguish it from the 'aesthetic metaphor' that will be discussed later on) is based on a different abstractive procedure. It does not consist in perceiving the order of a structure, but in 'forgetting,' in eliminating – really, in 'making us abstract from' – several attributes that the metaphorized term evokes in us in its normal usage. Accordingly, to call a line of people a 'queue' [literally 'tail' in French] is to neglect all its conceptual traits except its length; to say 'The roses in these cheeks have paled' is to forget many attributes present in 'This rose is fresh.' This theory of metaphorical abstraction anticipates the contemporary theories (to be examined in Study 5) that attempt to explain metaphor as an alteration in the semic composition of a lexeme, and more particularly, as a semic *reduction.*

But Konrad has observed rightly that abstraction is simply a foundational mechanism. Three other factors must still be added. First of all, through abstraction, the word loses its reference to an individual object and again takes on a *general* value; this sets metaphorical abstraction on a course opposite to that of the concept, since the latter, as we have seen, aims at designating an individual object. One can speak in this sense of metaphorical generalization. Hence, more than any other substantive, the metaphorized substantive resembles the name of an attribute. Nevertheless, the metaphorical term does not become the symbol of a logical 'species,' because (and this is the second added trait) 'it has become the name of the carrier of a general attribute and thus can apply to all objects that possess the general quality expressed' (88). Generalization is thus balanced by a concretization. Consequently, the transposed term is the one that appears to be most suited to the attribute in question, or in other words, the representative of a dominant attribute (which can vary among cultures and individuals as regards its content of meaning).[13] In this fashion the substantive function is preserved, the general aspect being designated by its representative: 'The metaphorical term designates the new object totally, with its whole structure, just as formerly it designated the object that alone was involved when it first became extended' (89). But this is still not all: metaphor acts as a sort of *classification*, as it were. It is precisely here that resemblance comes in. In effect, the common attribute, issuing from the abstraction, is the foundation for the similitude between the transposed meaning and the proper meaning. Accordingly, 'the two terms of a metaphor behave like two species joined by the representation of a genus' (91).[14]

But metaphorical classification itself also has differential traits that locate it midway between logical classification based on a conceptual structure and classification based on isolated features like that which Cassirer still attributes to 'primitives' at the end of volume 1 of *The Philosophy of Symbolic Forms*, and which Durkheim and Mauss also describe in their study *Primitive Classification.*[15] Metaphorical classification is distinguished from the classification ascribed to primitive peoples by the role of abstraction, which established a generic scope entirely absent from classification based on isolated features. Rather, metaphorical classification manifests the intersecting of the two other classifications, that based on structure (the logical) and that based on isolated features.

A conception that connects the functioning of resemblance to the three other traits of abstraction, generalization, and concretization is evidently a particularly full one. The whole of this conception is summed up in the following definition: 'Metaphor names an object with the help of the most typical representative of one of its attributes' (106).

The counterpart of this logico-linguistic treatment of metaphorical denomination is the disjunction that results between *linguistic* and *aesthetic* metaphor, the latter being the stylistic effect of metaphor. Only some of the functions of aesthetic metaphor correspond to those of linguistic metaphor (creating new words, making up for poverty of vocabulary). Aesthetic metaphor is essentially different. Its aim is to create illusion, principally by presenting the world in a new light. Now, to a great extent this effect puts into play an entire operation of unusual relationships, of connections between objects governed by a personal point of view – in brief, a creation of relationships.[16] The author claims that 'it is not just the grammatical relationship that functions here; a second relationship is evoked with the help of identical domains to which all these objects belong' (137). What arises here is the ontological dimension (which will be the object of Study 7). Illusion itself as 'quasi-reality' has this ontological dimension. Let us say for the moment that it is difficult to co-ordinate this aim with a simple process of denomination, and more so even with a process of unusual attributions.

Thus this work, which is so powerfully synthetic, ends up splitting the field of metaphor into a denominative function, hence one of delimitation (147), and an aesthetic function that only emphasizes a trait of an object in order to give 'a new impression' of the object (147). The abstraction at work in the one and the other is insufficient to preserve their unity.

This first doubt, raised by the opposition between linguistic and aesthetic metaphor, should make us question seriously the way the author has marshalled the facts. Is denomination truly the pivot of the problem of metaphor?

Even within the logico-linguistic viewpoint the author has assumed, the case of the metaphor-adjective and that of the metaphor-verb pose interesting problems which shatter the strict framework of denomination. Konrad again refers explicitly to Geoffroy de Vinsauf (17-18), whom she acknowledges for having taken into consideration the metaphor-adjective or metaphor-verb in conjunction with the substantive (*Dormit mare, nudus amicis*). Following his lead, she proposes (49) to fill the gap that she detects in her predecessors. In particular she corrects Meillet, who brought the adjective too close to the substantive, whereas it ought to be assimilated to the verb. They are both, in effect, functions of the substantive, which alone independently designates an object. Besides, they do not involve any complexity of elements: certainly they admit of species (which moreover are themselves nothing but attributes and actions) (69-71), but these are dependent terms and simple terms. It follows that the adjective and the verb cannot support the same abstraction as can the substantive: 'Abstraction here means forgetting the relationship between the adjective or verb and a defined substantive' (89). But – taking full account of the logical simplicity of adjectives and verbs – is this not a notable case of *application* of a predicate, a case of interaction?

The problem of interaction arises once the question of resemblance is introduced and, in its wake, that of classification. The sub-title itself is revealing: 'Metaphorical joining as classification' (91). Suddenly it is decided that one needs 'two coupled significations in one metaphor' (91), that 'two species [are there] joined by the representation of a genus' (91). Resemblance operates precisely here between these 'coupled significations,' these 'joined species.' The author is so careful to formulate her description within the framework of denomination that she has not noticed the predicative character of the operation. The result of the operation, which is simply an act of classification, is in effect a new way of naming. But is this not an equivocation on 'to name or denominate [*dénommer*]'? When one says that metaphor names an object with the help of the most typical representative of its attributes, 'to name' can sometimes mean giving a new name, and sometimes it can mean giving X the name of Y.[17] The act of naming has the second of these meanings when the author says that 'the metaphorical term *indicates the group of objects under which another object is to be subsumed, due to a characteristic trait that belongs to it*' (107). Here classification is no longer absorbed into denomination, but is linked to predication.

This implicit role of predication is attested to by the two facts of language that the author classes in the 'family of metaphor' (149), namely, comparison and subordination.

The author grants that simile and metaphor share a perception of otherness [*altérité*] : 'In both cases we see an object compared to another, not on the basis of a simple resemblance, but because this other appears to represent *par excellence* the base of comparison concerned' (149). The difference, then, is not that the one is one word long and the other needs two words. The difference lies rather in the fact that, as Le Guern strongly emphasizes, bringing two concepts together in simile does not destroy their duality, whereas it is destroyed in metaphor (or more exactly, in metaphor *in absentia*); so the correlation is not as close as in metaphor, where the transposed term replaces the proper term (150, note 1).[18]

Does this not indicate that the duality (and the tension, as we shall say later) between the terms is more evident in metaphor *in praesentia* than in metaphor *in absentia*, where substitution hides the correlation from view?

Indeed, it is the metaphor *in praesentia* that is in question under the term of 'substitution' (the form with 'is,' for example, 'The tree *is* a king') (150). Konrad agrees that this is 'the most frequent form of metaphor' (ibid.). In this case as well, a term is not *replaced* but 'expressed in the sentence and *subordinated* to the metaphorical term' (ibid.). In this functioning the author sees only the confirmation of the *generic* value resulting from metaphorical abstraction, the common foundation of subordination as species and of complete replacement of one term by another. She does not draw any conclusion from it concerning the predicative operation at work in subordination. Is it to be understood that subordination is an imperfect form of substitution? But then sentence order is being confused with an operation affecting signs.

Finally – and this is perhaps the most serious objection that can be addressed to a logico-linguistic theory of metaphorical denomination – it can be asked whether an explication centred entirely on denomination can distinguish between living and worn-out [*usée*] metaphor. Outside of examples borrowed from poets, which illustrate aesthetic metaphor alone, all the examples involve metaphorical usage in a state of advanced *lexicalization*. Further, the theory clarifies above all the phenomenon of lexicalization of metaphor, its power to enrich our vocabulary by adding to polysemy (which the theory does not take into account). This process hides another, that of metaphorical production.

3 / METAPHOR AS 'CHANGE OF MEANING'

Because of its *logico-linguistic* character, the work of Hedwig Konrad has remained in many ways without successor. The unity of its perspective succumbed to the pressure of the postulates of Saussurean semantics, which no longer looked to the concept (henceforth considered to be extralinguistic) for the measure of verbal meaning. But if the divorce between the semantics of the linguists and that of the logicians took place quite easily,[19] the dissociation of semantics from psychology has been much longer in taking hold.[20]

We will now locate our inquiry at a stage where semantics has not yet managed to dissociate itself from psychology; a stage where it is not the concept, in the German sense of *Begriffsbildung*, but association of ideas that provides semantics with a support of external origin.

I have chosen to take the semantics of Stephen Ullmann in its three successive versions[21] as principal witness, and a few related works as accessory evidence (Stern,[22] Nyrop[23]). There are many reasons for doing so. The general theses of semantics are supported here by a keen sense of empirical description, principally of the French language. Further, the long history of semantics since Bréal, Marty, and Wundt is not forgotten, although the Saussurean revolution provides the main axis of the description; but the linguistics of Bloomfield, of Harris, and of Osgood[24] are also taken into account. Finally, the most recent development of structuralism is looked at, without either hostility or over-enthusiasm. We look accordingly with special curiosity into the place and the role that might be assigned to metaphor in this firmly built as well as accommodating framework.

Metaphor is counted among the 'changes of meaning,' and thus figures in the 'historical' part of a treatise whose central axis is provided by the synchronistic constitution of states of language. Accordingly, metaphor brings into play the ability of synchronistic linguistics to take phenomena of meaning change into account. Our discussion of Ullmann's thought will accordingly be organized with reference to this specific problem.

The first thesis concerns the choice of the word as carrier of meaning. Of the four basic units within the purview of linguistics – phoneme, morpheme, word, locution (sentence) – it is the word that defined the lexical level of linguistics; and, at this level, semantics properly speaking is distinct from morphology in the way that meaning is from form.

This first thesis is not adopted without nuance or reservation. The definition of word according to Meillet, 'association of a given meaning with a given combination of sounds amenable to a given grammatical use,'[25] is taken rather as a concentration of all the accumulated difficulties surrounding the problem of the word. We will refer to some of them in section 4, especially those that concern the relationship between word meaning and sentence meaning. Diverse classical definitions of the word[26] testify that the separation of the word from the orbit of the sentence, at the very level of the identification of the word, is not accomplished without difficulty. The semanticist is always absolutely against any reduction of the meanings of words to their purely contextual values. For him the thesis that the word owes its semantic existence entirely to context is anti-semantic in principle. A lexical semantics is possible because the meaning of an isolated word can be understood (for example the title of a book – *La Peste, If, Nothing*); because one can learn the names of things and give their equivalents in another language; because dictionaries can be constructed; because a culture tends to understand itself by crystallizing its convictions in key-words (the 'honest man' of the seventeenth century).[27] It must be conceded, then, that whatever the importance of the various contexts (sentence, text, culture, situation, etc.), words have a permanent meaning by which they designate some referents and not others. It is the semanticist who contends that words have a hard core that contexts do not modify.

On the other hand, while it is possible to carry out the abstraction with respect to the word-sentence relationship in order to restrict study to individual isolated words as semantics demands, the problems attached to identifying the word prove to be considerable. Just the phonological demarcation of the word, that is, the steps taken by language to preserve the unity of the word at this level (Troubetzkoy's *Grenzsignale*), presents a wealth of problems that will not be explored here.[28] Similarly, it is very difficult to pinpoint the semantic core and the grammatical function that says what part of speech a word is (noun, verb, adjective, etc.), when, for example, the role of the word as part of speech is incorporated into its semantic core within the boundaries of the word as a lexical item. To this is added the problem of words that have meaning only in combination with other words (the 'asemic' words of the Greeks, the 'syncategorematics' of Marty, here called 'form-words'), as opposed to words that have meaning by themselves ('semic' words, the 'categorematics,' 'full words'). The semanticist evidently must hack his way through a forest of difficulties towards what he takes to be the word's unity of meaning, that is, the very object of his science.

The second thesis that such a semantics involves concerns the very status of meaning. Here Ullmann's position is deliberately Saussurean, except for two additions.

Following de Saussure, the third corner of the well-known triangle of Ogden and Richards[29] (symbol, thought or reference, referent or thing) is abandoned, and one stays within the boundaries of a two-sided phenomenon: signifier-signified (de Saussure), expression-content (Hjelmslev), name-sense (Gombocz).[30] Ullmann adopts the last-mentioned terminology, accentuating at the same time the phenomenon of naming. This is not unimportant for the later theory of changes of meaning, which, by prior rights, will be name-changes. The meaning of a word is the double unity of the name and the sense. In order to give the reciprocity of positions of speaker and hearer its due, the reciprocity and reversibility of the name-sense relation will be included within the definition of meaning. Meaning, then, will be defined as a 'reciprocal and reversible relationship between the name and the sense' (*Semantics* 67). It is because this two-fold access to the texture of the word is possible that both alphabetical and conceptual dictionaries can be compiled.

Ullmann makes two important additions to this nuclear thesis. First of all, except for the case of the highly codified vocabularies of science, technology, and administration, the name-sense relation is rarely a term-to-term relation, a name for a sense. Several names can correspond to one sense, the condition called synonymy; there can be several senses for one name, i.e. homonymy (although homonyms are really distinct words and not multiple senses of one and the same word); and above all, as we shall see later, there is the situation of polysemy.

Next, an 'associative field' must be added to every name as well as to every sense. This brings relationships of contiguity and resemblance into play, either in the sphere of the name, or in the sphere of the sense, or in both at once. This extension will allow us presently to distinguish four kinds of changes of meaning and to locate metaphor among them.

Such, then, is 'the infinite complexity of semantic relations' (*Semantics* 63). And this complexity will appear even greater if the 'emotive overtones' of words are added to what to this point is just a denotative value – that is, their expressive values with regard to the feelings and moods of the speaker, and at the same time the power of words to arouse the same states or processes in the hearer. A theory of meaning changes and especially of metaphor will not abandon contact with this emotive function, especially as metaphor could be one of the 'lexical devices' with regard to it (*Semantics* 136).

The third thesis that we extract from the semantics of Stephen Ullmann concerns the characteristics of meaning. These are accessible to a 'descriptive' linguistics, which the author always opposes to 'historical' linguistics; they can be retained within 'historical' linguistics under the heading of causes of change.

At the centre of all the descriptions and all the discussions reigns the key phenomenon of the entire semantics of the word, the phenomenon of *polysemy*; and the three works of Ullmann that we are considering abound with very emphatic statements on this point.[31] Polysemy is defined on the previously established base of the name-sense relation; it signifies that there is more than one sense for one name. The study of polysemy, however, is preceded by a more general commentary that includes it, and to which we will return in the next section. It speaks of a very general characteristic of language, called *vagueness* by Ullmann, which indicates the slight degree to which the lexical organization of a language is systematic. Vagueness is to be understood not exactly as that abstraction which is itself a phenomenon of order, a taxonomic feature, but in the 'generic' sense, that of not ordered, indefinite, and imprecise, which always demands that a further discrimination be made on the basis of actual context. We will return as well to this connection between vagueness and contextual discrimination. Let us say for the time being that most words in our ordinary language answer sooner to this feature, which Wittgenstein calls 'family resemblance,'[32] than to an implicit taxonomy within the lexicon itself. Polysemy is just an already more ordered and a more determinate characteristic of the more general phenomenon of lexical imprecision.

Another phenomenon comes into the understanding of polysemy, since it is its opposite. This is the phenomenon of synonymy, which is also of interest to a general reflection on the systematic and non-systematic features of language. It implies a partial semantic identity, which would be inadmissible in a system based only on oppositions; it points to overlapping of semantic fields, with the result that an acceptation of one word is synonymous with an acceptation of another word. The image of paving tiles or of a mosaic is deceptive in this regard: words are not just distinct from one another, that is, defined only by their opposition to other words, as are phonemes in a phonological system; they also trespass on one another. Certainly the art of speaking consists in distinguishing synonyms while applying them discriminatingly in appropriate contexts; but such contextual discrimination presupposes just this phenomenon of synonymy, as a descriptive trait of natural languages. To take the other side of the coin, so to speak, there would be no question of looking for the contexts in which synonyms are not interchangeable, if there were not contexts in which they are interchangeable. What defines synonymy is precisely the possibility of substituting words in given contexts without altering the objective and affective meaning. Inversely, the irreducible character of the phenomenon of synonymy is confirmed by the possibility of providing synonyms for the various acceptations of a single word (this is the commutative test of polysemy itself): the word *review* is the synonym sometimes of 'parade,' sometimes of 'magazine.' In every case a community of meaning is at the bottom of synonymy. Because it is an irreducible phenomenon, synonymy can play two roles at once: offering a stylistic resource for fine distinctions (*peak* instead of *summit, minuscule* for *minute*, etc.), and indeed for emphasis, for reinforcement, for piling-on, as in the mannerist style of Péguy; and providing a test of commutativity for polysemy. Identity and difference can be accentuated in turn in the notion of partial semantic identity.

So polysemy is defined initially as the inverse of synonymy, as Bréal was the first to observe: now not several names for one sense (synonymy), but several senses for one name (polysemy).

The case of homonymy must be set apart. Certainly homonymy and polysemy rest on the same principle of the combination of a single signifier with more than one signified (*Précis* 218). But while homonymy applies to a difference between two words and between their entire semantic fields, polysemy takes place within a single word whose several acceptations it distinguishes. Actually, although the boundary is easy to trace when homonyms by etymology are at issue (for example *locare* and *laudare* both give *louer* [laud]), it is more difficult to see in the case of semantic homonyms. These are explained in terms of the divergent evolution of senses of a single word beyond a point at which no community of meaning is to be perceived any longer, as in the case of the word *pupil.* Truly, notes Ullmann, 'there are border-crossings in both directions between polysemy and homonymy' (*Précis* 222).

The central phenomenon of descriptive semantics is polysemy (here also called lexical ambiguity, in order to distinguish it from grammatical ambiguity or amphibology). The theory of changes of meaning in historical semantics will deal essentially with the description of polysemy. This phenomenon signifies that in natural languages the identity of a word in relation to other words at the same time allows an internal heterogeneity, a plurality, such that the same word can be given different acceptations according to its contexts. This heterogeneity does not destroy the identity of the word (as does homonymy) because (1) these meanings can be listed, that is, identified by synonymy; (2) they can be classified, that is, referred to classes of contextual use; (3) they can be ordered, that is, they can present a certain hierarchy that establishes a relative proximity and thus a relative distance of the most peripheral meanings in relation to the most central meanings; (4) finally and above all, the linguistic consciousness of speakers continues to perceive a certain identity of meaning in the plurality of acceptations. For all these reasons, polysemy is not just a case of vagueness but the outline of an order and, for that very reason, a countermeasure to imprecision.

That polysemy is not a pathological phenomenon but a healthy feature of our language is shown by the failure of the opposite hypothesis. A language without polysemy would violate the principle of economy, for it would extend its vocabulary infinitely. Furthermore, it would violate the rule of communication, because it would multiply its designations as often as, in principle, the diversity of human experience and the plurality of subjects of experience demanded. We need a lexical system that is economical, flexible, and sensitive to context, in order to express the spectrum of human experience. It is the task of contexts to sift the variations of appropriate meanings and, with the help of polysemic words to devise discourse that is seen as relatively univocal – that is, giving rise to just one interpretation, that which the speaker intended to bestow on his ords.[33]

On this foundation of 'descriptive' semantics (synchronistic in the Saussurean sense), Ullmann plants his study of changes of meaning, of which metaphor is one species.

Being placed among changes of meaning, metaphor accordingly is part not of 'descriptive' but of 'historical' semantics.[34] Thus a methodological line is being crossed, one which the *Cours de linguistique générale* had etched firmly between two points of view too often confused in the past. Semantic constitution and semantic change belong to 'two orders of facts ... disparate even while interdependent' (*Précis* 236). Ullmann remains faithful to de Saussure when he writes: 'One can surely *combine* the two points of view – one even has to in certain situations, for example in the integral reconstitution of a homonymic collision; but the combination must never result in a *confusion*. To forget this precept would be to falsify at once the present and the past, description and history' (ibid.). Even more, by putting his study of changes of meaning at the end of his works, the author asserts his distance from the first semanticists, who not only defined semantics in the same breath as the study of the meaning of words and as the study of their changes, but put the principal accent on these changes. The opposite holds true for structural semantics, where it is the descriptive point of view that provides the guiding thread in the study of changes.

It is true that, as such, changes of meaning are innovations, and so phenomena of speech. Most often these innovations are individual and even intentional; unlike phonetic changes, which in general are hardly conscious, 'semantic modifications are often the work of a creative intention' (*Précis* 238). Furthermore, the blossoming of new meaning is sudden, without intermediate gradations: 'What intermediate stage can there be between a man's throat [*gorge*] and a mountain gorge [*gorge*] ?' (*Précis* 239). Like Minerva springing forth from Jupiter's head, metaphor issues wholly formed from an 'act of immediate apperception' (ibid.). Possibly its social diffusion will be slow; the innovation itself is always sudden.

But while changes of meaning are always innovations, the foundation of the explication of innovations lies in the descriptive point of view.

First of all, what allows changes of meaning is the nature of the lexical system, namely the 'vague' character of meaning, the indeterminacy of semantic boundaries, and, above all, the cumulative character proper to the meanings of words (a feature of polysemy that we have not yet highlighted). Indeed, it is not enough that a word should have several acceptations at a given moment in a state of a system, that is, variants belonging to several contextual classes. It should also be able to acquire a new meaning without losing its earlier meaning. This cumulative capability[35] is essential for understanding metaphor, in that it possesses the character of double or stereoscopic vision described in an earlier Study. More than anything else, this cumulative character of the word opens language to innovation. We will return later to the implications of this notion of meaning-accumulation for a discussion of Saussurean postulates. Let us now establish just one key characteristic: polysemy, the descriptive fact *par excellence*,

makes change of meaning possible; and within polysemy, it is the phenomenon of accumulation of meaning that does this. Polysemy attests to the
quality of openness in the texture of the word: a word is that which has
several meanings and can acquire more. Thus it is a descriptive trait of
meaning that leads into the theory of change of meaning – namely, that
there can be more than one sense for a name and more than one name for
one sense.

The theory of changes of meaning receives a new application in a 'descriptive' trait presented above, the union of each 'sense' and each 'name'
with 'associative fields' that permit shifts and substitutions at the level of
the name, at the level of the sense, or at both levels at once. Since these
substitutions by association take place on the basis of contiguity or of resemblance, four possibilities present themselves: association by contiguity
and association by resemblance in the realm of the name; and association
by contiguity and association by resemblance at the level of the sense. The
last two cases define metonymy and metaphor.[36]

Recourse within a semantic theory to psychological explanation should
not be surprising. Within the purely Saussurean tradition, this interference
presents that much less difficulty to the degree that both signifier and signified have a psychological status, as acoustic image and as concept.[37] Accordingly, no problem arises when the principle of a classification of
semantic changes is borrowed from the tradition of Wundt[38] and these
changes are incorporated into the Saussurean theory of the sign in such a
way that the explication of innovations remains in line with the broad articulations of the linguistic structure. Besides, there is a precedent right in
the *Cours de linguistique générale*, in the famous chapter on 'Mechanism
of Language,' for this marriage between associationist psychology and
structural linguistics. There, the syntagmatic and paradigmatic operations
are interpreted in terms of combination. Fifty years later, Roman Jakobson sees no difficulty in principle in these interchanges between semantics
and psychology, since he grafts his distinction between metaphorical process and metonymic process directly on to the Saussurean distinction, itself
interpreted in terms of association by resemblance and by contiguity.[39]

Hence a psychological mechanism regulates semantic innovations, and
that principle is association. Léonce Roudet in 1921[40] and Z. Gombocz in
1926[41] were the first to show how one can derive an explication of semantic changes – one that returns to the broad rhetorical categories – from a
purely psychological explication. Ullmann completes this movement to
bring the rhetorical classes into semantics by tightly linking the theory of
associative fields to the definition of meaning as correlation of name and
sense. Following a suggestion of Léonce Roudet in this procedure, he suggests that it is during the effort of expression, such as Bergson described in

the famous essay on 'L'effort intellectuel,'[42] that interference occurs between the two systems of senses and of names. The usual association between such a meaning and such a word is found wanting; the idea seeks expression through another word associated with the first, sometimes by resemblance, sometimes by contiguity; what results is sometimes metaphor, at other times metonymy. Ullmann notes judiciously that psychic associations do not 'set up' the change but only determine its 'direction'; in fact, the effort of expression remains the efficient cause (*Précis* 276).

This psychological mediation between semantics and rhetoric deserves attention. It carries very positive benefits, no matter what our later reservations might be. In the first place, a bridge is constructed between the individual activity of speech and the social character of language. The associative fields provide this mediation. They belong to the language, and they present the same character of latency as the 'storehouse of language' in de Saussure; at the same time, they demarcate a field of play for an activity that remains individual since it is an effort at expression: 'Whether it has to do with filling a real void, avoiding a verbal taboo, giving free play to the emotions or to the urge to express oneself, the associative fields are what will provide the primary material for innovation' (*Précis* 276-7).

Next, the psychology of association opens the door to uniting a classification with an explication, that is, a taxonomic principle with an operative principle. Dumarsais and Fontanier tried to do this by means of the distinction of tropes according to different sorts of relationships between objects or their ideas. The resemblance relationship of Fontanier is preserved unchanged. Only the two relationships of inclusion and exclusion are contracted into the idea of contiguity, as much on the plane of operations as on that of figures; thus, metonymy and synecdoche are reduced to metonymy.

Another advantage is that metaphor and metonymy derive their similarity from association itself. The only differentiating factor is the nature of the association. The distinction between figures is reduced to a psychological difference within a single general mechanism.

As for metaphor itself, it owes the preservation of its close kinship with the two-term comparison of simile to its rapprochement with association by resemblance. In other words, a psychologizing semantics gives metaphor *in praesentia* precedence over metaphor *in absentia* (as we shall see, this will not be the case any longer with a semantics that breaks all ties with psychology). In effect, the primacy of simile is properly psychological. Esnault[43] had emphasized this point: 'Metaphor is a condensed simile by which the spirit affirms an intuitive and concrete identity' (quoted in *Précis* 277). Ullmann remarks subsequently: 'In the final analysis, metaphor is an abridged simile. Rather than explicitly spelling out analogies, one compresses them into an image that has the air of an identification' (ibid.). Truly the key to metaphor is the perception of a resemblance between two ideas – in Aristotle's words *to homoïon theôrein*.[44]

On the other hand, the marriage with associationist psychology is not without grave complications. Besides the overall dependence of linguistics on another discipline (a dependence that subsequent linguistics will no longer tolerate), the mélange of the two disciplines carries harmful effects for the very analysis of figures of discourse. What is damaged primarily is its complexity. At first the distinction between two sorts of association might appear to be a simplification, and would thus satisfy the concern for economy. This is revealed quite quickly to be an impediment. By boxing the relationships of inclusion and exclusion together under the heading of contiguity, the associationist principle impoverishes the operations as well as the figures that result from it. Further, the reduction of synecdoche to metonymy is a flagrant case of reducing a logical difference (co-ordination versus subordination) into a single psychological procedure, that of contiguity. What survives this operation is a rhetoric of two figures, a 'restricted rhetoric' par excellence.[45]

The analysis of metaphor itself suffers from the psychological explication. One might have thought that the idea of 'abridged simile' would have introduced a description in terms of statement and of predication. Ullmann (*Semantics* 213) explicitly likens the conception of metaphor exposed here to that of I.A. Richards. The two compared terms that the associative fields bring into proximity are in the same relationship as Richards' tenor and vehicle. Instead of explicitly comparing two things, metaphor contrives a verbal short-circuit: instead of comparing a certain part of the anatomy to a little mouse, one says 'muscle' (the transference having occurred in the Latin origins of these words, cf. *Semantics* 213). Moreover, Ullmann accepts Richards' valuable idea that the greater the distance between tenor and vehicle[46] and the more unexpected their combination, the more striking and surprising is the metaphor.

But these remarks do not contribute to overthrowing the very principle of a description that remains within the boundaries of the word. Recourse to the process of association tends rather to strengthen these limits: in fact, operating as it does only with individual elements – meanings and words – associationism never confronts the truly predicative operation. (We will return later to this decisive point for the relationship between the semantics of the word and the semantics of the statement at the very heart of metaphor.) This is why the analysis is quick to reduce simile to substitution, which indeed takes place between psychic atoms, elements, or terms. The double play of association between senses and between names finally includes only substitutions resulting in novel naming: 'Instead of stating precisely that [the] elements [of a comb] are *like* teeth, one will simply call them the *teeth of the comb*. In doing this one will have transposed the name of a human organ in order to designate an inanimate object' (*Précis* 277). The resemblance between the two senses is what permits one to give the name of one to the other.

Confined thus within the realm of naming, the study of metaphor does not regain the breadth it used to have with the rhetoricians until the enumeration of its *species* is begun. Association is still the guiding thread. The innumerable borrowings that metaphor brings into play can indeed be assembled into broad classes that are themselves divided up according to which associations are the most typical, that is, the most usual; associations not only between senses, but between domains of sense, for example that of the human body and that of physical objects. Hence we again come upon the broad classes of Fontanier, where pride of place is held by the transposition of the animate to the inanimate and, less frequently, of the inanimate to the animate. Transposition from the concrete to the abstract forms another large group (for example, from *velum* 'veil' to 'reveal' [*Semantics* 215]). The 'sensorial transpositions,' joining two different perceptual domains (a *warm* colour, a *clear* voice), fit without difficulty into the great family of metaphors. The synaesthetics constitute a case of spontaneous perception of resemblances, which is nevertheless a function of the mental dispositions of speakers. Sensorial correspondences harmonize neatly with substitutions of names since both are cases of resemblance between 'senses.' The difference of level between sensorial and semantic resemblance is diminished by the fact that, as the famous sonnet 'Correspondances' by Baudelaire shows, the synaesthetic transpositions themselves become recognizable thanks to the mediation of language.

4 / METAPHOR AND THE SAUSSUREAN POSTULATES

At first glance, the theory of metaphor in the work of Ullmann and in that of post-Saussurean semanticists close to him appears to be nothing more than an application of the fundamental postulates of structural linguistics to a sector of historical linguistics, that of changes of meaning. In a second and more critical approximation their analysis is really something other than an application: it initiates, virtually at least, a correction of the postulates through consideration of their consequences. This rebounding of the consequences on the principle deserves attention, because it is the index of a certain latitude in a semantics that pretends to be solely a semantics of the word. To explore this further, an attempt will be made in the next section to co-ordinate the metaphor of the word, to which this Study and the following are restricted, with the statement-metaphor of the preceding Study.

The post-Saussurean treatment of metaphor shows after the fact that the *Cours de linguistique générale* constituted as much a stage as a disruption in the program of the semantics of the word. This trait is explained well enough by the nature of the methodological crisis that the *Cours* initiated at its heart.

It is really a two-fold crisis. On the one hand, the *Cours* eliminated confusions and equivocations in an essentially simplifying and purifying action. On the other hand, through the dichotomies that it instituted, it left a legacy of perplexities, ones for which the problem of metaphor, even if confined to lexical semantics, continues after de Saussure to be a good touch-stone. Indeed metaphor straddles most of the divisions instituted by de Saussure and reveals at what point these dichotomies today constitute antinomies to be reduced or to be mediated.

For de Saussure, accordingly, the gap between *language* and *speech* makes of language a completely homogeneous object contained within a single science, with the two faces of the sign – signifier and signified – falling on the same side of the gap.[47] But this dichotomy creates as many problems as it resolves; as Roman Jakobson observes in his synthesis of modern linguistics, 'although this restrictive program still finds its theoretical adherents, in fact the absolute separation of the two aspects turns into a recognition of two different hierarchic relations: an analysis of the code with due regard for the messages, and vice versa. Without a confrontation of the code with the messages, no insight into the creative power of language can be achieved.'[48] In addition to the examples of interchange between code and message that Jakobson proposes (the role of sub-codes freely chosen by the speaking subject on account of the communication situation, construction of personal codes supporting the speaking subject's identity, etc.), metaphor constitutes a magnificent example of exchange between code and message. As we saw, metaphor is to be classified among the changes of meaning; for 'it is within speech, the concrete realization of language, that the changes proclaim themselves' (Ullmann *Précis* 237). Moreover, the discrete character of these changes has been noted: however numerous the intermediary stages recorded by the history of semantic changes in a word, each individual change is a leap that attests to the dependence of innovation on speech. But on the other hand, metaphor depends on a characteristic of the code, namely polysemy. This is what metaphor will augment to some degree, when, having ceased to be an innovation, it enters into standard usage and then becomes a cliché; the circle is then completed between language and speech. The circle can be described in the following manner. Initial polysemy equals 'language,' the living metaphor equals 'speech,' metaphor in common use represents the return of speech towards language, and subsequent polysemy equals 'language.'

This circle is a perfect illustration of the untenability of the Saussurean dichotomy.

The second large dichotomy, which opposes the synchronistic and the diachronistic points of view,[49] was no less beneficial than the first. It not only put an end to a confusion by dissociating two distinct relations of linguistic fact to time (that of simultaneity and that of succession), it also put an end to the hegemony of the historical perspective precisely at the level of the principles of intelligibility, by imposing a new priority of system over evolution.

But the trouble created is as great as the advantages gained. A phenomenon like metaphor has some systematic aspects and some historical aspects. For a word to have more than one meaning is, strictly speaking, a synchronistic fact – it is *now*, in the code, that it signifies several things. Consequently, we must align polysemy with synchrony. But the alteration of meaning that adds to the polysemy and in the past had contributed to building up current polysemy is a diachronistic fact. Thus, as innovation, metaphor is to be set among changes of meaning, and thus among diachronistic facts; yet as accepted deviation, it is aligned with polysemy, and thus belongs in the synchronistic realm.[50] Once again, then, it is necessary to mediate too severe an opposition and to interrelate the structural and historical aspects. The word seems truly to stand at the crossroads of two orders of consideration, thanks to its capacity for acquiring new meanings and for retaining them without losing the old meanings. In its two-fold character, this cumulative process seems to call for a panchronistic point of view.[51]

Quite apart from the consideration of changes of meaning, the complete description of polysemy demands some such panchronistic point of view. It would appear to be rather difficult to describe polysemy without alluding to its origin; Ullmann, accordingly, despite his declarations to which I referred, discusses in the chapter on polysemy the 'four principal sources' on which it 'feeds.'[52] Now these four 'sources' have a more or less obvious diachronistic character. 'Shifts in meaning' are developments in divergent directions. 'Figurative expressions' grow out of metaphor and metonymy, which, acting in the present instant, are no less events of speech that engender polysemic series. 'Popular etymology,' a sort of popular semantic wisdom endorsing or conjuring connections that are frequently philologically unsound, leads to a situation of polysemy. And as the words themselves indicate, 'foreign influences' belong in the group of evolutions that create their situations by means of semantic imitation. The very notion of 'semantic copying' introduced here implies a return to analogy, itself treated as a factor in semantic change. Thus, despite every effort at partitioning description and history, the very description of polysemy makes reference to the possibility of semantic change. Polysemy as such, that is, regarded apart from consideration of its 'sources,' refers to possibilities of a diachronistic character: polysemy is simply the possibility of adding a new meaning to the previous acceptations of the word without having these former meanings disappear. Thus the open structure of the word, its elasticity, its fluidity, already allude to the phenomenon of change of meaning.[53]

If polysemy is so difficult to contain within the limits of synchronistic description, conversely changes of meaning that arise from the historical perspective cannot be identified completely until they are written into the synchronistic domain and show themselves to be a variety of polysemy. Thus Ullmann himself considers stylistic 'ambiguity' in the chapter on polysemy. Now this expression points out very precisely the rhetorical level of figures: 'dreaded by the foreigner, denounced by the logician, battled by the need for clarity that dominates everyday speaking, ambiguity is sometimes sought by the writer for stylistic purposes.[54] This assignment of stylistic ambiguity to the same division as polysemy is perfectly legitimate, since at a given time it will be inscribed into the current state of the language as a double meaning. Therefore, the synchronistic projection of a change of meaning is truly a phenomenon of the same order as polysemy.

In its turn, moreover, equivocation can be treated as one of the conditions of semantic changes.[55] By figuring in an ambiguous sentence, for which two interpretations remain possible, words receive new values. Thus the ambiguity of discourse clears the way for equivocity of the word, which can result in established changes of meaning that add to polysemy.

Nothing would be more accurate than to say that the Saussurean dichotomies create as many problems as they solve. Not even his most firmly fixed distinctions avoid being a source of perplexity. We know how insistently de Saussure contrasted the relation between signifier and signified (which is purely immanent to meaning) with the external sign-thing relation, which he repudiated. Henceforth, 'thing' is excluded from the factors involved in meaning; the linguistic sign does not unite a thing and a name, but a concept and an accoustic image.[56]

But even this disjunction, which has been adopted by all the post-Saussurean linguists, leads to an aporia. This is because discourse, through its referential function, sets signs fully into relation with things. Denotation is a sign-thing relation, whereas signification is a relation between signifier and signified.[57] What this leads to is an ambiguity within the very notion of meaning. As the Saussurean 'signified,' meaning is nothing other than the counterpart of the signifier; what defines one defines the other, as both sides of a sheet of paper are cut by the same motion of the scissors. But in relation to the reality denoted, meaning stands as mediator between words and things, i.e. it is that through which words relate to things – *vox significat mediantibus conceptis.*[58] This rift cuts across semantics, taken in its broad sense, and separates the semantics of Saussurean-school linguists from that of philosophers like Carnap, Wittgenstein, and so on, for whom semantics is fundamentally the analysis of the relationships between signs and the things denoted.

By holding the meaning-thing relationship at bay, linguistics emancipates itself with regard to the normative logico-grammatical sciences; and it establishes its autonomy by guaranteeing the homogeneity of its object, with the signifier and signified falling within the frontiers of the linguistic sign. All this has its unfortunate consequences, however. It becomes very difficult, if not impossible, to give an account of the denotative function of language within the framework of a theory of the sign that acknowledges only the internal difference between signifier and the signified. This denotative function, on the other hand, presents no problem in a conception of language that distinguishes from the start between signs and discourse and defines discourse, as opposed to the sign, by its relation to extra-linguistic reality. Thus the semantics of the English-language philosophers, which is a semantics of discourse, finds itself from the start in the territory of denotation, even when it is discussing words. This is because for it, words, as parts of discourse, are equally carriers of a part of the denotation.[59]

It is quite true that a semantics of the Ullmann variety succeeds in defining most of the phenomena it describes – synonymy, homonymy, polysemy, etc. – within the limits of a theory of the sign that does not involve any concession to extra-linguistic reality. But the denotative relationship, which puts the relation of sign to thing into play, is required as soon as the focus is concentrated on the operation of these differences within discourse. A purely virtual characteristic in the lexical sense, polysemy is screened in discourse. The same contextual mechanism (verbal or non-verbal) serves to separate the polysemic equivocations and determines the genesis of new meanings: 'It is the *context*, verbal and non-verbal, which makes deviations possible, the use of unusual acceptations.'[60] One really has to return to contextual uses to define the diverse acceptations of one and the same word, whether they be usual or unusual acceptations; so these are actually nothing but the contextual variations that can be classed according to their families of occurrence. And once one embarks on this mission, it is immediately apparent that the classes of these conceptual variations are dependent on the different possibilities of analysing objects, that is, things or their representatives. As the *Rhétorique générale* itself admits,[61] the material analysis of objects into their parts and the rational analysis of concepts into their elements both appeal to models of description from the universe of representations. Thus the consideration of denotation interferes necessarily with that of the signified as such when it takes account of the classes into which the polysemic variations of a single word are arranged, once they are characterized as contextual meanings. The adjective *contextual* reintroduces discourse, and with it the denotative purpose of language.

If polysemy as a synchronistic fact has such implications, so all the more does metaphor as change of meaning. Innovation properly speaking is a fact of speech, as Ullmann reminds us.[62] We have seen its consequences for the language-speech relation and the synchronistic-diachronistic relation; the implications are no less important for the signified-denotated relation. A semantic innovation is a way of responding in a creative fashion to a question presented by things. In a certain discourse situation, in a given social milieu and at a precise moment, something seeks to be said that demands an operation of speech, speech working on language, that brings words and things face to face. The final outcome is a new description of the universe of representations. We will return to this problem of redescription in a later Study.[63] What had to be shown right now was its insertion into a semantic theory that nevertheless wishes to restrict itself to changes of meaning, that is, to the study of the signified alone. Every change implicates the entire debate between man speaking and the world.

But no bridge can be laid directly between the Saussurean signified and the extra-linguistic referent; one must detour through discourse and pass through denotation of the sentence in order to arrive at denotation of the word. This detour alone allows one to interrelate the denotative operation at work in metaphor and the predicative operation that gives it the framework of discourse.

5 / BETWEEN SENTENCE AND WORD:
THE INTERPLAY OF MEANING

Rendering the broad methodological decisions of the theory problematic once again is not the only effect of applying the fundamental principles of Saussurean linguistics to metaphor. It reveals an uncertainty at the very heart of the semantics of the word, a stirring, a space for moving about, thanks to which it again becomes possible to forge a link between the semantics of the sentence and the semantics of the word, and correspondingly, between the interaction theory and the substitution theory of metaphor. If this extension should prove to be practicable, then the real location of metaphor in the theory of discourse would begin to define itself *between* the sentence and the word, *between* predication and naming.

I wish first to refer to three clues, within a semantics as deliberately given over to the word as that of Stephen Ullmann, that indicate the point of connection between this semantics and the semantics of the sentence discussed in the preceding Study.

(a) The first of these indications is given by the non-systematic aspects of the lexical system (if one can say such a thing). Let us go no further than the quantitative viewpoint: the lexical code bears features that distinguish it emphatically from the phonological code (45,000 words in the Oxford Dictionary against 44 or 45 phonemes!) as well as from the grammatical system (even if the lexical morphology of suffixes, prefixes, inflexions, compounds, etc., are included in it). The code is certainly beyond the capacity of the individual memory, and the lexical level does not need to be comprehended entirely within an individual consciousness in order to function. But the number of units in the two other codes is also not unrelated to the capacity of human memory. If one adds that this code is such that it is always possible to add new entities to it without changing it fundamentally, this absence of closure suggests the thought that the structure of vocabulary consists in 'a loose aggregate of an infinitely larger number of units'[64] than the other systems. If one considers given segments of this code, like those that have occasioned the most brilliant 'semantic field' analyses in the mode of J. Trier, it is evident that these sectors present extremely variable degrees of organization. Some present a subdivision of meaning such that each element exactly delimits its neighbours and is determined by them as if in a mosaic – colour names, kinship terms, military ranks, and some groups of abstract ideas like the triad *Wisheit-Kunst-List* in Middle High German of about 1200, as studied by Trier.[65] Other sectors are much less well ordered. These are most often 'incomplete patterns' with 'half-finished designs' (Ullmann here adopts Entwistle's phrases) where the overlapping of senses overrides neat delimitation. De Saussure himself saw in a given term, 'teaching' for instance, 'the centre of a constellation; it is the point of convergence of an indefinite number of co-ordinated terms.'[66] Obviously the idea of a twofold associative field, which continues this image of the constellation, does not take one in the same direction as the idea of mutual delimitation, which is rather a continuation of the mosaic image; thus the idea of an open system imposes itself a second time.

If one finally considers isolated words, all that was said above about synonymy and about polysemy comes together and points to the same notion of open texture. It repeats itself on the level of the lexical whole, on the regional level of semantic fields, and on the local level of the single word. The vague character of the word, the indecision about its frontiers, the combined action of polysemy, which disseminates the meaning of the word, and of synonymy, which discriminates the polysemy, and above all the cumulative power of the word, which allows it to acquire a new meaning without losing its previous meanings – all these traits indicate that the vocabulary of a language is 'an unstable structure in which individual words can acquire and lose meanings with the utmost ease.'[67] This renders meaning 'of all linguistic elements ... [the one which] is probably the least resistant to change.'[68]

In the words of an author cited by Ullmann, language *in toto* is 'neither systematic nor completely non-systematic.' This truly is why it is at the mercy not only of change in general, but of non-linguistic causes of change, among whose various effects is the prevention of the establishment of lexicology on an entirely autonomous base. The appearance of new natural and cultural objects in the field of naming; the deposit of beliefs in keywords; the projection of social ideals in emblematic words; the reinforcement or lifting of linguistic taboos; political and cultural domination by a linguistic group, by a social class, or by a cultural milieu – all these influences leave language, at least at the level of semantics of the word, which our authors have chosen, to the mercy of social forces whose effectiveness underlines the non-systematic character of the system.

At the limit, this character would lead one to doubt that the term *code* applies rigorously at the lexical level of language. In a text that we have already cited,[69] Jakobson suggests that the word *code* be put in the plural, so entangled are the sub-codes among which we learn to orient ourselves in order to speak in an appropriate manner, according to the milieux, the circumstances, and the situations where these sub-codes have currency. Perhaps one ought to go further and refuse to call 'code' a system about which, after all, so little is systematic.

(b) A second index of the opening of the semantics of the word towards the semantics of the sentence is provided by the properly contextual characteristics of the word. The predicative functioning of language is imprinted to some extent on the word itself; and this takes place in several ways.

First of all, the delimitation of the word cannot be done without reference to its eventual occurrence as a complete statement. To call the word the 'minimum free form' (Bloomfield) is to refer it ineluctably to the sentence, the model of the free form. That form is free that can constitute a complete statement ('Are you happy? ' – 'Very!').

Furthermore, in many languages the class of forms of discourse to which a word belongs (noun, verb, etc.) is announced within the perimeter of the word as entered in the dictionary. In any case, the word has the power of figuring in at least one class, for together the semantic kernel and the class define the word. In brief, the word is grammatically determined.[70]

Finally, the distinction reported earlier between categorematic and syn-categorematic words cannot be made without reference to the function of the word in discourse.

This imprint of the predicative operation on the word is so strong that certain authors define meaning in a way that is frankly contextual or, as Ullmann puts it, 'operational.'[71] Wittgenstein's theory in the *Philosphical Investigations* – to the extent that it is still valid to speak here of theory – is the most 'provocative' example of this conception: 'For a *large* class of cases – though not for all – in which we employ the word "meaning" it can be defined thus: the meaning of a word is its use in the language.'[72] The comparison of language to a toolbox from which one sometimes takes a hammer, sometimes pliers[73]; then the comparison (very Saussurean, at least in appearance) of the word to a piece in a chess set[74] – all these analogies tend to reduce lexical meaning to a simple function of the meaning of the sentence taken as a whole. This at least is the most general tendency in the semantics of English-speaking philosophers. Thus Ryle declares in a celebrated article: 'Understanding a word ... is knowing how to use it, i.e. make it perform its rôle in a wide range of sentences. But understanding a sentence is not knowing how to make it perform its rôle ... It has not got a rôle ...'[75]

These many reroutings of the word towards discourse do not in any way imply that the word has no semantic autonomy at all. The reasons listed earlier in favour of its independence still hold: I can say what something is called and look for an equivalent of its name in a foreign language; I can say the key-words of the tribe; I can point out the dominant elements of this or that moral code, the fundamental concepts of this or that philosophy; I can endeavour to name exactly the qualitative nuances of emotions and feelings; I can define a word by means of other words; and for purposes of classification, I must define genera, species, and sub-species, which is still to name them. In short, naming is an important 'language game,' which fully justifies the compiling of dictionaries and authorizes in large part the defining of meaning by the reciprocal relationship between name and sense. But, although naming is an important 'language game,' the overestimation of the word and even fascination with words, pushed to the point of superstition, reverence, or terror, are due perhaps to a basic illusion that Wittgenstein attacks at the beginning of the *Philosophical Investigations* – namely, the illusion that the naming game is the paradigm of all language games.[76]

When we begin to examine this naming-game in itself, context reappears within the very perimeter of the word. What we call the diverse acceptations of a word are contextual classes, which emerge from the contexts themselves after patient comparison of samples of usage. So the many meanings of a word can be identified as types of contextual values. Hence the semanticist is forced to make room for the contextual definition of meaning beside the properly analytical or referential definition; or rather, the contextual definition becomes a phase of the properly semantic definition: 'The relation between the two methods, or rather between the two phases of the inquiry, is ultimately the same as that between language and speech: the operational theory is concerned with meaning in speech, the referential with meaning in language.'[77] It would be hard to affirm more strongly that the definition of the word cannot appear except where speech and language intersect.

(c) The dependence of word-meaning on the meaning of the sentence becomes even more obvious when, no longer considering the word in isolation, we take up its actual, effective functioning in discourse. Taken in isolation, the word still has only a potential meaning, made up of the sum of its partial meanings, themselves defined by the types of contexts in which they can participate. They have actual meaning only in a given sentence, that is to say, in an instance of discourse, in Benveniste's sense. While the reduction of potential meaning to use is still open to discussion, that of actual meaning to use is completely beyond debate. This was noted by Benveniste: 'The meaning of a sentence is its idea, the meaning of a word is its use (always in the semantic acceptation). Based on the idea, which is particular in every case, the speaker assembles words which, in *this* employment, have a particular "meaning."'[78]

A consequence of this dependence of the actual meaning of the word on the actual meaning of the sentence is that the referential function that attaches to the sentence taken as a whole distributes in some fashion over the words of the sentence. In the language of Wittgenstein,[79] which in this instance is close to that of Husserl,[80] the referent of the sentence is a 'state of affairs' and the referent of the word is an 'object.' In a closely related sense, Benveniste calls the referent of the word 'the particular object to which the word corresponds in the concrete actuality of circumstance or of use.'[81] He distinguishes this from the sentence reference: 'If the meaning of the sentence is the idea it expresses, the "reference" of the sentence is the state of affairs it provokes, the discursive or factual situation to which it relates and which we can never foresee nor guess.'[82]

Taking this to its limit, if one puts the accent on the actual meaning of the word, to the point of identifying the word with this actual meaning in discourse, one comes to doubt that the word is a lexical entity; and one is led to say that the signs in the semiotic repertory stand this side of the threshold of what is properly semantic. The lexical entity is at most the lexeme, that is, the semantic kernel separated by abstraction from the mark indicating the class to which the word belongs as an element of discourse. This semantic kernel is what earlier we called the potential meaning of the word or its semantic potential; but this is nothing real or actual. The real word, the word as an occurrence in a sentence, is already something entirely different; its meaning is inseparable from 'its capacity to integrate a particular syntagma and to fill a propositional function.'[83]

It is not by chance, therefore, that earlier we had to incorporate the effect of context into the potential meaning itself, that is, into the word in isolation. As Benveniste remarks, 'what one calls polysemy is nothing but the institutionalized sum, let us say, of these contextual values, always instantaneous, continually apt to enrich, to disappear – in brief, without permanence, without constant value.'[84]

We are brought thus to picture discourse as a reciprocal interplay between the word and the sentence. The word preserves the semantic capital constituted by these contextual values deposited in its semantic treasury. What it brings to the sentence is a potential for meaning. This potential is not formless: the word does have an identity. Certainly, this is a plural identity, an open texture, as we said; but this identity is nevertheless sufficient for it to be identified and reidentified as the same in different contexts. The game of naming discussed just above is possible only because the semantic 'diversity' that the word consists in endures as a limited, rule-governed, and hierarchical heterogeneity. Polysemy is not homonymy. But this plural *identity* is also a *plural* identity. This is why, in the game of the word and of the sentence, the 'initiative of meaning,' as it were, passes over again to the sentence. The passage from the potential to the actual meaning of a word requires the mediation of a new sentence, just as the potential meaning issues from the sedimentation and institutionalization of previous contextual values. This trait is so important that Roman Jakobson unhesitatingly makes 'sensitivity to context' a criterion of natural languages as opposed to artificial languages, together with the two other criteria of plurivocity and mutability of meaning.[85]

This mediation of the new sentence is required especially if one considers (again with Ullmann) the 'vague' character of words and above all the phenomenon of polysemy. The word receives from the context the determination that reduces its imprecision. This is true even of proper names: Ullmann notes that while proper names have several aspects – 'Queen Victoria' as a young woman, the same person at the time of the Boer War – only one is appropriate to a given situation.[86] In like manner, Strawson notes that the proper name identifies one and only one person only if it is the abbreviation of some anterior descriptions present in the rest of the context (verbal or non-verbal) in which the name is mentioned.[87]

But, above all, it is the function of context to sift out polysemy by means of a 'conspiracy' (Firth) or 'coaptation' (Benveniste) effect of words on each other. This mutual selection of acceptations of semantically compatible meaning is most often effected so inconspicuously that, in a given context, the other inappropriate acceptations do not even cross one's mind. As Bréal remarked already about this, 'one does not even go to the trouble of suppressing the other meanings of the word: these meanings do not exist for us, they do not cross the threshold of our consciousness.'[88]

This action of the context – sentence, discourse, work, discourse situation – to reduce polysemy is the key to the problem that motivated this entire Study.

What takes place in a metaphorical statement can be understood perfectly in terms of the above phenomenon. If it is true that metaphor adds to polysemy, then the operation of discourse set in motion by metaphor is the inverse of that which we have just described. For a sentence to make sense it is necessary (it was claimed just above) that all the acceptations of the semantic potential of the word under consideration be eliminated except one, that which is compatible with the meaning, itself appropriately reduced, of the other words of the sentence. In the case of metaphor, none of the already codified acceptations is unsuitable; it is necessary, therefore, to retain all the acceptations allowed *plus one*, that which will rescue the meaning of the entire statement. The theory of the statement-metaphor puts the accent on the predicative operation. It seems now that it is not incompatible with the theory of the word-metaphor. The metaphorical statement achieves its statement of meaning by means of an *epiphora* of the word. A little while ago we said with Stephen Ullmann that the 'analytical' definition and the 'contextual' definition of the word are compatible with each other to the extent that the perspectives of language and of speech call for and complete each other. Now it must be said that the theory of the word-metaphor and the theory of the statement-metaphor relate to each other in just the same way.

The complementary value of the two theories can be demonstrated in the following manner, which cuts short any accusation of eclecticism. The theory of the statement-metaphor refers back to the word-metaphor through an essential trait that the preceding Study set into relief. Recalling the distinction proposed by Max Black between 'focus' and 'frame,' this trait can be called the *focalization* on the word. The 'focus' is a word, the 'frame' is a sentence. It is to the 'focus' that the 'system of associated commonplaces' is applied in the manner of a filter or a screen. It is, again, through a focalizing effect that interaction or tension polarizes on a 'vehicle' and a 'tenor'; they relate to each other within the statement, but it is the word that assumes each of the two functions. In the same vein I will strive in the next Study to show that deviation at the level of the word – through which, according to Jean Cohen,[89] a deviation at the predicative level, i.e. a semantic impertinence, comes to be reduced – is itself also an effect of focalization on the word. Its origin is in the establishment of a new semantic pertinence at the very level where the impertinence takes place, that is at the predicative level. In various ways, consequently, the dynamism of the statement-metaphor condenses or crystallizes into an operation of meaning whose focus is the word.

But the reverse is no less true. The changes of meaning for which the semantics of the word tries to give an account demand the mediation of a complete expression. To the focalization of the statement by the word corresponds the contextualization of the word by the statement. One can be led astray in this regard by the role played by associative fields in the semantics of Ullmann. Recourse to the association of ideas is even an effective way of avoiding the properly discursive aspects of change of meaning and of operating only with the elements – names and senses. In particular, in the case of metaphor, the operation of resemblance is carried on at the level of the elements, without quarter being given to the idea that this resemblance itself results from the application of an unusual and impertinent predicate to a subject that 'yields while protesting' (in the words of Nelson Goodman,[90] who will be discussed later).

The argument is not limited to proposing a different formulation in which predication would replace association. On at least two points, to my mind, the marriage between semantics and associationist psychology has ruinous results.

I hold first that the psychologizing interpretation of figures is responsible for the false symmetry between metaphor and metonymy that prevails in the 'restricted rhetoric' inspired by associationism. This symmetry is very deceptive. Only metonymy can be treated purely as a phenomenon of denomination, one word in place of another. In this sense, it alone satisfies a substitution theory, because it alone is located within the limits of naming. Metaphor does not differ from metonymy in that the association takes place by resemblance in this case instead of by contiguity. It differs by the fact that it takes place on two planes, that of predication and that of naming; and it takes place on the second only because it takes place on the first. This is what the English-language authors have perceived so well: words change meaning only because discourse must confront the threat of an inconsistency at the properly predicative level, and it re-establishes its intelligibility only at the price of what looks, in the framework of semantics of the word, like a semantic innovation. The theory of metonymy makes no appeal to such an exchange between discourse and the word. This is why metaphor has a role in discourse that metonymy never equals; their difference in fecundity brings into play more complex factors than the simple difference between two sorts of associations. Metaphor prevails over metonymy not because contiguity is less fruitful a relationship than resemblance, or again because metonymic relationships are external and given in reality whereas metaphorical equivalences are created by the imagination, but because metaphorical equivalences set predicative operations in motion that metonymy ignores.[91]

The psychologizing interpretation of figures has the even more serious drawback of impeding the full recognition of the interchange between word and sentence in the constitution of the figure. The role attributed to associative fields lets metaphor and metonymy be kept in the domain of denomination; and this helps reinforce the substitution theory, basing it on the psychological mechanism of the association by contiguity or by resemblance, which occurs sometimes between name and name, sometimes between sense and sense, and sometimes between both at once. On the other hand, if, like Max Black, one sees in association an aspect that envisages the 'application' of a strange predicate to a subject which itself consequently appears in a new light, then the association of ideas requires the framework of a complete expression.

Once this obstacle is cleared away, the same mechanism of exchange between the word and the sentence that was seen to be at work in the case of polysemy can be brought into play again to explain metaphor. Finally it becomes possible to formulate this mechanism first in terms of statement and then in terms of word. The two analyses become not just complementary but also reciprocal. Just as the statement-metaphor has as 'focus' a word whose meaning is changing, the change of meaning of the word has as 'frame' a complete expression whose meaning is in tension.

We can now state, at this point where our third and fourth Studies converge, that metaphor is the outcome of a debate between *predication* and *naming*; its place in language is between words and sentences.

Metaphor and the new rhetoric

For A.-J. Greimas

The common aim of the works of the new rhetoric to which this Study is devoted is to renovate the essentially taxonomic enterprise of classical rhetoric by founding the *species* of classification on the *forms* of the operations that take place at all levels of articulation in language. In this respect the new rhetoric is dependent on a semantics taken to its own highest degree of structural radicalism.

Because the period is too short and the works too recent, I will concentrate less on the historical succession of theses than on their major theoretical articulations, taking as immediate reference the *Rhétorique générale* published by Groupe μ (Centre d'études poétiques, Université de Liège).[1] This is not to say that all the partial analyses to be examined along the way are considered exhaustively here; nevertheless, all the problems that have given rise to special analyses are taken up in the synthesis of the *Rhétorique générale.*

The semantics of the word discussed in the preceding Study provides the background from which this ongoing investigation stands out. It inherits from this semantics the two foundational postulates set out at the beginning of Study 4: metaphor belongs in the semantics of the word; and the semantics of the word fits into the framework of a semiotics for which all the units of language are varieties of the sign – that is, negative, differential, oppositive entities – all of whose relations with the other homologous units are immanent within language itself.

But the structural semantics on which the new rhetoric is based is not a simple outgrowth of the semantics set out above. It proceeds from a revolution within the revolution, which confers a sort of crystalline purity on the postulates of Saussurism. In the first place, the definition of the sign is detached from its matrix, both psychological (acoustic image, mental content) and sociological (the societal storehouse of the language inscribed in the memory of each individual); the relation between signifier and signified is held to be a relation *sui generis*. Furthermore, all the consequences are drawn from the Saussurean distinction between form and substance (whether this be the sound-substance of the signifier or the psycho-social substance of the signified); the operations to be defined later all take place at the level of the form of language. Phonology, which de Saussure still held as a subsidiary science, provides the purest model of the oppositions, disjunctions, and combinations that allow linguistics to pass beyond the stage of description and of classification to that of explanation. But above all, the analysis of the signified finds itself pushed in a direction that assures the parallelism between the two planes of the signified and the signifier. Just as the analysis of the signifier since Troubetskoy has proceeded essentially as its decomposition into distinctive traits that no longer belong as such to the linguistic domain, the analysis of the signified with Prieto[2] and Greimas[3] is pursued beyond the distinct lexical type, beyond the semantic kernel of the word, to the level of *semes*, which are to the signified (that is, the lexical units of the preceding chapter) what distinctive traits are to the phoneme. Thus, the strategic level of structural semantics shifts from the word towards the seme in a step that is exclusively linguistic, for there is no speech-related consciousness, on the part of either the sender or the receiver of messages, accompanying the constitution of the word as a collection of semes. At the same time, it becomes possible to define not only entities at the semic level, but also operations at a purely semic level. These are principally binary oppositions, thanks to which one can display collections of semes as a hierarchy of disjunctions that give the form of a 'tree' or a 'graph' to all the repertories language offers at the properly linguistic level, the level at which speakers express themselves, signify, and communicate.

I will not consider here the results that semantics properly speaking has drawn from the application of the strictly structural method to semic analysis (just as the preceding Study did not consider in itself the 'semantic fields' theory of Josef Trier, which would be to semic analysis what the description of the phenotype is to the reconstruction of the genotype in the biological conception of organisms). I shall simply refer for an exposition of these works to the *Sémantique structurale* of Greimas, and shall focus essentially on the attempts at a redefinition of the domain of rhetoric on the basis of this purely structural semantics.

As indicated in the introduction to the preceding Study, one ought not to expect from neo-rhetoric a reshaping of the problematic of metaphor comparable to that which English-language authors have achieved in this domain. The radicalization of the semiotic model results rather in reinforcing the privilege of the word, in forging an even tighter pact between metaphor and the word, and in consolidating the substitution theory of metaphor. Furthermore, by changing the strategic level, structural semantics makes it more difficult to see the point where a bond is possible between semiotics of the word and semantics of the sentence, and at the same time obscures the locus of the exchange between naming and predication, which also serves as the anchorage of the word-metaphor in the statement-metaphor.

For all these reasons, the new rhetoric at first glance is nothing but a repetition of classical rhetoric, at least that of tropes, only at a higher level of technicity.

But this is just a first impression. The new rhetoric is far from being a reformulation of the theory of tropes in more formal terms; it proposes instead to restore the entire breadth of the theory of figures. We have alluded several times to the protest of modern writers against 'restricted rhetoric,'[4] that is, to put it more exactly, against the reduction of rhetoric to tropology and of tropology eventually to the pair of metonymy and metaphor, for the greater glory of metaphor, the pinnacle of the tropological edifice. Fontanier wanted to include the theory of tropes in a theory of figures; but, lacking an adequate instrument, he had to be content with reorganizing the entire field of the rhetoric of figures as a function of that of tropes and with giving the name *non-trope figures* to all other figures. Thus, trope survived as the strong concept and figure as the weak. The new rhetoric proposes explicitly to construct the notion of trope on that of figure, not the other way around, and to build up a rhetoric of figures directly. The trope will then be able to remain what it was in the ancient rhetoric, a substitution figure at the level of the word. At least it will be enframed by a more general concept, that of *deviation*.

This concept took shape first in Aristotle's *Rhetoric*, where metaphor is defined, among other uses of words – rare word, shortened word, lengthened word, etc. – as a deviation in relation to the norm of the 'standard' meaning of words. Gérard Genette shows easily in his introduction to *Les Figures du discours* by Fontanier that deviation is the telling trait of the figure.[5]

But it is contemporary stylistics that has paved the way for a generalized concept of deviation. Jean Cohen provides this reminder in his *Structure du langage poétique*: 'Deviation is the very definition that Charles Bruneau, reviving Valéry, gave for the fact of style ... [style] is a deviation in relation to a norm, and so a fault, but, as Bruneau also said, a voluntary fault' (13).

The whole effort of neo-rhetoric, therefore, is directed towards incorporating deviation among the other operations that take place, as structural semantics shows, at all the levels of articulation of language – phonemes, words, sentences, discourse, etc. Hence, deviation at the level of the word, i.e. the trope, appears somewhat as a local item in the general table of deviations. This is why, on the one hand, one can see in the new rhetoric a rather uninstructive repetition of classical rhetoric as far as the actual description of metaphor is concerned (which remains what it was, namely a substitution of meaning at the level of the word); and on the other hand, one can see in it a highly clarifying explanation resulting from the integration of the trope into a general theory of deviations. It is worth the effort to grant full scope to these new aspects of the theory of figures in general, before returning to the problems posed by the purely repetitive aspect of the theory of metaphor in particular.

I propose to order the problems posed by a general theory of figures in the following manner:

(1) First, deviation from what? Where is the 'rhetoric degree zero' from which the distance could be felt, appreciated, even measured? Did not classical rhetoric die from (among other mortal weaknesses) having left this preliminary question unanswered?

(2) Next, what does one mean by 'deviation'? Can the corporeal metaphor of *figure* and the spatial metaphor of *deviation* clarify each other, and, taken together, what do they say?

(3) And if deviation and figure are to mean something together, what are the rules of the meta-language in which one can speak of deviation and of figure? Put differently, what are the criteria of deviation and of figure in rhetorical discourse? This third question will bring to light a new factor, that of reduction of deviation, which does not limit itself to specifying the concept of deviation, but which rectifies it to the point of inverting it. This raises the question of what is important in the figure: is it deviation or the reduction of deviation?

(4) The search for the criterion leads to problems that set one outside the consciousness of speakers, since from this point onwards one operates with infralinguistic units, the semes. How, then, is the effect of meaning at the level of discourse linked to the operations applied to atoms of meaning at the infralinguistic level? This fourth question will lead us back to our initial problem, that of the insertion of the word-metaphor into discourse-metaphor.

A problem pertaining to the object of further investigation will be left on the border of this inquiry. One can ask why language in operation has recourse to the play of deviations. What defines the rhetorical intention of figurative language? Is it the introduction of new information that would enrich the referential function of discourse, or rather, must the apparent surplus of meaning be referred to another non-informative, non-referential function of discourse? This last question will be answered only in Study 7, which is devoted more specifically to the referential scope of discourse.

1 / DEVIATION AND RHETORIC DEGREE ZERO

The first question is a considerable one just on its own. Properly speaking, it governs the demarcation of the rhetorical object.[6] Perhaps classical rhetoric died through not having resolved this question; but neo-rhetoric has not arrived at its complete answer. Everyone agrees in saying that figurative language exists only if one can contrast it with another language that is not figurative. There is even agreement on this point with the English-language semanticists. As we saw, a metaphorical word functions only when it is contrasted and combined with other non-metaphorical words (Max Black);[7] the self-contradiction of literal interpretation is necessary for the unfolding of metaphorical interpretation (Monroe Beardsley).[8] What, then, is this other language, unmarked from the rhetorical point of view? One must first admit that it cannot be found. Dumarsais identified it with etymological meaning; but then all derivative meanings (which is to say, all actual usage) are figurative, and rhetoric is confused with semantics or, as was said then, with grammar.[9] Or, to put the same thing in another way, an etymological and thus diachronic definition of the non-figurative tends to identify figures with polysemy itself. This is why Fontanier contrasts figurative meaning with proper meaning and no longer with primitive meaning, by giving 'proper' a value derived from use, and not from origin. Figurative meaning contrasts with proper meaning within current usage. The line of separation falls between two levels of meaning. Rhetoric says nothing about 'the ordinary and common manner of speaking' – that is about meanings to which single words alone correspond – a feature that makes the path of usage forced and necessary. Rhetoric will be concerned with the non-proper alone, that is, with borrowed, circumstantial, and freed meanings. This line, unfortunately, cannot be drawn within current usage: neutral language does not exist. The upcoming examination of criteria will confirm this fact.

Must one then just note this impasse and bury the question alongside rhetoric itself? The new rhetoric has to be given credit for refusing to capitulate in the face of this question which is, in some ways, the watchdog at the threshold of rhetoric.

Three answers have been proposed, ones which, moreover, are not mutually exclusive. With Gérard Genette[10] it will be said that the opposition of figurative and non-figurative is that of a real language to a virtual language, and that the evidence for the reference of one to the other is the self-awareness of the speaker or the listener. Consequently, this interpretation links the virtuality of language of rhetorical null degree to its mental status. The deviation is between what the poet thought and what he wrote, between meaning and letter. Unfortunately, the author identifies the detection of this virtual meaning with the idea that every figure can be translated, and therefore with the theory of substitution; what the poet thought can always be re-established by another thought that translates the figurative expression into a non-figurative expression. The best way to put it is to say that this recourse to an absent term is completely dependent on a substitutive conception of metaphor and of the figure in general, and consequently is at one with the thesis according to which 'every figure is translatable' (*Figures I* 213). The real word is *put in for* an absent word, which, however, can be restored by translation.[11]

This manner of linking the consciousness of deviation to translatability in fact condemns the very thing one wants at least to describe, if not to save. The non-translatability of poetic language is not just a pretension of romanticism, but an essential trait of the poetic. It is true that one can save the thesis by saying, with Genette himself, that the figure is translatable with respect to meaning, and not translatable with respect to signification, that is, with respect to the 'more' that the figure entails; and one assigns the study of this increase to another theory, not now of denotation but of connotation. We will come back to this point further on. What creates difficulty here is the idea that 'every figure is translatable,' an idea that is inseparable from that of a deviation between actual signs and virtual or absent signs. I wonder whether one ought not to dissociate the postulate of deviation from the postulate of implicit translation, and to say with Beardsley[12] that what the figure contrasts with is a literal interpretation of the sentence as a whole, the impossibility of which motivates the constitution of the metaphorical meaning. This impossible virtual interpretation is in no way the translation of a present word by an absent word, but a way of making sense with the words present, and a way that destroys itself. I shall say, then, that a theory of interaction and of metaphor as a phenomenon of discourse resolves the problem of the status of the non-figurative better than a substitution theory with its continual fealty to the primacy of the word ('sail' in place of 'ship'!). The idea prevails, because it is profoundly right, that figurative language seeks to be opposed to a non-figurative, purely virtual language. However, this virtual language cannot be restored by a translation at the level of words, but only by an interpretation at the level of the sentence.

A second manner of resolving the paradox of the undiscoverable degree zero of rhetoric is that of Jean Cohen, whose work will be explored at greater length in the third section from the viewpoint of the notion of reduction of deviation. It consists in choosing as point of reference not absolute degree zero, but a relative degree zero, i.e. that stratum of language usages that would be the least marked from the rhetorical point of view, and thus the least figurative. This language exists; it is the language of science.[13]

The advantages of this working hypothesis are numerous. First, one avoids having to go back to the consciousness of the speaker in order to measure the deviation between the sign and the meaning. Next, one takes account of the fact that the rhetorical point of view is not without form. It already has a grammatical form, which the preceding theory acknowledges; and above all, it has a semantic form, which the preceding theory presupposes but does not thematize. For there to be deviation between the virtual sign and the actual sign, there must also be semantic equivalence, or, as was said, there must be a meaning that stays the same while significations alter. Thus, one must be able to point, if not to an absolutely neutral language (which Todorov considers 'colourless and dead'), at least to the closest approximation of this neutral language; this is what permits the choice of scientific language as relative degree zero. Finally, the adoption of this level of reference allows one to give a quantitative value to the notion of deviation and to introduce statistical instrumentation into rhetoric. Instead of metaphorizing the spatial aspect of deviation, let us measure it. What one measures in this way will be not only the deviation of all poetic language in relation to scientific language, but also the relative deviation of some poetic language systems in relation to others. By such means a diachronic study of the evolution of deviation, for example from classical to romantic and then to symbolist poetry, can avoid impressionism and subjectivism and achieve scientific status.[14]

Perhaps the theoretical difficulties are not resolved, but they are neutralized. They are unresolved, in that the style of scientific prose already marks a deviation: 'Deviation is not absent from its language, but it certainly is minimal' (*Structure* 22). Where can the 'natural language' be found, that is, the negative pole of null deviation? (23) What defines this minimum of deviation, and how are we to speak of the frequency of deviation proper to this style? The difficulty is merely neutralized by the affirmation that deviation is not at the zero level in scientific language but tends toward zero, and thus that such a language offers the best approximation of a 'writing degree zero' (23). A bit later, dealing with the content, i.e., with the signified, Jean Cohen returns from another angle to the notion of degree zero of style. Absolute prose is content, as distinct from expression. Translatability, whether into another language or in the same language, permits the definition of the semantic equivalence of two messages, that is, identity of information. On this basis, translatability can be taken as the criterion that differentiates the two types of language. 'Absolute prose' is the substance of the content, the signification that guarantees the equivalence of the messages in the 'before' and the 'after' languages. The zero degree is the signification defined by identity of information (16). Now is the difficulty eliminated? Not entirely, if one considers that absolute translation is itself an ideal limit.

To my mind, the merit of the method is undeniable; its results speak for it. But I would not say that the measurement of deviations replaces the consciousness of deviation possessed by speakers; it only provides an equivalent. Moreover, Jean Cohen asks only that his method 'verify an hypothesis,'[15] one which supposes a prior identification of the poetic fact and its consecration by the 'vast public called posterity' (17). It is not a replacement because the term of comparison is taken outside of the poetic statement itself, in another discourse belonging to other speakers, to scientists. At the same time the rhetorical consciousness vanishes with the internal tension between two lines of meaning. This is why it seems more legitimate to me to preserve Gérard Genette's idea of a virtual, filigreed language, and to pay the price of a correction eliminating the idea of word-for-word translation in favour of that of an inconsistent literal interpretation of the entire statement. In order that the dynamism of the tension between two interpretations remain immanent within the statement itself, what Genette says of translation must be said of literal interpretation, namely that the figure brings about 'visibility in transparency, like a filigree or a palimpsest, beneath its apparent text.'[16] A theory of the figure must not lose the valuable idea of this 'duplicity of language.'[17]

This is why I say that the calculation of the deviation of poetic language in relation to another language offers only an equivalent, with respect to an internal term of reference, of what takes place in the statement between two levels of interpretation. And the elaboration of this objection is not all that unjust to Jean Cohen's enterprise in that his most interesting contribution is elsewhere, in the relation between deviation and its reduction. Moreover, this relation resides within the poetic statement, and consequently it too leads on to a comparison between an actual level and a virtual level of reading at the heart of the poetic statement itself.

Another way to give an account of rhetoric's degree zero is to take it as a metalinguistic construction – neither virtual in the sense of Genette, nor actual in the sense of Cohen, but constructed. This is the position adopted by the authors of the *Rhétorique générale*.[18] Just as decomposition into smaller and smaller units reveals components on the side of the signifier, the distinctive traits, that have no explicit and independent existence in language, so too the decomposition of the signified reveals entities, the semes, that do not belong to the level where discourse manifests itself. In both cases, the end-state of the decomposition is infra-linguistic: 'The units of signification, as they manifest themselves in discourse, begin at the immediately higher level' (*Rhétorique générale* 30). One should not be restricted then to the manifest lexical level, but should transfer the analysis to the semic level. Genette's virtual is not to be linked to some speaker-consciousness but to a construction of the linguist: 'Degree zero is not contained in the language as it is given to us' (35). 'Accordingly, degree zero would be a discourse brought down to its essential semes' (36). However, since these are not distinct lexical types, this reduction is a metalinguistic step (36). It supports the distinction of two parts in figurative discourse: that which has not been modified, or the 'base,' and that which has undergone rhetorical deviation (44). In turn, the latter conserves with its degree zero a certain relation, not gratuitous but systematic, which entails that invariants can be discerned in this other part. While the base has the structure of the syntagma, these invariants have the constitutive structure of a paradigm: that in which degree zero and the figured degree exist together at the same time.

We will leave discussion of the fundamental theses of the *Rhétorique générale* for a later investigation (section 4). Let us just note here that, as concerns the practical determination of degree zero, the problems are the same as in the preceding interpretations. In effect, deviation as such belongs to the level of the manifestation of discourse: 'In the rhetorical sense, we will understand deviation as the detected alteration of degree zero' (41). This definitely is as it should be, if the reduction of deviation (section 3) is more important than deviation; for this is what makes deviation a 'meaningful alteration' (39). Besides, in all discourse, the essential semes are enrobed by lateral semes that carry supplementary, inessential information. This fact is what prevents the practical degree zero – that which can be registered in discourse – from coinciding with the absolute degree zero that a semic analysis could eventually recognize and to which it assigns the 'place outside of language' (37). Recourse to subjective probabilities – fulfilled expectation, etc. – also implies a return to the plane of manifestation. The same holds for the notion of isotopy in Greimas,[19] taken as the semantic norm of discourse: in effect, this notion implies the rule that every message seeks to be taken as a meaningful whole.

Hence, the solution of the problem of deviation at an infralinguistic level does not substitute for its description at the level where discourse manifests itself. At this level, rhetoric needs to note a practical degree zero in language itself. It is in relation to this that deviation is a 'detected alteration'; for 'without doubt it is impossible to decide at what degree of accumulation of inessential semes a deviation begins to be perceived' (42). These difficulties concern precisely the domain of word figures – the metasememes – to which metaphor belongs.

In addition, only those deviations are disclosed by the reader or hearer that have some warning *mark*; this is a greater or lesser departure from the normal level of redundancy, which 'is something known implicitly by every user of a language' (41). Thus, we are brought back to the virtual of the previous interpretation. The characterization of deviation and of its reduction in terms of base and invariant leads back to it ineluctably. Base, it was said, is a particular form of syntagma; as for the invariant, it belongs to the order of the paradigm. Now 'the syntagma is actual and the paradigm is virtual' (44).

2 / THE SPACE OF THE FIGURE

But what does deviation mean? The word itself is a metaphor on the road to extinction, and a spatial metaphor at that. Rhetoric battles valiantly with this metaphoricity of metaphor, which leads it to remarkable discoveries about the actual status of the literal in discourse and thus about 'literature' as such.

We faced this problem already once with the Greek expression *epiphora.*[20] *Epiphora* 'spatializes' in many ways: it is a transfer of meaning 'from (*apo*) ... to (*epi*)'; it runs alongside (*para*) standard usage; it is a replacement (*anti*, in place of). Furthermore, if one compares these spatializing values of transfer of meaning with other properties of metaphor – for example, that it 'sets (something) before the eyes'[21] – and if one also adds the remark that *lexis* makes discourse 'appear,'[22] one constructs a converging cluster that calls for the unifying thread of an enquiry into the figure as such.

A passing remark by Fontanier concerning the word *figure* itself comes very close to wrapping up this issue: 'It appears that, originally, the word *figure* was to be said only of bodies, or, equivalently, of man and of animals considered as physical and with respect to the limits of their extension. And, in this first acceptation, what does it signify? Contours, features, the exterior form of man or of an animal or of any palpable object whatsoever. Addressed only to the intelligence of the soul, discourse is not, properly speaking, a body, even when considered in terms of the words that transmit it through the spirit and the senses. Therefore it has no *figure*, properly speaking; but still, in its different ways of signifying and expressing, it has something analogous to the differences in form and features to be found in real bodies. Without doubt, it was on the basis of this analogy that the *metaphor* "the figures of discourse" was coined. But this *metaphor* ought not be considered a true *figure*, because we have no other words in the language for the same idea.'[23]

Two ideas of space are suggested here, a quasi-corporeal exteriority, and contour, feature, form. The expression *exterior form* unites them in the suggestion of something like a milieu of spatiality overlaid by a design. And these two values of spatiality seem to be implied jointly, if figures are to be defined as 'the features, forms, or contours [second value] by which means discourse, in the expression of ideas, thoughts, or sentiments, assumes a more or less distant position [first value] from what would have been the simple and common expression.'[24]

Roman Jakobson's interpretation of the poetic function in language, in his famous remarks to an Interdisciplinary Conference on Style,[25] provides the bridge between these fleeting remarks and the more concentrated investigations of the neo-rhetoricians. After having enumerated the six factors of communication – addresser, message, addressee, context (which is or can be verbalized), common code, contact (physical or psychic) – Jakobson enumerates functions in parallel fashion, according to which factor dominates. In this way he defines the poetic function as the function that puts the accent on the message for its own sake, and he adds: 'This function, by promoting the palpability of signs, deepens the fundamental dichotomy of signs and objects' (356). The two spatial values brought out above are interpreted here in a completely original fashion. On the one hand, the notion of a contour, of a configuration of the message, rising to top rank, is attached to a precise functioning of the signs in messages of poetic quality, namely, a very particular interlacing of the two fundamental modes in which signs are arranged – selection and combination.[26] Accordingly, with the introduction of two orthogonal axes in place of the simple linearity of the spoken chain endorsed by de Saussure, it is possible to describe the poetic function as a certain alteration in the relation between these two axes. The poetic function projects the principle of equivalence, which belongs to the selection axis, onto the axis of combination. In other words, in the poetic function equivalence is promoted to the rank of constitutive procedure of the sequence. Thus, recurrence of the same phonic figures, rhymes, parallels, and other related procedures in some way introduce a semantic resemblance.

It is evident in what new sense the quasi-corporeality of the message is interpreted – as an adherence of meaning to sound. At first this idea seems to be opposed to that of deviation between letter and meaning; but if one remembers that this meaning is virtual, one can say that sound and real meaning intermingle in the letter of the poem, giving rise to figure according to the process described by Jakobson.

On the other hand, no longer occupying a place between the tonal form and the semantic content, the very notion of a spatiality of deviation is directed elsewhere, and takes up a position between the message accentuated for itself and things – what Jakobson calls the dichotomy of signs and objects. This point is spelled out, following the communication model that is its framework, as a different division of the functions: 'Poeticalness is not a supplementation of discourse with rhetorical adornment but a total re-evaluation of the discourse and of all its components whatsoever' (377). The message is accentuated at the expense of the referential function. Because the message is centred on itself, the poetic function prevails over the referential function; prose also produces this effect ('I like Ike') once the message begins to exist for itself instead of being crossed by the purpose that carries it towards the context it verbalizes. I shall reserve for a separate discussion the question whether the referential function is abolished in poetry or whether, as Jakobson himself suggests, it rather is 'split.'[27] This is a huge question in itself; it involves a properly philosophical decision about what 'reality' signifies. It could be that the everyday reference to the real must be abolished in order that another sort of reference to other dimensions of reality might be liberated. This, when the time comes, will be my thesis. The idea of a shrinking of the referential function – in the form, at least, that ordinary discourse makes use of it – is entirely compatible with the ontological conception that will be set out in the last Study. Hence, we may retain it for our reflection on the spatiality of the figure. The 'conversion of a message into an enduring thing' (371) is what constitutes the quasi-corporeality suggested by the metaphor of the figure.

Taking advantage of Jakobson's breakthrough, neo-rhetoric attempts to reflect on the *visibility* and *spatiality* of the figure. Expanding Fontanier's remark on the metaphor of the figure, Todorov proclaims figure to be what makes discourse appear by making it opaque: 'Discourse that simply brings thought to our cognition is invisible and, by the same token, nonexistent.'[28] Instead of disappearing in its mediating function and making itself 'invisible' and 'nonexistent' as 'thought,' discourse points to itself as discourse: 'The existence of figures equals the existence of discourse' (102).

The remark is not without its difficulties. Firstly, 'transparent discourse,' which would be the rhetoric degree zero of which we spoke earlier, would not be formless from another point of view, for it is said that it 'would be what allows signification to be visible' and that its only purpose is 'to make itself heard' (102). It must be possible, then, to speak of signification quite apart from figure. But in a semiotics that does not turn to the description of the operation as such of the discourse sentence, the very notion of signification remains suspended. Further, the opacity of discourse is identified too quickly with its lack of reference. In opposition to transparent discourse, it is said that 'there is opaque discourse so well covered with "designs" and "figures" that it lets nothing be seen behind it;

this would be a language that does not refer to reality at all, that is complete in itself' (102). The problem of reference is dismissed without a theory of the relations of sense and reference in discourse at the sentence level. It is entirely conceivable that the opacity of words implies some *other* reference and not *no* reference at all (Study 7).

What remains, however, is the very valuable idea that one function of rhetoric is to 'make us take notice of the existence of discourse' (103).

Gérard Genette claims to push to the limit the spatial metaphor of figure, according to its two aspects of distantiation and configuration.[29] There are really two ideas, then: deviation between sign and virtual meaning, which constitutes 'the inner space of language'; and the contour of the figure ('the writer draws the limits of this space'), which here is opposed to the absence of form, at least of rhetorical form, of virtual language. In these two aspects, spatiality is defined here, in the tradition of ancient rhetoric, in relation to virtual language, which would be rhetoric degree zero ('the simple and common expression has no form, the figure does have one,' 209). In this manner, justice is done to Roman Jakobson's idea of an accentuation of the message centred on itself.

But why stay with the metaphor of space instead of translating it, in line with Genette's own stand that every metaphor is translatable? The reason is, essentially, to leave in play the surplus of meaning that constitutes the connotation of the metaphor but does not belong to its denotation (that is, the meaning common to the figure and its translation). Accordingly, the metaphor of a space of discourse is partially translatable. Its translation is the very theory of denotation. What is untranslatable in it is its power to evoke an affective tone, a literary dignity. By calling a ship a sail, my connotation indicates the desire (in the case of synecdoche) to designate the thing by means of a sensible detail, or (in the case of metaphor) to designate it by means of a similarity – in both cases, therefore, by a detour through the sensible. This motivation is 'the very soul of figure' (219). In this sense Genette contrasts the 'surface' of rhetorical form, 'that which the two lines of the present signifier and the absent signifier demarcate,' with the simple linear form of discourse, which is 'purely grammatical' (210). In its first sense, space is a void; in its second sense, it is a design.

To exhibit this motivation, and thus to 'signify poeticalness,' is the connotative function of the figure. Here again we encounter Roman Jakobson's idea of the message centred on itself. What deviation brings to light, beyond the meaning of words, are the values of connotation. These are what the old rhetoric codified: 'Once outside the living speech of personal invention and within the code of the tradition, the sole function of every figure is to hint, in its particular way, at the poetic quality of the discourse that contains it' (220). In the *emblem* that the classical 'sail of the ship' has become for us, we can read at once both '*This* is a *ship*' and 'Look: poetry!' (220).

Thus, the theory of figures blends into a whole current of thought for which literature is auto-significative. The code of literary connotations, which the rhetoric of figures joins, is to be linked to the codes under which Roland Barthes puts the 'signs of literature.'[30]

The metaphor of the interior space of discourse, then, must be treated like every figure. It denotes the distance between the letter and virtual meaning; it connotes a whole cultural orientation, that of a person who highlights in contemporary literature its self-signifying function. Because of these untranslatable connotations, Genette is in no hurry to translate the metaphor of the space of language and is happy to stay with it. The space of language, in effect, is a connoted space, 'connoted, manifested more than pointed to, speaking rather than spoken of, which betrays itself in metaphor like the surfacing of the unconscious in a slip or a dream.'[31]

Is it unfair to apply to this declaration what the author just said about the symbolic value of the word 'sail'? – and to cry 'Look: modernity!'? Genette's discourse on the spatiality of discourse connotes the preference of contemporary man for space, following the Bergsonian inflation of duration ('man prefers space to time' [107]). On this basis, when the author writes 'one could almost say that it is space that speaks' (102), his own speaking is to be interpreted more in terms of what it connotes than in terms of what it denotes: 'Today, literature – thought – no longer articulates itself except in terms of distance, horizon, universe, surroundings, place, area, routes, and home-ground: naive figures, but characteristic, figures *par excellence*, in which language *spatializes itself* in order that space, having become language, may speak and inscribe itself in it' (108). In fashioning this brilliant maxim, the author produces the sign of his allegiance to the school of thought for which the meaning of literature is found in literature.

I should like to ask whether what is really denoted by this meditation on space, and not only what is connoted, is entirely satisfactory. What seems to me to be gained is the idea of an opacity of discourse centred on itself, the idea that figures render discourse visible. What I question are the two consequences drawn from it. It is supposed, first, that the suspension of the referential function, as it operates in ordinary discourse, implies the abolition of all referential function; this leaves literature to signify itself. Once again, we are faced with a decision concerning the signification of 'reality' that goes beyond the resources of linguistics and rhetoric and belongs properly to the philosophical order. The affirmation of the opacity of poetic discourse and its corollary, the obliteration of ordinary reference, are merely the starting-point of an immense inquiry on the topic of reference, one which cannot be dismissed so summarily.

The second reservation has to do with the very distinction between denotation and connotation. Can one say that figurative language signifies poetry alone, that is, the particular quality of discourse that possesses figure? The surplus of meaning would then remain generic, as is moreover the alarm 'Look: poetry!.' If one wanted to preserve the notion of connotation, it would be necessary in any case to treat it in a more specific fashion, in terms of the uniqueness of each poem. One might reply that this generic quality can be analysed in turn into epic quality, lyric quality, didactic quality, oratorical quality, and so on. Would this mean then, that to call something literature is to point to the multiple, distinct qualities – the figures – that rhetoric lists, then classifies and orders in systems? But this is again designation of species, of types. Genette says so himself: rhetoric cares little about the originality or the novelty of figures, 'which are qualities of individual speech, and which, as such, do not concern it' (220). What interests it are the codified forms whose system would make a second language out of literature. What is to be said, then, of the singular connotations of this or that poem? Northrop Frye is closer to the truth when he says that the structure of a poem articulates a 'mood,' an affective value.[32] However (as I will argue in Study 7), this 'mood' is quite a bit more than a subjective emotion. It is a way of being rooted in reality; it is an ontological index. With it the referent returns, but in a radically new sense in comparison to ordinary language. This is why the denotation-connotation distinction has to be maintained to be entirely problematic and linked to a properly positivistic presupposition according to which only the objective language of scientific prose would be able to denote. To deviate from it would be to no longer denote anything. This presupposition is a prejudice that must be exposed to direct interrogation.

Unable to carry out this process here, we will note only that the affirmation that the figure's surplus of meaning depends on connotation is the exact counterpart of the affirmation discussed earlier that the figure is translatable with regard to its sense – in other words, that it carries no new information. Now this thesis is eminently debatable. I believe that, with the English authors, I have shown that it is of a piece with a substitutive conception of metaphor, which in turn remains restricted to a word-focused conception of metaphor. But if metaphor is a statement, it is possible that this statement would be untranslatable, not only as regards its connotation, but as regards its very meaning, thus as regards its denotation. It teaches something, and so it contributes to the opening up and the discovery of a field of reality other than that which ordinary language lays bare.

3 / DEVIATION AND REDUCTION OF DEVIATION

Is figure nothing but deviation? With this question we enter into a criterio-logy of properly rhetorical deviations. This question cannot be dissociated from the one dealt with in the first section, about the rhetoric degree zero in relation to which deviation takes place. Instead of returning to this pro-blem, we will concentrate on one of a different sort: are there criteria of figurative language? The ancients, Todorov remarks, were unable to give any meaning to the idea of a 'deviation towards the alogical,'[33] not having defined the logical character of everyday discourse and not having ex-plained the rule of infractions in which usage sets limits on the overly inde-terminate boundaries of logic. The criterion of 'frequency' (101) falters before the same paradox. Figure is opposed to the common and usual ways of speaking. But figures are not always rare; moreover, the most unusual of all discourses would be one devoid of figure. More interesting is the remark of ancient and classical authors that figures are what render discourse de-scribable by making it appear in discernible forms. I spelt out above the idea that figure makes discourse 'perceptible.' Let us now add: makes it 'describable.'

But the author says himself that this third criterion, of 'describability,' is only a weak criterion. Figure here is not contrasted with a rule but with a discourse that one does not know how to describe. This is why, to the extent that this weak criterion is applicable to it, a good part of the classi-cal theory of figures is really just an anticipation of linguistics and of its four domains – sound-meaning relation, syntax, semantics, sign-referent relation (113). We will return to this point in the fifth section.

A strong criterion is not provided by the idea of describability but by that of rule-breaking. Subsequently, however, if transgression itself is to be regulated, the idea of deviation understood as violation of a code must be completed by the idea of reduction of deviation, in order to give form to deviation itself, or, in the language of Genette, to mark off the space opened up by deviation.

It was Jean Cohen who introduced – in decisive fashion, to my mind – the notion of reduction of deviation. His identification of metaphor with all reduction of deviation is more debatable, but it does not affect the sub-stance of his discovery. Nowhere is the confrontation with the interaction theory more illuminating or fruitful.

I shall not return to Jean Cohen's stylistic definition of deviation, nor its statistical treatment (cf. section 1). I shall take up his work at the point where the notion of deviation allows him, at the very core of the signified, to distinguish the signified substance (that is, the information produced) from the 'form of the meaning' (38), in the words of Mallarmé. 'The *poetic fact* is born the moment Valéry calls the sea "roof" and boats "doves." That constitutes a violation of the language code, a linguistic deviation, which (with ancient rhetoric) can be called "figure" and which alone gives the poetic its true object' (44).

Two methodological decisions are made at this point. The first concerns distribution in levels and functions, and the second the introduction of the notion of reduction of deviation, which is of more particular interest to us.

Through the first methodological decision the theorist can claim to assume again the task of the old rhetoric at the point where the latter stopped. It is necessary, after having classified the figures, to extract their common structure. The old rhetoric had identified only the rationale proper to each figure, whereas 'structural poetics is located at a superior level of formalization. It seeks a form of forms, a general poetic operator of which all the figures would just be so many particular virtual realizations, specified according to the level and the linguistic function in which the operator actualizes itself' (50). The analysis of figures (setting aside the second theme, the reduction of deviation) will first be accomplished according to levels – the phonic level and the semantic level – and then according to functions. Thus rhyme and meter are two distinct phonic operators, the one relating to the function of diction, the other to the function of contrast. At the semantic level, the identification of the three functions of predication, determination, and co-ordination permits the distinction of a predicative operator, metaphor; a determinative operator, epithet; and an operator of co-ordination, incoherence. Accordingly metaphor is opposed on the one hand to rhyme, as semantic operator versus phonic operator, and on the other hand to epithet among the semantic operators. In this way poetics rises from a simple taxonomy to a theory of operations.

The second methodological decision must now be taken. The notion of deviation as it has been defined up until now, that is as a systematic violation of the language code, is in effect nothing but the other side of another process: 'Poetry destroys ordinary language only to reconstruct it on a higher level. The "de-structuring" done by the figure is followed by a "re-structuring" of another order' (51).

By joining the two rules of method, it is possible to come up with a theory of figure that would not be a mere extension of the theory of tropes. Here, in its deep structure, the verse is a figure like others. But is the phenomenon of reduction of deviation to be seen there as well as the phenomenon of deviation? The latter is strongly evident, represented first in versification by the contrast between phonic and semantic segmentation (divisions of the verse and of the sentence respectively); the insertion of a metric pause without semantic value constitutes a disruption of the phonosemantic parallelism. Now does versification offer at the same time something like a reduction of deviation that subdues the conflict between meter and syntax? The quantitative analysis of Jean Cohen claims only that, from classical to romantic and then to symbolist poetry, 'versification did not stop increasing the divergence between meter and syntax; *it has always gone further in the direction of agrammaticalism*' (69). Verse, concludes Cohen, is the anti-sentence. But it is not apparent where the reduction of deviation is located. The comparative study of rhyme presents the same phenomenon of increase of deviation, calculated in terms of the frequency of non-categorial rhymes (85). The same holds for meter, and for the split it creates between homometry (and homorythmics) at the level of the signifier and a homosemy that does not exist in the poem: 'By this the parallelism of sound and sense is broken, and it is within this rupture that verse fulfils its true function' (93).

Truly, then, it seems that at the phonic level deviation operates alone, without reduction of deviation. Must one conclude that the counterpart is treated only by omission – 'we have ... examined in this study only the first phase of a mechanism which, we feel, entails two phases' (51) – or that reduction of deviation is a semantic phenomenon *par excellence*? This sort of conclusion will be particularly interesting for the later discussion of the phenomena of semantic impertinence and pertinence.[34]

Now the author himself remarks that the resistance of intelligibility is what prevents the total destruction of the message by the phonic figure. So prose is present at the very heart of poetry: 'In fact, the verse is constituted by antimony. For it is not unidirectional;* it doubles back. If it were, it would not be able to carry meaning. Because it signifies, it remains linear. The poetic message is at once verse and prose' (101). Accordingly, I do not think it is forcing the author's thought to conclude that what reduces the phonic deviation is the meaning itself – that is, what at the semantic level reduces another sort of deviation that itself is properly semantic. Therefore, the phenomenon of reduction of deviation should be sought essentially at the semantic level.

The conception of a deviation – and a reduction of deviation – proper to the semantic level of discourse depends on the elucidation of a code of pertinence [meaningfulness or relevance, *pertinence*] governing the interrelationships of signified entities. It is this code that the poetic message violates. Syntactically correct sentences can be absurd, that is incorrect with respect to meaning, through impertinence [calculated error, *impertinence*] of the predicate. A law exists demanding that in every predicative

* 'L'antinomie constitue le vers. Car il n'est pas tout entier vers, c'est-à-dire retour.' The English does not capture the pun on *vers* the noun (verse) and the adverb (towards). (Trans.)

sentence the predicate must be pertinent in relation to the subject, that is, should be semantically capable of fulfilling its function. Plato called on this law when, in the *Sophist*,[35] he noted that communication of 'kinds' rests on the distinction between genera that are entirely incompatible with each other and those that can accommodate each other partially. This law is more restrictive than the general condition of 'grammaticality' defined by Chomsky, at least before the properly semantic developments of his theory since 1967.[36] The law of semantic pertinence, according to Jean Cohen, designates the combinatory permissions that the *signified* must satisfy among themselves if the sentence is to be received as intelligible. In this sense, the code governing semantic pertinence is properly a 'code of speech' (109).

On this basis it is possible to characterize Mallarmé's expression 'The sky is dead' as flagrant predicative impertinence, since the predicate *is dead* is compatible only with individuals belonging to the category of living beings.

We turn now to metaphor, which has not yet been mentioned, but supposedly embodies the fundamental characteristic of poetic language – that is, metaphor is not deviation itself, but the reduction of deviation. Deviation exists only if words are taken in their literal meaning. Metaphor is the process through which the speaker reduces the deviation by changing the meaning of one of the words. As the rhetorical tradition established, metaphor is truly a trope, that is, a change of the meaning of words; but the change of meaning is the answer of discourse to the threat of destruction represented by semantic impertinence. And this answer in turn consists of the production of another deviation, namely in the lexical code itself. 'Metaphor intervenes in the interests of reducing the deviation created through impertinence. The two deviations are complementary, but precisely because they are not situated on the same linguistic plane. Impertinence is a violation of the code of speech, and is located on the syntagmatic level; metaphor is a violation of the language code, and belongs to the paradigmatic level. There is a sort of dominance of speech over language, with the latter agreeing to change in order to give meaning to the former. The totality of the procedure comprises two inverse and complementary phases – (1) situation of deviation: *impertinence*; (2) reduction of deviation: metaphor' (114).

This conception of a counterbalanced operation, bringing the two domains of speech and of language into play, is applied in the three adjoining regions of predication, determination, and co-ordination, which functional analysis distinguishes at one and the same semantic level. Predication and determination actually overlap, since the attribution of a characteristic to a subject in the name of a property is studied, for 'the convenience of the analysis' (119), in the epithet form. The essence of the study of the first function is an inquiry into *impertinent epithets* ('the clenched-fist wind of morning,' 'he ascended the ruthless stairs').

According to the second function, determination, the epithet has the precise meaning of a quantification and a localization that cause the epithet to apply only to a segment of the subject's extension. Rhetorical, and so impertinent, use of the epithet will be that which violates this rule of determination – in other words, redundant epithets; for example, 'pale death.' At first sight redundancy is the opposite of impertinence (the 'verte émeraude' of Vigny, the 'azur bleu' of Mallarmé). This would be the case were determination not a function distinct from predication. If, on the other hand, the two figures are distinct, they each have their own type of deviation and (in this broad sense) of impertinence. The rule that the redundant epithet breaks is that it should bear new information in determining its subject. The violation of this rule through redundancy results in absurdity, since it makes the part equal to the whole. Where, then, is the reduction of deviation? It can consist in a change in grammatical function (the detached epithet becomes apposition, it loses its determinative function to resume a predicative function); the trope is then grammatical. But the reduction can also consist in a change in word meaning; the tautology in 'azure blue' disappears if 'the blue, on account of the metaphor, takes on a meaning that is no longer that of the code' (155). And this leads back to explanation in terms of impertinent epithets.[37]

The function of co-ordination takes the analysis beyond the sentence and to the level of the succession of sentences in discourse. It is grounded in the semantic level, to the extent that the constraints that codify it borrow from the semantic homogeneity of ideas 'set together.' In violating this demand for thematic unity, nonsense, as well as disconnected or incoherent style, refers back to the rules of semantic pertinence that govern the first predicative function. One can speak of deviation through inconsequence. Consider, for example, nature's unexpected invasion of the human drama in Victor Hugo's famous verse in *Booz endormi* ('Asphodels breathed a fresh perfume; / Whispers of night brushed o'er Galgala'), and every unexpected combination of the physical and the spiritual ('Here are fruit, flowers, leaves and branches. And then here is my heart which beats only for you' – Verlaine, quoted p. 177). Discovery of a homogeneity, therefore, will reduce the deviation caused by terms not all belonging to the same universe of discourse; the procedure here is the same as in the case of predication.

Thus, the same two-phase process rules in the three regions of predication, determination, and co-ordination. Each time 'the figure is the conflict between syntagma and paradigm, discourse and system ... Poetic discourse runs counter to the system, and in this struggle it is the system that backs down and agrees to transform' (134).

The critical remarks that follow aim at situating the analysis by Jean Cohen in relation to the interaction theory set out in the third Study. This comparison brings out a convergence, then a divergence, and finally a possible co-ordination.

Let us begin with the convergence. Nowhere is the structural treatment of metaphor as close to the interaction theory. To start with, the properly semantic aspect of metaphor is fully recognized here as a phenomenon of the predicative order. In this connection, the concept of semantic impertinence in Cohen and that of self-contradictory statement in Beardsley correspond perfectly. Cohen's analysis even has the advantage over that of Beardsley of distinguishing absurdity from contradiction, by distinguishing the code of semantic pertinence from the codes of grammaticality and of logical coherence.

Moreover, the theory addresses itself directly to newly invented metaphor, since metaphor in common use is not a case of poetic deviation.[38]

Finally, the breadth of the problem of *epiphora* in Aristotle is restored by a theory that propounds the universality of the double process of production and reduction of deviation. Given that, one may well quarrel with the author's terminology. Was it necessary to reserve the word *metaphor* to designate those changes of meaning where the relationship is one of resemblance, or to give it the generic meaning of 'change of meaning'? This, though, is a peripheral issue: Jean Cohen is in good company with Aristotle.[39]

And yet Cohen's theory, despite its extraordinary merit in comparison to the rest of French-language writing on the subject, is significantly inferior in relation to the corresponding English-language work. As was noted, the only phenomenon of the syntagmatic order is impertinence, the violation of the code of speech. Metaphor properly speaking does not belong to the syntagmatic order; as a violation of the language code, it is situated on the paradigmatic plane. With this bias, we remain within the rhetorical tradition of the one-word trope and under the sway of the theory of substitution. It seems to me that the theory contains a serious omission, that of the new pertinence, which is properly syntagmatic and of which the paradigmatic deviation is but the reverse side. Jean Cohen writes: 'The poet plays upon the message in order to change the language' (115). Should he not also write: 'The poet changes the language in order to play upon the message'? Does he not come close to doing so when he adds: 'If the poem transgresses the code of speech, it is in order that the language re-establish it by transforming it' (115)? But then, it is untrue that 'the goal of all poetry' is to 'establish an alteration in language that at the same time, we shall see, is a mental metamorphosis' (115). Rather, it seems that the goal of poetry is to establish a new pertinence by means of an alteration in the language.

The force of the interaction theory lies in keeping together the two stages of the process, production and reduction of deviation, on the same level, namely that of predication. In changing the lexical code, the poet 'makes sense' with the entire statement containing the metaphorical word. The metaphor as such is a case of application of the predicate. The structural theory of Jean Cohen rids itself of such a concept, in order to operate with just two sorts of deviations. It succeeds through this conceptual economy in shepherding metaphor into the fold of the word and under the care of the substitution theory; the problem posed by the initiation of a new pertinence is thus avoided.

Yet it seems to me that Cohen's own analysis calls for this absent term. The production of deviation brings to light impertinent epithets (Cohen is justified in bringing predication itself into the 'epithetic form' (119), that is, the attribution of a characteristic in the guise of property of a logical subject), without as a consequence giving epithet properly speaking a distinct function of determination (137 ff.). Should he not have set up the new compatibility as epithet face to face with the paradigmatic deviation, i.e. lexical deviation – and thus, have spoken of a metaphorically pertinent epithet?

It is true that Cohen himself states that poetry creates 'a new linguistic order founded on the ruins of the old, through which ... a new type of signification is built' (134). But the author, as we shall see, like Genette and others, seeks this order not in the area of objective information but in that of affective values of a subjective character. Can one not hypothesize that it is because he has not reflected on the new pertinence at the very level of predication that the author joins the idea of a new type of signification lacking referential import to the idea of a paradigmatic deviation?

In this fashion the author confronts (only to dismiss it immediately) the properly semantic treatment of co-ordinative deviation (the third type at the semantic level): 'Between heterogeneous terms, homogeneity must be discovered' (178). Will the new pertinence be considered? No: this case was assimilated immediately into that of predicative deviation; and all that is pointed out in addition is the 'affective resemblance' that takes us completely outside the semantic domain, to the conclusion that 'emotional unity is the obverse side of notional inconsequence' (179).

Nevertheless, the missing term is sighted several times. The author holds that poetry, like all discourse, must be intelligible for its reader; like prose, poetry is a discourse that the author offers to his reader. Cannot then reduction of deviation unfold on the same plane on which deviation arose?

'Poetizing is a process with two correlative and simultaneous faces: deviation and reduction, destruction and restructuring. For the poem to function poetically, it is necessary that in *the consciousness of the reader, the signification be at once lost and recovered*' (182, author's emphasis). But must one then assign to other disciplines, 'psychology or phenomenology,' the task of determining the nature of this 'transmutation' (182) that draws meaning out of non-sense?

After having created a place for predicative pertinence and impertinence, Cohen's theory realigns with the other structural theories that operate with signs or collections of signs alone and ignore the central problem of semantics: the constitution of meaning as a property of the undivided sentence.

This omission of the properly predicative moment of metaphor is not without consequences. Since the theory thematizes just the lexical mutation, the study of the function of poetic language will be deprived of its essential support, namely the mutation of meaning at the same level at which the semantic impertinence takes place. It is not surprising, then, that one falls back into a theory of connotation and, at the same time, to an emotionalist theory of poetry. Recognition of the new semantic pertinence achieved through the lexical mutation is the only thing that could lead to an investigation of the new referential values attached to the innovation in meaning and open the way to an examination of the heuristic value of metaphorical statements.

But I would not want to end on this critical note. The addition of the predicative moment, which I call the *new pertinence*, at the same time allows one to say at what level a theory of paradigmatic deviation acquires meaning and validity. My critique will have been misunderstood if the conclusion is drawn from it that the notion of paradigmatic deviation is to be rejected.

On the contrary, it is invested with its full value if it is attached to the term missing from the theory, to the new pertinence. Indeed, Cohen proposes to show how the syntagmatic and the paradigmatic planes, far from being opposed, complete each other. Now, only the inception of a new pertinence within the metaphorical statement clears the way for linking a lexical deviation with a predicative deviation.

Returned thus to its place, paradigmatic deviation recovers its full value. It corresponds, in the interaction theory, to the phenomenon of *focalization* on the word described at the end of the previous Study.[40] Metaphorical meaning is an effect of the entire statement, but it is focused on one word, which can be called the metaphorical word. This is why one must say that metaphor is a semantic innovation that belongs at once to the predicative order (new pertinence) and the lexical order (paradigmatic deviation). In its first aspect it depends upon a 'dynamics' of meaning; under the second, upon a 'stasis' or non-dynamic state of a system. It is under this second aspect that it is addressed by a structural theory of poetry.

Accordingly, there is no conflict, properly speaking, between the theory of substitution (or of deviation) and the interaction theory. The latter describes the dynamics of the metaphorical statement; it alone deserves to be called a *semantic* theory of metaphor. The substitution theory describes the impact of this dynamic on the lexical code, where it sees a deviation; in doing so, it offers a *semiotic* equivalent of the semantic process.

The two approaches are grounded in the double character of the word. As a lexeme, the word is a difference in the lexical code. In this first guise it is affected by the paradigmatic deviation that Jean Cohen describes. As a part of discourse, it bears a part of the meaning that belongs to the entire statement. In this second role, it is affected by the interaction described by the interaction theory.

4 / THE FUNCTIONING OF FIGURES: 'SEMIC' ANALYSIS

The question of criteria of rhetorical deviation may still be posed at the level at which discourse appears. The question of operation or procedures calls for a change of level comparable to that which led to the decomposition of phonemes, the last distinctive units in the order of the signifier, into pertinent traits at the infralinguistic level. In the same way, the *signified* can be decomposed into semantic atoms, called semes, that do not belong to the surface level of discourse. The *Rhétorique générale* of the Liège group, and to a lesser degree the work of Le Guern,[41] will serve as my guide. We have already referred to this methodological decision in connection with the determination of the rhetoric degree zero, but we postponed examination of the problem posed by this strategy until later. We shall examine it now, at the same time as we pass from a simple criteriology to a theory of procedures.

At stake in this enterprise is the possibility of linking functional concepts (deviation, redundancy, etc.) to simple operations, such as *suppressing* and *adding*, that are at work at all the levels at which discourse is effected. In this way justice would be done to the universality of the notion of figure and to the generality of rhetoric itself.

But this involves the presupposition, which precedes all the other analyses and which the authors pass over very quickly (*Rhétorique générale* 37), that all the levels of decomposition (in the 'descending' sense) and of integration (in the 'ascending' sense) are homogeneous. We recognize in this what we have called the *semiotic postulate*.[42] Certainly this borrows from Benveniste's idea of the hierarchy of levels, but one destroys his point by depriving it of its fundamental corollary, the duality between semiotic units or signs and semantic units or sentences. The level of the sentence is just one among others (cf. table I, 31); the minimal complete sentence 'is defined by the presence of two syntagmas, the one nominal and the other verbal, by the relative order of these syntagmas, and by the complementarity of their markings' (68). But this order and this complementarity do not constitute a heterogeneous factor in a system where addition and suppression are to be the fundamental operations. These operations demand that one work only with collectivities. Phonemes, graphemes, words, and so on are collectivities (see the definitions, 33). So too the sentence; it is defined, at least in French, 'by the minimal presence of certain constituents, the syntagmas' (33); and these 'are defined in turn by morphemes that belong to them and divide them into classes' (33-4). As for morphemes, they subdivide into phonemes on the one hand, then into distinctive traits (which are infralinguistic); and on the other hand, into sememes (words) and then into (infralinguistic) semes. No discontinuity is allowed, either in the ascending or the descending scale. This is why all the units at all levels can be considered as 'collections of elements built upon preexisting stocks' (31). The sentence is no exception; it is defined, as to its grammatical side, as a 'collection of syntagmas and of morphemes, endowed with an order and admitting of repetition' (34). This order is what Benveniste calls predicate and what breaks up the monotony of the hierarchy. From a semiotic point of view, order is just an aspect of collection.

The table of *metaboles* (that is, of all operations on language) presents the same homogeneous character. It is established on the basis of a double dichotomy, which on the one hand distinguishes the signifier from the signified (expression and content in the terminology of Hjelmslev), and on the other hand distinguishes entities smaller than or as large as the word from larger entities.

Four domains are distinguished in this way. The domain of *metaplasmes* covers figures that act on the sound or graphic aspect of words and of smaller units. That of *metataxes* contains figures that act on the structure of the sentence (as defined above). *The third domain contains metaphor.* The authors of the *Rhétorique générale* call it the domain of *metasememes*, which they define as follows: 'A metasememe is a figure that replaces one sememe by another, that is, modifies the groupings of degree-zero semes. This type of figure supposes that the word is equal to a collection of *nuclear semes*, without internal order and not admitting of repetition' (34). Finally we have the domain of *metalogismes*; these are figures that modify the logical value of the sentence (according to the second definition cited above).

It is granted from the outset that metaphor is to be sought among the metasememes, and so among the word-focused figures, as in classical rhetoric. With such a beginning, it will be difficult to connect its functioning to a predicative character of statements, since the metataxes constitute a distinct class and the sentence-structure they modify is considered from the perspective of the collectivity of its constituents (syntagmas or semes). The path of the statement-metaphor is thus blocked. It is granted at the same time that, as in classical rhetoric, the metasememes are substitutive phenomena, replacing one sememe with another. So the originality of the work, as it deals with metaphor, does not consist in the definition of metaphor as a word-focused figure, nor in the description of this figure as substitution; it lies in the explanation of substitution itself in terms of a modification bearing on the collectivity of nuclear semes. Put differently, all of its originality lies in the change in the level of analysis, in the descent to the infra-linguistic level of semes, which are to the signified what distinctive traits are to the signifier.

The whole apparatus of functional concepts and operations brought into play will not bring with it any essential change in the theory of metaphor, but only a higher level of technical finesse and the reduction of word-figures to a basic type of functioning common to all figures.

One can anticipate, nevertheless, that the framework adopted by the new rhetoric will break down in the same way as that of the old rhetoric, under the very pressure of the description that, whether we like it or not, reintroduces the predicative aspects of metaphor.

The change of strategic level permits the introduction of operative concepts and then of operations that act at all the levels where units of signification have managed to be brought together into collectivities of elements. Accordingly, one will come across them again at work in the four classes of metaboles.

We have already spoken of these operative concepts in connection with the notion of degree zero. The operative concepts are those of information theory (the concept of semantic information being that of Carnap and Bar-Hillel: the identification of a piece of information is determined by the number of binary choices one must make in order to arrive at it; thus, one will be able to give a numerical signification to the addition and suppression of units in which the transformations applied to units of signification consist). It then becomes possible again to take up the notions of deviation and its reduction, discussed in the two previous sections, as well as the notion of convention, which is a systematic deviation, and express these notions in terms of redundancy and self-correction. Deviation diminishes redundancy, and so predictability. Reduction of deviation is a self-correction that re-establishes the integrity of the message. Every figure alters the amount of redundancy in discourse whether by reducing it or by adding to it. From the point of view of redundancy, conventions operate in the reverse manner to deviation properly speaking, since they reinforce redundancy (38-45). As for reduction, it involves two conditions. (1) In figurative discourse one can distinguish on the one hand a part, or 'base,' that has not been modified and is a particular form of syntagma; and on the other hand, a part that has undergone rhetorical alterations. (2) The second part retains with its degree zero a certain relation that falls under certain paradigms of articulation of degree zero and of figurative degree. This point is important for the theory of metaphor. The invariant in the paradigmatic order will be the virtual term common to degree zero and the figurative degree. Here we encounter again a postulate that we have shown to belong to the same model as the other postulates of deviation and of substitution. Metaphor is a substitution within a sphere of selection that is here called the invariant and has the status of paradigm, whereas the base, which has the status of syntagma, remains unmodified. This amounts to saying that no information comes through the figure. That is why its positive function is consigned to the study of *ethos*, that is, of the specific aesthetic effect taken as the true object of aesthetic communication.

'In sum, rhetoric is a collection of *deviations* capable of *self-correction*, that is to say, modifying the normal level of *redundancy* of language, by breaking rules or by inventing new ones. The deviation created by an author is perceived by the reader thanks to a *mark* and subsequently is reduced thanks to the presence of an *invariant*' (45). (I am intentionally ending the quotation before the introduction of the notion of *ethos*, which, along with those of deviation, mark, and invariant, completes the list of 'operative concepts' [35-45].)

The operations that interest the whole of the field of figures and have provisionally been called transformations – the metaboles – divide into two large groups, according to whether they alter the units themselves or their position, that is, the linear order of units. Thus, they are either substantial or relational. Word-figures have an interest in the first type of transformation. The key idea – at which the notion of 'collection' hinted – is that the operations of this group reduce to additions and suppressions; that is, because of the operative concepts adopted, to an increase or decrease of information. The second kind of operation does not interest us, since the word is a collection of nuclear semes without internal order. Hence, metaphor will bring into play neither syntagmatic operation nor the concept of order implied by the sentence.

The theory of *metasememes* – a new name given to tropes or one-word figures to indicate symmetry with the 'metabole' and 'metaplasme' already adopted (33) and, further, in order to designate the nature of the operation in question – is the rigorous application of these operations of addition and suppression to the collection of semes or minimal units of meaning, which constitute the word. Classical rhetoric knew only the effect on meaning, namely, the fact that the figure 'replaces the *content* of one word by another' (93). General rhetoric takes this nominal definition as established; but it explains substitution as an arrangement of semes resulting from addition and suppression, with a portion of the initial meaning – the base – remaining unchanged.[43]

The enterprise encounters a major difficulty, however: how are figure and polysemy to be distinguished? A word is defined in lexicological terms, indeed, by the enumeration of its semantic variants or sememes. These are contextual classes, that is, types of occurrence in possible contexts. The dictionary word is the *corpus* constituted by these sememes. Now this field already includes the phenomenon of deviation, but internal to the corpus, between a principal meaning and peripheral meanings (the *Rhétorique générale* cites the semic analysis of the word *tête* ['head'] in *Sémantique structurale* by Greimas).[44] And so the word considered as paradigm of its possible uses appears as an area of substitution, in which all the variations have equal status (each use of the word *tête* is a metasememe equivalent to all the others). If the deviations that constitute word-figures are also substitutions, and if the lexicalized word carries deviations within itself, semantic process and rhetorical process become indistinguishable. Moreover, as we shall see, this is the direction of the notion of metaphorical process in Jakobson: all paradigmatic selection becomes metaphorical.[45]

The authors of the *Rhétorique générale* are conscious of this difficulty; but it seems to me that the answer they offer makes an implicit appeal to a theory of the figure of discourse that is foreign to their system.

In order 'to restore to the rhetorical process its specificity in relation to the purely semantic process' (95), it is necessary first to introduce the idea of a tension between two variations of meaning. Figure occurs only if, through the change of meaning, 'a tension endures, a distance, between the two sememes, of which the first remains present, even if implicitly' (95). What is this tension? Let us grant that it can be contained within the boundaries of one and the same word. But what about its mark? (The figure, in fact, is a sensed deviation; the word must be 'felt' to be filled with a new meaning [96].) It is here that a syntagmatic factor, a context, must necessarily intervene: 'If it remains true to say that the metasememe can be reduced to modification of the contents of a single word, one must add for the sake of completeness that the figure will not be perceived except in a sequence or sentence' (95). Is this really only 'for the sake of completeness'? Is the sentence merely the condition of the mark's perception, or is it involved in the very constitution of the figure? We have reiterated that there are no metaphors in the dictionary; even though polysemy is lexicalized, metaphor, at least newly created metaphor, is not; and when it does become lexicalized, it means that the metaphor in common use has become part of polysemy. Now it certainly seems that a syntagmatic factor from the order of the sentence should be at the origin of the figure, and not just of its mark. Within the figure, the message is perceived to be linguistically incorrect. Now this incorrectness is immediately a fact of discourse; if this is not granted, one cannot (as do the authors of the *Rhétorique générale*) integrate Jean Cohen's notion of semantic impertinence with the theory of metasememes ('Here we join Jean Cohen, who very neatly formulated the complementarity of these two operations, perception and reduction of deviation. The first is clearly located on the syntagmatic plane, the second on the paradigmatic plane' [97].) But how is it not seen that this 'dissonance ... of a semantic order' (96) is a fact of predication that corrupts the very notion of metasememe? The *Rhétorique générale* dismisses the difficulty by rejecting among the 'extrinsic conditions' (96) those that are manifestly intrinsic to the production of the meaning effect. I would account in the following manner for the ease with which the authors proceed to this reduction of the syntagmatic conditions of word figures to a simple extrinsic condition: it could be that synecdoche, to which metaphor presently will be reduced, lends itself better to this reduction than metaphor itself and that the dissymmetry between the two figures resides precisely in a difference at the level of operation of the sentence. We will come to this later.

So, as Jean Cohen says as well, it is reduction of deviation, unfolding (it is granted) only on the paradigmatic level, that carries the entire burden of explanation. How do addition and suppression operate?

The reply to this question cannot be given directly; it requires that the question of semantic segmentation first be resolved. Now the latter passes via the detour of the *object* and its linguistic counterpart, the *concept*. This perambulation is foreshadowed from the beginning of the work: 'One can equally take the view that certain words refer mediately to an object = collection of co-ordinated parts, and that this decomposition of the object into its parts (at the level of the referent) has its linguistic counterpart (at the level of concepts), the one like the other being designable by words ... the results of these two decompositions are completely different' (34).[46] Later these two decompositions are called 'models of representation,' that is 'models capable of aiding the description of the universe of representations' (97). Material analysis of the object and notional analysis of the concept do not coincide; the first results in a parcelling up of classes, its analysis resting on similarities, while the second results in a tree of disjunctions with its analysis resting on differences.

It certainly seems that the properly linguistic model (the endocentric series described on pages 99-100) is not independent of these 'purely cognitive' models (97), since the descending linear itineraries that the series of words follow are 'traced in the pyramid of nested classes or in the disjunctive tree' (99). Furthermore, the authors affirm this clearly: 'It is always the semantic universe itself that is at the bottom of this structuring of vocabulary' (99).

The two types of semantic *decomposition* considered, accordingly, are copied from the nesting of classes and from decomposition on the model of the disjunctive tree. The conceptual mode and the material mode of decomposition give two different statuses to the notion of an individual: a given tree will be either 'poplar' *or* 'oak' *or* 'willow,' but it will also be 'branches' *and* 'leaves' *and* 'trunk' *and* 'roots.' The semic analysis is thus dependent on the laws that 'govern the collective whole of the semantic universe.' This dependence particularly affects the theory of the noun, placed at the centre of the word figures. In effect, the distinction between concrete nouns and abstract nouns can be equated with the two modes of decomposition: the concrete 'tree' is the empirical conjunction of all its parts, the abstract 'tree' is the rational disjunction of all its modalities.[47]

It is to these two modes of decomposition that the two operations of suppression and of addition apply. The classification of tropes (synecdoche, metaphor, metonymy) undergoes a profound alteration due to this fact. The guiding thread is no longer to be sought at the level of effects of meaning but of operations: the notions of suppression of semes, of addition, and of suppression *plus* addition will now guide.

The principal result – the one that concerns our investigation directly – is that *synecdoche* takes first place and metaphor is reduced to synecdoche through an addition and a suppression making metaphor the product of two synecdoches.

This outcome could have been foreseen at the point at which the metasememe was considered within the limits of the word and its activity restricted to a modification of the collection of semes. Indeed, the partial suppression of semes gives us directly the generalizing synecdoche, most often of type Σ: species to genus, particular to general (e.g. when one says 'mortals' for 'men'). Total suppression would lead to asemy – 'stuff,' 'thing' for anything and everything. Simple addition gives us the particularizing synecdoche, most often of type π (e.g. 'sail' for 'vessel'). Synecdoche, in fact, is the figure that best verifies the theory, because of (1) the conservation of a foundation of essential semes whose suppression would render discourse incomprehensible; (2) the operation of simple addition and suppression; (3) the application of these operators in mode Σ and mode π; and (4) the extrinsic status of contextual factors.

The reduction of metaphor to a product of two synecdoches demands very close and detailed examination.

Three factors are brought into consideration in connection with these operators of suppression and addition. First, they are not mutually exclusive; they can be cumulative. Next, their combination can be partial or total. Partial combination gives us metaphor, and total combination metonymy. This analysis, accordingly, puts the two figures in the same class, as opposed to Jakobson.[48] Finally, the combination has 'degrees of presentation': in metaphor *in absentia* (true metaphor according to the Ancients), the substitutable term is absent from discourse; in metaphor *in praesentia*, the two terms are present together, as well as the mark of their partial identity.

So to discuss metaphor properly speaking is to consider (1) suppression-addition, (2) partial, and (3) *in absentia*.

According to the foregoing presentation, it is metaphor *in absentia* that is analysed as a product of two synecdoches.

But the proof of this thesis reveals immediately that only the reduction of deviation, Jean Cohen's second operation, is taken into consideration. In fact, the production of deviation brings the entire statement into play. The authors readily agree: 'Formally, metaphor reduces to a syntagma in which, contradictorily, the identity of two signifiers and the non-identity of the two corresponding signified things appear together. This affront to (linguistic) reason gives rise to a reduction procedure through which the reader seeks to validate the identity' (106-7). But once again, the initial operation is relegated to 'conditions extrinsic to rhetorical consciousness' (107). Thus reduced to the operation of validating identity alone, the explanation focuses on the stage that Cohen had placed on the paradigmatic plane.

And so the problem presents itself as follows: 'To find a limit class such that the two objects are both counted in together, but are separate in all inferior classes'; or again, 'to establish the shortest route by which two objects can reconnect' (107). Therefore, metaphorical reduction is the search for a virtual, hinge-like third term; the reader conducts this search 'by exploring any tree or any pyramid whatever, speculative or realistic' (ibid.).

The discovery of this zone of intersection can be broken down into two synecdoches, from the starting term to the intermediary term and from this latter to the destination term. The sought-for invariant is the narrow path; the rest of the semantic areas that lie outside the intersection maintain the consciousness of deviation. The only constraints are, on the one hand, that the synecdoches be complementary, that is that they function in opposite directions with respect to the level of generality so that the common term is at the same level on both sides (generalizing *plus* particularizing and vice-versa); and on the other hand, that the two synecdoches be homogeneous as to mode of decomposition, whether by semes or by parts. The interaction takes place in a conceptual metaphor or in a referential metaphor.

It goes without saying that the reader of a metaphor is not conscious of these two operations. He is conscious only of the transfer of meaning from the first term to the second; it is for the semic analysis that this transfer consists of 'the attribution, to the combination of the two collections of semes, of properties that strictly apply only to their intersection' (109). This is why the reader of metaphor does not sense the impoverishment involved in passing through 'the narrow path of the semic intersection,' but on the contrary feels a sense of enlargement, an opening up, an amplification.

The same theory that demonstrates the close relationship between synecdoche and metonymy also shows that the difference between metaphor and metonymy reduces to a difference between the partial and the total character of the self-same addition-suppression operation.

Indeed, the difference between metaphor and metonymy is not a difference of operation, as is the case between resemblance and extrinsic relation. There is a movement in both of them from a starting term to a destination term *via* an intermediate term. In metaphor, this intermediate term constitutes a semic intersection of the two classes; therefore, it belongs to the semantic field of each of them. This is why the supplementary addition of semes is partial. In the well-worn case of contiguity, there is no such semic intersection. From this point of view, metonymy 'rests on a void' (117); one can speak of a null intersection. Nevertheless, there is a common inclusion, but of the two terms in a larger domain, whether of semes in the case of conceptual decomposition or of things in the case of material decomposition. In short, 'in metaphor the intermediate term is encompassed, whereas in metonymy it is encompassing' (118). To put it differently, the third, absent term is to be sought in a contiguous region of semes and of things. One can say, in this sense, that metaphor calls upon only denotative semes, that is, nuclear semes, included in the definition of the terms, while metonymy calls upon connotative semes, that is, 'contiguous to the array of a larger grouping and combining to define this grouping' (118).

It seems to me that this theory leaves out what constitutes the specificity of metaphor, namely the reduction of an initial semantic impertinence. Synecdoche, indeed, lacks this function completely; there is no need, in accounting for synecdoche, to diverge from a predicative character of discourse. The status of the impertinent epithet, essential to metaphor, is of no concern whatsoever to synecdoche, which confines itself within the bare limits of a substitutive operation applied to the word.

Having dismissed the predicative condition of impertinence, the theory can dismiss the properly predicative status of the new pertinence more easily than does Jean Cohen. The whole interplay of 'focus' and 'frame' that dominates the investigation of intersection is also dispersed, along with everything that arises from the predicative plane. All that is noted is the result of this attributive dynamic that *produces* the intersection. It is this implied product as *given* (with its 'virtual' status) that is decomposed after the fact into two synecdoches. The only function of this activity is to submit metaphor to the system that admits of additions and suppressions alone and omits predicative operations. To this extent it is utterly valid: it ensures the simplicity of the system, that is, in one stroke, the homogeneous character of the hierarchy among the levels of units of signification (from phoneme to sentence and to text), and the applicability of the same operative concepts (deviation, redundancy, correction, etc.) and the same operators (addition, suppression) at all the levels. Now, it is certainly possible to decompose a *given* metaphor into two synecdoches; but one cannot *produce* a metaphor with two synecdoches. The 'double logical operation' (111) is only the reformulation, in the terms of the semic arithmetic, of an operation whose dynamism puts into play the predicative operation of the sentence.

My objections are confirmed by an examination of metaphor *in praesentia* and of oxymoron. Their reduction to metaphor *in absentia* is an important condition of the success of the theory: 'We did justice at the appropriate point to the illusion created by the figures *in praesentia* and those which appear to involve several words: it is always possible to reduce them to a figure *in absentia* (cf. metaphor and oxymoron)' (132). The authors introduce the difference between metaphor *in absentia* and metaphor *in praesentia* under the title of 'degrees of presentation,' that is, of the extension of the units considered. In the case of metaphor *in absentia*, the semic intersection is between the absent degree zero and the figurative term, thus within the word. With metaphor *in praesentia*, the semic intersection is a mutual approach of two equally present terms: a simile, with or without the grammatical mark of comparison.

One might have thought that the precisely predicative structure of metaphor *in praesentia* would have turned attention towards the equally predicative conditions of metaphor *in absentia*, and consequently to the intersection of the metaphorical term with the other terms equally present in the metaphorical statement. One sees, indeed, that metaphors *in praesentia* reduce to syntagmas in which two sememes are assimilated improperly, whereas metaphor properly speaking does not manifest assimilation (114). The opposite is the case: 'We know that tropes, in Fontanier's sense, involve one word alone. In our category of metasememes, which encom-

passes all of the tropes of Fontanier, metaphor *in praesentia* would constitute an exception to this rule. In fact, this figure can equally be analysed
as a figure by addition that involves a single word, that is, as synecdoche'
(112). In the passage taken from Edmund Burke, 'l'Espagne – une grande
baleine échouée sur les plages d'Europe (Spain – a great whale stranded on
the beaches of Europe),' introduction of an absent degree zero, the swollen
outline on the map, is all one needs in order to have a particularizing
synecdoche (whale – swollen outline). In this way one eliminates the
operation of the metaphor as impertinent predicate (or epithet). The
authors have no trouble admitting that here the description bows to the
imperatives of the system: 'Despite the undeniable metaphorical functioning of the example cited, we think that the synecdochic reduction is to
be preferred, for reasons of method and of generality. It has the advantage,
moreover, of insisting on the strict relation, discussed earlier, between
metaphor and synecdoche' (112).

One may doubt that metaphorical comparison (discussed again on page
114) can be equated in this way with synecdochic reduction. In effect,
what it presents is first and foremost a deviation that itself is of the predicative order, namely the incompatibility of a term with the rest of the
message. The same holds for the rest of the message, the term of comparison re-establishing compatibility by reducing the degrees of identity, that
is, by asserting a weak equivalence. This is why the term of comparison belongs to the order of the copula, as the authors also agree (114-16). There
is even the case where the comparison contracts into an 'is' of equivalence:
'Nature is a temple where living columns ...' In the face of this example,
the authors concede that 'this use of the verb to be is distinct from the
"is" of determination: "the rose is red" is a process that is synecdochic
and not metaphorical in nature' (115). How then are we to understand the
reduction of metaphor *in praesentia* to metaphor *in absentia* and of the
latter to a double synecdoche? Must not the reverse also be said, that
metaphor is a syntagma contracted into a paradigm (substitution of a figurative meaning for an absent degree zero)? It is quite apparent to me that
metaphor *in praesentia* requires one to modify the categorical affirmation
that 'the definition of paradigm is, structurally, identical with that of
metaphor: as a result, it is permissible to consider this last as a paradigm
deployed as a syntagma' (116).

The theory confronts an analogous difficulty in oxymoron ('This obscure clarity that falls from the stars' [120]). Oxymoron is an impertinent
epithet par excellence, where impertinence is heightened to the point of
antithesis. Reduction, for this figure, consists in a contradiction being
assumed in full, according to the expression of Léon Cellier.[49] The economy of the *Rhétorique générale* prescribes a search for the degree zero

that allows one to consider the figure as *in absentia*: 'There is real question whether oxymoron is actually a figure, that is, whether it has a degree zero' (120). In the example quoted, the degree zero would be 'luminous clarity' and the transition to the state of figure would be accomplished through *negative* suppression-addition. But what is a negative suppression-addition? This operator on an operator (itself already complex: suppression-addition) is all the more unusual as it operates on an expression, luminous clarity, 'that already constitutes a figure: i.e., epithet, as understood by J. Cohen' (120). Does not this remark also lead us back to predication? It would be necessary to study the parallels in metalogisms, irony, and paradox.

At the end of this discussion, it might seem that the predication theory of metaphor of the English-language authors and the theory of the word-metaphor are equal in force and differ only in the choice of a different system of fundamental axioms, in the one case regulating the activity of 'bizarre' predicates and in the other case governing purely arithmetical operations applied to semic collections. Nevertheless, the theory of the statement-metaphor seems to me to have an undebatable advantage on two counts.

First of all, it alone gives an account, through the interaction of all the terms present at the same time in the same statement, of the *production* of the intersection that the theory of the word-metaphor postulates. The crucial phenomenon is the *augmentation* of the initial polysemy of words by means of an instance of discourse. What compels the addition of a semantic variant that did not exist before is the recoil shock where the predicative structure and the semantic field meet. The *Rhétorique générale* does well to say that 'the reader of poetry elaborates ... seeks ... traverses ... finds ...' – so many words attesting to a certain invention; but this no longer finds a place in the concept of semic intersection, which operates only with semantic fields that are already completely constituted.

One can question whether semic analysis, which, by definition, applies to terms already lexicalized, can give an account of the augmentation of polysemy by means of discourse.

Here the present doubt mingles with those of Jean Cohen, who nevertheless sets great store by this procedure.[50] Can one say that 'fox' analyses into 'animal' *plus* 'sly' in the same way as 'mare' analyses into 'horse' *plus* 'female'? The parallel is misleading, because the example is that of a metaphor in common use and the predicate *sly* is practically a part of the already lexicalized network of contextual significations (which, with Max Black, I have called the 'system of associated commonplaces'). Jean Cohen, from whom I borrow the example of the sly fox, which he treats according to the rules of semic analysis, notes himself: '"Fox" could signify "sly" [*ruse*] only because "cunning deceit" [*la ruse*] was, in the minds of speakers, one of the semantic components of the term' (127). There is, of course, no clearly marked border between the lexical code and the cultural code: expressions which are called figurative register the partial inscription of the latter in the former. But this semi-lexicalized status of commonplaces is not ignored by linguistic consciousness, which, even in the case of metaphor in common use, still distinguishes between literal meaning and figurative meaning.[51] This is certainly why the trope alone provides the criterion of extension of meaning: 'Perhaps the study of tropes would provide – let us say in passing – the linguistic criterion required by structural semantics' (127).

With newly invented metaphor, uncertainty is no longer possible. In relation to the lexical code, the new value constitutes a deviation that semic analysis cannot contain. Even the cultural code of commonplaces is insufficient, according to Max Black.[52] Indeed, one must call forth a system of *ad hoc* references that comes into existence only with the metaphorical statement itself. Neither the lexical code nor the code of clichés contains the new constituent trait of the signified, which is deviatory in relation to the two codes. If it was true that the metaphor rests on a common seme already present at the infralinguistic level, even if in a virtual state, then not only would there be no new information, no invention, but there would not even be any need for a paradigmatic deviation in order to reduce a syntagmatic deviation. A simple subtraction of semes – which is precisely what synecdoche does – would be enough. It is clear why it was necessary at all costs to reduce metaphor to synecdoche: the latter is truly the one-word figure that completely satisfies the rules of semic analysis.

The newly invented metaphor is not alone in resisting semic analysis. Jean Cohen, of whose partial agreement with componential analysis we just spoke, raises the case of indecomposable predicates, like colours (the 'bleus angelus' of Mallarmé), to which he adds synaesthetic metaphors and affective resemblances. These metaphors, he notes, constitute deviations of second degree in relation to those (which he calls first-degree) whose impertinence can be submitted to semic analysis and reduced by simple subtraction of inappropriate elements of the signified. With deviations of second degree, it is necessary to look *outside* the signified for the reason for the metaphorical usage, for example among the subjective effects (appeasement, or others) produced by the figure. The evocation of this subjective effect would serve to diminish impertinence. Now, this value or effect 'in no way constitutes a pertinent trait of signification' (129). This acknowledgment is important if it is true that 'the fundamental resource of all poetry, the trope of tropes, is the synaesthetic metaphor, or affective ressemblance' (178). Is it not necessary, then, to return to the case of first-degree deviations? Is it true that 'sly' is an objective characteristic of 'fox' just as 'green' is of 'emerald,' and that we derive one from the other by a simple subtraction of inappropriate semes? In my opinion, the deviations of first degree must be reinterpreted as a function of second-degree deviations. If not, the explanation of reduction breaks down into two parts: on one side, a type of reduction motivated by internal relations; on the other side, a type motivated by an external relationship. It is not enough to say that the distance increases from the first to the second degree and that the first metaphors are 'closer' and the second more 'distant' (130); interiority and exteriority in relation to a semic collection designate two different statuses of the metaphorical use of a word in relation to semic analysis.

This is why I prefer to say, precisely in order to save the idea of code violation and paradigmatic deviation, that in the first place the impertinent predicate is outside the code. Let us repeat: there are no metaphors in dictionaries. Metaphor is not polysemy. Semic analysis produces a theory of polysemy directly, and only indirectly a theory of metaphor, to the extent that polysemy attests to the open structure of words and their capacity to acquire new significations without losing their old ones. This open structure is only the condition of metaphor and not yet the reason for its production. The appearance, with the impertinent predicate, of extra-code values that the prior polysemy could not contain by itself requires an event in the realm of discourse.

The second aspect of superiority of the theory of statement-metaphor over a theory of word-metaphor lies in the fact that it takes into account the kinship of the two domains of metasememes and metalogisms, which the *Rhétorique générale* dissociates.

The *Rhétorique générale* has ample reason to characterize metalogism as a deviation, not between words and meanings, but between the meaning of words and reality, the reality term being taken in the most general sense of extra-linguistic referent of discourse: 'Whatever its form, the metalogism necessarily has reference to something extra-linguistically given as its criterion' (125). Hence, a rhetoric aspiring to generality cannot operate merely in the 'interior' space that (according to the metaphor of Gérard Genette) lies deep between sign and meaning. It must also consider the 'exterior' space between sign and referent in order to account for figures such as litotes, hyperbole, allegory, and irony, which disturb not only the lexicon but also the referential function.

Now, one may be surprised to see Gilbert Ryle's famous 'category mistake' (presentation of certain facts arising in one category in the terms of a category that is not their own) appearing under the rubric of metalogisms, and to read the following: 'In particular, it is not an accident that the theories of Ryle serve as foundation for the study of metaphor by several English-language authors. His "category mistake," which is used to denounce the absurdity of cartesianism, is rebaptized "category-confusion" by Turbayne, who opposes it to "category-fusion," in which he sees the process by which metaphor is elaborated' (129-30). If 'it is not an accident,' then truly there must be a method for passing from trope to metalogism.

The *Rhétorique générale* itself demands this, and not just the historical rapprochement with the English-language theories: 'Doubtless the metaboles do not always present themselves in the predicative format, but it is always possible to reduce them to it. In this case, the metasememe is always a "pseudo-proposition," because it presents a contradiction to which logic objects and that rhetoric accepts. This is true of metaphor, it is also true of the other metasememes' (131). This belated admission is an important one, and reinforces our thesis. In fact, only this reduction to the predicative form allows a bridge to be laid between metasememe and metalogism. We saw the necessity of this recourse to the predicative form when we discussed the 'is' of equivalence in 'nature is a temple where living columns ...' (115). This is certainly what the authors have in mind when they remark: 'Under the predicative form, the metasememe uses the copula in a way that the logician judges illicit, because in this case "to be" signifies "to be and not be" ... In this manner, one can reduce all metasememes to ... the formula of contradiction, with the difference that this is not a contradiction' (131). But then metaphor is no longer a trope in one word only. The necessity of this reduction to the predicative form results again from this remark, that the constitution of the referent is quite often necessary for the identification of a metaphor: 'Metaphor *in absentia* especially does not appear as a metaphor unless its referent is known' (128).

Certainly the distinction in principle that the authors establish between metasememe and metalogism is not abolished, but their relatedness demands that one compare them as different types of statements (131).

This kinship is particularly close when one compares metaphor and *allegory* (137-8).[53] The former is a trope for these authors, the latter a metalogism. The first changes the meaning of words, the second enters into conflict with reality. Thus 'bateau ivre' [drunken boat], as a metaphor of Rimbaud, is a one-word trope; only the lexicon is upset. But the expression 'the drunken boat has rejoined the great and lonely sailor' is an allegory because the referents (Malraux and de Gaulle) are neither boat nor sailor. But if, as was just admitted, metaphor can be reduced to a statement, 'drunken boat' will have to enter into a composition with some other expression – for example, 'the drunken boat finally ended its days in Ethiopia.' The difference between metaphor and allegory, therefore, will not be between word and sentence, as is proposed here, but will consist in the fact that the metaphorical statement incorporates non-metaphorical terms ('end its days in Ethiopia') with which the metaphorical term ('the drunken boat') interacts, whereas allegory is made up only of metaphorical terms. Hence, the tension is not in the proposition but in the context. This is what leads to the belief that metaphor concerns words alone and only allegory is in conflict with a referent. But the structural difference between the two statements does not keep the reduction of absurdity from following the same path: when a reading of the complete sentence does not offer an acceptable or interesting meaning at the literal level, one investigates, provoked by this deception, 'whether a second, less banal isotopy might not perhaps exist' (137).

This is the direction in which the English-language authors have advanced their research. They say of metaphor and allegory, parable and fable as a group what the *Rhétorique générale* says only of allegory and the neighbouring figures: 'When the first isotopy appears to us to be insufficient, this is due to the impertinence of the relationships in relation to the elements to which they are connected (absence, for example, of Court or a tribunal among animals)' (138). But it is because metaphor has been separated from the complete statement that it appears to be another sort of figure, and that only its incorporation into a metalogism lets it participate in the referential function recognized in allegory, fable, and parable, while the metasememe as such remains a transformation operating at the level of every element of discourse, of every word (figure 16, page 138).

The theory of the statement-metaphor is more suited to display the profound relationship, at the level of statements, between metaphor, allegory, parable, and fable. For this very reason, it allows one to open up, for this entire set of figures – metasememes and metalogisms – the problematic of the referential function that the *Rhétorique générale* reserves for metalogisms alone.[54]

What remains true in the distinction between metasememes and metalogisms is that the metasememe designates the deviation at the level of the word through which the metaphorical statement re-establishes meaning. But if one admits, with the conclusion of the preceding Study, that this deviation is only the impact on the word of a semantic phenomenon that concerns the entire statement, then one must call 'metaphor' the entire statement with its new meaning, and not just the paradigmatic deviation that focuses the mutation of meaning of the whole statement on one word.

The work of resemblance

For Mikel Dufrenne

This Study is devoted to the examination of a problem that seems to be the counterpart of the very success of the semantic theory set out in the preceding Studies. This problem concerns the role of resemblance in the explanation of metaphor. There is no doubt surrounding this role in classical rhetoric. On the other hand, it seems to be progressively obscured as the discursive model becomes more refined. Does this imply that resemblance is linked exclusively to a theory of substitution and is incompatible with an interaction theory? Such is the question to be taken up in this Study, which I will preview by saying that I propose to dissociate the fate of resemblance from that of the substitution theory and to reinterpret the role of resemblance within the guidelines of the theory of interaction set out in the third Study. But before attempting this, we must test the common bonds between substitution and resemblance and measure the obstacles to a new pact between interaction and resemblance.

1 / SUBSTITUTION AND RESEMBLANCE

In the tropology of classical rhetoric, the place assigned to metaphor among the figures of signification is defined specifically by the role that the relationship of resemblance has in the transference from initial idea to new idea. Metaphor is the trope of resemblance *par excellence.* This pact with resemblance is not just an isolated trait; in the model underlying the theory of classical rhetoric, it is intimately connected to the primacy of naming or denomination and to the other traits that follow from this primacy. Now resemblance operates first between the ideas named by words. Subsequently, in the model, the theme of resemblance is closely united with those of borrowing, deviation, substitution, and exhaustive paraphrase. Indeed, resemblance first of all motivates the borrowing; next, it is the positive side of the process whose negative side is deviation; further, it is the internal link within the sphere of substitution; finally, it guides the paraphrase that annuls the trope by restoring the proper meaning. To the extent that the postulate of substitution can be taken to be representative of the whole chain of postulates, resemblance is the foundation of the substitution that is set in motion in the metaphorical transposition of names and, more generally, of words.

This pact between metaphor and resemblance is reinforced by an initial argument. The relation that Aristotle saw between metaphor and simile was subsequently reversed; simile is no longer a sort of metaphor, but metaphor a sort of simile, namely an abbreviated simile. Only the elision of the term of comparison distinguishes metaphor from simile. Now the latter brings resemblance itself into discourse, and by this means points out the grounds of metaphor.[1]

We will dwell on a more modern argument that consolidates the pact. In its binarist zeal, structural linguistics has been extreme in its tendency to simplify the complicated table of tropes, to the point where metaphor and metonymy alone remain in play – that is, it is alleged, contiguity and resemblance. We explained while discussing the rhetoric of Fontanier how far the ancient rhetoricians were from identifying metonymy and synecdoche (to speak only of tropes that can be set in opposition to metaphor). Even more, with Fontanier, 'correspondence' (which underlies metonymy) brings together ideas of objects each of which forms an absolutely separate whole. But the variety of relations satisfying this general condition of correlation cannot in any way be reduced to contiguity. As for the 'connection' relation, which involves the idea of inclusion of two things in a whole, it is opposed directly to the relationship of correlation, which implies a certain mutual exclusion of related terms. Only with contemporary neo-rhetoricians is tropology restricted to the opposition of metaphor and metonymy. At the same time, the role of resemblance is confirmed and amplified by a simplifying operation that makes it the sole counterpart of a single opposite, namely contiguity. But this is not all, nor is it the most important thing. Thanks to his famous article of 1953, 'Two Aspects of Language and Two Types of Aphasic Disturbances,' the coupling of metaphor and metonymy has been linked permanently with the name of Roman Jakobson. It was his stroke of genius to have connected this properly tropological and rhetorical duality with a more fundamental polarity that concerns the very functioning of language and not just its figurative use. Henceforward, metaphor and metonymy do not merely define figures and tropes; they define general processes of language. The analysis of Roman Jakobson is referred to at this stage of the investigation because, by generalizing the distinction between metaphor and metonymy far beyond tropology, and so the change in meaning of words, the famous linguist has

strengthened the idea that substitution and resemblance are two inseparable concepts, since they rule together over processes that work on the
numerous levels at which language is effected. It is this reinforcement of
the link between substitution, resemblance, and metaphor that will be at
stake in the following discussion.

The new linkage of the metaphorical and the metonymic in Jakobson
builds on a distinction (to be found in the *Cours de linguistique générale*
of Ferdinand de Saussure) between two ways in which signs are arranged –
combination and selection.[2] According to Jakobson, however, Saussure
would have sacrificed the second of these to the old prejudice that regards
the signifier as having a purely linear character. Nevertheless, the kernel of
the theory remains Saussurean. The primary mode of arrangement unites
in praesentia two or more terms *in absentia* in a virtual mnemonic series.
Hence, this concerns entities associated in the code but not in the given
message, whereas in the case of combination the entities are associated in
both places or only in the actual message. Now, where there is selection
between alternative terms, there is the possibility of substituting one for
the other, which is equivalent to the first in one aspect and different from
it in another. Selection and substitution, accordingly, are the two faces of
a single operation. All that remains is to link up combination and contiguity, substitution and similarity – which Jakobson does not hesitate to
do. Indeed, contiguity and similarity characterize the status of the constituents, in the context of a message on the one hand, within a substitution group on the other. From this point on, the correlation with tropes
presents no difficulty, if it is granted that metonymy rests on contiguity
and metaphor on resemblance. Thanks to this series of correlations, one
can for short call combination itself the metonymic pole and selection the
metaphoric pole of linguistic operations. These operations can be represented only with the help of orthogonal axes, of which only one, that of
combination, corresponds to the linearity of the signifier.

In this manner, the tropological distinction provides the vocabulary,
but not the key. Indeed, the two tropes are reinterpreted in the light of a
distinction that prevails on the most abstract plane conceivable by linguistic analysis – that of *any and all* linguistic identities or units. 'Any linguistic sign,' it is stated, 'involves two modes of arrangement: (1) combination
... (2) selection ...' (243). The distinction is thus profoundly semiological.

This point deserves to be dwelt upon for a moment. Jakobson's analysis
completely bypasses the distinction introduced by Benveniste between
semiotics and semantics, between signs and sentences. This monism of the
sign is characteristic of a purely semiotic linguistics. It confirms the fundamental hypothesis of this work, that the model to which a substitution
theory of metaphor belongs is one that ignores the difference between

semiotics and semantics and takes the word and not the sentence as the basic unit of tropology. This is a model that recognizes in the word only its character as a lexical sign, and in the sentence only the double characteristic of combination and selection, which it has in common with all signs from the distinctive trait, through phonemes, words, expressions, and sentences, right up to the text. The combination of these linguistic units truly presents an ascending scale of freedom, but it does not contain any discontinuity in kind like that which Benveniste sees between the order of the sign and that of discourse. The word is simply the highest among the linguistic units that must be encoded, and the sentence is just more freely composed than words. Hence, the notion of context can be used to designate equally the relationship of morpheme to phoneme and the relationship of sentence to morpheme. As a result, metaphor will characterize a general semiotic process and definitely not a form of attribution whose prerequisite is the distinction between discourse and sign.

The confirmation of the universally semiotic character of the polarity under consideration lies in the fact that the notion of semantics, which is not only recognized but vigorously defended against the attempts of a faction of American linguists to exclude meaning from the linguistic field, in no way constitutes an order distinct from the one, semiotic order. Semantics is incorporated into the bipolar schema at the same time as it receives its justification from it. Indeed, by adding new linkages to the preceding ones, it is possible to superimpose the pair 'syntax-semantics' onto the pair 'combination-selection,' therefore onto the pair 'contiguity-similarity,' and so also onto the pair comprising the metonymic and metaphorical poles. Indeed, the facts of combination within a message are facts of syntax, or syntagmatic facts (so as not to reduce syntax to grammar nor to include in it the composition of words or even phonematic sequences for instance). Contextual combination and syntagmatic combination overlap. The bonds between selection and semantics, on the other hand, are just as tight: 'For years and decades we have fought for the annexation of speech sounds to linguistics, and thereby established phonemics. Now we face a second front – the task of incorporating linguistic meaning into the science of language ... Let us, within the framework of synchronic linguistics, examine: what is the difference between syntax and semantics. Language entails two axes. Syntax is concerned with the axis of concatenation, semantics with the axis of substitution.'[3] This link between semantics and selection had already been perceived by de Saussure. In the constitution of a message, one word is chosen among other similar words within a group that constitutes a paradigm based on similarity. So it is possible to replace the Saussurean pair of the syntagmatic and the paradigmatic with that of syntax and semantics, and to arrange these on the orthogonal axes of combination and selection.

Some new correlations are revealed by the divergence of the two functional modes that characterize aphasia. Indeed, these disorders can be divided into those having to do with similarity and those related to contiguity. With regard to the latter, characterized by its agrammaticality (loss of syntax, inflections, derivations in the formation of words, etc.), the word survives the obliteration of syntax. Selection operations continue even while the contextual structure disintegrates; metaphorical shifts proliferate. On the other hand, in the case of disorders in similarity, connective chains are preserved while substitutive operations are destroyed. Metaphor disappears together with semantics; the aphasic fills the gaps left by metaphor with metonymies, thereby extending the drift of the context over that of substitution and selection. But the metaphorical use of language is not alone in being affected; other operations suffer the same fate, and their kinship with metaphor is thus revealed. For example, consider the power to define words, that is, to provide an equational definition, projecting a substitution group from the lexical code of the language into the context of a message. Consider also the capacity to give a name for an object that one can point to or manipulate, hence the power to give a linguistic equivalent for a gesture. This twofold approximation enriches our concept of metaphorical process: definition, naming, synonymy, circumlocution, and paraphrase are metalinguistic operations through which I designate elements of my code by means of equivalent elements within the same code. Even code-changing operations depend upon equivalence of terms from one code to another. All these operations are related profoundly to the capacity of words to receive additional, displaced, and associated meanings on the basis of their resembling the fundamental meaning. The same characteristic resides in the construction of paradigmatic series, of inflections or of tenses, in that the same semantic content is presented here from different points of view associated by their similarity. The same holds for the semantic unity common to the root word and its derivations.

Other interesting correlations add still more to the richness of the polarity of metaphoric process and metonymic process. Personal styles and verbal behaviour themselves also evince a preference for one type of arrangement or the other. Poetic forms also show a predominance sometimes of metonymy, as in realism, and sometimes of metaphor, as with romanticism and symbolism. The correlation is even more striking when the artist shows indications of the sort of pathological problems described above. The polarity is also so general that it finds a parallel in non-linguistic sign systems. In painting, one can speak of metonymy in connection with cubism, of metaphor with surrealism. In film, the synecdochic close-ups and the metonymic montage of D.W. Griffith contrast with the metaphorical montage of Charlie Chaplin. The same polarity can be found again in unconscious symbolic processes, such as those that Freud described in dreaming. Jakobson suggests that displacement (which would be metonymic) and condensation (synecdochic) be put on the side of contiguity, and identification and symbolism on the side of similarity.[4] Finally, in the area of the unconscious use of symbolism, we may find in *The Golden Bough* Sir James Frazer's two types of magic, the one working by contagion, and the other by imitation.

The article ends with an interesting remark that refers back to something noted earlier in connection with disorders concerning similarity. It is due to the fact that the same relation of similarity is at work in the trope *metaphor* where one term substitutes for another, and in metalinguistic operations where the symbols of a second-order language resemble those of the object language, that tropology, which itself is also a metalanguage, has favoured metaphor regularly over metonymy and has given a special place to symbolism in poetry. This remark could be read as a plea for metonymy, although such an interpretation would run counter to the criticism of de Saussure for favouring combination over selection in the name of the linearity of the signifier.

The strength of Jakobson's schema[5] is also its weakness. The strength of the bipolar scheme lies in its extreme generality and its extreme simplicity. The last correlations demonstrated its validity, since it extends beyond the sentence into the realm of style, beyond intentional use of linguistic signs into dreaming and magic, and beyond linguistic signs themselves into the use of other semiotic systems. The gains appear to be immense as far as metaphor is concerned. Formerly confined to rhetoric, the procedure itself is generalized beyond the sphere of the word and even beyond tropology.

But a heavy price must be paid. First of all, when applied to the domain of rhetoric, the binarism of the schema needlessly restricts its field to two figures. It is true that synecdoche is mentioned several times, but as a case of contiguity, sometimes in parallel with metonymy (metonymic displacement and synecdochic condensation in Freud), and sometimes as a species of metonymy (the Russian novelist Uspenski is said to have 'had a particular penchant for metonymy, and especially for synecdoche' ['Two Aspects' 257]). Now, the most extreme restriction that tropology seems previously to have undergone involved at least three figures: metonymy, synecdoche, and metaphor. (Dumarsais allowed a fourth fundamental figure, irony.) In a tripartite schema, resemblance is opposed not to contiguity but to the pair formed by inclusive and exclusive relations. Paradoxically, therefore, the generalization of the concept of metaphor beyond the linguistic field is paid for by the restriction of this field to two tropes.

But above all, those differences that derive from the cleft between discourse and the sign in the hierarchy of linguistic entities are obliterated in vague resemblances and in equivocations affecting the concept of combination as much as that of selection. As to the first, it can be doubted whether the logical operations that preside over the syntax of predication, and consequently over that of the co-ordination and subordination of statements, come from the same sort of contiguity as, for example, the concatenation of phonemes within morphemes. In one sense, predicative synthesis is the opposite of contiguity. Syntax represents the order of the necessary, ruled by completely formal laws concerning the condition of the possibility of well-formed expressions. Contiguity stays in the order of the contingent, and moreover, of the contingent at the level of objects themselves, where each thing forms a completely independent whole. So metonymic contiguity appears to be quite different from syntaxic liaison.

Regarding the notion of metaphorical process, it is not only equivocal, and in that sense too wide; in addition, it is cut off paradoxically from an essential trait – so that, despite its extremely general character, it remains too narrow.

The notion is too wide when one considers the heterogeneity of substitution and selection operations from one level to another. The linking of metaphorical procedure and meta-linguistic operations has been noted in passing. The first makes use of a virtual resemblance inscribed in the code and applies it in a message, whereas the equational definition, for example, talks only about the code. Can the use of resemblance in discourse and a totally different operation requiring a hierarchy of levels be put into the same class?

The notion of metaphorical process is even more emphatically too narrow if one considers that there is no place for the phenomenon of interaction, specifically of metaphorical statements, in the orbit of the selection-substitution phenomenon, even though this orbit is excessively extended. What is left out, ultimately, is the predicative character of metaphor.

In the end, metaphor settles into the status of substitution of one term for another, just as in classical rhetoric: 'Similarity connects a metaphorical term with the term for which it is substituted.'[6] It is legitimate to ask whether metonymy is not a substitution, more precisely a substitution of names, rather than metaphor. Fontanier triggered this thought earlier with his definition of 'metonymy, that is, changes of names, or names for other names.'[7] If the essence of metaphor is to 'present an idea under the sign of another idea that is more striking or better known,' does not the procedure consist as much in combining as in substituting? Let us go further: is it legitimate to reduce the semantic aspect of language to substitution? One is reminded of Jakobson's declaration, inspired by Peirce, that 'the meaning of a sign is the sign it can be translated into ... in all these cases we substitute signs.'[8] Is that not a semiotic definition where the central problem of predication has vanished? And if, with Benveniste, one defines semantics by predication, must it not be sought in the area of combination as well as in that of substitution, or better, outside this purely semiological distinction?

Finally, the fundamental problem of the difference between newly invented metaphor and metaphor in common use vanishes with the omission of the predicative character of metaphor, to the same extent that the degrees of freedom in combination affect the syntagmatic and not the paradigmatic side of language. In this connection, one should remember the force with which Fontanier contrasted catachresis with metaphor. One is constrained to use the former, one is free to use or not use the latter. It appears to be very difficult to do justice to this important difference if one cannot contrast phenomena of discourse with phenomena of language – indeed, catachresis is ultimately an extension of denomination and, by virtue of that, a phenomenon of language. Metaphor, and above all newly invented mataphor, is a phenomenon of discourse, an unusual attribution. Jakobson's generalized model cannot but completely obliterate this difference because, in a semiological monism, the difference between sign and discourse is itself minimized. It should be noted that for Jakobson, combination takes place in the code or in the message, whereas selection operates between entities associated in the code. In order that selection itself be free, it must result from an original combination created by the context and therefore distinct from pre-formed combinations within the code. In other words, it is in the region of unusual syntagmatic liaisons, of new and purely contextual combinations, that the secret of metaphor is to be sought.

We must now ask whether Michel Le Guern's reformulation[9] of Jakobson's theses is better able to meet the foregoing criticisms of the initial model. I have already made many separate references to this important work, but the time has now come for a systematic analysis.

Le Guern offers at once both a reinterpretation of the categories of Jakobson and two important additions, which, more than the reinterpretation itself, set forth a partial reply to our recent objections to Jakobson's analysis.

The reinterpretation concerns the very definition of the two processes of selection and combination. If one is based on 'internal' relations and the other on 'external' relations, then 'internal' must be understood in the sense of intralinguistic and 'external' in the sense of a relationship to the extra-linguistic order of reality. If this is so, it is possible to superimpose a Fregean distinction between sense and reference on the distinction, borrowed from Jakobson, between selection-substitution and combination-structure. Metaphor concerns only the substance of the language, i.e. meaning (sense) relations, while metonymy modifies the referential relation itself (44). The advantage of this reinterpretation is that it completely liberates an analysis in terms of sense from the yoke of the logic that holds sway in the order of the referent. The changes of meaning that the mechanism of metaphor puts into play concern only the internal groupings of the constitutive *semes* of the *lexeme* employed. Once the hold of the referent is broken, the semic analysis given by Greimas[10] can be applied directly to the operation of selection, whose close relationship with operations of a metalinguistic character applied to the code was demonstrated by Jakobson. It is on this basis that metaphor can be construed as the 'suppression, or more exactly as the *bracketing of one portion of the constitutive semes of the lexeme employed*' (*Sémantique* 15; my italics). In contrast, metonymy calls upon a syntagmatic choice that goes outside the limits of the paradigmatic structures internal to language. Let us recall the difference between the two orders: to say 'eating cake' rather than 'eating fruit' is to establish a connection between a linguistic entity and an extra-linguistic reality that cannot here be distinguished easily from the mental representation of the material object as perceived (14). Such is the level at which metonymy operates; indeed, it consists in 'a shift of reference between two objects connected by an extra-linguistic relation, which is brought to light by a common experience that is not linked to the semantic organization of a particular language' (25). The role of the reference is verified in the activity of interpreting a message that contains a metonymy. In order to understand it, one must always return to information furnished by the context and interpolate this information into the message, which then takes on the appearance of an ellipsis. If metonymy is regarded as a deviation, in the same way as other tropes, this deviation is nothing other than an ellipsis of the very relation of reference.

Introduction of the notion of reference into the explanation of metonymy provides a solid foundation for the reduction of synecdoche to metonymy. This reduction was implicit in Jakobson; it is explicit in Le Guern. However, a necessary prelude is th dismembering of synecdoche into two figures: synecdoche of the part and the whole (*sail* for ship); and synecdoche of the species and genus (eating *an apple* for eating a fruit). Only the first involves the same shift of reference and the same ellipsis of the statement as does metonymy. There is the important reservation, however, that in metonymy the shift of reference prevails over the ellipsis process.

In this manner, the bipolarity of metaphor and metonymy required by Jakobson's schema is safeguarded.

I would argue that this reinterpretation adds new difficulties without really resolving those raised by Jakobson's drastic reduction to a bipolar scheme. One is left perplexed by the liaison perceived between syntactic combination and referential function. The author asserts that what he calls here 'referential relation' has a 'bivalent' character, since 'at one and the same time it calls into play combination, interior to language, which links the elements on the syntagmatic axis, and correspondence, which is established between one element of the spoken chain and a reality exterior to the message itself' (24). Thus, we are further removed than the author imagines from the Fregean distinction between sense and reference, since reference in Frege's scheme coincides only with the second aspect of this bivalent relation. A certain ambiguity results with respect to the relationship between syntagmatic combination and the referential relation.[11]

If one must divide in this manner what is here called referential function, why could not the same bivalent character be found on the side of the metaphorical operation? Why would the latter not call into play simultaneously a semic composition internal to language and correspondence with a reality external to the message? In this same vein, the authors of the *Rhétorique générale* were seen to introduce consideration of the object in semic constitution.[12]

Le Guern's analysis, therefore, clarifies that of Jakobson only at the price of a supplementary difficulty concerning the work of reference in a semantic analysis. On the other hand, the objections addressed to Jakobson's analysis of metaphor still stand. To a purely lexematic analysis, metaphor is just a phenomenon of abstraction. But this points merely to the culmination of a process that involves the dynamics of the entire statement. Indeed, there would not be any metaphor if no deviation were detected between the figurative meaning of a word and the isotopy of the context, that is, in the language of Greimas, the semantic homogeneity of a statement or part of a statement. Le Guern is forced at once to connect the two phenomena of semic abstraction and deviation in relation to isotopy by relating them to two different moments of the theory. It is from the perspective of producing the message that the mechanism of metaphor is explained as the 'bracketing of one portion of the constitutive semes of the lexeme employed.' But it is 'from the perspective of interpretation of this message by the reader or hearer' (15-16) that consideration of the context imposes itself. Indeed, interpretation of metaphor is not possible unless one first perceives the incompatibility of the non-figurative meaning of the lexeme with the rest of the context. The author considers this to be an important difference from metonymy. The lexeme constituting metonymy is not generally perceived to be foreign to the isotopy: 'Metaphor, on the other hand, on condition that it be a living and image-triggering metaphor, strikes one immediately as being foreign to the isotopy of the context in which it is inserted' (16). Consequently, in order to interpret a metaphor, one must purge the proper meaning of traits that are incompatible with the context.

If this is the case, can one confine the function of deviation in relation to the isotopy of the context to *interpretation* of the message and keep the mechanism of semic abstraction for the *production* of the message? If something is essential to interpretation of the message, was not the same thing already essential for its production? Everything indicates that by distinguishing between production and interpretation in this way, the author has avoided the problem of the relationship between the dynamic of the statement and its meaning-effect at the level of the word. Eliminated from the purely semantic definition of the production of figure, semantic incompatibility at the level of the entire statement is spurned by an explanation of the mechanism of interpretation, which by that very fact becomes simply psychological: 'Semantic incompatibility plays the role of a signal that invites the receiver to select, among the constitutive meaning elements of the lexeme, those not incompatible with the context' (16). Yet the most remarkably detailed analyses by Le Guern suggest that semantic incompatibility is more than a signal for interpretation, and is in fact a component of the production itself.

Extension of the nuclear analysis of the *noun*-metaphor to the *adjective*-metaphor and *verb*-metaphor heralds the first consideration of context in the production of the figure (16-20). When the verb and adjective constitute one and the same metaphor with the substantive (*light ... a fire*), the effect of the verb-metaphor and adjective-metaphor is to attenuate the abruptness of the logical disruption produced by the substantive-metaphor. Therefore, semantic incompatibility is here an essential moment of the metaphor's production. (This is suggested by the author himself: 'Its specific character in relation to the substantive-metaphor is then a lesser degree of autonomy in relation to the context' [19].) Given this, suppression of semes is only one moment in a process that brings the entire statement into play. Jean Cohen describes this moment as reduction of deviation, which itself presupposes production of the deviation, or, as is said here, abrupt change of isotopy. It is this prior moment that is ignored in the definition of metaphor as semic reduction.

The excellent analysis of the difference between metaphor and comparison (52-65), to which we will return later from the point of view of the role of analogy, again necessitates incorporation of the disruption of isotopy into the very definition of metaphor. Indeed, it is impossible to discuss the relationship between metaphor and comparison without bringing the role of isotopy into play. Quantitative comparison, or comparison properly speaking (is *more* than, is *as much* as), is based in the isotopy of the context (only comparable things are compared). Qualitative comparison or simile (is *like*) shows the same deviation with regard to isotopy as does metaphor; the role of isotopy is fundamental in both cases, with the difference between metaphor and simile (as we shall see) lying elsewhere. It is best put by saying that deviation in relation to the context is not only a signal that orients the interpretation, but a constitutive element of the metaphorical message. It is hard to maintain the specificity of semantics in relation to logic with the same force as Le Guern displays (63 ff.), if semantics, within its own structure, does not retain the incompatibilities and compatibilities proper to its level and irreducible to those that bring the logic of comparison into play.

The relation between *denotation* and *connotation*, which constitutes the first important addition by Le Guern to Jakobson's thesis, provides a final reason for incorporating change of isotopy into the definition of metaphor. For Le Guern, metaphor combines a purely *denotative* aspect, the very one that was defined by semic reduction, and an aspect of *connotation*, which is external to the properly logical or informative function of the statement. This connotative function is expressed, in metaphor's case, by the role of the *associated image*, thus, a *psychological* connotation and, in addition, a connotation that is not free but *demanded* (21). The author emphasizes that this factor adds nothing to the information, properly speaking, of the message.[13] Indeed, the link between semic abstraction and evocation of an associated image is effected by 'the introduction of a foreign term into the isotopy of the context' (22). But how is this known, if the isotopy as such is not taken into account within the definition of metaphor?

Thus, the reinterpretation of Jakobson's dichotomizing model by Le Guern and his first important addition to it have brought us to the same issue as did the critique of Jakobson's own work, namely, the need to reintroduce the phenomenon of semic reduction at the end of a fundamentally syntagmatic process that affects the entire statement.

A second addition to Jakobson's theory calls for some separate remarks.

Over and above delimiting the language facts described by rhetoric and adding the distinctions between sense and reference, connotation and denotation, a semantics of metaphor and metonymy has the task of situating metaphor in relation to the set of procedures founded on similarity – symbol and synaesthesis on the one hand, comparison on the other. Now, as opposed to Jakobson, Le Guern does not consider the question of resemblance to be settled by the analysis of selection procedures. Moreover, the notion of similarity is not introduced at the point where semic selection is studied; the reason no doubt is that this consists less in a selection within a sphere of similarity, as was the case already with de Saussure, than in an alteration of the semic composition, as the structural semantics of Greimas suggests. The question of resemblance is put better in the context of the positive procedure that offsets the more exactly negative phenomenon of semic abstraction, namely, the operation of the *associated image*, which (as we just said) is based on connotation and not on denotation.

The way in which the workings of resemblance are incorporated into the dynamism of the statement as a whole will be explored later. Nevertheless, numerous traits of this analysis are anticipated in the framework of a substitution theory, by the interplay of denotation and connotation. But the important point for the present discussion is that analogy be introduced at the same time as the associated image, as a relationship between a term belonging to the isotopy and another, the image, that does not belong to it. Indeed, the basis for ordering the set of language facts related to similarity is provided by the manner in which the image operates in relationship to the logical or denotative kernel of significance (it will be noted that the author's word *analogy* is what we mean here by 'similarity'). Le Guern's contribution to semantics on this point is novel and invaluable.

First, three phenomena are compared – symbol, metaphor, and synaesthesis. In the symbol ('Faith is a great tree' writes Péguy), the analogical correspondence through which the symbol represents something else depends upon an extra-linguistic relationship that, to develop this correspondence, brings into play the mental representation of 'tree.' It is this very perception of the image that sustains the logical information of the statement. In other words, the symbol is an intellectualized image. What is meant here is that the image provides the basis for a 'reasoning by analogy, which remains implicit, but which is necessary to the interpretation of the statement' (45). I should say that the symbol according to Le Guern corresponds to Aristotle's metaphor by analogy or proportional metaphor. The situation is completely different in the case of metaphor properly speaking. The semic selection does not depend here on the image being evoked ('the metaphorical image does not intervene in the logical texture of the statement' [43]). This is the sense in which the image is an *associated* entity. No appeal is made to the conscious logic of reasoning by analogy. For this reason, the image, which is not part of the denotation, tends to become attenuated to the point where it is no longer perceived, as the metaphor enters into common usage. Finally, as for synaestheses, they depend upon purely perceptual analogies between the qualitative contents of the different senses (as in Rimbaud's 'Sonnet of the Vowels' with its analogies between vowels and colours). Accordingly, we are presented with three modalities of analogy. The semantic analogy of the metaphor is to be situated between the logical and extra-linguistic analogy of the symbol and the perceptual and infra-linguistic analogy of synaesthesis.

The specificity of semantic analogy in relation to 'analogy that is grasped intellectually' (47) is clarified once more by another distinction, between metaphor and comparison, where the latter is taken in the qualitative sense of *similitudo* or simile (like ...) and not as the quantitative *comparatio* (more, less, as much ...). Metaphor is not an abbreviated simile, as a formal analysis of surface structures may lead one to believe. Simile is related to metaphor rather than to quantitative comparison, since both disrupt the isotopy of the context. But simile and metaphor do not restore that isotopy in the same way. No transfer of meaning takes place in the case of comparison as simile (Jim is *as stubborn as a mule*); all the words retain their meaning, and the representations themselves remain distinct and coexist with fairly equal degrees of intensity. This is why 'no semic incompatibility is detected' (56). Since the terms remain distinct, they also retain their essential features, obviating the need for further semic abstraction. For the same reason, the imagistic accompaniment can remain very rich and the images themselves highly coloured. On the other hand, as we have already seen, perception of incompatibility is essential to the interpretation of the message in the case of metaphor. The incompatibility is expressed in metaphor *in praesentia* (Jim *is an ass*), and implicit in metaphor *in absentia* (*what an ass!*); but, even if implicit, it is still the grounds for figurative interpretation. Formally, then, analogy constitutes the common ground of metaphor, symbol, and simile, but the intellectualization involved increases as one passes from metaphor to symbol and from symbol to simile. The analogical relation is a logical tool in comparison; it belongs to the semantic and not the logical order when it is presented in an image.

However, a suggestion that I find even more important than this ordering of the vast and complex domain of analogy is the one that brings semantic analogy into view as the counterpart of semantic incompatibility. It is 'imposed ... as the only means of suppressing semantic incompatibility' (58). As opposed to logical comparison, which by definition does not break out of the isotopy of the context – only what is comparable is compared quantitatively – semantic analogy institutes a relationship 'between an element belonging to the isotopy of the context and an element that is foreign to this isotopy and for this reason produces an image' (58).

I consider this to be the most important observation of the entire work. But it is my feeling that its full value can be exercised only in a theory of statement-metaphor and not one of lexeme-metaphor. As the rest of this

Study will show, the image does not receive its properly semantic status unless it is attached not only to the perception of deviation but also to its reduction, that is, to the initiation of the new relevance, of which reduction of deviation at the level of the word is but an effect. This is what the last quotation from Le Guern suggests.

To follow this lead, however, one must further clarify the very status of the image and of the notion of associated image, as the fifth and sixth sections of this Study will attempt to do. With Le Guern, the image is defined above all by its negative relationship with isotopy; it is called 'an element that is foreign to this isotopy and for this reason produces an image' (58). 'Strangeness vis-à-vis the isotopy of the context' is, therefore, 'a typical feature of the image' (ibid.). The role of the image is assimilated to 'the use of a lexeme that is foreign to the isotopy of the immediate context' (53). But this negative definition of image leaves the very *iconicity* of the image in suspense. Is the image a 'mental representation that is alien to the informational purpose motivating the statement,' or rather 'a lexeme that is foreign to the isotopy of the immediate context' (ibid.)? In brief, in what sense is the image at once both representation and lexeme?

By the same stroke, the 'associated' character of the image itself remains in suspense. Is it a psychological trait or a semantic trait? If, as a factor belonging to the realm of connotation, it designates a characteristic that is extrinsic from the perspective of logical information, then the image is externally linked to the content of signification. In this position, however, how can it assist in suppressing semantic incompatibility? In short, how can it be outside the isotopy *and* semantic? But this asks twice how an analogy can 'produce an image.' Indeed, what aspect of the analogy at work in metaphor warrants the name *semantic*? For it to be convincing, Le Guern's analysis needs to be rounded out at this point by another analysis that will incorporate the role of the image more thoroughly into the reduction of deviation. With Le Guern, the associated image as image runs the risk of remaining an extra-linguistic fact; and if it is recognized as a fact of language, it runs the risk of remaining an extrinsic factor with regard to the statement, in that it is only associated. This extrinsic position concerns only the first phase, the perception of deviation; it no longer holds for the second, that of the reduction of deviation. Nevertheless, it is this second phase that holds the solution of the problem and justifies the terminology of semantic analogy when defining the role of the associated image.[14]

2 / THE 'ICONIC' MOMENT OF METAPHOR

Can the pact forged in the course of the history of rhetoric between substitution and resemblance be broken? The possibility of dissociating resemblance from a substitution theory and associating it with one of interaction seems to be denied by the brief history of this doctrine. To my knowledge, only one important author has attempted to do so. That author is Paul Henle,[15] whose influence in English-language circles has been substantial, although it has not equalled that of I.A. Richards. But since Henle, in the interaction theories put forward by Richards, notions of tension and then of logical absurdity seem to supplant resemblance, which by the same stroke is banished in an apparently unequivocal manner from the realm of substitution. So it is interesting to return to Paul Henle's analysis in order to ascertain the scope and the import of the refutation that it later suffers.

Henle begins by reformulating the definition of Aristotle in a way that, without expressly constituting a predicative theory of metaphor, nevertheless presents all the features that force it to be detached from naming and attached to predication.

Let us call any 'shift from literal to figurative sense' a metaphor. If the general sweep of this definition is to be preserved, it is necessary, first, that the notion of change of meaning be not restricted to names, or even to words, but extended to all signs. Furthermore, one must dissociate the notion of literal meaning from that of proper meaning. Any lexical value whatsoever is a literal meaning; thus, the metaphorical meaning is non-lexical: it is a value created by the context. It remains necessary to conserve the generic amplitude of Aristotle's definition, which also encompasses synecdoche, metonymy, irony, and litotes, that is, all shifts from literal meaning to figurative meaning that occur through discourse and in discourse. An implicitly discursive trait follows, which at the same time prepares for the entrance of resemblance: every metaphorical meaning is mediate, in the sense that the word is 'an *immediate sign* of its literal sense and a *mediate sign* of its figurative sense' (175). To speak by means of metaphor is to say something different 'through' some literal meaning. This trait says more than 'shift,' which could still be interpreted in terms of deviation and substitution. In turn, this intermediacy lays the foundation for the possibility of paraphrasing a metaphor by means of other words, some taken literally and others not. Not that the paraphrase could exhaust its meaning: for it is not necessary that a paraphrase be finalized for it to begin. The difference between trivial metaphor and poetic metaphor is not that one can be paraphrased and the other not, but that the paraphrase of the latter is without end. It is endless precisely because it can always spring back to life. If metaphor engenders thought throughout a long discourse, is this not because it is itself a brief discourse?

It is at this point that Henle introduces the iconic character that, according to him, specifies metaphor among all the tropes. One is thus undertaking to describe the fourth species of metaphor in Aristotle's breakdown, metaphor by analogy or proportional metaphor. But this trait too must be generalized well beyond the four-term proportion; it has to do with a parallel between two thoughts, such that one situation is presented or described in terms of another that is similar to it.[16] The author borrows the concept of *icon* from Charles Sanders Peirce to signal this very general analogical character. The essential role of the icon is to contain an internal duality that at the same time is overcome. In Keats' verse 'When by my solitary hearth I sit, / And hateful thoughts enwrap my soul in gloom'[17] the metaphorical expression *enwrap* consists in presenting sorrow as if enveloping the soul in a cloak. Thus, 'we are led [by figurative discourse] to think of something by a consideration of something like it, and this is what constitutes the iconic mode of signifying' (177). There is a danger here, which Henle clearly sees, that the theory of metaphor may be led into the impasse of a theory of the image, in the Humean sense of a weakened sensorial impression. This danger is coped with by the remark that 'if there is an iconic element in metaphor, it is equally clear that the icon is not presented, but is merely described' (ibid.). Nothing is displayed in sensible images, therefore; everything, whether associations in the writer's mind or in that of the reader, takes place within language. Henle continues very cautiously: 'What is presented is a formula for the construction of icons' (178). This calls to mind the 'productive' imagination that Kant distinguishes from the 'reproductive' in order to identify it with the schema, which is a method for constructing images.

Metaphor is analysed, therefore, in accordance with two modalities of semantic relationship. In effect, the expression first functions literally. It is (to continue with the description of symbol in the restricted sense of Peirce) a rule for pinpointing an object or situation. Subsequently, it functions iconically, by indirectly designating another, similar situation. Precisely because the iconic representation is not an image, it can point towards original resemblances, whether of quality, structure or locality, of situation or, finally, of feeling. In every case, the thing in focus is thought of as what the icon describes. Thus, the iconic representation harbours the power to elaborate, to extend the parallel structure.

This tendency towards further development distinguishes metaphor from the other tropes, which are exhausted in their immediate expression. On the other hand, metaphor is capable in the first place of extending vocabulary, whether by providing a guide for naming new objects or by offering concrete equivalents for abstract terms (thus the word *cosmos*, after having signified 'a pleasing sort of array such as a woman's headdress or the trappings of a horse's harness' [188], came to designate the disposition of an army and, finally, the order of the universe). Extension of vocabulary, however, is but the least effect of this penchant for development.

It is resemblance that allows us to function in new situations. If metaphor adds nothing to the description of the world, at least it adds to the ways in which we perceive; and this is the poetic function of metaphor. This still rests upon resemblance, but at the level of feelings. In symbolizing one situation by means of another, metaphor 'infuses' the feelings attached to the symbolizing situation into the heart of the situation that is symbolized. In this 'transference of feelings,' the similarity between feelings is induced by the resemblance of situations. In its poetic function, therefore, metaphor extends the power of double meaning from the cognitive realm to the affective.

It is regrettable that, by opposing feeling and description in this manner, the author gives in ultimately to an emotionalist theory of metaphor and loses part of the benefit of an analysis that had nevertheless recognized perfectly the connection between the workings of resemblance and the capacity for further development on the cognitive plane itself.[18]

However one regards this final interpretation of the role of metaphor, the major interest of Henle's analysis is that it does not force us to choose between a predicative theory and an iconic theory. This is, to my mind, the essential point of the present Study. Moreover, it is difficult to see how an iconic theory could be articulated, if not in terms of predication. Henle perceives clearly that metaphor as trope is a species of 'metaphoric statement' (181). In effect, only a complete statement can refer to a thing or a situation 'by symbolizing its icon' (as above, symbolizing is taken in the sense of Peirce, that is, in the sense of conventional sign). In such a statement, 'some terms symbolize the icon and others symbolize what is iconized' (ibid.).[19] (Max Black says nothing different: metaphor requires a complex of words in which some terms are taken literally and others metaphorically.) So important is this contrastive constitution that it suffices to distinguish metaphor from simile on the one hand (in which no term is taken in a figurative sense and where the parallelism operates between two sequences of literal terms) and allegory on the other (in which all of the terms are taken figuratively, giving rise accordingly to two parallel interpretations, each equally coherent).

This analysis also does not force a choice between a theory of logical absurdity and an iconic theory. It is the 'clash' (183) on the literal level that leads one to seek out a meaning beyond the lexical meaning; while the context allows one to maintain the literal sense of certain terms, it prevents one from doing so for others. However, metaphor is not quite the clash itself, but rather its resolution. One must decide, on the basis of various 'clues' (ibid.) provided by the context, which terms can be taken figuratively and which cannot. One must therefore 'work out' (185) the parallelism between situations that will guide the iconic transposition of one to the other. This activity has become useless in the case of conventional metaphors, where cultural usage decides on the figurative sense of certain expressions. It is only in living metaphors that one sees this activity at work.

We are not far from recognizing that semantic clash is just one side of a process whose other side is the iconic function.

3 / THE CASE AGAINST RESEMBLANCE

Despite the penetrating suggestions contained in the article by Paul Henle, the later history of the predicative theory of metaphor reflects an obliteration of interest in the problem of resemblance and the development of an explanation in which it plays no decisive role. The brief against resemblance can be drawn up as follows.

The keystone of the case is the long association between substitution and resemblance in the history of the problem of metaphor. The brilliant generalization by Roman Jakobson only confirms this assessment: every substitution of one term for another takes place within a sphere of resemblance. On the other hand, interaction is compatible with any sort of relation. The tenor-vehicle relationship still refers to resemblance between 'what is really thought or said' and 'that to which it is compared'; but the broader idea of 'transaction between contexts' does not require this reference.[20] Max Black follows this direction. By strongly opposing theory of interaction to substitution theory, and by connecting the outcome of the latter with that of the theory of comparison, he leads up to the conclusion that there are 'all kinds of "grounds" for shifts of meaning with context – and even no ground at all, sometimes.'[21] As for the application of the system of associated commonplaces to the principal subject, it can be described without recourse to analogy of terms. With Monroe Beardsley, the withdrawal of resemblance is complete. Everything takes place as if logical absurdity had replaced analogy in the explanation of metaphor. It is logical absurdity that forces one to leave the plane of primary meanings and seek, in the network of connotations, the one that can give rise to a meaningful attribution.[22]

A second argument can be stated thus: even though analogy is the relation metaphorical statement puts into play, it explains nothing, since it is more the result of the statement than its cause or reason. A resemblance suddenly becomes visible between two things that previously one had never dreamed of juxtaposing and comparing. This is why the interaction theory is forced to take account of resemblance itself, but does so without including it in its explanation for fear of falling into a vicious circle. Rather, the application of the metaphorical predicate to the principal subject is compared to a screen or a filter that selects, eliminates, and organizes meanings in the principal subject; and analogy is not involved in this application.

Thirdly, it can be argued that resemblance and analogy are equivocal terms, which cannot help introducing confusion into the analysis. Their use in Aristotle appears to confirm this criticism of the logical weakness of resemblance.[23] At least three uses of the term can be found in Aristotle – four even, if one considers the supplementary meaning that will be set out in the fourth argument. The one rigorous use of the term corresponds to what Aristotle continually calls analogy, which is a relationship of proportionality. It is defined in the *Nichomachean Ethics* (5: 6) as 'equality of ratios, and involves four terms at least' (1131 a 31). But proportional metaphor does not define metaphor generically, but only the fourth type. Comparison of simile (*eïkôn*) comes close to this first meaning; *Rhetoric* 3: 4 (1407 a 17-20) mentions this kinship specifically, despite the fact that the relationship in comparison is simple and not two-fold. But simile is not the foundation of metaphor: the *Poetics* ignores it, and the *Rhetoric* subordinates it to metaphor.

Without any detectable allusion to the logic of proportion and comparison, Aristotle states at the end of the *Poetics*: 'But the greatest thing by far is to be a master of metaphor. It is the one thing that cannot be learnt from others; and it is also a sign of genius, since a good metaphor implies an intuitive perception of the similarity in dissimilars' (1459 a 5-8). This general statement encompasses the four species of metaphor and therefore covers the entire domain of *epiphora*. But what is it to perceive similarity? There seems to be a hint in *Rhetoric* 3 that 'similar' is 'same,' that is, generic identity: 'Metaphors should be drawn ... from objects closely related [*apo oïkeïôn*] but not obvious to every one at first sight [*mê phanerôn*]; just as in philosophy also, to observe the resemblance [*to homoïon*] in widely distant things is characteristic of a sagacious penetrating intellect: like Archytas' saying, that arbitrator and altar were the same thing [*tauton*]; because both are the refuge of the injured or wronged' (1412 a 11-14). How is this universal role of resemblance to be squared with the specific reasoning of analogy or simile? And how are 'similar' and 'same' to be reconciled at the level of this universal role?

The focus of a fourth argument is a more serious equivocation that affects if not *resemblance* itself, then one term that is most often associated with it. To resemble is, in a sense, to be the image of. Do we not say interchangeably that a portrait or photograph 'is the image of' or 'resembles' the original? This connection between resemblance and image is reflected in a certain approach to literary criticism – a former approach, to be sure – for which to enquire into an author's metaphors is to hunt down his typical images, by which is understood his visual, auditory, and generally sensorial images. The resemblance here moves from the abstract to the concrete, with the concrete image resembling the abstract idea it illustrates. Resemblance, therefore, is precisely the property of that which depicts, of the portrait broadly speaking. This new equivocation would appear to find some support in Aristotle himself. Does he not say that a vivid metaphor is one that 'sets something before the eyes'? As it happens, this property is mentioned in the same context as proportional metaphor, without the author indicating any link whatsoever between these two traits. Now, what is there in common between positing an equality of relationships and setting something before the eyes, in other words, between calculating and making visible? It would be fair to ask whether this equivocation does not also underlie the description Paul Henle gives of the iconic character of metaphor. Is not the presentation of one thought in terms of another always, in one way or another, to make visible, to show the first in the light of the more vivid appearance of the second? Going further, is it not the property of figure as such to convey visibility, to make discourse appear?[24] If this is the case, what link remains between the two extremities of the range thus opened, between the logic of proportionality and the imagery of iconicity?

All these ambiguities seem to converge on a central point: what constitutes the metaphoricity of metaphor? Does the notion of resemblance have the power to encompass proportion, comparison or simile, the bond of similarity (or sameness), and iconicity, without destroying itself? Or must one rather admit that it just hides the initial embarrassment of a definition and an explanation that can produce nothing but a metaphor of metaphor – metaphor of transference in Aristotle, of vehicle with Richards, of screen, filter, and lens with Max Black? Do all these metaphors not bring us back ironically to our point of departure, to the metaphor of displacement, of change of location?[25]

4 / IN DEFENCE OF RESEMBLANCE

I propose to demonstrate:

(a) that the factor of resemblance is of even greater necessity in a tension theory than in a substitution theory;

(b) that resemblance is not only what the metaphorical statement fashions, but also what guides and produces this statement;

(c) that resemblance can accommodate a logical status capable of overcoming the equivocity criticized above; and

(d) that the iconic character of resemblance must be reformulated such that imagination becomes itself a properly semantic moment of the metaphorical statement.

(a) The first mistake on the part of the reasoning directed against including resemblance in the logical status of metaphor is to believe that the notions of tension, interaction, and logical contradiction make every possible role of resemblance superfluous. Let us turn to the strategy of language at work in a metaphorical expression as simple as an oxymoron (a *living* death, *obscure* clarity). In its literal sense, the expression constitutes an enigma to which the metaphorical meaning offers the solution. Now, the tension and contradiction point only to the form of the problem within the enigma, what one could call the semantic challenge or, in Jean Cohen's terms, the 'semantic impertinence.' The metaphorical meaning as such is not the semantic clash but the new pertinence that answers its challenge. In the language of Beardsley, the metaphor is what forms a meaningful self-contradictory statement from a self-destructive self-contradictory statement. It is in this mutation of meaning that resemblance plays its part. But this role cannot come to light unless one turns away from the alliance between resemblance and substitution, which is purely semiotic in character, towards a properly semantic aspect of resemblance – I mean, towards a functioning that is inseparable from the instance of discourse constitutive of the sentence (or from the complex expression at play in oxymoron). In other words, if it serves some purpose in metaphor, resemblance must be a characteristic of the attribution of predicates and not of the substitution of names. What constitutes the new pertinence is the kind of semantic 'proximity' established between the terms despite their 'distance' apart. Things that until that moment were 'far apart' suddenly appear as 'closely related.'[26] Aristotle was aware of this strictly predicative effect of resemblance when he considered, among the 'virtues' of good metaphors, that of being 'appropriate' (*Rhetoric* 3: 1404 b 3). He saw in this a sort of 'harmony' (1405 a 10). On guard against 'far-fetched' metaphors, he recommends that metaphors be derived from material that is 'kindred' (*sungenôn* and 'of like form' (*homoeïdôn*), such that once the expression is produced, it will appear clearly that the 'names' involved are 'near of kin' (*hoti sungenes*) (1405 a 37).[27]

This notion of generic relatedness is valuable; and since we acknowledge that metaphors instruct, there is no great drawback in the fact that it is expressed metaphorically. Besides, the metaphor of 'far' and 'near' merely continues that of 'transfer' or 'conveyance' [*transport*]; to transfer is to ap-proximate, to suppress distance [*dés-éloigner*]. In a preconceptual fashion, the notion of generic relatedness points towards the idea of a 'family resemblance,' to which the logical status of resemblance in the metaphorical process could be linked.

The following paragraphs will capitalize on this breakthrough. A first point at least has been made: namely, that tension, contradiction, and controversion are nothing but the opposite side of the reconciliation in which metaphor 'makes sense.' And a second point is established as well: that resemblance is itself a fact of predication, which operates between the same terms that contradiction sets in tension.[28]

(b) The objection here is that resemblance is not a good candidate to serve as the reason or cause of the new pertinence, because it is what results from the statement and from the rapprochement it effects. The reply to this objection takes us into a sort of paradox that is quite capable of shedding new light on the theory of metaphor. Phillip Wheelwright comes very close to this paradox in his work *Metaphor and Reality*[29] (to which I will devote more time in Study 7). The author proposes to distinguish between *epiphor* and *diaphor*. *Epiphora*, we recall, is Aristotle's term. It is transposition, transference as such, that is, the unitive process, the sort of assimilation that occurs between alien ideas, ideas distant from one another. As such, this unitive process arises from an apperception – an insight – that belongs to the order of *seeing*. Aristotle was pointing to this apperception when he said: 'To metaphorize well is to see – to contemplate, to have the right eye for – the similar.' *Epiphora* is this glance and this genius-stroke, unteachable and impregnable.[30] But there is no epiphor without diaphor, no intuition without construction. Indeed, the intuitive process, bringing together what is disparate, contains an irreducibly discursive moment. The same Aristotle who 'contemplates the similar' is also the theoretician of that proportional metaphor in which resemblance is more constructed than seen (even though the similar is at work there is some fashion, as the Greek expression *homoïôs ekheï*, to behave in a similar way, indicates [*Poetics* 1457 b 20]). Max Black captures this discursive moment again in another metaphor, that of the screen, filter, or lens, in order to express the way the predicate chooses and organizes certain aspects of the principal subject. There is no contradiction, therefore, in giving an account of metaphor now in the language of apperception, that is, of vision, and then in the language of construction. It is at once the 'gift of genius' and the skill of the geometer, who sees the point in the 'ratio of proportions.'

Perhaps this constitutes a divorce from semantics and remarriage to psychology. In the first place, however, there is no shame in being taught by psychology, especially when it is a psychology of process and not of elements. Gestalt psychology is very instructive in this respect, when, dealing with the phenomenon of invention, it shows that every change of structure passes through a moment of sudden intuition in which the new structure emerges from the obliteration and modification of the prior configuration. Furthermore, this paradox of psychological attraction between genius and calculation, between intuition and construction, is really a purely semantic paradox, which has to do with the unusual character of allocation of predicates in the instance of discourse. Nelson Goodman provides an interesting apologue in this connection (again a metaphor of metaphor!): metaphor, he says, is the 'reassignment of labels,' but a reassignment that fashions its figure from 'an affair between a predicate with a past and an object that yields while protesting.'[31] To yield while protesting is, in metaphorical form, our paradox. The protest is what remains from the former marriage, the literal assignation, destroyed by contradiction; the yielding is what finally happens thanks to the new rapprochement. Diaphor of the epiphor is this very paradox. It underlies the 'glance' that perceives the similar beyond the divorce.

(c) This last paradox may contain the key for a reply to the objection concerning the logical status of resemblance. That is, what holds for the operation of assimilation can hold for the relation of similarity, but only if it can be shown that the relation of similarity is another name for the operation of assimilation described earlier.

The argument accusing resemblance of logical weakness is, we know, that anything resembles anything else ... except for a certain difference!

The solution that remains is to construct the relationship on the model of the operation and relate the paradox of the operation to the relation. It then becomes apparent that the conceptual structure of resemblance opposes and unites identity and difference. It is not due to oversight that Aristotle assimilates 'similar' to 'same': to see sameness in what is different is to see similarity.[32] Now, metaphor reveals the logical structure of 'the similar' because, in the metaphorical statement, 'the similar' is perceived *despite* difference, *in spite of* contradiction. Resemblance, therefore, is the logical category corresponding to the predicative operation in which 'approximation' (bringing close) meets the resistance of 'being distant.' In other words, metaphor displays the work of resemblance because the literal contradiction preserves difference within the metaphorical statement; 'same' and 'different' are not just mixed together, they also remain opposed. Through this specific trait, enigma lives on in the heart of metaphor. In metaphor, 'the same' operates *in spite of* 'the different.'

This feature has been seen in one way or another by various authors,[33] but I would like to take the idea a stage – or rather, two stages – further.

If, in metaphor, resemblance can be construed as the site of the clash between sameness and difference, cannot this model serve as basis for an account of the diversity of species of metaphor, from which the alleged equivocity seems to be derived? We should ask in what sense transference from genus to species, from species to genus, and from species to species are all forms of *epiphora*, reflecting the same polemical unity of the similar.

Turbayne broaches the answer in *The Myth of Metaphor.*[34] He observes that what takes place in the metaphorical statement is comparable to what Gilbert Ryle calls 'category mistake,' which consists in the 'presentation of facts belonging to one category in the idioms appropriate to another.'[35] Indeed, the definition of metaphor does not differ radically from this; metaphor consists in speaking of one thing in terms of another that resembles it. It is tempting to say that metaphor is a planned category mistake. According to this perspective, the four Aristotelian species are brought together again. This is clear for the first three (giving the name of the genus to the species, etc.) – they manifestly transgress the conceptual boundaries of the terms considered. Moreover, proportional metaphor involves the same sort of error, because for Aristotle the metaphor is not the analogy itself (i.e. equivalence of the relations) but rather the transference of the name of the second term to the fourth and vice versa, on the basis of the proportional relationship. Aristotle's four types, therefore, are planned category mistakes.

The same structure allows us to understand the primacy of metaphor over simile in Aristotle. In effect, metaphor says 'this is that' directly (*Rhetoric* 3: 1410 b 19). This application of a predicate despite the incompatibility involved constitutes the instruction that metaphor provides. Simile is already something more; it is a paraphrase, which dissipates the force of the unusual attribution. This is why the attack on simile by Max Black and Monroe Beardsley does not reach metaphor, which is not merely the abridged form of simile, but on the contrary, its dynamic principle.[36]

The idea of category mistake brings us close to our goal. Can one not say that the strategy of language at work in metaphor consists in obliterating the logical and established frontiers of language, in order to bring to light new resemblances the previous classification kept us from seeing? In other words, the power of metaphor would be to break an old categorization, in order to establish new logical frontiers on the ruins of their forerunners.

Advancing still another step, can we not hypothesize that the dynamic of thought that carves its way through already established categories is the same as that which engenders all classification? (I speak here of hypothesis because we have no direct access whatsoever to any such origin of genera and classes. Observation and reflection always arrive too late. So it is by means of a sort of philosophical imagining, proceeding by extrapolation, that one can propose that the figure of speech we call metaphor, and that appears first of all as a phenomenon of deviation in relation to an established usage, is homogeneous with a process that has given rise to all the 'semantic fields,' and thus to the very usage from which metaphor deviates.) The same operation that lets us 'see the similar' also 'conveys learning and knowledge through the medium of the *genus.*' This too is in Aristotle. But if it is true that one learns what one does not yet know, then to make the similar visible is to produce the genus within the differences, and not elevated beyond differences, in the transcendance of the concept. This is what Aristotle signified through the idea of 'generic relationship.' Metaphor allows us to intercept the formation of the genus at this preparatory stage because, in the metaphorical process, the movement towards the genus, which is checked by the resistance of difference, is captured somehow by the rhetorical figure. In this manner, metaphor reveals the dynamic at work in the constitution of semantic fields, the dynamic Gadamer calls the fundamental 'metaphoric,'[37] which merges with the genesis of concepts through similarity. A family resemblance first brings individuals together before the rule of a logical class dominates them. Metaphor, a figure of speech, presents in an *open* fashion, by means of a conflict *between* identity and difference, the process that, in a *covert* manner, generates semantic grids by fusion of differences *into* identity.

This last generalization allows us to take up our suspended discussion of the concept of metaphorical process in Roman Jakobson. Like Jakobson, indeed, but in a different sense from his, we form a concept of 'metaphorical process' for which the rhetorical trope plays the role of agent of revelation. But we part ways with Jakobson in that what can be generalized in metaphor is not its substitutive essence but its predicative essence. Jakobson generalized a semiotic phenomenon, the substitution of one term for another. We are generalizing a semantic phenomenon, assimilation to each other of two networks of signification by means of an unusual attribution. At the same time, being properly predicative or attributive in essence, the 'metaphorical pole' of language does not have a metonymic pole as its counterpart. The symmetry of the two poles is broken. Metonymy – one name for another name – remains a semiotic process, perhaps even the substitutive phenomenon *par excellence* in the realm of signs. Metaphor – unusual attribution – is a semantic process, in the sense of Benveniste, perhaps even the *genetic* phenomenon *par excellence* in the realm of the instance of discourse.

(d) The same paradox of vision and discursiveness that served as a model in constructing the relation of resemblance can now serve as a guide in answering the fourth objection. This concerns the status of resemblance as a figurative presentation, as an image depicting abstract relationships. The issue, we remember, comes from a remark by Aristotle concerning the power of metaphor to 'set before the eyes'; and it is posed in its full scope by the iconic theory of Paul Henle and by the notion of 'associated image' of Michel Le Guern. For, as we also saw, the more a semantic analysis surrenders to a logical grammar, the greater its reluctance to return to the notion of image, which is considered too enmeshed with bad psychology.

The question then is whether the iconic moment of metaphor stands outside every semantic approach, and whether it is not possible to account for it starting from the paradoxal structure of resemblance. Would not imagination have something to do with the conflict between identity and difference?

We should make clear that we are not yet speaking here of imagination in its sensible, quasi-sensual aspect, which we will consider in the following section. It is advisable first to bracket this *non-verbal* kernel of imagination, that is, imagery understood in the quasi-visual, quasi-auditory, quasi-tactile, quasi-olfactory sense. The only way to approach the problem of imagination from the perspective of a semantic theory, that is to say on a verbal plane, is to begin with productive imagination in the Kantian sense, and to put off reproductive imagination or imagery as long as possible. Treated as a schema, the image presents a verbal dimension; before being the gathering-point of faded perceptions, it is that of emerging meanings. In the same way, therefore, that the schema is the matrix of the category, the icon is the matrix of the new semantic pertinence that is born out of the dismantling of semantic networks caused by the shock of contradiction.

Integrating this new viewpoint with those we have already accepted, I would suggest that the iconic moment involves a verbal aspect, in that it constitutes the grasping of identity within differences and in spite of differences, but based on a preconceptual pattern. Aristotelian seeing – 'to see the similar' – does not appear to be different from the iconic moment, when clarified in this way by the Kantian schema: for to teach the genus, to grasp the relatedness of terms that are far apart, is to set before the eyes. Accordingly, metaphor is established as the schematism in which the metaphorical attribution is produced. This schematism turns imagination into the place where the figurative meaning emerges in the interplay of identity and difference. And metaphor is that place in discourse where this schematism is visible, because the identity and the difference do not melt together but confront each other.

Furthermore, this notion of a schematism of metaphorical attribution allows us to take up again a question that was left in abeyance. It will be recalled that Aristotle said that *lexis* makes discourse appear, and that Fontanier compared the figure to the face of the body. Now, the idea of a

schematism of metaphorical attribution does proper justice to this phenomenon, since the schema is what makes the attribution appear, what gives
it body. This predicative process 'creates image' and is itself the carrier of
the semantic analogy. In this way, it helps to resolve the semantic incompatibility perceived at the level of the literal meaning.

Does this mean that the problem posed by the image has been completely solved? To tell the truth, we have incorporated only the verbal
aspect of the image, in the guise of schema of the synthesis of the identical
and the different. What is the status of the *making-seen* as such? Of 'setting
before the eyes'? Of the figurative ability of the figure? We must admit
that, after this analysis, the residue left behind is the image itself!

Nevertheless, it may be possible, by concentrating on the schematism of
productive imagination, at least to explore the frontier between semantics
and psychology where one finds the junction of verbal and non-verbal, if
not to incorporate the image as such into semantic theory.[38]

5 / PSYCHOLINGUISTICS OF METAPHOR

A radical way of exploring the frontier between semantics and psychology
is to set up a combined discipline, *psycholinguistics*, at that boundary. The
need for this move is not shown only by the concern that the image be incorporated into the properly semantic operation of metaphor. The very
notion of transposition, the constant theme of a theory of tropes, brings
operations into play that legitimate a mixed approach involving psychology *and* linguistics. We will deal with this motif in the present section,
leaving till later the psycholinguistic consideration of the *image* itself.

The very principle of a psycholinguistic approach to operations involved
in metaphor deserves examination. Will we not fall again into just that
style of description and explanation from which linguistics with very great
effort freed itself? Not at all: the psycholinguistics to be encountered is
not pre-linguistic but post-linguistic; its aim is, in fact, to join in a new discipline the componential analysis of semic fields and the mental operations
that traverse these fields. Hence, this discipline would not be subject to the
former, justified criticism of a psychology whose two faults were to concentrate more on contents (image, concept) than on operations, and to
provide a mechanical representation of the relationships between contents
(thus the successive versions of association of ideas). It is a new discipline
born from the contribution of an entirely specific semic analysis and from
a description of operations investigated at their sublinguistic level.

As far as figures are concerned, Gaston Esnault was a forerunner.[39] He
saw that the operations brought into play by figures reduce to the capacity
to increase or restrict extension (i.e., the number of entities to which a

notion applies) or comprehension (i.e., the number of characteristics that make up a notion). According to him, synecdoche is nothing but a modification of extension, and metaphor and metonymy a variation in comprehension. The difference between these two figures is that metonymy follows the order of things and proceeds analytically, whereas metaphor plays on comprehension in a synthetic and intuitive manner, by means of a reaction that begins and ends in imagination. This is why the imaginative equivalence instituted by metaphor does more violence to the real than does metonymy, which respects the links inscribed in the facts. But Esnault lacked the methodological tool of psycholinguistics, which is (as stated above) the combination of a theory of operations and of a theory of fields.

Métonymie et Métaphore by Albert Henry attempts to satisfy this twofold requirement (at the same time, it addresses a properly stylistic concern which is outside our sphere of interest). Indeed, he considers 'the psycholinguistic foundations' that he proposes to be the 'indispensible basis for a sound stylistic analysis' (21). This work, accordingly, is to the psycholinguistics of metaphor what that of Hedwig Konrad was to the logico-linguistics of metaphor. For Henry, a single mental operation is at work in the synecdoche-metonymy-metaphor triad; and this operation appears in its first degree in metonymy (and synecdoche), and in its second degree in metaphor. This is why one must study it first in metonymy.

As Esnault saw, this operation is the perceptive synthesis that allows the mind to focus or to diffuse its inquiring searchlight (23). Figures are only the various ways in which the meaning-results of this unique operation are institutionalized on the linguistic plane.

What is to be said now of metonymy, if it is true that it exemplifies the simple level of the operation? The semic analysis of Pottier[40] and Greimas[41] is relevant at this point. If 'semic field' is the name we give to the collection of elementary constituents of a concept-entity, then a semic field is something that can be traversed. 'In the case of metonymy, the mind, traversing a semic field, focuses on one of its semes and labels the concept-entity that is the object of its contemplation with the word that, in pure linguistic reality, would name this seme, were it itself considered as a concept-entity' (25). Accordingly, we call a certain coin a *Louis* because it bears the portrait of a king by that name. Three aspects are to be considered, therefore: articulation of the semic field as a state of language, 'more or less free and more or less felicitous mental inspection' (25), and the naming of the object considered by the seme on which the mind focuses.[42]

This perspective is interesting for our present research because, by approaching the phenomenon from the operational side and not only from that of structure, one can distinguish from dead figures other figures in the process of being born, new metonymies that bring into play an 'active, selective perception' (30) – as in the expression of the Marquis de Brinvilliers, who said of her locket of poisons that 'many successions were contained in that box' (ibid.). Stylistics has much to expect from this differentiation based on the difference of operations.[43]

At the same time, the role of predication in the operation can be noted in passing, for example, when the figurative word is in the adjectival position ('to have a *lively* wine'): 'Predication is the linguistic process that allows the semantic phenomenon called metonymy to affirm itself' (33). Our critique will not lose sight of this trait.[44]

Semic focalization, then, is the fundamental 'creative mechanism.' And metonymy, furthermore, is the simple expression of this mechanism on the level of figures.

In what sense is metaphor a variant, as Esnault saw, of the same capacity for altering the understanding? Here again, this forerunner lacked technical means, and that is why he could not overcome the purely psychological opposition between the analytical mode and a synthetic, intuitive, imaginative mode. The linguistic shift permits the construction of metaphor on the basis of metonymy as a double and superimposed metonymy.[45]

To take this route is to pass up another, the traditional one in rhetoric, which identifies metaphor with an abbreviated simile. On this point, the author precedes Le Guern by developing the argument that simile is not a figure because it presents neither deviation nor substitution; that it results in no new naming; and lastly that it is a *bona fide* intellectual operation which leaves the compared terms intact (59-63).

If metaphor is not an abbreviated simile, how can it be considered to be 'the synthesis of a short-circuited double metonymy' (66)?

In order to show how this can be, let us begin with Aristotle's fourth class of metaphor, metaphor by analogy, which the author holds to be fundamental (whereas Konrad, with her logico-linguistic point of view, gave first place to the relationship of species to species). When Victor Hugo writes: 'Malta's armour was threefold [*trois cuirasses*], its fortresses, its ships, and the valour of its knights,' he achieves a first metonymy by crossing the semic field of *fortress* and focalizing on the seme *to protect*. He proceeds to a second metonymy with the word *armour*, and then posits the equivalence of the two retained characteristics. Finally, the intended equivalence is expressed in the name of the object (armour), that is, by the symbol of the entire semic field that possesses the common characteristic (to protect).

But where does the synthesis lie? At this point, the author offers a set of synonyms, themselves metaphorical as were the 'screen,' 'filter,' 'lens,' and 'stereoscopic vision' of the English-language critiques. He will speak in like fashion of 'metonymic superposition creating a subjective synonymy in discourse' (66). This superposition is to be represented graphically by two planes (the semic fields) showing two centres of focalization, and by an arrow piercing the two planes through their two centres. The author's comment on this diagram is that 'in metaphor, there is a double focalization and precision of vision along the longitudinal perspectival axis' (68). This is exactly the same as the 'stereoscopic vision' of W.B. Stanford.[46] The image can be completed by saying that the metaphorical term 'loads down the metaphorized term with all of its own *connotation* – some of it clear and precise, some of it vague and fuzzy' (67); and the image of overload leads to that of 'metaphoric density' (67). This is the dominant image in the formula that neatly summarizes the entire thesis: 'The sole fundamental figure is the figure of contiguity: at its first degree, it is realized in metonymy and in synecdoche; at the second degree, it multiplies and thickens into metaphor' (69).

Before proposing several critical thoughts specifically concerning the psycholinguistic foundation of the work, I should admit that I have not done enough justice to this work, which does not just lay these psycholinguistic foundations but builds a genuine stylistic edifice on them. I must explain why I thus cut away the work's crowning feature and its incomparably rich analyses concerning 'the stylistic status of metaphor' (115–39). Once a stylistic point of view is adopted, a new unit of discourse is taken as reference point, the literary *work*. Now, our whole discussion has been located between the word and the sentence; new problems are linked specifically to this change of level, and we will discuss them in Study 7. This is why I restrict my view to the analyses that support the transition from the semantic level to the stylistic level (although actually the work talks about the relationship between psycholinguistics and stylistics).

As with metonymy, the stylistic point of view puts the focus on combinations of figures. Along with those of contrasts and redundancies, one finds twinnings, concatenations, rings, and plaitings, such as in Saint-John Perse. This takes one close to Riffaterre's analysis of metaphoric series (121). The integration of these metaphoric complexes into a work is mediated either by a narrative structure or, more simply, by a vast, metaphorically detailed semic field. So it is at the level of the work that one can understand that metaphor belongs to 'a complex stylistic organism' (139). At this level too, the value of metaphor as personal expression and its properly poetic function of indirect language (132) are made precise, without overlooking its purely intellective and dialectical function (132). Accordingly, a whole metaphorical complex is required so that, in the two quatrains of *Les Fleurs du Mal* (superbly analysed on page 135), the conjunction of two figures (*sea / mane-like hair* and *ship / soul*) achieves 'cosmic opening from these waving tresses up to the over-arching sky' (135). An entire poem is needed in order to open up a world and create, 'in convergence, the harmony of a universe in motion' (135). We will come across this sort of problem again in Study 7.

My criticism is not directed at all against the principle of a psycholinguistics of metaphor. To repeat, the mixed method is perfectly justified, on the one hand by the operation constituted by transposition, and on the other hand by the conjunction of this operation and the image. The work under analysis provides almost no occasion at all for considering the latter side; but it is perfectly suited to a discussion of the former.

I am inclined to say that, in the mixture of psychology and linguistics, only one part of the resources of linguistics is exploited, namely, semic analysis; and another part is neglected, the very aspect that Jean Cohen recognized, i.e. the domain of semantic impertinence and pertinence. The reduction of metaphor to metonymy is the outcome of this unequal mingling of a theory of operations and a theory of semic fields in which a properly semantic aspect is missing.

Let us begin with a preliminary remark, which may only be a quibble over words but will receive greater weight in the remainder of the discussion: does the name *metonymy* apply strictly speaking to the two partial operations of focalization on a seme, on which the constitutive equivalence of metaphor is built? If one relies on the definition given above, metonymy is a figure only if the focalization results in a name change. Without that change, there is no longer deviation, nor figure. Now, this is not the case here: metonymy is not incorporated into metaphor as a figure, but only as focalization, which is an abstraction performed on the new naming. So the metaphor itself is a figure only when it is the outcome of the entire process. One can speak of course of metonymic focalization (76), as a reminder that this focalization is the same as that which gives rise to the figure called metonymy; nevertheless, metaphor and metonymy remain two distinct figures.

But the principal difficulty concerns the status of the equivalence itself, that central phenomenon which we saw bounded by a series of expressive metaphors: superposition, overloading, thickening. On one occasion, it is called, in a more direct manner, an 'integrating identification' (71). One would expect a psycholinguistic analysis (that is, psychological and linguistic at the same time) of this integrating identification. In fact, the linguistic aspect would not reduce to the naming, by application to the thing considered, of 'the linguistic sign that designates the whole semic field' (69). As Vinsauf and later Konrad both saw, substitution at the level of expression is only the final phase, itself grounded in the equivalence that is the essential phase. Nor would the linguistic aspect reduce to double metonymy. Equivalence arises of itself when the double metonymy is given, whereas the whole art of metaphor is to achieve the rapprochement that motivates the search for semes capable of identifying what was 'alien.' Thus, it is the operation of equivalence that summons the two partial operations imprecisely called metonymies. If the mind scans various semic fields and focalizes on this or that seme, it is because the entire process is stretched (as Jean Cohen perceived) between an impertinence to be neutralized and a new pertinence to be instituted. The two 'metonymies' are merely abstract phases of a concrete process, ruled by the interplay of distance and proximity. Their status here is not that of figures, therefore, but of segments in a process whose unity belongs to the semantic order (in the sense that we give to this word opposing it to the semiological).

The above suggests that the semantic character of the integrating identification comes to light if it is set in relation to the semantic character of the 'distance' that rapprochement overcomes. In this sense, a psycholinguistics of metaphor would have to include the concept of semantic impertinence in its theory of operations. But just as the theory of Jean Cohen lacks a correspondingly semantic analysis of the establishment of pertinence (a lack not satisfied by the idea of a deviation of language reducing a deviation in discourse),[47] the 'integrating identification' of Albert Henry, as it happens, is capable of filling in for the concept of new pertinence missing in Cohen's work.

Now, although this psycholinguistic node of equivalence is not a conscious target of the study of the 'mechanism' of metaphor, it is approached indirectly in the study of its 'morphology,' the topic of a separate chapter (74-114). Indeed, this study shifts the accent quite sharply from double metonymy towards the equivalence itself of the two metonymic relationships. There could be legitimate apprehension that morphology – precisely because it is morphology and not just a mechanism – might enclose itself in an algebra that retains only a trace of operations, especially if its guide is the 'number of terms expressed' (85). Indeed, the equation

$$\frac{a}{b} = \frac{a'}{b'},$$

where the metaphorizing term properly speaking is always placed in position a, is taken by the author as 'a prelinguistic or sublinguistic representational schema, which the expression will actualize and flesh out' (82). With this groundwork, all the theoretical possibilities are exhausted by the successive examination of metaphor in four terms, in three terms, in two terms (and even in one term). There is great danger that this schema will contain nothing but the formula of the resolved problem.

And yet the detail of the analysis lets through several less formal operational traits. Thus, metaphor in two terms reveals something concerning the scope of equivalence that distinguishes it from mathematical equality – as verified consistently, moreover, by our remarks on metaphor *in praesentia*. Formally, metaphor in two terms involves the ellipsis of two terms from the complete relationship. If these terms are a and a', then in *burning bush (a) of your lips (a')*, the terms to be restored are *flicker of flames (b)* and *red (b')*. The terms can be a and b', as in the genitive forms, the verbal or adjectival metaphors, as seen in the example *the sea smiled on him*. Here, too, the four terms can be completed: *to smile (a)* is to *man (b)* as *to shine (a')* is to *sea (b')*. However, even if formally the formula is that of metaphor in four terms, there is something specific in the way metaphor in two terms functions because of the link created between the two terms brought into each other's presence. In this way, the predicative value that a' acquires from a is not that of identification but that of subordination (91). In the case of b', it receives a specifically different signification of identification from a: identity, fundamental characterization of identity, belonging, etc. Above all, it is notable that 'no identification is possible between the substantive and the verb or adjective' (93); the nominal metaphor of a based on b' itself must be assimilated to verbal and adjectival metaphors (94). Now, it is insufficient here to invoke linguistic servitude, which demands that the verb apply to a substantive taken according to its proper meaning – with the result that the verb metaphorizes alone – in order to conclude that the verbal or adjectival metaphor does not constitute a particular category of metaphor (95). This deep linguistic structure accounts only for the normal type of such a metaphor being ab'; it does not explain why the predicative relation is not an identification. This is the trait that sets it apart. Generally speaking, neither 'is,' nor 'to call,' nor 'to name,' nor 'to do,' nor 'to have in the place of,' nor 'to stand for' is an identification. The nature of these relations is that of the copula.

Ultimately, 'properly metaphorical semantic fusion' (108) is revealed to be more highly singular than the algebraic identity of two relationships.

One last comment will orient us along the axis of the second psycholinguistic problem mentioned at the beginning of this section. Henry sees three aspects in 'the central problem of metaphoric expression: double metonymic operation, identification, and imaginative illusion' (82). We have discussed the relation of the second to the first aspect. We must still touch on the relation of the third to the second, a relation that is not the object of any special observations in the fundamentally psycholinguistic stylistics of Albert Henry.

6 / ICON AND IMAGE

Is a psycholinguistics of imaginative illusion possible? If, as the analysis of section 4 shows, semantics goes no further than the verbal aspect of imagination, could psycholinguistics perhaps cross over this line and join the properly *sensual* aspect of the image to a semantic theory of metaphor? This is the aspect that was bracketed in order to integrate the aspect of image closest to the verbal plane, namely (in quasi-Kantian language) the 'metaphoric schematization.'

I propose to examine this problem in the light of the interesting contribution of Marcus B. Hester.[48] True, this work does not claim to be 'psycholinguistic.' It is linguistic in the Wittgensteinian sense of the word, and psychological in the Anglo-American tradition of philosophy of mind. Nevertheless, the problem it addresses, the intersection between '*saying*' and '*seeing as ...*', is psycholinguistic in the terms set out at the beginning of the preceding section.

At first sight, the orientation of this exploration is opposite to that of the semantic theory set out in Study 3. That theory opposed not only any reduction of metaphor to mental imagery, but also any intrusion of the image, considered as a psychological factor, into a semantic theory conceived as logical grammar. This was the price for containing the interplay of resemblance within the limits of the predicative operation, and therefore of discourse. But, ruling out a passage from the imaginary to discourse, the question remains whether one cannot or ought not to attempt the reverse, and *proclaim the image to be the final moment of a semantic theory* that objected to it as a starting point.

This question is called for by the preceding analysis, which, on an essential issue, suffers from a fundamental shortcoming that may well identify the gap that the image is to fill. What remains to be explained is the *sensible* moment of metaphor. This moment is designated in Aristotle by the lively character of metaphor, by its power to 'set before the eyes.' In Fontanier, it is implicit in the very definition of metaphor as something that presents one idea under the sign of another, better known idea. Richards also approaches it with his idea of the *tenor-vehicle* relationship. The relationship of resemblance between vehicle and tenor is not like the relationship of one idea to another, but like that of an image to an abstract meaning. The moment of the image is recognized more succinctly by Paul Henle in connection with the iconic character of metaphor. In the French-language literature on the subject, Le Guern is the one who has gone furthest in this direction with his notion of 'associated image.'

On the other hand, it is precisely this concrete, sensible side of the *vehicle* and *icon* that is eliminated in the interaction theory of Max Black. All that remains from Richards' distinction is the predicative *focus-frame* relationship, which itself is analysed into 'principal subject' and 'auxiliary subject.' Finally, neither Black's notion of 'system of associated common-places' nor that of 'network of connotations' in Beardsley necessarily involves reference to any use of images. All these expressions designate aspects of *verbal* meaning.

Now, it is true that my plea on behalf of resemblance ended with a certain rehabilitation of the iconic moment of metaphor. But this rehabilitation does not go beyond the verbal aspect of the icon, nor beyond a purely logical concept of resemblance, conceived as the unity of identity and difference. It is true as well that a certain concept of imagination returns with the iconic moment, but this concept of imagination is restricted prudently to the Kantian productive imagination. In this sense, the notion of *schematism of metaphoric attribution* does not violate the boundaries of a semantic theory, that is, of a theory of *verbal* meaning.

Can one go further and affix to a semantic theory that sensible element without which the productive imagination itself would not be imagination? The resistance to this proposal is understandable: by doing so, will one not be opening the gate of the semantic sheepfold to the wolf of psychologism? This is a significant objection. But must one not also ask the inverse question – must there remain indefinitely a moat between semantics and psychology? Now, the theory of metaphor would seem to provide the perfect instance for recognizing their common frontier. Indeed, a logical moment and a sensible moment, or if one prefers, a *verbal* moment and a *non-verbal* moment co-operate in it in the unique manner shortly to be discussed. Metaphor owes to this liaison its seemingly essential concreteness. So fear of psychologism should not impede a search, in the transcendental manner of Kantian critique, for the point where the psychological is inserted into semantics – the point in language itself where meaning and sensibility are articulated. My own working hypothesis is that the idea elaborated above of a schematism of attribution constitutes the point on the frontier of semantics and psychology where the imaginary is anchored in a semantic theory of metaphor. It is with this hypothesis in mind that I approach the theory of Marcus B. Hester.

This theory draws support from analyses relating to English-language literary criticism and applied more to poetic language in general than to metaphor in particular. The common characteristic of these analyses is an exaltation of the sensible, sensorial, even sensual aspect of poetic language – the very aspect that the logical grammar of metaphor removes from its purview. Hester retains three principal themes from this mass of analyses.

First of all, poetic language presents a certain 'fusion' between meaning or sense and the senses. This distinguishes it from non-poetic language, where the arbitrary and conventional nature of the sign separates meaning from the sensible as much as possible. This first trait constitutes in Hester's eyes a refutation, or at least a correction, of the Wittgensteinian concept of meaning contained in the *Philosophical Investigations* (this theory, laid out in detail in Hester's first chapter, accentuates the distance between meaning and its carrier and between meaning and object). Hester claims that Wittgenstein constructed a theory of ordinary language alone, to the exclusion of poetic language.

The second theme is that, in poetic language, the pairing of sense and the senses tends to produce an object closed in on itself, in contrast to ordinary language and its thoroughly referential character. In poetic language, the sign is looked at, not through. In other words, instead of being a medium or route crossed on the way to reality, language itself becomes 'stuff,' like the sculptor's marble. We might note here, foreshadowing a longer treatment in the next Study, that this second theme is close to the characterization of the 'poetic' in Jakobson, for whom the poetic function consists essentially in accentuating the message as such at the expense of the referential function.

The third characteristic, finally, is that this closure of poetic language allows it to articulate a fictional experience. As Susanne Langer says,[49] poetic language 'presents an experience of virtual life.' This feeling, which is given form by a centripetally, non-centrifugally oriented language, and which is precisely what this language articulates, is called mood by Northrop Frye.[50]

These three traits – fusion of sense and senses, density of language that has become 'stuff,' virtuality of the experience articulated by this non-referential language – can be summed up in a notion of icon palpably different from that of Paul Henle (on which W.K. Wimsatt lavished praise in *The Verbal Icon*). Like the icon of the Byzantine cult, the verbal icon consists in this fusion of sense and the sensible. It is also that hard object, similar to a sculpture, that language becomes once it is stripped of its referential function and reduced to its opaque appearance. Lastly, it presents an experience that is completely immanent to it.

Hester adopts this point of departure, but his purpose is to lodge the notion of the sensible firmly within the meaning of imagery. The context of this modification is a very original conception of reading, applied to the poem as a whole as well as to the somewhat localized metaphor. The poem, he says, is a 'read object' (117). The author compares reading to the Husserlian *epoché*, which restores the original claim of all the data by suspending any position with respect to natural reality. Reading is also a suspension of all reality and 'an active openness to the text' (131). It is this concept of reading as suspension and openness that introduces the complete rearrangement of the previous themes.

With respect to the first theme, the act of reading shows that the essential trait of poetic language is not the fusion of sense with sound, but the fusion of sense with a wave of evoked or aroused images. This fusion constitutes the true 'iconicity of sense.' Hester fully accepts an understanding of images as sensorial impressions evoked in memory or, as Wellek and Warren put it, as various 'vestigial representations of sensations.'[51] Poetic language is that language game (to use Wittgenstein's terms) in which the aim of words is to evoke, to arouse images. Not only do sense and sound function iconically in relation to each other, but the sense itself is iconic through this power of developing in images. The two traits of the act of reading, suspension and opening, are presented truly by this iconicity. On the one hand, the image is the achievement *par excellence* of neutralization of natural reality; on the other hand, the deployment of images is something that 'occurs' and towards which the sense opens indefinitely, giving unlimited scope to interpretation. One can say truly, in connection with the flux of imagery, that to read is to grant original right to all the data. In poetry, openness to the text is openness to the imagery as liberated by the sense.

Correction of the first theme, borrowed from what can be called the sensualist conception of *verbal icon*, brings with it correction of the second and third themes. This object that Wimsatt, Frye, and others describe as closed in on itself and non-referential is the meaning clothed in imagery. For nothing is obtained from the world except imagery unchained by meaning. From this point of view, not only must the metaphorical be identified with the iconic, but the iconic must also be interpreted as the fictive as such, before a non-referential theory of poetic language can be complete. Once again, it is *epoché*, the suspension proper to the imaginary, that withdraws all reference to empirical reality from the verbal icon. It is also imagery, through its quasi-observational character, that grounds the characteristic of quasi-experience or virtual experience – in short, the *illusion* attendant to reading a poetic work.

In the discussion that follows, I will set aside altogether the two themes of non-referentiality and the aspect of virtual experience. They concern the problem of reference, reality, and truth, which we decided to bracket when making a thoroughgoing distinction between the problem of sense and the problem of reference.[52] Furthermore, Hester's denial of the referential character of poetry is not as free from ambiguity as may appear. The notion of virtual experience indirectly brings back a 'relatedness' to reality, which paradoxically offsets the difference and the distance from reality that characterize the verbal icon. Hester is even seduced in passing by the distinction proposed by Hospers between truth about and truth to.[53] When, for example, Shakespeare likens time to a beggar, he is faithful to the profoundly human reality of time. Therefore, we must reserve the possibility that metaphor is not limited to suspending natural reality, but that in opening meaning up on the imaginative side it also opens it towards a dimension of reality that does not coincide with what ordinary language envisages under the name of natural reality. This is the perspective that I will try to develop in Study 7. Accordingly, following a suggestion by Hester himself,[54] we will restrict ourselves here to the problem of meaning, to the exclusion of the problem of truth. This delimitation of the problem puts us back by the same stroke inside the limits of the first theme: the fusion of 'sense' and 'sensa,' understood from now on as an iconic unfurling of sense in imagery.

The fundamental question posed by the introduction of image or imagery (Hester uses the two terms interchangeably) into a theory of metaphor concerns the status of a sensible, thus non-verbal, factor inside a semantic theory. The difficulty is amplified by the fact that image, as opposed to perception, cannot be related to any 'public' realities, and seems to reintroduce the sort of 'private' mental experience condemned by Wittgenstein, Hester's chosen master. So the problem is to bring to light a liaison between sense and sensa that can be reconciled with semantic theory.

A first trait of the iconicity of meaning seems to facilitate this accord. Images evoked or aroused in this way are not the 'free' images that a simple association of ideas would join to meaning. Rather, to return to an expression of Richards in *The Principles of Literary Criticism* (118-19), they are 'tied' images, that is, connected to poetic diction. In contrast to mere association, iconicity involves meaning controlling imagery. In other words, this is imagery involved in language itself; it is part of the game of language itself.[55] It seems to me that this notion of imagery tied by meaning is in accord with Kant's idea that the schema is a method for constructing images. The verbal icon in Hester's sense is also a method for constructing images. The poet, in effect, is that artisan who sustains and shapes imagery using no means other than language.

Does this concept of 'tied' image entirely escape the objection of psychologism? That can be doubted. The manner of Hester's detailed explanation of the fusion of sense and sensa, even when understood as tied images rather than as real sounds, leaves the sensible moment very much outside the verbal moment. In order to account for the aura of images surrounding words (143), he invokes, in turn, association in memory between words and the images of their referents; historical and cultural conventions (for example, determining that the Christian symbol of the Cross develops such and such a sequence of images); and the stylization that the author's intention imposes on diverse images. All these explanations remain more psychological than semantic.

The most satisfying explanation, and in any case the only one that can be reconciled with semantic theory, is the one that Hester links to the notion of 'seeing as' (which is Wittgensteinian in origin). *This theme constitutes Hester's positive contribution to the iconic theory of metaphor.* It is because he expressly brings resemblance into play that it seemed possible to discuss him at the end of this Study.

What is 'seeing as'?

The factor of 'seeing as' is exposed through the act of reading, even to the extent that this is 'the mode in which such imagery is realized' (21). The 'seeing as' is the positive link between vehicle and tenor. In poetic metaphor, the metaphorical vehicle is *as* the tenor – from one point of view, not from all points of view. To explicate a metaphor is to enumerate all the appropriate senses in which the vehicle is 'seen as' the tenor. The 'seeing as' is the intuitive relationship that makes the sense and image hold together.

With Wittgenstein,[56] the 'seeing as' concerns neither metaphor nor even imagination, at least in its relationship to language. Considering ambiguous figures (like the one that can be seen as a duck or a rabbit), Wittgenstein remarks that it is one thing to say 'I see this ...' and another to say 'I see this as ...'; and he adds: 'seeing it as ...' is 'having *this* image.' The link between 'seeing as' and imagining appears more clearly when we go to the imperative mood, where, for example, one might say 'Imagine this,' 'Now, see the figure as this.' Will this be regarded as a question of interpretation? No, says Wittgenstein, because to interpret is to form a hypothesis which one can verify. There is no hypothesis here, nor any verification; one says, quite directly, 'It's a rabbit.' The 'seeing as,' therefore, is half thought and half experience. And is this not the same sort of mixture that the iconicity of meaning presents?[57]

Following Virgil C. Aldrich,[58] Hester proposes to have the 'seeing as' and the imaging function of language in poetry clarify each other. The 'seeing as' of Wittgenstein lends itself to this transposition because of its imaginative side; conversely, as Aldrich puts it, thinking in poetry is a picture-thinking. Now this 'pictorial' capacity of language consists also in 'seeing an aspect.' In the case of metaphor, to depict time in terms of the characteristics of a beggar is to see time as a beggar. This is what we do when we read the metaphor; to read is to establish a relationship such that X is like Y in some senses, but not in all.

It is true that the transfer from Wittgenstein's analysis to metaphor introduces an important change. In the case of the ambiguous figure, there is a *Gestalt* (B) that allows a figure A or another figure C to be seen. Thus the problem is, given B, to construct A or C. In the case of metaphor, A and C are given in reading – they are the tenor and vehicle. What must be constructed is the common element B, the *Gestalt*, namely, the point of view in which A and C are similar.

Whatever the case with this reversal, 'seeing as' proffers the missing link in the chain of explanation. 'Seeing as' is the sensible aspect of poetic language. Half thought, half experience, 'seeing as' is the intuitive relationship that holds sense and image together. How? Essentially through its selective character: '*Seeing as is an intuitive experience-act by which one selects from the quasi-sensory mass of imagery one has on reading metaphor the relevant aspects of such imagery*' (180). This definition contains the essential points. 'Seeing as' is an experience and an act at one and the same time. On the one hand, the mass of images is beyond all voluntary control; the image arises, occurs, and there is no rule to be learned for 'having images.' One sees, or one does not see. The intuitive talent for 'seeing as' (182) cannot be taught; at most, it can be assisted, as when one is helped to see the rabbit's eye in the ambiguous figure. On the other hand, 'seeing as' is an act. To understand is to do something. As we said earlier, the image is not free but tied; and, in effect, 'seeing as' orders the flux and governs iconic deployment. In this way, the experience-act of 'seeing as' ensures that imagery is implicated in metaphorical signification: 'The same imagery which *occurs* also *means*' (188).

Thus, the 'seeing as' activated in reading ensures the joining of verbal meaning with imagistic fullness. And this conjunction is no longer something outside language, since it can be reflected as a relationship. 'Seeing as' contains a ground, a foundation, that is, precisely, resemblance – no longer the resemblance between two ideas, but that very resemblance the 'seeing as' establishes. Hester claims emphatically that similarity is what results from the experience-act of 'seeing as.' '*Seeing as*' defines the resemblance, and not the reverse. This priority of 'seeing as' over the resemblance relationship is proper to the language-game in which meaning functions in an iconic manner. That is why the 'seeing as' can succeed or fail. It can fail as in forced metaphors, because they are inconsistent or fortuitous, or on the contrary, as in banal and commonplace metaphors; and succeed, as in those that fashion the surprise of discovery.

Thus, 'seeing as' quite precisely plays the role of the schema that unites the *empty* concept and the *blind* impression; thanks to its character as half thought and half experience, it joins the light of sense with the fullness of the image. In this way, the non-verbal and the verbal are firmly united at the core of the image-ing function of language.

Besides this role of bridging the verbal and the quasi-visual, 'seeing as' ensures another mediative service. Semantic theory, as we remember, puts the accent on the tension between the terms of the statement, a tension grounded in contradiction at the literal level. In the case of banal, even dead, metaphor, the tension with the body of our knowledge disappears. (This may also be the case with myth, if one agrees with Cassirer that myth represents a level of consciousness where tension with the body of our knowledge has not yet appeared.) In living metaphor, on the other hand, this tension is essential. When Hopkins says 'Oh! The mind has mountains,' the reader knows that, literally, the mind does not have mountains; the literal *is not* accompanies the metaphorical *is*. (We will return to this theme at length in Study 7.) Now, a theory of fusion of sense and the sensible, adopted prior to the revision proposed by Hester, appears to be incompatible with this characteristic, of tension between metaphorical meaning and literal meaning. On the other hand, once it is re-interpreted on the basis of 'seeing as,' the theory of fusion is perfectly compatible with interaction and tension theory. 'Seeing X *as* Y' encompasses 'X is *not* Y'; seeing time *as* a beggar is, precisely, to know also that time is *not* a beggar. The borders of meaning are transgressed but not abolished. Barfield[59] pictures metaphor well as 'a deliberate yoking of unlikes by an individual artificer.' Hester therefore is justified in saying that '*seeing as*' permits harmonization of a tension theory and a fusion theory. I should personally go further; I should say that *fusion* of sense and the imaginary, which is characteristic of 'iconized meaning,' is the necessary counterpart of a theory of interaction.

Metaphorical meaning, as we saw, is not the enigma itself, the semantic clash pure and simple, but the solution of the enigma, the inauguration of the new semantic pertinence. In this connection, the interaction designates only the *diaphora*; the *epiphora* properly speaking is something else. It cannot take place without fusion, without intuitive passage. The secret of *epiphora* then appears truly to reside in the iconic nature of intuitive passage. Metaphorical meaning as such feeds on the density of imagery released by the poem.

If this is how things really stand, then 'seeing as' designates the *nonverbal* mediation of the metaphorical statement. With this acknowledgment, semantics finds its frontier; and, in so doing, it accomplishes its task.

If semantics meets its limit here, a *phenomenology of imagination*, like that of Gaston Bachelard,[60] could perhaps take over from psycholinguistics and extend its functioning to realms where the verbal is vassal to the nonverbal. Yet it is still the semantics of the poetic verb that is to be heard in these depths. Bachelard has taught us that the image is not a residue of impression, but an aura surrounding speech: 'The poetic image places us at the origin of the speaking being.'[61] The poem gives birth to the image; the poetic image 'becomes a new being in our language, expressing us by making us what it expresses; in other words, it is at once a becoming of expression, and a becoming of our being. Here expression creates being ... one would not be able to meditate in a zone that preceded language.'[62]

If, then, the phenomenology of imagination does extend beyond psycholinguistics and even beyond the description of 'seeing-as,' this is because it follows the path of the 'reverberation'[63] of the poetic image into the depths of existence. The poetic image becomes 'a source of psychic activity.' What was 'a new being in language' becomes an 'increment to consciousness,' or better, a 'growth of being.'[64] Even in 'psychological poetics,' even in 'reveries on reverie,' psychism continues to be directed by the poetic verb. And so, one must attest: 'Yes, words really do dream.'[65]

Metaphor and reference

For Mircea Eliade

What does the metaphorical statement say about reality? This question carries us across the threshold from the *sense* towards the *reference* of discourse. But does the question itself have any meaning? This must be established first.

1 / THE POSTULATES OF REFERENCE

The question of reference can be posed at the two different levels of semantics and of hermeneutics. At the first level, it deals only with entities belonging to the order of the sentence. At the second level, it addresses entities that are larger than the sentence. It is at this level that the problem reaches its full amplitude.

As a postulate of semantics, the requirement of reference takes as given the distinction between semiotics and semantics, which the preceding Studies have already introduced. As we saw, this distinction first sets in relief the essentially synthetic character of predication, the central operation of discourse, and opposes this operation to the mere interplay of differences and oppositions among signifiers and among the signified in the phonological code and in the lexical code of a given language. Moreover, it means that what is *intended* by discourse [*l'intenté*], the correlate of the entire sentence, is irreducible to what semiotics calls the signified, which is nothing but the counterpart of the signifier of a sign within the language code. The third implication of the distinction between semiotics and semantics that concerns us here is the following: grounded on the predicative act, what is intended by discourse [*l'intenté*] points to an extra-linguistic reality which is its referent. Whereas the sign points back only to other signs immanent within a system, discourse is about things. Sign differs from sign, discourse refers to the world. Difference is semiotic, reference is semantic: 'One is never concerned in semiotics with the relation between the sign and the things denoted, nor with relationships between language and the world.'[1] But we must go beyond the simple opposition between the semiotic and the semantic viewpoint, and clearly subordinate the former to the latter. Not only are the two planes of the sign and of discourse distinct, but the first is an abstraction of the second; in the last analysis, the sign owes its very meaning as sign to its usage in discourse. How would we know that a sign *stands for...* if its *use* in discourse did not invest it with the scope that relates it to that very thing *for which* it stands? To the extent that it restricts itself to the closed world of signs, semiotics is an abstraction from *semantics*, which relates the internal constitution of the sign to the transcendent aims of reference.

This distinction between sense and reference, which Benveniste establishes in all its generality, had already been introduced by Gottlob Frege, but within the limits of a logical theory. Our working hypothesis is that the Fregean distinction holds in principle for all discourse.

Let us recall the distinction that Frege proclaimed between *Sinn* (sense) and *Bedeutung* (reference or denotation).[2] The sense is *what* the proposition states; the reference or denotation is *that about which* the sense is stated. So what must be grasped, says Frege, is 'the regular connexion between a sign, its sense, and its reference' (58). This regular connection is 'of such a kind that to the sign there corresponds a definite sense and to that in turn a definite reference, while to a given reference (an object) there does not belong only a single sign' (ibid.). Accordingly, 'the reference of "evening star" would be the same as that of "morning star," but not the sense' (57). This lack of a one-to-one relationship between sense and reference is characteristic of common languages and distinguishes them from a system of perfect signs. The possibility that no reference corresponds to the sense of a grammatically well-formed expression does not weaken the distinction; rather, not to have a reference is another trait of reference that confirms that the question of reference is always opened by that of sense.

One might object that Frege, as opposed to Benveniste, applies his distinction initially to words and more precisely *to proper names*, not to the entire proposition – in Benveniste's terminology, to what is intended by the entire sentence. Indeed, what Frege first defines is the reference of the proper name, which 'is the object itself which we designate by its means' (60). The entire statement, considered from the point of view of its reference, plays the role of a proper name with regard to the state of affairs it 'designates.' Hence it can be said that 'a proper name (word, sign, sign combination, expression) *expresses* its sense, *stands for* or *designates* its reference' (61). Indeed, when we use a proper name ('the moon') we do not restrict ourselves to talking about our idea (that is, about a specific mental event); however, 'nor are we satisfied with the sense alone' (that is, the ideal object irreducible to any mental event); 'We presuppose besides a reference' (ibid.). It is precisely this presupposition that causes us to err; but if we are wrong, it is because a reference is demanded by 'our intention in speaking or thinking' (61-2). This intention is 'the striving for truth,' which 'drives us always to advance from the sense to the reference' (63). This striving for truth suffuses the entire proposition, to the extent that it can be assimilated to a proper name; but it is via the proper name as intermediary that, for Frege, the proposition has a reference: 'For it is of the reference of the name that the predicate is affirmed or denied. Whoever does not admit the name has reference can neither apply nor withhold the predicate' (62).

There is less than total opposition, therefore, between Benveniste and Frege. For Frege, the reference is communicated from the proper name to the entire proposition, which, with respect to reference, becomes the proper name of a state of affairs. For Benveniste, the reference is communicated from the entire sentence to the word, by subdivision within the syntagma. Through its *use*, the word takes on a semantic value, which is its particular sense in *this* use. In this manner the word has a referent, 'which is the particular object to which the word corresponds in the concrete situation of circumstance or of usage.'[3] Word and sentence are thus the two poles of the same semantic entity; it is in conjunction that they have sense (always in the semantic acceptation) and reference.

The two conceptions of reference are complementary and reciprocal, whether one rises by synthetic composition from the proper name towards the proposition, or whether one descends by analytic dissociation from the sentence down to the semantic unit of the word. At their intersection, the two interpretations of reference make apparent the polar constitution of reference itself, which can be called the *object* when the referent of the name is considered, or the *state of affairs* if one considers the referent of the entire statement.

Wittgenstein's *Tractatus Logico-Philosophicus* gives an exact presentation of this polarity of the referent. He defines the world as 'the totality of facts (*Tatsachen*), not of things (*Dinge*)' (1.1), and then defines fact as 'the existence of states of affairs (*das Bestehen von Sachverhalten*)' (2); next, he proposes that a state of affairs is 'a combination of objects (things) (*eine Verbindung von Gegenständen, Sachen, Dingen*)' (2.01). Thus, the pair of object and state of affairs corresponds, on the side of the world, to the noun-statement pair in language. On the other hand, Strawson returns in *Individuals*[4] to the strict Fregean position. Reference is linked to the function of singular identification, itself *carried by* the logically *proper* name. The predicate, which does not identify but characterizes, does not refer as such to anything that exists; to accord existential value to predicates would be to make the same mistake as the realists make in the argument over universals. The identifying function and the predicative function are totally asymmetrical: only the first poses a question of existence; the second does not. In this way, then, the proposition refers globally to something via the function of singular identification of one of its terms. In *Speech Acts*,[5] John Searle postulates without hesitation the thesis that something must be in order that something may be identified. In the last analysis, this postulate of existence as the foundation of identification is what Frege had in mind when he said that we are not satisfied with a sense, we presuppose a reference.

The postulate of reference requires a separate discussion when it touches on those particular entities of discourse called texts, that is, more extensive compositions than the sentence. The question henceforth arises in the context of hermeneutics rather than of semantics, for which the sentence is at once the first and the last entity.

The question of reference is posed here in terms that are singularly more complex; for certain texts, called literary, seem to constitute an exception to the reference requirement expressed by the preceding postulate.

The text is a complex entity of discourse whose characteristics do not reduce to those of the unit of discourse, or the sentence. By text I do not mean only or even mainly something written, even though writing in itself poses original problems that bear directly on the outcome of reference; I mean principally the production of discourse as a work. With the work, as the word implies, new categories enter the field of discourse. Essentially these are pragmatic categories, categories of production and of labour. To begin with, discourse is the arena of a work of composition or arrangement, 'disposition' (to echo *dispositio*, the term in ancient rhetoric), which makes of a poem or novel a totality irreducible to a simple sum of sentences. Next, this 'disposition' obeys formal rules, a codification that belongs no longer to language but to discourse, and fashions from discourse what we have just called a poem or a novel. This code is the one of literary 'genres,' that is, of genres that regulate the praxis of the text. Finally, this codified production ends in a particular work: this poem, that novel. Ultimately this third trait is the most important. It can be called style, where this is understood (with G.G. Granger)[6] as what makes the work a singular, individual thing. It is the most important trait because it distinguishes practical categories in an irreducible manner from theoretical categories. Granger refers in this connection to a famous text in Aristotle according to which to produce is to produce individual things;[7] conversely, an individual thing, opaque to theoretical consideration that stops at the last species, is the correlate of a making.

Such, then, is what the labour of interpretation addresses. It is the text as work. Arrangement, belonging to genres, achievement in a particular style, are the categories proper to the production of discourse as work.

This specific realization of discourse calls for an appropriate reformulation of the postulate of reference. It would seem enough at first glance to reformulate the Fregean concept of reference just by substituting one word for another: instead of saying that we are not satisfied with the sense and so presuppose reference besides, we would say that we are not satisfied with the structure of the work and presuppose a world of the work. The structure of the work is in fact its sense, and the world of the work its reference. This simple substitution of terms is sufficient as a first approximation. Hermeneutics then is simply the theory that regulates the transition from structure of the work to world of the work. To interpret a work is to display the world to which it refers by virtue of its 'arrangement,' its 'genre,' and its 'style.' In another publication, I contrast this postulate with the romantic and psychologizing conception of hermeneutics originating with Schleiermacher and Dilthey, for whom the supreme law of interpretation is the search for a harmony between the spirit of the author and that of the reader. To this always difficult and often impossible quest for an intention hidden behind the work, I oppose a quest that addresses the world displayed before the work. But the issue in the present discussion is not the quarrel with romantic hermeneutics, but the right to pass from the structure (which is to the complex work what sense is to the simple statement) to the world of the work (which is to the work what the denotation is to the statement).

This passage requires a distinct postulate because of the specific nature of certain works, those called literary. The production of discourse as 'literature' signifies very precisely that the relationship of sense to reference is *suspended*. 'Literature' would be that sort of discourse that has no denotation but only connotations. This rejection is supported not only by an internal examination of the literary work (as we shall see later), but also by Frege's own theory of denotation (or reference). This theory includes, in effect, an internal principle of limitation that defines its own concept of truth. The desire for truth motivating the push from sense towards reference is ascribed expressly by Frege only to scientific statements, and seems quite clearly to be denied to poetic statements. Considering an example from epic poetry, Frege holds that the proper name *Ulysses* has no reference; 'We are interested,' he says, 'only in the sense of the sentences and the images and feelings thereby aroused' (63). In contrast to scientific inspection, therefore, artistic pleasure seems linked to 'senses' without any 'reference.'

My whole aim is to do away with this restriction of reference to scientific statements. Therefore, a distinct discussion appropriate to the literary work is required, and a second formulation of the postulate of reference, more complex than the first, which simply mirrored the general postulate that every sense calls for reference or denotation. The second formulation is stated as follows: the literary work through the structure proper to it displays a world only under the condition that the reference of descriptive discourse is suspended. Or to put it another way, discourse in the literary work sets out its denotation as a second-level denotation, by means of the suspension of the first-level denotation of discourse.

This postulate brings us back to the problem of metaphor. It may be, indeed, that the metaphorical statement is precisely the one that points out most clearly this relationship between suspended reference and displayed reference. Just as the metaphorical statement captures its sense as metaphorical midst the ruins of the literal sense, it also achieves its reference upon the ruins of what might be called (in symmetrical fashion) its literal reference. If it is true that literal sense and metaphorical sense are distinguished and articulated within an interpretation, so too it is within an interpretation that a second-level reference, which is properly the metaphorical reference, is set free by means of the suspension of the first-level reference.

Whether or not, in the course of this process, our concepts of reality, of world, and of truth vacillate is a question reserved for Study 8. Do we actually know what 'reality,' 'world,' and 'truth' signify?

2 / THE CASE AGAINST REFERENCE

The possibility that the metaphorical statement might aspire to truth value meets considerable objections that do not reduce to the pre-judgment originating in the rhetorical conception discussed in the earlier Studies, namely, that metaphor carries no new information and is purely ornamental. The strategy of language that characterizes the production of discourse in the form of 'poetry' seems in itself to constitute a formidable *counter-example* to the alleged universality of the referential relationship of language to reality.

This strategy of language does not appear distinctly until one stops considering units of discourse, or sentences, and moves to totalities of discourse, or works. Here the question of reference is located not at the level of each sentence, but at the level of the 'poem' considered on the lines of the three criteria of the work: 'arrangement,' subordination to a 'genre,' and production of a 'singular' entity. If the metaphorical statement is to have a reference, it is through the mediation of the 'poem' as an ordered, generic, and singular totality. In other words, metaphor says something about something to the extent that it is, to quote Beardsley,[8] a 'poem in miniature.'

The strategy of language proper to poetry, that is, to the production of the poem, does indeed seem to consist in constituting a sense that intercepts reference and, in the limiting situation, abolishes reality.

The proper level of argument is that of 'literary criticism,' that is, a discipline scaled to discourse realized as a work. However, literary criticism draws support from a purely linguistic analysis of the poetic function, which Roman Jakobson sets into the more general framework of linguistic communication. As we remember, Jakobson[9] attempts with a powerfully synthetic exactitude to embrace the totality of linguistic phenomena within the scope of six 'factors' that contribute to the process of verbal communication. These six 'factors' of communication – addresser, addressee, code, message, contact, context – are matched by six 'functions,' any one of which may predominate at any time ('The verbal structure of a message depends primarily on the predominant function' [353]). Thus, the emotive function corresponds to the addresser, the conative function to the addressee, the phatic function to contact, the 'metalingual' or metalinguistic function to the code, and the referential function to the context. As for the 'poetic' function, the one that interests us, it corresponds to the highlighting of the message for its own sake: 'This function, by promoting the palpability of signs, deepens the fundamental dichotomy of signs and objects' (356). This definition directly places the poetic function of language in opposition to the referential function through which the message is oriented towards the non-linguistic context.

Two observations are required at this point. First of all, it should be understood clearly that this analysis concerns the 'poetic function' of language and does not define the 'poem' as a 'literary genre.' Even isolated statements such as 'I like Ike' can interrupt the flow of a prosaic referential discourse and present this accentuation of the message and this obliteration of the referent that characterize the poetic function. Therefore, one must not identify 'poem' with 'the poetic' in Jakobson. Furthermore, the predominance of one function does not mean that others are abolished, only that their hierarchy is altered. To carry this further, the poetic genres themselves are distinguished by the way in which the other functions mix with the poetic function: 'The particularities of diverse poetic genres imply a differently ranked participation of the other verbal functions along with the dominant poetic function. Epic poetry, focused on the third person, strongly involves the referential function of language; the lyric, oriented toward the first person, is intimately linked with the emotive function; poetry of the second person is imbued with the conative function and is either supplicatory or exhortative, depending on whether the first person is subordinated to the second one or the second to the first' (357). Hence, this analysis of the poetic function constitutes only a preparatory stage in the determination of the poem as work.

The linguistics of Roman Jakobson does offer, it is true, a second analytical instrument that relates the theory of the poetic function to that of the strategy of discourse proper to the poem. The poetic function is distinguished by the manner in which the two fundamental arrangements, selection and combination, relate to each other. We referred already to this theory of Jakobson within the framework of the Study on 'The work of resemblance.'[10] It is taken up again here in the somewhat different context of the issue of reference. Let us recall the principal claim. The operations of language can be represented by the intersection of two axes at right angles to each other. The relations of contiguity, and consequently the operations that are syntagmatic in character, occupy the first axis, that of combinations. The operations grounded in resemblance, and constitutive of all paradigmatic organizations, are played out along the second axis, that of substitutions. The elaboration of every message depends upon the interplay of these two modes of arrangement.

What characterizes the poetic function, then, is the alteration of the relationship of the operations located on one or the other axis: '*The poetic function projects the principle of equivalence from the axis of selection into the axis of combination*' (358). In what sense? In ordinary language, the language of prose, the principle of equivalence plays no part in constituting the sequence but only in the choice of appropriate words within a sphere of resemblance. The anomaly of poetry is precisely that equivalence plays a part in connection as well as selection. In other words, the principle of equivalence serves to constitute the sequence. We can speak in poetry of a 'reiteration of equivalent units' (the role of rhythmic cadences, of resemblance and opposition between syllables, of metric equivalence, of periodic repetition of rhymes in rhymed poetry, of alternation of long and short feet in stressed poetry). As for relations of meaning, they are introduced somehow by this recurrence of phonic form. A 'semantic propinquity' (367) and even a 'semantic equivalence' (368) result from the sounding of rhymes: 'In poetry, any conspicuous similarity in sound is evaluated in respect to similarity and/or dissimilarity in meaning' (372).

What is the upshot of all this for reference? The question is not settled by the preceding analysis, whose topic might be called the strategy of sense. What has just been called semantic equivalence concerns the interplay of sense. But it is precisely this interplay of sense that ensures the accentuation of the message for its own sake (as Jakobson put it in 'Linguistics and Poetics') and thus the obliteration of reference. The projection of the principle of equivalence from the axis of selection onto the axis of combination is what ensures the highlighting of the message. So what was treated as effect of sense in the above-mentioned essay is treated as process of sense in Jakobson's 'Two Aspects of Language and Two Types of Aphasic Disorders.'

Literary criticism comes in at just this point.

But let us not leave Roman Jakobson without accepting a valuable suggestion from him, which will not reveal its whole meaning until the end of this Study. The semantic equivalence brought about by phonic equivalence brings with it an ambiguity that affects all the functions of communication. The addresser is split (the 'I' of the lyrical hero or of the fictitious narrator), and so too the addressee (the 'you' as supposed addressee of dramatic monologues, supplications, epistles). The most radical consequence of this is that what happens in poetry is not the suppression of the referential function but its profound alteration by the workings of ambiguity: 'The supremacy of poetic function over referential function does not obliterate the reference but makes it ambiguous. The double-sensed message finds correspondence in a split addresser, in a split addressee, and what is more in a split reference, as is cogently exposed in the preambles to fairy tales of various peoples, for instance, in the usual exordium of the Majorca storytellers: "Aixo era y no era" (It was and it was not)' (371).

Let us keep this notion of *split reference* in mind, as well as the wonderful 'It was and it was not,' which contains *in nuce* all that can be said about metaphorical truth. But first, the case against reference must be pressed to the limit.

The dominant current of literary criticism, European as well as American, does not have split reference in mind, but more radically the destruction of reference – a theme, indeed, that appears better attuned to the principal trait of poetry, namely 'this capacity for reiteration whether immediate or delayed, this reification of a poetic message and its constituents, this conversion of a message into an enduring thing ...' (371).

This last expression – conversion of a message into an enduring thing – could serve as the subtitle of a whole series of works on 'Poetics,' for which the essence of the strategy of discourse in poetry is the attainment of meaning within the haven of sound. The idea is an old one; Pope said 'The sound must seem an echo to the sense.' Valéry sees the dance, which travels nowhere, as the model of the poetic act. For the reflecting poet, the poem is a prolonged oscillation between sense and sound. Like sculpture, poetry converts language into matter, worked for its own sake. This solid object is not the representation of some thing, but an expression of itself.[11] Indeed, the mirror-play between sense and sound somehow absorbs the movement of the poem, which does not spend its energy externally but within itself. To capture this mutation of language, Wimsatt forged the very suggestive expression of *verbal icon*,[12] which recalls not only Peirce but also the Byzantine tradition for which the icon is a thing. The poem is an icon and not a sign. The poem is. It has an 'iconic solidity' (*The Verbal Icon* 231). Language takes on the thickness of a material or a *medium*. The sensible, sensual plenitude of the poem is like that of painted or sculptured forms. The combination of sensual and logical ensures that expression and impression coalesce within the poetic thing. Poetic signification fused thus with its sensible vehicle becomes that particular and 'thingy' reality we call a poem.

The fusion of sense and sound is not alone in presenting an argument against reference in poetry. An additional and perhaps even more radical attack lies in the fusion of sense and images, which at one and the same time proliferate from the sense as source and are ruled from within by it. We have already discussed the work of Hester[13] and praised it for the role it gives the image in the constitution of metaphorical meaning. His argument is taken up again at the point where reference is at issue. Poetic language, says Hester, is the language in which 'sense' and 'sound' function in an iconic manner, creating accordingly a fusion of 'sense' and 'sensa' (96). These 'sensa' are, essentially, the ebb and flow of images allowed to be by the *epoché* of the referential relation. Therefore, the fusion of sense and sound is no longer the central phenomenon, but occasion for an unfolding of the imaginary that is bound to the sense. Now with the image comes the fundamental moment of 'suspension,' of *epoché*, Husserl's notion borrowed by Hester and applied to the non-referential interplay of imagery in poetic strategy. The abolition of reference, which belongs to the achievement of poetic sense, is thus *par excellence* the work of the *epoché* that makes the iconic functioning of sense and of sensa possible, itself achieved by the iconic functioning of sense and sound.

It is Northrop Frye, however, who approaches the limit most radically. In *Anatomy of Criticism*, Frye generalizes his analysis of poetry to all works of literature. Whenever a sort of signification oriented in the opposite direction to the centrifugal orientation of referential types of discourse can be opposed to informative or didactic discourse, exemplified by the language of science, then we can speak of literary signification. In effect, centrifugal or 'outward' movement takes us outside discourse, from words towards things. Centripetal or 'internal' movement of words presses towards the broader verbal configurations that constitute the literary work in its totality.

In informative or didactic discourse, the 'symbol' (Frye's term for any discernible unit of meaning) functions as a sign that 'stands for,' 'points to,' 'represents' something. In literary discourse, the symbol represents nothing outside itself but links the parts to the whole within the discursive framework: 'Verbal elements understood inwardly or centripetally, as parts of a verbal structure, are, as symbols, simply and literally verbal elements, or units of a verbal structure' – compare the 'motifs' of a musical composition (73-4). As against the striving for truth of descriptive discourse, Frye asserts with Sir Philip Sidney that 'the poet affirmeth' (76). Metaphysics and theology affirm, assert; poetry ignores reality and limits itself to forging a 'fable' (Frye revives here the expression of Aristotle who, in the *Poetics*, characterizes tragedy by its *muthos*). Were it necessary to compare poetry with something other than itself, that other would be mathematics: 'The poet, like the pure mathematician, depends, not on descriptive truth, but on conformity to his hypothetical postulates' (ibid.). Thus, the appearance of the ghost in *Hamlet* corresponds to the hypothetical conception of the play. No claim is made concerning the reality of ghosts – yet there must be a ghost in *Hamlet*! To begin reading is to accept this fiction; any paraphrase that approximates a description of something misconstrues the rules of the game. In this sense, meaning in literature is literal; it says what it says and nothing else: 'Understanding a poem literally means understanding the whole of it, as a poem, and as it stands' (77). One's only task is to perceive its unitary structure through the concatenation of its symbols.

One encounters at this point an analysis in the same style as that of Jakobson. The literality of the poem is established by recurrence in time (rhythm) and in space (pattern). Literally, its meaning is its pattern or its integrity. The internal verbal relations absorb the variability of the sign's external meaning to some extent: 'So literature in its descriptive context is a body of hypothetical verbal structures' (79).

Frye, it is true, introduces a moderately different factor, onto which our own reflections will be grafted: 'The unity of a poem,' he says, 'is ... a unity of mood' (80); 'Poetic images ... express or articulate the mood' (81). Now the mood '*is* the poem, not something else still behind it' (ibid.) All literary structure is ironic in this sense: '"What it says" is always different in kind or degree from "what it means"' (ibid.).

Such, then, is poetic structure, 'a self-contained "texture"' (82) – that is, a structure entirely dependent on its internal relationships.

I would be loath to leave this case against reference without pointing to the *epistemological argument*, which, while augmenting the linguistic argument (for example, Jakobson) and the argument of literary criticism (for example, Frye), at the same time reveals their hidden presupposition. Critiques shaped by the school of logical positivism state that all language that is not *descriptive*, in the sense of giving information about *facts*, must be *emotional*. Furthermore, the suggestion is that what is 'emotional' is sensed purely 'within' the subject and is not related in any way whatsoever to anything outside the subject. Emotion is an affect which has only an inside, and not an outside.

This argument – which thus has two sides to it – did not arise originally in the course of consideration of literary works; it is a postulate imported from philosophy into literature. And this postulate decides on the meaning of truth and reality. It says that there is no truth beyond the pale of possible verification (or falsification), and that in the last analysis all verification is empirical, as defined by scientific procedure. This postulate functions in literary criticism as a prejudgment. Besides the alternative between 'cognitive' and 'emotive,' it imposes the alternative between 'denotative' and 'connotative.' The 'emotivist' theories in ethics are an adequate demonstration that this prejudice is not restricted to poetics. It is so powerful that the authors who are most hostile to logical positivism often fortify it while fighting it. To say, with Suzanne Langer, that to read a poem is to grasp 'a piece of *virtual life*,'[14] is to remain within the verifiable-unverifiable dichotomy. To say with Northrop Frye that images suggest or evoke the mood that informs the poem is to confirm that the 'mood' is itself centripetal, like the language that informs it.

The new rhetoric in France confronts us with the same scene: literary theory and positivist epistemology support each other. For example, the notion of 'opaque discourse' in Todorov is identified immediately with that of 'discourse without reference': over against transparent discourse, he says, 'there is the discourse so well covered with patterns and figures that no vision can penetrate behind it. This would be a language that does not point to any reality, a language satisfied in itself.'[15]

The concept of 'poetic function' in Jean Cohen[16] proceeds from the same positivist convictions. It is self-evident to this author that cognitive response and affective response overlap: 'The function of prose is denotative, the function of poetry is connotative' (205). It is no accident that Cohen recognizes himself in his quotation of Carnap: 'The aim of a lyrical poem in which occur the words "sunshine" and "clouds" is not to inform us of certain meteorological facts, but to express certain feelings of the poet and to excite similar feelings in us' (cited 205).

Nevertheless, doubts arise. How is one to explain that the emotion in poetry is 'linked to the object' (205)? Indeed, poetic sadness is 'felt as a quality of the world' (206). Carnap is not the one to quote at this stage, but Mikel Dufrenne, who tells us: 'To feel is to experience a feeling as a property of the object, not as a state of my being.'[17] How can one reconcile with the positivist thesis the admission that poetic sadness is 'a modality of consciousness of things, an original and specific way of seizing the world' (206)? And how is a bridge to be built between the purely psychological and affectivist notion of connotation and this opening of language towards a 'poetics of things' (226)? Must not the expressivity of things (to take up a notion of Raymond Ruyer)[18] find in language itself, and specifically in its power of deviation in relation to its ordinary usage, a power of designation that escapes the alternative of denotative and connotative? Is the issue not closed if the connotation is held to be a substitute for the denotation ['the connotation takes the place of the denotation which defaults' (211)]? This stumbling block is admitted in the pages of Čohen's work. Pointing to this 'evidence of feeling,' which, for the poet, is 'as compelling as empirical evidence,' he notes: 'This evidence is surely wellgrounded: subjectivity is linked up with the profound objectivity of being – but that question belongs to metaphysics, not to poetics' (213). This is why Cohen finally beats a retreat and returns to the dichotomy of subjective and objective, which projects the task of an 'aesthetics that would like to be scientific' (207). 'The poetic sentence,' he says, 'is objectively false, but subjectively true' (212).

The *Rhétorique générale* of the Groupe de Liège confronts the same problem under the title 'The Ethos of Figures.'[19] Although systematic study of this topic is reserved for another work, the present volume can provide a preliminary sketch. Moreover, this study in fact could not be put off entirely because the specific aesthetic effect of figures, 'which is the real object of artistic communication' (45), is part of the complete description of a rhetorical figure, together with the descriptions of its deviation, its sign, and its invariant (45). The sketch of the theory of Ethos (145-56) leads one to anticipate an investigation alligned essentially to the response of the reader or listener, putting the metaboles in the position of *stimuli*, of signals, engendering a subjective impression. Now among the effects achieved by figurative discourse, the primordial effect 'is to neutralize the perception of the literality (in the wide sense) of the text in which it appears' (148). We are here truly on terrain marked out by Jakobson with his definition of the poetic function and by Todorov with his definition of opaque discourse. Yet the authors of the *Rhétorique générale* proclaim: 'This is where it all stops; our work, indeed, demonstrates that there is almost no necessary relationship between the structure of a figure and its Ethos' (148).

As for Le Guern,[20] he does not differ at all from the authors just cited as far as this point is concerned. We saw earlier that the distinction between *denotation* and *connotation* is even one of the major axes of his semantics: semic selection is assigned to denotation, the associated image arises from connotation.

3 / A GENERALIZED THEORY OF DENOTATION

The thesis to be argued now does not deny the preceding thesis, but rather draws support from it. It proposes that the suspension of reference in the sense defined by the norms of descriptive discourse is the negative condition of the appearance of a more fundamental mode of reference, whose explication is the task of interpretation. At stake in this explication is nothing less than the meaning of the words *reality* and *truth*, which themselves must vacillate and become problematical.

There were meaningful clues for this search for another reference in the preceding analysis devoted to the poetic function in all its generality, quite apart from the particular role of metaphor. First let us take up the notion of 'the hypothetical' in Northrop Frye. The poem, he says, is neither true nor false; it is hypothetical. But 'the poetic hypothesis' is not the mathematical hypothesis; it is the suggestion or proposal, in imaginative, fictive mode, of a world. Hence, suspension of real reference is the condition of access to the virtual mode of reference. But what is a virtual life? Can there be a virtual life without a virtual world capable of being inhabited? Is it not the function of poetry to establish another world – another world that corresponds to other possibilities of existence, to possibilities that would be most deeply our own?

There are other indications in Frye that point in the same direction. As was said before, 'The unity of a poem ... is a unity of mood';[21] and again: 'Poetic images do not state or point to anything, but, by pointing to each other, they suggest or evoke the mood which informs the poem' (81). Under the name of mood, an extra-linguistic factor is introduced, which is the index of a manner of being (on condition that it is not treated psychologically). A mood or 'state of soul' [*état d'âme*] is a way of finding or sensing oneself in the midst of reality. It is, in the language of Heidegger, a way of finding oneself among things (*Befindlichkeit*).[22] Here again, the *epoché* of natural reality is the condition that allows poetry to develop a world on the basis of the mood that the poet articulates. It will be the task of interpretation to elaborate the design of a world liberated, by suspension, from descriptive reference. The creation of a concrete object – the poem itself – cuts language off from the didactic function of the sign, but at the same time opens up access to reality in the mode of fiction and feeling.

A last indicator concerns Jakobson. As we saw, he links the notion of split reference to that of ambiguous meaning: 'Poeticalness is not a supplementation of discourse with rhetorical adornment but a total re-evaluation of the discourse and of all its components whatsoever' ('Closing Statements' 377).

It is within the very analysis of the metaphorical statement that a referential conception of poetic language must be established, a conception that takes account of the elimination of the reference of ordinary language and patterns itself on the concept of split reference.

Initial support comes from the very notion of metaphorical meaning; the way in which metaphorical meaning is constituted provides the key to the splitting of reference. We can start with the point that the meaning of a metaphorical statement rises up from the blockage of any literal interpretation of the statement. In a literal interpretation, the meaning abolishes itself. Next, because of this self-destruction of the meaning, the primary reference founders. The entire strategy of poetic discourse plays on this point: it seeks the abolition of the reference by means of self-destruction of the meaning of metaphorical statements, the self-destruction being made manifest by an impossible literal interpretation.

But this is only the first phase, or rather the negative counterpart, of a positive strategy. Within the perspective of semantic impertinence, the self-destruction of meaning is merely the other side of an innovation in meaning at the level of the entire statement, an innovation obtained through the 'twist' of the literal meaning of the words. It is this innovation in meaning that constitutes living metaphor. But are we not in the same motion given the key to metaphorical reference? Can one not say that, by drawing a new semantic pertinence out of the ruins of the literal meaning, the metaphoric interpretation *also* sustains a new referential design, through those same means of abolition of the reference corresponding to the literal interpretation of the statement? A proportional argument, therefore: the other reference, the object of our search, would be to the new semantic pertinence what the abolished reference is to the literal meaning destroyed by the semantic impertinence. A metaphorical reference would correspond to the metaphorical meaning, just as an impossible literal reference corresponds to the impossible literal meaning.

We have posited this unknown reference through analogy (specifically, as the fourth term of a proportional argument); but can we do more? Can the reference itself be seen at work?

The semantic study of metaphor contains a second hint in this connection. As we saw, the interplay of resemblance, which we held within the strict limits of an operation of discourse, consists in the initiation of a *proximity* between formerly 'remote' meanings. 'To see the similar,' we said with Aristotle, 'is to metaphorize well.' Why would not this proximity of meaning be at the same time a proximity between the things themselves? Is it not from this proximity that a new way of seeing springs forth? Accordingly, it would be the category mistake that clears the way to a new vision.

This suggestion is not just added to the preceding, it is developed with it. The vision of the similar that produces the metaphorical statement is not a direct vision, but one which itself can also be called metaphorical. Using Hester's terms, metaphorical seeing is a 'seeing as.' Indeed, the former classification, linked to the previous use of words, resists and creates a sort of stereoscopic vision in which the new situation is perceived only in the depths of the situation disrupted by the category mistake.

Such is the schema of split reference. Essentially, it sets up a parallel between metaphorization of reference and metaphorization of meaning. This is the schema to which we will try to give some body.

Our first task is to overcome the opposition between denotation and connotation and to insert metaphorized reference into a *generalized* theory of *denotation*.

This general framework is developed in *Languages of Art* by Nelson Goodman. But Goodman does more than this; within that framework, he also designates the place of a frankly denotative theory of metaphor.

Languages of Art begins by situating all symbolic operations, verbal and non-verbal (including pictorial among others), within the boundaries of a single operation, the referential function by which a symbol 'stands for' or 'refers to.' The universality of the referential function is guaranteed by the universality of the organizing power of language and, more generally, of symbolic systems. This theory appears on the horizon of a general philosophy that has certain affinities with the philosophy of symbolic forms of Cassirer, but even more with the pragmatism of C.S. Peirce. Moreover, it draws the consequences, for a theory of symbols, of the nominalist positions taken in Goodman's *The Structure of Appearance* and *Fact, Fiction and Forecast*. The title of the first chapter, 'Reality Remade,' is very significant in this regard: symbolic systems 'make' and 'remake' the world. Beyond its imposing technicality, the entire work is a homage to a militant attitude, as the last chapter says,[23] of 'reorganizing the world in terms of works and works in terms of the world' (241). Work and world mirror each other. The aesthetic attitude 'is less attitude than action: creation and re-creation' (242).

We will return later to the nominalist and the pragmatist tone of the work. Let us focus for the moment on the important corollary, the refusal to distinguish between cognitive and emotive: 'In aesthetic experience the *emotions function cognitively*' (248). The rapprochement that occurs throughout the book between verbal and non-verbal symbols is grounded in an emphatic anti-emotionalism. This is not to say that the two sorts of symbols function in the same way. On the contrary, it is a matter for difficult argumentation, attempted only in the last chapter of the book, to distinguish between 'description' by language and 'representation' by the arts. What is important is that the four 'symptoms' of the aesthetic – syntactic density, semantic density, syntactic repleteness, role of exemplification (i.e. showing rather than saying) – are distinguished within a single, unique symbolic function. Distinguishing these traits concedes nothing to immediacy. Under one or another mode, 'Symbolization ... is to be judged fundamentally by how well it serves the cognitive purpose' (258). Aesthetic excellence is a cognitive excellence. One must even speak of the truth of art, if truth here is defined as 'fit with a body of theory' and between hypotheses and the facts at hand – briefly, as the 'appropriateness' of a symbolization (264). These traits hold for the arts as well as for discourse. 'My aim,' concludes the author 'has been to take some steps toward a systematic study of symbols and symbol systems and the ways they function in our perceptions and actions and arts and sciences, and thus in the creation and comprehension of our worlds' (265).

This enterprise is akin to that of Cassirer, therefore, although there is no progression from art to science. Only the use of the symbolic function is different; the symbolic systems coexist simultaneously.

Metaphor is an essential piece of this symbolic theory, inserted directly into the framework of reference. What must be shown is the difference, on the one hand, between what is 'metaphorically true' and what is 'literally true,' and, on the other hand, between metaphorical and literal truth together and 'mere falsity' (51). Broadly speaking, metaphorical truth concerns the application of predicates or of properties to something by a sort of transference, as for example the application of predicates borrowed from the domain of sound to something coloured (significantly, the chapter containing the theory of transference is entitled 'The Sound of Pictures' [45 ff.]).

But what is the literal application of predicates? The response to this question involves setting in place an important conceptual network comprising notions such as denotation, description, representation, and expression.[24] Reference and denotation coincide on first approximation. But later it will be necessary to introduce a distinction between two ways of referring, by denotation and by exemplification. Initially, then, we can regard reference and denotation as synonymous. Denotation must be defined fairly widely from the start, so as to subsume what art does – represent something – and what language does – describe. To say that representing is one way of denoting is to assimilate the relation between a picture and what it depicts to that between a predicate and that to which it is applied. At the same time, it says that representing is not imitating in the sense of resembling or copying. Therefore, the preconception that representation is imitation by resemblance should be carefully broken down and dislodged from one of its seemingly safest refuges, the theory of perspective in painting.[25] But if to represent is to denote and if our symbolic systems 'remake reality' through denotation, then representation is one of the modes through which nature becomes a product of art and discourse. So too, representation can depict a non-existant (the unicorn, Pickwick); in terms of denotation, this is a situation of null denotation, as distinct from multiple denotation (the eagle design in the dictionary to depict all eagles) and singular denotation (the portrait of so-and-so). Will Goodman draw from this distinction the conclusion that the non-existant also helps to fashion the world? Curiously, the author backs away from this consequence, which the upcoming theory of models will impel us to accept. To talk about the picture *of* the Unicorn is to talk about the unicorn-picture, that is, about a picture classified by the term associated with it. To learn to recognize a picture is not to learn to apply a representation (asking *what* it denotes) but to distinguish it from another (asking *which* species it is).

No doubt the argument carries the day against the confusion between characterizing and copying. However, if to represent is to classify, it is difficult to see how, in the case of null denotation, symbolization can make[26] what it depicts: 'The object and its aspects depend upon organization; and labels of all sorts are tools of organization ... a representation or description, by virtue of how it classifies and is classified, may make or mark connections, analyze objects, and organize the world' (32). By linking *fiction* and *redescription* very tightly, an analysis borrowed from the theory of models will allow us to correct an incompatibility, apparent at least in Goodman, between the theory of null denotation and the organizing function of symbolism.

Up until this point, denotation and reference have been treated as synonymous. This identification caused no inconvenience so long as the distinctions considered (description and representation) fell within the concept of denotation. A new distinction must be introduced concerning the orientation of the concept of reference, according to which its direction is from symbol to thing or from thing to symbol. As long as we identify reference and denotation, we take account only of the first direction, which consists in applying 'labels' to events. (Let us note in passing that the choice of the term *label* is appropriate to the conventionalist nominalism of Goodman – there are no fixed essences giving a tenor of meaning to verbal and non-verbal symbols. At the same time, the way of the theory of metaphor becomes smoother, for it is easier to replace a label than to reform an essence – habit is the only barrier!)

The second direction in which reference operates is no less important than the first. It consists in exemplifying, that is, in pointing out a meaning or property that something 'possesses.'[27] The reason why Goodman would appear to be so greatly interested in exemplification is that metaphor is a transference that affects the possession of predicates by some specific thing, rather than the application of these predicates to something. We arrive at metaphor in the midst of examples where it is said, for instance, that a certain picture that *possesses* the colour grey *expresses* sadness. In other words, metaphor concerns an inverted operation of reference plus an operation of transference. Close attention must be paid, therefore, to this series – reversed reference, exemplification, (literal) possession of a predicate, expression as metaphorical possession of non-verbal predicates (e.g. a sad colour).

Let us go back up the chain from (literal) possession[28] before descending towards (metaphorical) expression.

For a painted figure to possess greyness is to say that it is an *example* of greyness; but to say that this, here, is an example of greyness is to say that greyness *as such* applies to ... this thing, hence denotes it. Accordingly, the denotation relation is reversed. The picture denotes what it describes; but the colour grey is denoted by the predicate 'grey.' If, then, to possess is to exemplify, possession differs from reference only as to its direction.

The term symmetrical in this context to 'label' is 'sample' (for instance, a sample of fabric). The sample 'possesses' the characteristics (colour, texture, etc.) designated by the label. It is denoted by that which it exemplifies. The sample-label relation, if it is well understood, holds for non-verbal as well as verbal systems; predicates are labels in verbal systems, but non-linguistic symbols can also be exemplified and function as predicates. Thus, a gesture can denote or exemplify or do both: the motions of the orchestral conductor denote the sounds to be produced without being sounds themselves; sometimes they exemplify the speed or cadence of the sounds; the gymnastics instructor provides samples that exemplify the movement called for that denotes the movement to be produced; dance denotes the motions of everyday life or of a ritual and exemplify the prescribed stance that in turn reorganizes experience. The opposition between representing and expressing will not be a difference of domain (for example the domain of objects or events and the domain of feelings, as in an emotionalist theory), since representing is a case of denoting, and expressing is a variant by transference of possessing, which is a case of exemplifying; and since exemplifying and denoting are cases of making reference, with only a difference of direction. A symmetry by inversion replaces an apparent heterogeneity, by means of which the ruinous distinction of the cognitive and the emotive – from which that of denotation and connotation is derived – could creep back in again.

What has been gained with respect to the theory of metaphor?[29] We find it bound solidly to the theory of reference, linked by transference of a relation, which itself is the inverse of denotation, of which representation is a species. Indeed, if one acknowledges what will be shown later, that metaphorical expression (the sadness of the grey picture) is transference of possession; and if it is proven already that possession, which is nothing other than exemplification, is the inverse of denotation, of which representation is a species, then all the distinctions fall within the bounds of reference, with the proviso that their orientations differ.

But what is a transferred possession?

Let our starting point be the suggested example – the painting is literally grey, but sad metaphorically. The first statement concerns a 'fact,' the second a 'figure' (whence the title of chapter 2, section 5, 'Facts and Figures,' which contains the theory of metaphor). But 'fact' must be taken in the sense of Russell and Wittgenstein, where fact is not to be confused with a given but understood as a state of affairs, that is, as the correlate of a predicative act. For the same reason, 'figure' is not the ornament of a word but a predicative usage in a reversed denotation, that is, in a possession-exemplification. 'Fact' and 'figure,' therefore, are different ways of applying predicates, of using labels as samples.

Metaphor is an unusual application for Goodman, that is, application of a familiar label (whose usage consequently has a past) to a new object that resists at first and then gives in. Goodman's droll formulation states that 'applying an old label in a new way ... is a matter of teaching an old word new tricks ... metaphor is an affair between a predicate with a past and an object that yields while protesting' (69); later, it is 'a happy and revitalizing, even if bigamous, second marriage' (73). (Metaphor is again being spoken of in terms of metaphor – but this time the screen, filter, grill, and lens give way to carnal union!)

Here, within a theory of reference and no longer just of sense, we rediscover the essential points of the semantic theory of metaphorical statement of Richards, Beardsley, and Turbayne. Ryle's idea of category-mistake is retained as well, which moreover was also referential; I say that the painting is sad rather than gay, *even though* only sentient beings are gay or sad. Nevertheless, there is a metaphorical truth here, for the mistake in label application is equivalent to the reassignment of a label, such that 'sad' is more appropriate than 'gay.' The literal falsity, through misassignment of a label, is transformed into metaphorical truth through reassignment of the label.[30] I will show later how the intermediary of the theory of models allows one to interpret this reassignment in terms of redescription. The heuristic device of fiction must be inserted between description and redescription, and this will be accomplished by the theory of models.

But first, an interesting extension of metaphor must be considered. Metaphor does not cover just what we have called 'figure,' that is, ultimately, transference of an isolated predicate operating in opposition to another (the alternative 'red' or 'orange'). It also covers what must be called 'schema,' which stands for a group of labels with the characteristic that a corresponding group of objects, a 'realm,' is picked out by it (for example, colour).[31] Metaphor's power of reorganizing our perception of things develops from transposition of an entire 'realm.' Consider, for example, sound in the visual order. To speak of the sonority of a painting is no longer to move about an isolated predicate, but to bring about the incursion of an entire realm into alien territory. The well-worn notion of 'transporting' becomes a conceptual migration, if not an armed and luggage-laden overseas expedition. The interesting point is that the organization brought about in the adopted region is *guided by* the use of the entire network in the region of origin. This means that even if the territory to be invaded is chosen arbitrarily (whatever closely resembles whatever else), the usage of the labels in the new field of application is governed by the previous practice. In this vein, the use of the expression *high numbers* may guide the use of 'high sounds.' The use of schemata is governed by the law of 'precedence.' Here again, Goodman's nominalism will not allow him to look for affinities in the nature of things or in an eidetic constitution of experience. Nothing is explained in this regard by etymological geneologies or reappearances of animistic confusions (for example, between the animate and the inanimate), because the application of a predicate is metaphorical only if it conflicts with an application governed by present practice. Ancient history and repressed memory can break through to the surface. Still, an expatriate according to the present laws remains an alien even when back in his homeland. A theory of application comes to life in the present.[32]

It is fruitless, therefore, to look for something to justify the metaphorical application of a predicate. The difference between literal and metaphorical can introduce dissymmetry in any way at all into compatible combinations. Are a person and a picture alike in being sad? Yet one is sad literally, the other metaphorically, according to the established usage of our language. If one still wishes, nevertheless, to speak of resemblance, one must join Max Black in saying that metaphor creates the resemblance rather than finding and expressing it.[33]

For a nominalist perspective, the problem posed by metaphorical application of predicates is no different from that posed by their literal application: 'The question why predicates apply as they do metaphorically is much the same as the question why they apply as they do literally' (78). Metaphorical sorting under a given schema conveys information just as a literal sorting does. Application in both cases 'is fallible and thus subject to correction' (79). Literal application is simply the one that has been endorsed by usage. This is why the question of truth is not restricted or peculiar. Only metaphorical application is peculiar; for extension in the application of a label or a schema must satisfy opposed demands – it must be new but fitting, strange but evident, surprising but satisfying. A simple 'labeling' does not equal a 're-sorting'; new discriminations, new organization must result from emigration of a schema.[34]

Finally, if all language, all symbolism consists in 'remaking reality,' there is no place in language where this work is more plainly and fully demonstrated. It is when symbolism breaks through its acquired limits and conquers new territory that we understand the breadth of its ordinary scope.

Two questions then occur with respect to the boundaries of the metaphorical phenomenon. The first concerns enumeration of 'modes' at the level of discourse. For Goodman as for Aristotle, metaphor is not one figure of discourse among others, but the transference principle common to all of them. If one's guideline is the notion of 'schema' or 'realm' rather than that of 'figure,' a first group will include all transfers from one realm to another, non-intersecting realm – thus, personification, from person to thing; synecdoche, from whole to part; antonomasia, from thing to property (or label). All transfers between intersecting realms will be put in a second group: upward displacement or hyperbole, downward displacement or litotes. A last group is kept for transfers that do not alter extension; here we have the reversing of irony (81-3).

Thus, Goodman takes the same route as other authors who, like Jean Cohen, subordinate taxonomy to functional analysis. Transference as such occupies the first level of consideration. Now it is merely an option of naming whether the general function or one of the figures is called metaphor. We saw earlier that everything that diminishes the role of resemblance also diminishes the singularity of metaphor the figure and reinforces the generality of metaphor as function.

The second question relative to the delimitation of the phenomenon of metaphor concerns the operation of the metaphorical function outside of verbal symbolism. We return here to our initial example, the sad expression of a painting. We find it at the end of a series of distinctions and linkages: (1) exemplification as the inverse of denotation, (2) possession as exemplification, (3) expression as the metaphorical transference of possession. Now this same series, denotation-exemplification-possession, must be considered not only in the order of verbal symbols and so in the order of description, but also in the order of non-verbal symbols (pictures, etc.), and thus in the order of representation. *Expression* is the name of a metaphorical possession of the representational order. In our example, the sad painting is a case of metaphorical possession of a representational 'sample,' which exemplifies a representational 'label.' In other words, 'what is expressed is metaphorically exemplified.'[35] The expression (sad), therefore, is no less real than the colour (blue). The fact that it is neither verbal nor literal, but representational and transferred, does not make the expression any less 'true,' so long as it is appropriate. Expression is not constituted by the effects on the spectator, for I can perceive the sadness of a picture without being made sad by it. 'Metaphorical importation' is able to make this predicate an acquired property; the expression is truly the possession of the thing. A painting expresses properties that it exemplifies metaphorically in virtue of its status as pictorial symbol: 'Pictures are no more immune than the rest of the world to the formative force of language even though they themselves, as symbols, also exert such a force upon the world, including language' (88).

In this way, *Languages of Art* solidly links verbal metaphor and non-verbal metaphorical expression to the plane of reference. Goodman succeeds in arranging the governing categories of reference in orderly fashion: denotation and exemplification (label and sample), description and representation (verbal and non-verbal symbols), possession and expression (literal and metaphorical).

I suggest the following assessment of Goodman's categories in application to the poetics of discourse:

(1) The distinction between denotation and connotation is not a fruitful principle of differentiation with respect to the poetic function, if connotation is understood as a set of associative and emotional effects without referential value. As a symbolic system, poetry has a referential function just as much as does descriptive discourse.

(2) The *sensa* – sounds, images, feelings – that adhere to the 'sense' are to be treated on the model of expression in Goodman's sense. These are representations and not descriptions, which exemplify instead of denoting and which transfer possession instead of retaining it by primordial right. Qualities in this sense are no less real than the descriptive traits that scientific discourse articulates; they belong to things over and above being effects subjectively experienced by the lover of poetry.

(3) Poetic qualities, through their status as transferred, add to the shaping of the world. They are 'true' to the extent that they are 'appropriate,' that is, to the extent that they join fittingness to novelty, obviousness to surprise.

On these three points, however, the analysis of Goodman calls for complements that will progressively turn into far-reaching alterations, in that they will affect his foundations in pragmatism and nominalism.

(1) Insufficient account is given of the strategy proper to poetic discourse, that of the *epoché* of descriptive reference. Goodman does proclaim the notion of a longstanding marriage that resists the initiation of a new and bigamous union, but he sees nothing in it except the resistance of habit to innovation. It seems to me that one must go further, up to the eclipse of one referential mode as the condition for the emergence of another referential mode. It is this eclipse of primary denotation that the theory of connotation had in view, without realizing that what it called connotation was still referential in its fashion.

(2) Poetic discourse faces reality by putting into play *heuristic fictions* whose constitutive value is proportional to their power of denial. Here again, Goodman offers a first step with his concept of null denotation, but he is too concerned to show that the *object* of null denotation serves to classify labels to see that precisely in this way, it helps redescribe reality. The theory of models will allow us to tighten the link between fiction and redescription.

(3) The 'appropriateness' of metaphorical as well as literal application of a predicate is not fully justified within a purely nominalist conception of language. Although such a conception has no trouble explaining the choreography of labels, since there is no essence to block re-labelling, it has greater difficulty accounting for the air of *rightness* that certain more fortunate instances of language and art seem to exude. To my mind, this is the place to part ways with Goodman's nominalism. Does not the fittingness, the appropriateness of certain verbal and non-verbal predicates, indicate that language not only has organized reality in a different way, but also made manifest a way of being of things, which is brought to language thanks to semantic innovation? It would seem that the enigma of metaphorical discourse is that it 'invents' in both senses of the word: what it creates, it discovers; and what it finds, it invents.

What must be understood, therefore, is the interconnection of three themes. In the metaphorical discourse of poetry referential power is linked to the eclipse of ordinary reference; the creation of heuristic fiction is the road to redescription; and reality brought to language unites manifestation and creation. This Study can explore the first two themes; it will be up to the eighth and final Study to clarify the conception of reality postulated by our theory of poetic language.

4 / MODEL AND METAPHOR

A detour through the theory of models constitutes the decisive stage in this Study. The idea of a kinship between model and metaphor is so fruitful that Max Black took it as the title of the collection containing 'Models and Archetypes,' the essay devoted specifically to this epistemological problem (the introduction of the concept of archetype will be explained later).[36]

The central argument is that, with respect to the relation to reality, metaphor is to poetic language what the model is to scientific language. Now in scientific language, the model is essentially a heuristic instrument that seeks, by means of fiction, to break down an inadequate interpretation and to lay the way for a new, more adequate interpretation. In the language of Mary Hesse,[37] another author close to Black, the model is an instrument of redescription. I will retain this expression for the duration of my analysis. Further, it is important to understand its meaning in its primitive epistemological usage.

The model belongs not to the logic of justification or proof, but to the logic of discovery. Again, it must be understood that this logic of discovery does not reduce to a psychology of invention without authentic epistemological interest but rather involves a cognitive process, a rational method with its own canons and principles.

The properly epistemological dimension of scientific imagination does not appear unless models are first distinguished according to their make-up and their function. Black arranges the hierarchy of models into three levels.

'Scale models' occupy the lowest level; examples are a model of a ship, enlargement of something very small (a limb of a mosquito), a slow-motion sketch of a manœuvre, simulation in miniature of social processes, etc. These are models in that they are models *of* something to which they refer in an asymmetrical relationship. Their purpose is to show how something looks, how it works, what laws govern it. It is possible to decode the model and, by reading off its properties, arrive at the properties of the original. Finally, only some features are relevant in a model, others are not. The model purports to be faithful only in respect to its relevant features. It is these relevant features that distinguish the scale model from other models. They are the counterparts of rules of interpretation that specify the way they are to be read. For everything with a spatial or temporal dimension, these conventions rest on partial identity of properties and invariance of proportions. For this reason, the scale model imitates its original, reproduces it. Black claims that the scale model corresponds to the 'icon' in Peirce. The scale model, through its sensible quality, adjusts what is too large or too small to our level and size.

At the second level Black situates *analogue models*: 'hydraulic models of economic systems, or the use of electrical circuits in computers,' etc. Two aspects are to be considered – change of medium, and representation of structure, that is, the 'web of relationships in an original.' Rules of interpretation determine the translation in this case from one system of relationships into another. The pertinent correlative traits of this translation constitute what in mathematics is called 'isomorphism.' The model and the original resemble each other in their structures and not through sensible features.

Identity of structure also characterizes *theoretical* models, which constitute the third level. However, one cannot point at them, nor are they to be constructed. They are not things at all; rather, they introduce a new language, like a dialect or idiom, in which the original is described without being constructed. An example would be Maxwell's 'representation of an electrical field in terms of the properties of an imaginary incompressible fluid.' The imaginary medium is here nothing more than a mnemonic device for grasping mathematical relationships. The important thing is not that one has something to view mentally, but that one can operate on an object that on the one hand is better known and in this sense more familiar, and on the other hand is full of implications and in this sense rich at the level of hypotheses.

The great interest of Black's analysis is that it escapes the alternative relative to the existential status of the model that seems to be imposed by the variations of Maxwell himself, the concretizing interpretations of ether by Lord Kelvin, and the savage rejection of models by Duhem. The issue is not whether and how the model exists, but what are the rules for interpretation of the theoretical model and, correspondingly, what are its pertinent features. The important point is that the model's only properties are those assigned to it by language convention, beyond any influence of a real construction. This is what the opposition between description and construction emphasizes: 'The heart of the method consists in *talking* in a certain way' (229). Its fruitfulness consists in our knowing how to make use of it; its 'deployability' – the expression is Stephen Toulmin's[38] – is its *raison-d'être*. To speak of intuitive grasp is only a shorthand way of indicating ease and rapidity in mastering the far-reaching implications of models. Recourse to scientific imagination in this regard does not signal a deflection of reason, distraction by images, but the essentially verbal power of trying out new relationships on a 'described model.' This imagination mingles with reason by virtue of the rules of correlation governing the translation of statements concerning the secondary domain into statements applicable to the original domain. Once more, it is the isomorphism of relationships that grounds the translatability of one idiom into another and, in so doing, provides the 'rationale' of the imagination (238). But the isomorphism does not hold now between the original domain and something constructed, but between that domain and something 'described.' Scientific imagination consists in seeing new connections via the detour of this thing that is 'described.' To remove the model from the logic of discovery, or even to reduce it to a provisional measure as the best substitute available for direct deduction, is ultimately to reduce the logic of discovery itself to a deductive procedure. The scientific ideal underlying this tendency, says Black, is finally that of 'Euclid as reformed by Hilbert' (235). The logic of discovery, let us say, is not a psychology of invention, because investigation is not deduction.

This epistemological outcome is highlighted well by Mary Hesse when she says that 'the deductive model of scientific explanation should be modified and supplemented by a view of theoretical explanation as metaphoric redescription of the domain of the *explanandum*' (249). This thesis incorporates two special emphases. The first applies to the word *explanation*. If the model, like metaphor, introduces a new language, its description equals explanation. This implies that the model operates precisely on the deductivist epistemological plane, modifying and completing the criteria of deductibility of scientific explanation as spelled out, for example, by Hempel and Oppenheim.[39] According to these criteria, it must be possible to deduce the *explanandum* from the *explanans*, which must contain at least one general law that is not redundant for the deduction; it must not yet have been empirically falsified; it must be predictive. Recourse to metaphorical redescription is a consequence of the impossibility of obtaining a strictly deductive relationship between *explanans* and *explanandum* – one can hope at most for an 'approximate fit' (257). This condition of acceptability is closer to the interaction at work in the metaphorical statement than is deductibility pure and simple. So too, the insertion of rules of correspondence between the *theoretical explanans* and the *explanandum* fits in with criticism of the ideal of deductibility; to have recourse to models is to interpret rules of correspondence in terms of extension of the language of observation through metaphorical usage. As for predictability, it cannot be conceived on a deductive model, as if general laws already present in the *explanans* were to incorporate events that are not yet observable, or as if the set of rules of correspondence were to need no addition. According to Mary Hesse in *Models and Analogies in Science*, there is no rational method for complementing the correspondence rules in a purely deductive way and for formulating new observational predicates. Prediction of new observational predicates requires a displacement of meanings and an extension of primitive observational language; so only the domain of the *explanandum* can be redescribed in the terminology transferred from the secondary system.

The second emphasis of the thesis of Mary Hesse focuses on the word *redescription*. This signifies that the ultimate problem posed by the use of models is 'the problem of metaphoric reference' (254-9). Things themselves are 'seen as'; they are *identified*, in a way that remains to be specified, with the descriptive character of the model. The *explanandum* as ultimate referent is itself changed by adoption of the metaphor. One must be willing, therefore, to reject the idea of an invariance of meaning with respect to the *explanandum* and move towards a 'realistic' view (256) of the theory of interaction. Not just our conception of rationality, but at the same time that of reality, is thrown open to question: as Hesse says, 'rationality consists just in the continuous adaptation of our language to our continually expanding world, and metaphor is one of the chief means by which this is accomplished' (259).

We will return later to the implications for the verb *to be* itself of this affirmation that things *are* 'as' described by the model.

What benefit does this detour through the theory of models bring to the theory of metaphor? The authors cited devote greater care to extending their original theory of metaphor to models than to considering the impact of their epistemological application to poetry. It is this reaction, the theory of models reflecting back on the theory of metaphor, that interests me here.

Extension of the theory of metaphor to that of models has other consequences besides confirmation of the principal traits of the original theory – interaction between secondary predicate and principal subject, cognitive value of the statement, production of new information, nontranslatability, inexhaustibility through paraphrase. The reduction of model to a psychic aid parallels the reduction of metaphor to a mere decorative process – misconception and recognition follow the same course in both cases. The procedure they possess in common is 'analogical transfer of a vocabulary' (Black 238).

The reflection of model back on metaphor results in exposure of new traits of metaphor not discovered in the foregoing analysis.

First of all, what on the poetic side corresponds exactly to the model is not precisely what we have called the 'metaphorical statement,' that is, a short bit of discourse reduced most often to a sentence. Rather, as the model consists in a complex network of statements, its exact analogue would be the extended metaphor – tale, allegory. What Toulmin calls the 'systematic deployability' of the model finds its equivalent in a metaphoric network and not in an isolated metaphor.

This first observation takes up the one made at the beginning of this Study, to the effect that it is the poetic work as a whole, the poem, that projects a world. The change of scale separating metaphor as a 'poem in miniature' (Beardsley) from the poem itself as an expanded metaphor calls for an examination of the constitution of the metaphoric universe as a network. The article by Max Black should be read in this context. The isomorphism that constitutes the 'rationale' of imagination in the use of models has its equivalent only in one kind of metaphor, which Black calls archetype (hence the title of the article, 'Models and Archetypes'). With this choice of terms, Black points out two aspects of certain metaphors, their 'radical' character and their 'systematic' character. Furthermore, these two aspects are linked; 'root metaphors,' to borrow the term of Stephen C. Pepper,[40] are also those that organize metaphors into networks (for example, in the work of Kurt Lewin, the network that inter-relates words like *field, vector, phase-space, tension, force, boundary, fluidity*, etc. – Black 241). By virtue of these two characteristics, the archetype has a less local, less pin-point existence than does metaphor; it covers an 'area' of experience or of facts.

The observation is excellent. We saw the need, with Nelson Goodman, to subordinate isolated 'figures' to 'schemas' that govern 'regions,' like that of sounds transferred in a group together to the visual order. It is to be expected that the referential function of metaphor should be carried by a metaphoric network rather than by an isolated metaphorical statement. (I prefer to speak of 'metaphoric network' rather than of 'archetype' because of the use of the latter term in Jungian psychoanalysis.) The paradigmatic power of these two kinds of metaphor comes as much from their 'radical' character as from their 'inter-connections.' To the simple idea of 'to see new connections,' a philosophy of imagination must add that of a break-through that is both profound and far-reaching, thanks to 'radical' and 'inter-connected' metaphors respectively (Black 237, 241).[41]

The second benefit of the detour via models is that it throws into relief the connection between heuristic function and description. This linkage suddenly takes us back to the *Poetics* of Aristotle. We recall how Aristotle linked *mimêsis* and *muthos* in his concept of tragic *poiêsis*.[42] Poetry, he said, is an imitation of human actions; but this *mimêsis* passes through creation of a plot, a tale, which shows signs of composition and order lacked by the dramas of everyday life. On these grounds, should not the relationship between *muthos* and *mimêsis* in tragic *poiêsis* be understood in the same way as that of heuristic fiction and redescription in the theory of models? In fact, tragic *muthos* evinces all the traits of 'radicality' and 'organization into a network' that Max Black accords to archetypes, that is, to metaphors with the same standing as models. Metaphoricity is a trait not only of *lexis* but of *muthos* itself; and, as in the case of models, this metaphoricity consists in describing a less known domain – human reality – in the light of relationships within a fictitious but better known domain – the tragic tale – utilizing all the strengths of 'systematic deployability' contained in that tale. As for *mimêsis*, it stops causing trouble and embarrassment when it is understood no longer in terms of 'copy' but of redescription. Both directions of the relationship between *muthos* and *mimêsis* must be appreciated: if tragedy achieves its effect of *mimêsis* only through the invention of the *muthos*, *muthos* is at the service of *mimêsis* and its fundamentally denotative character. In the terms used by Mary Hesse, *mimêsis* is the name of the 'metaphoric reference.' What Aristotle himself emphasized through this paradox is that poetry is closer to essence than is history, which is preoccupied with the accidental. Tragedy teaches us to 'see' human life 'as' that which the *muthos* displays. In other words, *mimêsis* constitutes the 'denotative' dimension of *muthos*.

This conjunction of *muthos* and *mimêsis* is not the work of tragic poetry alone. It is just easier to detect it there because, on the one hand, the *muthos* takes the form of a 'story' and the metaphoricity is attached to the plot of the tale, and because, on the other hand, the referent consists in human action which, due to its motivational course, has a certain affinity to the structure of the story. The conjunction of *muthos* and *mimêsis* is the work of all poetry. Let us recall Northrop Frye's linking of the poetic and the hypothetical. Now what is this 'hypothetical'? According to his perspective, poetic language, with its 'internal' and not 'outward' turn, constructs a mood, which has no existence outside the poem itself: this is what receives form from the poem as an arrangement of signs. Must we not say, first of all, that the mood is the hypothetical created by the poem, and that, as such, it occupies the place in lyric poetry that *muthos* occupies in tragic poetry? And ought we not to add that this lyric *muthos* is joined by a lyric *mimêsis*, in the sense that the mood created in this fashion is a sort of model for 'seeing as' and 'feeling as'? I will speak in this sense of lyric redescription, in order to introduce the fictive element highlighted by the theory of models into the heart of expression (in Goodman's sense). The feeling articulated by the poem is no less heuristic than the tragic tale. The 'internal' movement of the poem, therefore, could not be opposed purely and simply to 'outward' movement. What it signifies is only the disconnection of customary reference, the elevation of feeling to the hypthetical, and the creation of an affective fiction. But lyric *mimêsis*, which can be taken if desired as an 'outward' movement, is the very work of the lyric *muthos*; it is the consequence of the fact that the mood is no less heuristic than fiction in the form of a story. The paradox of the poetic can be summed up entirely in this, that the elevation of feeling to fiction is the condition of its mimetic use. Only a feeling transformed into myth can open and discover the world.

If this heuristic function of mood is so difficult to recognize, it is doubtless because 'representation' has become the sole route to knowledge and the model of every relationship between subject and object. Yet feeling has an ontological status different from relationship at a distance; it makes for participation in things.[43]

This is why the opposition between exterior and interior ceases to be valid here. Not being internal, feeling in like measure is not subjective. Metaphorical reference links rather with what Douglas Berggren calls 'poetic schemata of inner life' and 'the objectivity of poetic textures.'[44] By potetic schema he understands 'some visualizable phenomenon, whether actually observable or merely imagined, which serves as a vehicle for expressing something about the inner life of man, or non-spatial reality in general' (248); thus, for example, the 'lake of ice' at the bottom of Dante's *Inferno*.[45] To say with Frye that the poetic statement has a 'centripetal' direction is only to say how not to interpret the poetic schema, namely, in a cosmological fashion; but something is said about the sort of being of some spirits which, *in truth*, are of ice. Later I will discuss the meaning of the expression *in truth*, and will propose a *tensional* conception of metaphorical truth itself. It is enough for now to say that the poetic verb metaphorically 'schematizes' feelings or emotions only in depicting 'textures of the world,' 'non-human physiognomies,' which become actual portraits of our inner life. What Berggren calls 'textural reality' supports 'the schema of inner life,' which would be equivalent to those 'moods' that, for Northrop Frye, substitute for every referent. The 'joyous undulation of the waves' in Hölderlin's poem[46] is neither an objective reality in the positivist sense nor a mood in the emotivist sense. Such a contrast applies to a conception in which reality is first reduced to scientific objectivity. Poetic feeling in its metaphorical expressions bespeaks the lack of distinction between interior and exterior. The 'poetic textures' of the world (joyous undulations) and the 'poetic schemata' of interior life (lake of ice), mirroring one another, proclaim the reciprocity of the inner and the outer.

Metaphor raises this reciprocity from confusion and vagueness to bipolar tension. The intropathic fusion that precedes the conquest of subject-object duality is something different, as is the reconciliation that overcomes the opposition of subjective and objective.

The question of metaphorical truth has thus been raised. The meaning of the word *truth* is in question. The comparison of model and metaphor at least shows us the direction: as the conjunction of fiction and redescription suggests, poetic feeling itself also develops an experience of reality in which invention and discovery cease being opposed and where creation and revelation coincide. But what then does reality mean?

5 / TOWARDS THE CONCEPT OF 'METAPHORICAL TRUTH'

The discussion at hand has the following conclusions in view (the first and second merely record the advances made by the preceding discussion, whereas the third bears a consequence that calls for its own justification):

(1) The poetic function and the rhetorical function cannot be fully distinguished until the conjunction between fiction and redescription is brought to light. Each function now appears to be the other's inverse. The second seeks to persuade men by adorning discourse with pleasing ornaments; it is what emphasizes discourse in its own right. The first seeks to redescribe reality by the roundabout route of heuristic fiction.

(2) In service to the poetic function, metaphor is that strategy of discourse by which language divests itself of its function of direct description in order to reach the mythic level where its function of discovery is set free.

(3) We can presume to speak of metaphorical truth in order to designate the 'realistic' intention that belongs to the redescriptive power of poetic language.

This last conclusion needs clarification. In effect, it implies that the theory of tension (or of controversion), which has been the constant guiding thread of this investigation, might be extended to the referential relationship of the metaphorical statement to reality.

Three applications have in fact been given to the idea of tension:

(a) tension within the statement: between tenor and vehicle, between focus and frame, between principal subject and secondary subject;

(b) tension between two interpretations: between a literal interpretation that perishes at the hands of semantic impertinence and a metaphorical interpretation whose sense emerges through non-sense;

(c) tension in the relational function of the copula: between identity and difference in the interplay of resemblance.

These three applications of the idea of tension remain at the level of meaning immanent to the statement, even while the second involves a function external to the statement and the third already concerns the copula (but in its relational function). Our new application concerns reference itself and the claim of the metaphorical statement to reach reality in some particular manner. In the most radical terms possible, tension must be introduced into metaphorically affirmed being. When the poet says that 'nature is a temple where living columns ...' the verb *to be* does not just connect the predicate *temple* to the subject *nature* along the lines of the threefold tension outlined above. The copula is not only relational. It implies besides, by means of the predicative relationship, that *what is* is redescribed; it says *that* things really are this way. This is something we learned from Aristotle's treatise *On Interpretation*.

Are we now falling into a trap prepared for us by language, which, as Cassirer reminds us, does not go so far as to distinguish between two senses of the verb *to be*, the relational and the existential?[47] This would be the case if we were to take the verb *to be* itself in its literal sense. But is there not a metaphorical sense of the verb *to be* itself, in which the same tension would be preserved that we found first between words (between 'nature' and 'temple'), then between two interpretations (the literal and the metaphorical), and finally between identity and difference?

In order to elucidate this tension deep within the logical force of the verb *to be*, we must expose an 'is not,' itself implied in the impossibility of the literal interpretation, yet present as a filigree in the metaphorical 'is.' Thus, the tension would prevail between an 'is' and an 'is not.' This tension would not be marked grammatically in the example above. In any case, even if not marked, the 'is' of equivalence is distinct from the 'is' of determination ('the rose is red,' which is synecdochic in nature). That distinction, characteristic of the metaphorical process, issues from the *Rhétorique générale* of the Groupe de Liège.[48]

So it is not just the compared terms that are affected by this process, nor even the copula in its referential function, but the existential function of the verb *to be*. The same must be said of the 'to be like (or as)' of explicit metaphor or simile, which ancient rhetoric, in a departure from Aristotle, took to be the canonical form of which metaphor would be the abbreviation. 'To be like/as' must be treated as a metaphorical modality of the copula itself; the 'like/as' is not just the comparative term among all the terms, but is included in the verb *to be*, whose force it alters. In other words, the 'like/as' must be brought alongside the copula, as in 'her cheeks *are-like* roses' (one of the examples of the *Rhétorique générale*, 114). In this way, we would remain faithful to the tradition of Aristotle, which was not followed by later rhetoric. As we recall, for Aristotle metaphor is not an abbreviated simile, but simile is a weakened metaphor. Our primary focus, therefore, must truly be on the 'is' of equivalence. And my reason for trying to pinpoint within the very force of the verb *to be* that tension given three other applications by the preceding analysis is to distinguish its use from the 'is' of determination.

The question may be formulated in the following manner: does not the tension that affects the copula in its relational function also affect the copula in its existential function? This question contains the key to the notion of *metaphorical truth*.

In order to demonstrate this 'tensional' conception of metaphorical truth, I will proceed dialectically. First, I will point out the inadequacy of an interpretation that gives in to ontological *naïveté* in the evaluation of metaphorical truth because it ignores the implicit 'is not.' I will then portray the inadequacy of an inverse interpretation that, under the critical pressure of the 'is not,' loses the 'is' by reducing it to the 'as-if' of a reflective judgment.

The legitimation of the concept of metaphorical truth, which preserves the 'is not' within the 'is,' will proceed from the convergence of these two critiques.

Prior to any properly ontological interpretation, like the one we will try to initiate in the eighth Study, we will restrict ourselves to a dialectical discussion of opinions, as Aristotle does at the beginning of his analyses of 'first philosophy.'

(a) The first tendency – naïve and uncritical – is that of ontological *vehemence*. I will not renounce it, I will only mediate it. Without it, the critical moment would be weak. To state 'that is' – such is the moment of *belief*, of *ontological commitment*, which gives affirmation its 'illocutionary' force. There is no better testimony to this affirmative vehemence than the poetic experience. Along one of its dimensions, at least, this experience expresses the *ecstatic* moment of language – language going beyond itself. It seems, accordingly, to attest that discourse prefers to obliterate itself, to die, at the confines of the being-said.

Can philosophy take account of the non-philosophy of ecstasy? And at what price?

In a mélange of non-philosophy and Schellingian philosophy, Coleridge proclaims the *quasi-vegetal* power of imagination, concentrated in the symbol, to draw us to the growth of things: 'While it enunciates the whole, [a symbol] abides itself as a living part of that unity of which it is the representative.'[49] Thus, metaphor accomplishes an exchange between poet and world, thanks to which individual life and universal life grow together. In this way, the growth of plants becomes the metaphor for metaphorical truth, being itself 'a symbol established in the truth of things' (Coleridge in Richards 111). Just as the plant reaches towards the light and into the earth and draws its growth from them, and just as 'it becomes the visible *organismus* of the whole silent or elementary life of nature and therefore, in incorporating the one extreme becomes the symbol of the other; the natural symbol of that higher life of reason' (ibid.), so too the poetic verb enjoins us to participate in the totality of things via an 'open communion.' And all this moves I.A. Richards to repeat a question posed much earlier by Coleridge: 'Are not words parts and germinations of the plant?' (112).

Thus, the price that philosophy pays for countenancing poetic ecstasy is the reintroduction of philosophy of nature into philosophy of spirit, along the lines of Schelling's philosophy of mythology. But then imagination, according to the vegetal metaphor, is no longer the fundamentally discursive blending of identity and difference that we discussed earlier (Study 6). The ontology of 'correspondences' seeks support in the 'sympathetic' attractions of nature, prior to the interposition of dissecting understanding.

Coleridge combined philosophy with non-philosophy. With Bergson, the unity of vision and life is carried to the pinnacle of philosophy. The philosophical character of his enterprise is preserved by the critique of critique, through which understanding reflecting back on itself creates its own process. Thus, the status of the image is established by a proof *a contrario*, through the interconnection between conceptual atomization, spatial dispersion, and pragmatic interest. So too, the superiority of image over concept, the priority of undivided temporal flux over space, and the disinterestedness of the vision turned towards life's concerns are to be restored together. And it is in a philosophy of life that the pact between image, time, and contemplation is sealed.

There is one particular theory of literary criticism, influenced by Schelling, Coleridge, and Bergson, that tries to give an account of this ecstatic moment of poetic language.[50] We owe several romantic pleas focused specifically on metaphor to this critique. One of the most worthy is that of Wheelwright in *The Burning Fountain* and *Metaphor and Reality*. The author does not limit himself to connecting his ontology to generalized considerations concerning the power of imagination; he ties it closely to traits privileged by his semantics. These traits call directly for expression in terms of life. Language, says the author, is 'tensive' and 'alive.' He plays on all the contrasts between perspective and openness, designation and suggestion, imagery and significance, concreteness and plural signification, precision and affective resonance, etc. More particularly, this 'tensive' character of language is focused in metaphor, as opposed to 'epiphor' and 'diaphor': epiphor juxtaposes and fuses terms by means of immediate assimilation at the level of the image, whereas diaphor proceeds mediately and through combination of discrete terms. Metaphor is the tension between epiphor and diaphor. This tension guarantees the very transference of meaning and gives poetic language its characteristic of semantic 'plus-value,' its capacity to be open towards new aspects, new dimensions, new horizons of meaning.

Hence, all these traits call for expression directly in terms of life – 'living,' 'alive,' 'intense.' In the expression *tensive aliveness*[51] (which I will put to my own use, but in a rather different sense), the accent is put on the vital rather than the logical aspect of tension; 'connotative fullness' and 'tensive aliveness' are opposed to the rigidity, the coldness, the deadening effect of 'steno-language.'[52] 'Fluid-language' contrasts here with 'block-language,' which triumphs with the abstractions shared by several minds due to habit or convention. This is a language that has lost its 'tensional ambiguities,' its 'fluid uncaptured meanings.'[53]

These are the semantic marks of the affinity of 'tensive' language with a reality that presents corresponding ontological traits. Indeed, Wheelwright has no doubt that man, given that he is alert, has a constant concern for 'What Is.'[54] The reality brought to language by metaphor is termed 'presential and tensive'; 'coalescent and interpenetrative'; 'perspectival and hence latent'; in brief, 'revealing itself only partially, ambiguously, and through symbolic indirection' (154). Indistinctness bathes all these traits – presence is inflamed by a 'responsive-imaginative' act (156) and itself responds to this response in a sort of encounter. The author allows, it is true, that this sense of presence does not go unchallenged; but he adds right away that these contrastive elements are subordinated to the totality in view. As for 'coalescence,' Wheelwright opposes it to the selectivity of intelligence, which leads to the dichotomies of objective and subjective, physical and spiritual, particular and universal. The 'plus-value' of poetic expression causes each term to participate in its opposite, to metamorphose into it. Language itself, through the passage achieved in this way from one meaning to another, evokes 'something of a metaphorical character in the world which it [the poem] salutes' (169). Finally, the 'perpectival' character of poetic language evokes the excess that surpasses the angle of vision. Is this not what Heraclitus suggests when he says: 'The Lord whose oracle is at Delphi neither speaks nor conceals, but gives signs'? With the Hindu *guru* of the Upanishads, must we not whisper *'neti-neti,'* 'not quite that, not quite that'? Lastly, broaching the 'poeto-ontological question,' the author is quite agreeable to see his 'metapoetics' as an 'ontology not so much of concepts as of poetic sensitivity' (152, 20).

It is astonishing that Wheelwright should be brought quite close to a tensional conception of truth itself by his semantic conception of the tension between diaphor and epiphor. But the dialectical inclination of his theory is dissipated by the intuitionist and vitalist tendency that takes him finally into the metapoetics of the 'What Is.'

(b) The dialectical counterpart of ontological *naïveté* is presented by Turbayne in *The Myth of Metaphor*. He attempts to delimit the valid 'use' of metaphor by taking 'abuse' as his critical theme. Abuse is the 'myth' of his title, in a more epistemological than ethnological sense, scarcely differing from what we just called ontological *naïveté*. The myth, in fact, is 'believed poetry' – metaphor taken literally, I would put it. Now, there is something in the use of metaphor that inclines it towards abuse, and so towards myth.

What is this? Let us look back at Turbayne's semantic foundations (discussed above, Study 4). Metaphor is close to what Gilbert Ryle calls category mistake, which consists in presenting facts belonging to one category in idioms appropriate to another. Metaphor too is a calculated error, a 'sort-crossing.' The author builds his referential theory on this semantic base, where the inappropriateness of metaphorical attribution is underlined more strongly than the new semantic pertinence. Turbayne alleges that belief is led by a spontaneous movement from a 'pretence' that something is so, although such is not the case (13), to the corresponding 'intention' – I *in*tend what I *pre*tend (15) – and thence, from the intention, to 'make-believe' (17). Thus sort-crossing becomes a sort-trespassing, category-fusion becomes category-confusion (22); and belief, taken up in its pretending, is converted subtly into 'make-believe.'

Therefore, what earlier we called heuristic fiction is not an innocent pretence. It tends to lose sight of its nature as fiction and take on the dimensions of perceptual belief (this is close to how Spinoza described belief in countering Descartes: so long as imagination has not been limited and denied, it is indistinguishable from true belief). It is notable that the absence of grammatical markings serves here as a warning regarding this shift in belief. There is no grammatical feature that distinguishes metaphorical attribution from literal attribution. For example, grammar makes no distinction between Churchill's calling Mussolini 'That utensil!' and the use of the same phrase in a frying-pan advertisement (14); only the impossibility of taking the algebraic sum of the two statements raises our suspicion. Not marking the difference, and, in this sense, hiding it, is precisely the trap that grammar sets. This is why a critical instance must be applied to the statement in order to flush out the unmarked 'as if,' that is, the virtual mark of the 'pretence' immanent within the 'believe' and the 'make-believe.'

This dissimulative trait – one might almost say 'bad faith,' except that Turbayne does not use those terms – calls for a critical rejoinder. A line of demarcation should be drawn between 'to use' and 'to be used,' lest we fall victim to metaphor, mistaking the mask for the face. In brief, we must 'expose' metaphor, unmask it. This proximity between use and abuse leads to a correction of the metaphors about metaphor. We have spoken of transference or transporting. That is true: facts are reallocated by metaphor; but such reallocation is also a misallocation. Metaphor has been compared to a filter, a screen, and a lens, in order to say that it places things under a perspective and instructs us to 'see as ...' Yet it is also a mask that disguises. It was said that metaphor integrates diversity; but it also leads to categorial confusion. It was said that it 'stands for ...'; it must be said as well that it is 'taken for.'

But what is it to 'ex-pose' metaphor (54-70)? It must be noted that Turbayne is more inclined to reflect on scientific models than on poetic metaphors. This certainly does not disqualify his contribution to the concept of metaphorical truth, since, as we ourselves agreed above, the referential function of models is itself a model for the referential function of metaphor. But there is a strong possibility that the nature of critical vigilance differs from one situation to the other. Indeed, the examples of epistemological 'myths' are scientific theories where the index of the heuristic fiction has always been lost to view. Accordingly, Turbayne discusses at length the reification of mechanical models in Descartes and Newton, that is, their immediate ontological interpretation. The tension between metaphorical and literal, therefore, is absent from the very start. On this basis, 'to explode a myth' is to expose the model as metaphor.

Turbayne thus takes up the old tradition that began with Bacon denouncing the 'idols of the theatre' 'because in my judgment all the received systems are but so many stage-plays representing worlds of the creation ... which by tradition, credulity, and negligence have come to be received.'[55]

Nevertheless, this does not abolish metaphorical language. Quite the contrary, it confirms it, while adjoining to it the critical index of the 'as if.' It is not in fact possible to present 'the literal truth,' to say 'what the facts are,' as logical empiricism demands; every 'attempt to re-allocate the facts by restoring them to where they "actually belong" is vain' (64). 'We cannot say what reality is, only what it seems like to us' (ibid.). If there can be a non-mythic state, there can be no non-metaphorical state of language. So there is no other issue than to 'replace the masks,' but to do so consciously. We will not say 'non fingo hypotheses' but 'I feign hypotheses.' In brief, critical consciousness of the distinction between use and abuse leads not to disuse but to re-use of metaphors, in the endless search for other metaphors, namely a metaphor that would be the best one possible.

The limitations of Turbayne's thesis have to do with the specificity of his examples, which concern precisely that which is least transposible from models to metaphor.

In the first place, the author installs himself in an order of reality homogeneous with that of the positivism criticized by his thesis. The concern is always with 'facts' and therefore also with truth in a verificationist sense, and this is not fundamentally altered. There is no escaping this ultimately neo-empiricist character of the thesis, if we consider that the examples of model-metaphors are borrowed not from restricted areas of physics but from the order of meta-scientific world views, where the border between model and scientific myth tends to be erased, as we know since the *Timaeus* of Plato. The mechanicism of Descartes and that of Newton are cosmological hypotheses that are universal in character. The question is precisely whether poetic language does not break through to a pre-scientific, ante-predicative level, where the very notions of fact, object, reality, and truth, as delimited by epistemology, are *called into question* by this very means of the vacillation of literal reference.

Furthermore, the author speaks of a mastery of models that is not to be found in poetic experience, where something other than the poet speaks even as he speaks, and where, beyond the control of the poet, a reality comes to language. Turbayne's metaphor still belongs to the order of the manipulable. It is something we choose to use, to not use, to re-use. This power to decide, coextensive with the absolute hold of the 'as if,' is without analogue on the side of poetic experience, in which imagination is 'bound' (according to the description by Marcus Hester). It is difficult to harmonize this experience of being seized, instead of seizing, with the deliberate mastery of the 'as if.' The problem afflicting Turbayne is that of demythologized myth: does it still have its power as speech? Is there something like metaphor-faith beyond demythologization? A second *naïveté* beyond iconoclasm? The question requires different replies for epistemology and for poetry. A lucid, mastered, concerted employment of models may be conceivable, even though it seems difficult to maintain the ontological abstinence of the 'as if' without believing in the descriptive and representative value of the model. The experience of creation in poetry seems truly to ignore the lucidity required for any philosophy of the 'as if.'

These two limits appear truly to be related. The kind of vision that, *a parte rei*, penetrates beyond 'facts' dissected by methodology, and the kind of self-implication that, *a parte subjecti*, escapes the vigilance of the 'as if,' together designate the two faces of an experience of creation in which the creative dimension of language is consonant with the creative aspects of reality itself. Can one create metaphors without believing them and without believing that, in a certain way, 'that is'? So it is the relationship itself, and not just its extremes, that is at issue: it is still the correspondence concept of truth that rules between the 'as if' of self-conscious hypothesis and the facts 'as they seem to us.' It is only modulated by the 'as if,' without being altered in its basic definition.

(c) My twofold critique of Wheelwright and Turbayne is very close to that of Douglas Berggren in 'The Use and Abuse of Metaphor,' to which my own owes a great deal. No other author to my knowledge has gone as far in the direction of the concept of metaphorical truth. Not content, indeed, with recapitulating the principal theses of the theory of tension, Berggren tries to arbitrate (as I do too) between ontological *naïveté* and the critique of mythified metaphor. Thus he carries the tensional theory of the internal

semantics of the statement forward to the subject of truth and dares to
speak of the tension between metaphorical truth and literal truth (245).
Earlier I used his combined analysis of 'poetic schemata' and 'poetic textures,' the first offering the portrait of interior life and the second the
physiognomy of the world. What I did not say then is that for Berggren,
these tensions affect not only the meaning but also the truth-value of
poetic assertions concerning 'inner life' schematized in this way, and concerning 'textural reality.' Poets themselves, he says, 'often seem to think
that they are making what are in some sense true assertions' (249). In
which sense? Wheelwright is not wrong to speak of 'presential reality,' but
he neglects to distinguish poetic truth from mythic absurdity. He who
does so much to have the 'tensional' character of language recognized
misses the 'tensional' character of truth, by simply substituting one notion
of truth for another; accordingly, he goes over to the side of abuse by ap-
proximating poetic textures simply to primitive animism.

But the poet himself does not commit this error; he 'preserves the ordinary differences between the principal and subsidiary subjects of his metaphors, even while such referents are also being transformed by the process
of metaphorical construing' (252). Again, 'unlike the child and the primitive native, the poet does not mythically confuse the textural feel-of-things
with actual things-of-feeling' (255). 'It is only by the use of textural metaphor that the poetic feel-of-things can in a sense be liberated from prosaic
things-of-feeling, or be properly discussed' (ibid.). This is why the phenomenological objectivity of what commonly is called emotion or feeling is
inseparable from the tensional structure of the truth of metaphorical statements that express the construction of the world by and with feeling. The
possibility of textural reality is correlative to the possibility of a metaphorical truth of poetic schemata; the possibility of one is established at the
same time as that of the other (257).

And so the convergence of the two internal critiques, that of ontological *naïveté* and that of demythologization, culminates in a reiteration of
the thesis of the 'tensional' character of metaphorical truth and of the 'is'
that carries affirmation. I do not say that this twofold critique proves the
thesis. The internal critique only helps us recognize the assumptions and
commitments of one who speaks and uses the verb *to be* metaphorically.
At the same time, it underlines the inescapably paradoxical character surrounding a metaphorical concept of truth. The paradox consists in the fact
there there is no other way to do justice to the notion of metaphorical
truth than to include the critical incision of the (literal) 'is not' within the
ontological vehemence of the (metaphorical) 'is.' In doing so, the thesis
merely draws the most extreme consequence of the theory of tension. In
the same way that logical distance is preserved in metaphorical proximity,

and in the same way as the impossible literal interpretation is not simply abolished by the metaphorical interpretation but submits to it while resisting, so the ontological affirmation obeys the principle of tension and the law of 'stereoscopic vision.'[56] It is this tensional constitution of the verb *to be* that receives its grammatical mark in the 'to be like' of metaphor elaborated into simile, at the same time as the tension between *same* and *other* is marked in the relational copula.

Now, what are the repercussions of such a concept of metaphorical truth on the very definition of reality? This question, constituting the ultimate horizon of the present Study, will be the object of the next inquiry. For it falls to speculative discourse to articulate, with its own resources, what is assumed spontaneously by the storyteller who, according to Roman Jakobson,[57] 'marks' the poetic intention of his tales by saying 'Aixo era y no era.'

Metaphor and philosophical discourse

For Jean Ladrière

The final Study in this collection sets out to explore the philosophical confines of an investigation that, in its passage to the plane of hermeneutics, has seen its centre of gravity shift from rhetoric to semantics and from problems of sense to problems of reference. The last shift involved, in the form of postulates, a certain number of philosophical presuppositions. Now, no discourse can claim to be free of presuppositions for the simple reason that the conceptual operation by which a region of thought is thematized brings operative concepts into play, which cannot themselves be thematized at the same time. No discourse can be radically stripped of presuppositions; nevertheless, no thinker is dispensed from clarifying his presuppositions as far as he is able. We began to do this at the beginning of the preceding Study, when we put forward the semantic and the hermeneutic postulates functioning in the theory of metaphorical reference. At the end of the same Study, these postulates justified our carrying the ontological aim of metaphorical utterance back to the copula, understood in the sense of *being-as.* These postulates have still to be thematized in themselves. The question, therefore, is this: *what* philosophy is *implied* in the movement that carries the investigation from rhetoric to semantics and from sense towards reference? The question appears simple; actually it is twofold. We are asking, in fact, both whether a philosophy is *implied* – and *which one.* The strategy of the present Study will be to pursue our inquiry into both questions simultaneously. The question of the *ontology* to be made explicit will accompany the question of the *implication* at work in the interplay of implicit and explicit.

The second question, more deeply hidden from us, requires a global decision concerning the collective unity of modes of discourse as modes of use, such as poetic discourse, scientific discourse, religious discourse, speculative discourse, and so on. Taking the notion of discursiveness as such as our theme, I should like to plead for a relative pluralism of forms and levels of discourse. Without going as far as the notion, suggested by Wittgenstein, of a radical heterogeneity of language games – which would exclude the very cases of interaction with which the closing part of this Study will be concerned – it is important to recognize in principle the *discontinuity* that assures the autonomy of speculative discourse.

It is only on the basis of this difference in discourse, established by the philosophical act as such, that we can elaborate the modalities of interaction or, more precisely, of interanimation between modes of discourse required for the task of making explicit the ontology that underlies our investigation.

The first three sections argue for discontinuity between speculative discourse and poetic discourse, and are a refutation of some of the ways in which, in our opinion, the implication binding metaphorical and speculative discourse is misunderstood.

(1) A philosophy could be said to be *brought about* by metaphorical functioning, if one could show that it simply reproduced the semantic workings of poetic discourse on the speculative plane. We shall take as our touchstone the Aristotelian doctrine of the analogical unity of the multiple meanings of being, ancestor of the medieval doctrine of the analogy of being. Aristotle's doctrine will provide the occasion for showing that there is no direct passage from the semantic functioning of metaphorical expression to the transcendental doctrine of analogy. On the contrary, the latter furnishes a particularly striking example of the autonomy of philosophical discourse.

(2) If categorial discourse leaves no place for any transition from poetic metaphor to transcendental equivocalness, is it the union of philosophy and theology in a composite discourse that creates the conditions for a confusion between analogy and metaphor, and therefore the conditions for an implication that would be only a *subreption*, to borrow Kant's expression? The Thomist doctrine of the analogy of being is an excellent counter-example for our thesis of the discontinuity of modes of discourse. If it can be shown that the composite discourse of onto-theology allows no confusion with poetic discourse, the way is opened for an examination of figures of intersection that presuppose the difference in modes of discourse, primarily a difference between the speculative mode and the poetic mode.

(3) A completely different – even inverse – manner of involving philosophy in the theory of metaphor must also be considered. It is the inverse of that investigated in the two earlier sections in so far as it establishes philosophical presuppositions at the very source of the distinctions that make a discourse on metaphor possible. This hypothesis does more than reverse the order of priority between metaphor and philosophy: it reverses the

pattern of philosophical argumentation. Our earlier discussion will be seen to have been situated at the level of the stated intentions of speculative – even onto-theological – discourse, and thus to have had at issue only the order of its argumentation. For another 'reading,' it is the undeclared movement of philosophy and the unseen play of metaphor that are in complicity. Instructed by Heidegger's assertion that *'the metaphorical exists only inside the metaphysical,'* we shall take Jacques Derrida's essay 'White Mythology' as our guide in this 'second navigation.' This is indeed a second navigation: the pivotal point of the discussion will shift in fact from living metaphor to *dead metaphor*, metaphor that is not declared but hidden in the 'elevation' of the concept that is expressed as such. Basing my analysis on the preceding Studies, I hope to show that the problematic of the dead metaphor is derivative, and that the required response is to climb back up the slope of this sort of entropy of language by means of a new act of discourse. Only revivifying the semantic aim of metaphorical utterance in this way can recreate the conditions that will permit a confrontation that is itself enlivening between the modes of discourse fully recognized in their difference.

(4) It is to this interanimation of philosophical and poetic discourse that I should like to contribute in the two final stages of this investigation. Taking first the perspective of the phenomenology of semantic aims, I shall attempt to show that the possibility of speculative discourse lies in the semantic dynamism of metaphorical expression, and yet that speculative discourse can respond to the semantic potentialities of metaphor only by providing it with the resources of a domain of articulation that properly belongs to speculative discourse by reason of its very constitution.

(5) We can hope to clarify the postulates of reference assumed in Study 7 only through a labour of speculative discourse turned back upon itself and spurred on by metaphorical utterance. I shall try to say in what way the concepts of truth and reality, and ultimately the concept of being, have to be reworked in order to respond to the semantic claim of metaphorical utterance.

1 / METAPHOR AND THE EQUIVOCALNESS OF BEING: ARISTOTLE

The first *counter-example* opposing our initial hypothesis – that philosophical and poetic discourse are different – is provided by the type of speculation that Aristotle was the first to apply to the anological unity of the multiple meanings of being. The question can be put this way: whenever philosophy tries to introduce an intermediate modality between *univocity* and *equivocalness*, is speculative discourse not forced to reproduce, on its own level, the semantic functioning of poetic discourse? If this were the case, speculative discourse would be brought about or *induced* in some way by poetic discourse. The very vocabulary used supports the hypothesis of an initial confusion of kinds. The word *analogy* seems to belong to both discourses. In poetics, analogy in the sense of 'proportion' is at the root of the fourth class of metaphor, which Aristotle termed metaphor 'by analogy' (or, in some translations, 'proportional' metaphor). To this day, some theorists do not hesitate to subsume metaphor and simile under the generic term of analogy, or to place the family of metaphor under this common heading. In philosophy, this same word is at the centre of a certain discourse that claims its source in Aristotle and continues through the neo-Thomists.

I should like to show that, contrary to appearances, the intellectual labour that later crystallized in the concept of the analogy of being stems from an initial divergence between speculative and poetic discourse. I shall reserve for the second stage of the discussion the question whether it was possible to preserve this initial difference in the mixed forms to which discourse on God gave rise in philosophy and theology.

It is necessary therefore to begin at the greatest point of divergence between philosophy and poetry, the position established by Aristotle in the treatise on the *Categories* and in books Γ, E, Z, and Λ of the *Metaphysics*.

The *Categories*, in which the term *analogy* does not actually appear, produces a non-poetic model of equivocalness and thus suggests the necessary conditions for a non-metaphorical theory of analogy. Since Aristotle, through the neo-Platonists and the Arab and Christian medieval philosophers, down to Kant, Hegel, Renouvier, and Hamelin, this act of ordering that the *Categories* represents has remained the perennial signal task of speculative discourse. But the *Categories* raises its question of the connection between the meanings of being only because the *Metaphysics* poses the question that breaks with poetic discourse just as with ordinary discourse – what is being?

This question is entirely outside the bounds of all language games. For this reason, when the philosopher is confronted by the paradox that 'being is said in several ways' and when, in order to rescue the diverse meanings of being from dispersal, he establishes between them a relation of reference to a first term that is neither the univocity of a genus nor the mere chance equivocalness of a simple word, the plurivocity that is thus brought to philosophical discourse is of a different order than the multiplicity of meaning produced by metaphorical utterance. It is a plurivocity of the same order as the very question that opened up the speculative field. The first term – *ousia* – places all the other terms in the realm of meaning outlined by the question: what is being? For the moment, it is of little importance whether these other terms are in a relation to the first term that could, justly or not, be called analogy. What is important is that a connection be identified among the multiple meanings of being, one which, though not proceeding from the division of a genus into species, nevertheless constitutes an order. This order is an order of categories, to the extent that it is the necessary condition for the ordered extension of the sphere of attribution. The regulated polysemy of being orders the apparently disordered polysemy of the predicative function as such. In the same way that categories other than substance can be 'predicated' of substance and thus add to the first meaning of being, so too, for every given being, the sphere of predication presents the same concentric structure extending progressively farther from a 'substantial' centre, and the same expansion of meaning through the addition of determinations. This ordered process has nothing in common with metaphor, not even with analogical metaphor. The ordered equivocalness of being and poetic equivocalness move on radically distinct levels. Philosophical discourse sets itself up as the vigilant watchman overseeing the ordered extensions of meaning; against this background, the unfettered extensions of meaning in poetic discourse spring free.

The lack of a common point of contact between the ordered equivocalness of being and poetic metaphor is attested to indirectly by the charge Aristotle levelled at Plato. Ordered equivocalness is to be substituted for Platonic participation, which is only metaphorical: 'And to say that [the Forms] are patterns and the other things share in them is to use empty words and poetical metaphors' (*Metaphysics* A 9, 991 a 19-22). Thus philosophy must neither use metaphors nor speak poetically, not even when it deals with the equivocal meanings of being. But can it help doing what it must not do?

It has been argued that the Aristotelian treatise on the *Categories* forms a self-contained position only to the extent that it is supported by a concept of analogy that is itself compelled to draw its logical force from a domain other than the speculative order. But it can be shown that these objections prove at most that the *Categories* should be reworked, doubtless on a basis other than that of analogy; however, they do not prove that the semantic aim guiding the treatise is borrowed from a field other than the speculative.

First, one may object that the alleged categories of thought are only categories of language in disguise. This is the contention of E. Benveniste.[1] Beginning with the general claim that 'linguistic form is not only the condition for transmissibility, but first of all the condition for the realization of thought' (56), the author attempts to demonstrate that Aristotle, 'reasoning in the absolute, is simply identifying certain fundamental categories of the language in which he thought' (57).[2]

The correlation established by Benveniste is irrefutable as long as one is considering only the passage from Aristotle's categories as enumerated by him to the categories of language. But what about the inverse path? For Benveniste, the entire table of the categories of thought is merely 'transposed from categories of language' (61), 'the conceptual projection of a given linguistic state' (ibid.). As for the notion of *being* 'which envelops everything,' this concept 'reflects' (ibid.) the wealth of uses of the verb *to be*.

Evoking 'the magnificent images of the poem of Parmenides as well as the dialectic of *The Sophist*' (61), however, the linguist is forced to concede that 'the language did not, of course, give direction to metaphysical definition of "being" – each Greek thinker has his own – but it made it possible to set up "being" as an objectifiable notion that philosophical thought could handle, analyze and define just as any other concept' (62). And again: 'All we wish to show here is that the linguistic structure of Greek predisposed the notion of "being" to a philosophical vocation' (63).

The problem is then to understand what principle of philosophical thought, applied to grammatical being, produces the series of meanings of the term *to be*. Between what would be merely a list and what would be a deduction in the Kantian sense, there is room for an ordering, which in the post-Aristotelian tradition – and even in a few rare suggestions by Aristotle himself – came to be thought of as analogy.

Jules Vuillemin demonstrates in the second study of his work *De la logique à la théologie: Cinq études sur Aristote*[3] that the Aristotelian treatise on the *Categories* has a logical construction and that in grasping this, 'one will perhaps find the thread of Aristotelian deduction, which up to now seems to have escaped analysis' (77).

It is not without importance that the treatise on the *Categories* begins with a semantic distinction that, instead of marking a dichotomy, makes room for a ·third class. In addition to things that have only the name (*onoma*) in common but not the notion (*logos*), which Aristotle calls homonyms, and those that share both a common name and a notional identity – synonyms – there are also paronyms, that is, those things that derive their name from some other name, but differ from it in termination (*ptōsis*). Thus the grammarian derives his name from the word *grammar*, and the courageous man from the word *courage* (*Categories* 1 a 12-15). Here for the first time an intermediate class is inserted between homonymous and synonymous items, and consequently between expressions that are merely equivocal and expressions that are absolutely univocal. The entire following analysis will attempt to widen the gap opened up by paronyms in the solid front of equivocalness and to lift the general ban on equivocalness laid by one of Aristotle's own theses, namely that 'to mean more than one thing is to mean nothing at all.'

There would be no point to this distinction, which still refers to things named and not directly to meanings, if it did not shed light on the formal organization of the table of categories. In fact, the decisive distinction, introduced in the second paragraph of the treatise, is the one that opposes and combines two senses of the copula *is*: namely, *being-said of* (thus man, secondary substance, is said of Socrates, primary substance) and *being-in* (for example, musician, accident of the substance Socrates). This key distinction, around which the rest of the treatise is organized, makes the distinction between synonyms and paronyms functional: only the relation *said-of* allows synonymous attribution (the particular man is identically man).[4]

We said above that the two senses of the copula involved in the relations *being-said-of* and *being-in* are both opposed and combined. Indeed, by arranging these two features in a table noting absence and presence, one can derive four classes of substantives, two concrete (Socrates, man) and two abstract (a certain white, science). Aristotelian morphology is thus based on the intersection of two fundamental oppositions: the opposition of particular to general, which permits predication in the strict sense (*being-said of*) and that of concrete to abstract (which permits predication in the broad sense). The first opposition, understood in the realist sense, founds the irreducible obscurity of the copula, bound to the materiality of individual substances (with the exception of separate beings). The second opposition, understood in a conceptualist sense, replaces the alleged participation of Platonic ideas, which Aristotle denounced as simply metaphorical. The abstract is in the concrete potentially; its inherence too is tied to the obscure ground of individual substances.

How does analogy enter into this, if not explicitly (since the word is never mentioned), at least implicitly? Its avenue is this, that as the modalities of the copula become more varied, they progressively weaken the sense of the copula in the passage from primordial, essential predication – which alone is held to have a synonymous sense – towards derived, accidental predication.[5] A correlation suggests itself, therefore, between the distinction made in the *Categories* on the level of morphology and predication, and the great passage of *Metaphysics* Γ on the reference of all categories to a first term, texts read by medieval thinkers within the framework of the analogy of being. This correlation is set forth in *Metaphysics* Z, the text *par excellence* on substance, which explicitly relates the various forms of predication – and hence the categories – to possible equivocation in regard to the first category, *ousia*.[6] But it is because 'predication can be interpreted neither as the relation of element to set nor as the relation of part to whole' that it remains 'an ultimate intuitive given, whose meaning moves from inherence to proportion and from proportion to proportionality.'[7] It is this outcome that we shall consider later when we examine the passage from the analogy of proportion to the analogy of attribution, which is achieved explicitly only with medieval philosophers.

Before this, however, it is important to show that within the limits traced by the distinction made in paragraph two of the *Categories*, the subsequent series of categories is constructed soundly (in paragraphs three to nine of this work) on the basis of a non-linguistic model. The text Z 4, referred to earlier, offers a key: 'For it must be either by an equivocation that we say [things] *are*, or by adding to and taking from the meaning of "are."' Substance, the primary category, is circumscribed by a set of criteria resulting from prolonged thought on the conditions of predication. A comparative study of the *Categories* and *Metaphysics* Z 3 renders no less than seven. Three are properly logical criteria of predication: as primary substance, it is not said-of and is not in; as secondary substance, it is the subject of synonymous and primordial attribution. Four are ontological criteria. Three of these are secondary – substance is a determined 'this,' it has no contrary, it does not involve degree. The last is essential: substance is capable of receiving contraries. On this foundation, the organization of Aristotle's *Categories* proceeds by weakening the criteria, as the deduction moves from that which resembles substance most to that which resembles it least.[8]

The entire problem of analogy (but not the word itself!) is contained *in nuce* in this derivation by means of diminishing criteria. Essence, taken as the first term in Z 4, is imparted by degrees to all the categories: 'Essence will belong, just as "what a thing is" does, primarily and in the simple sense to substance, and in a secondary way to the other categories also – not essence in the simple sense, but the essence of a quality or of a quantity' (*Metaphysics* Z 4, 1030 a 29-31; then follows the passage cited above, that opposes to mere homonymy the process of adding or subtracting various qualifications from being). This transcendental mode of predication can indeed be called paronym, by reason of its parallelism with *Categories* 1, and analogy, at least implicitly.[9] Analogy designates virtually this progressive weakening of the precision of the predicative function as one moves from primordial predication to derived predication and from essential predication to accidental predication (which is paronymous).[10]

What will later be termed analogy of attribution is precisely this relation of progressively extended derivation, which Aristotle bounds on one side by essential predication – which alone provides the exact or approximate forms of proportionality and for which, we shall see, Aristotle reserves the term *analogy* – and on the other side by homonymy pure and simple or equivocity.

It was therefore of critical importance to show that the tripartite division – homonym, synonym, paronym – did indeed mark the opening of the treatise, thereby providing an introduction to the problem of analogy.[11]

Yet Aristotle does not call analogy what we have just termed a relation of progressively extended derivation. What is more, if the table of categories formed 'by adding to and taking from the meaning of "are"' does permit us to order the series of allegedly given terms, it does not show us why there must be other terms than the first nor why they are as they are. If we reread the canonical text of Γ 2,[12] we see that the other categories are so termed with reference 'to one central point (*pros hen*), one definite kind of thing (*kata mian phusin*)' (1003 a 33). But we do not see that the multiple meanings form a system. Aristotle may well declare that the lack of notional unity does not prevent there being a *single* science of the multiple senses of being. He may well affirm that terms that 'are related to one common nature' give rise to a *single* science, for 'even these in a sense have one common notion' (Γ 2, 1003 b 14). For, in this case, 'science deals chiefly with that which is primary, and on which the other things depend, and in virtue of which they get their names' (Γ 2, 1003 b 16-18). These statements do not prevent this enigmatic relation of dependence from being merely alleged, nor what Aristotle offers as a solution from being perhaps just a problem hypostatized in the form of a reply.

It might perhaps be a wise step, at this point in our study, to ignore the medieval interpretation and draw all we can from the fact that Aristotle did not call this *ad unum* reference 'analogy,' in order to lay bare what is thought under this term. An 'aporetic' reading of Aristotle, like that proposed by Pierre Aubenque,[13] combined with the logical and mathematical reading of Jules Vuillemin, permits us to isolate the operation by which medieval scholars, following a suggestion they found in other Aristotelian texts on analogy, tried to lessen the aporia of the 'many meanings of being.' From the perspective of my own inquiry into the heterogeneity of discourses in general and into the irreducibility of transcendental or speculative discourse to poetic discourse in particular, the aporetic interpretation applied to Aristotle's ontological discourse attests better than the medieval interpretation to the radical nature of the question, which for lack of a response is thus better exposed as a question.

Vuillemin has stated that primary attribution – that of a secondary substance to a primary substance – since it cannot be interpreted as the relation of element to set or as the relation of part to whole, is therefore 'an ultimate intuitive given, the meaning of which moves from inherence to proportion and from proportion to proportionality' (229). It is thus the very opacity of primary attribution that suggests analogy. For Aubenque, it is the absence of a generic unity – the sole support of Aristotelian science – and the resulting impossibility of generating categories other than *ousia*, which prevent attributing any determined meaning to *ad unum* reference. Discourse on being is the site henceforth of an unending investigation. Ontology continues to be the 'sought after science.'

Whatever the status of the arguments that finally develop all the reasons, well known from Aristotle, for which being is not a genus, and adding as well those reasons of which Kant made us aware, which determine that the table of categories cannot form a system but remains in a state of 'rhapsody';[14] it nonetheless remains that the aporia in question, if indeed this is an aporia, results from an aim, a requirement, an exigency, the original character of which ought to be recognized. It is because ontology aims at a non-generic science of being that even its failure is specifically its own. To develop the aporia – *diaporein* – as Aubenque wishes to do (221) is not to say nothing. For the effort that fails displays a particular structure, circumscribed by the very expression *pros hen, ad unum*. Something is required by the declaration even when it is put in the form of an aporia: 'But everywhere science deals chiefly with that which is primary, and on which the other things depend, and in virtue of which they get their names' (*Metaphysics* Γ 2, 1003 b 16). And a bit further: 'Therefore, since there are many senses in which a thing is said to be one, these terms also will have many senses, but yet it belongs to one science to know them all; for a term belongs to different sciences not if it has different senses, but if it has no one meaning *and* its definitions cannot be referred to one central meaning' (ibid. 1004 a 22-5). The search for this unity cannot be totally in vain for the very reason that the *pros hen* constitutes, 'in a certain sense,' one common notion, one definite kind of thing. If the science sought after were not structured in this way by the very form of the question, one could not even oppose, as Aubenque does, the reality of the failure to the 'ideal' of the investigation (240), or the actual analysis to the 'program.' The very disproportion between the analysis and its ideal attests to the semantic aim of this project, and it is on the basis of this aim that one could begin to look for something like a non-generic unity of being.

In this respect, the *rapprochement* between ontology and dialectic, which the aporetic character of the doctrine of being seems to impose (Aubenque 251-302), cannot, in the author's own opinion, be pursued very far. Between dialectic and ontology, the 'difference in intention' (301) is complete: 'Dialectic provides us with a universal technique of questioning, without concern for man's ability to answer; but man would not pose questions if he had no hope of answering them ... For this reason, the absence of prospective resolution required by the neutral character of the art of the dialectic is one thing; the actual incompletion of a project that by definition includes the very prospect of its accomplishment is something else again' (302).

One can pursue this point even further in an effort to understand the internal reasons why analogy presented itself as the solution to the central aporia of ontological discourse. If it is true, as Aubenque maintains, that this discourse receives its 'prospect,' its 'ideal,' and its 'program' from outside, namely from the theology inherited from Plato, it becomes even more urgent for ontology to reply to this external appeal with its own resources.

I am all the more willing to delve into this problem of the encounter between theological and ontological discourse, which Aubenque opposes to the hypothesis of a simple chronological succession between two states of Aristotle's system (an hypothesis first presented, as we know, by Werner Jaeger), as I find in it a compelling illustration of my own thesis regarding the plurality of spheres of discourse and the fecundity of the intersection of their semantic aims.

Let us therefore grant that what feeds the problematic of unity are properly theological considerations applied to 'separate realities' – the supralunar astral order, unmoved mover, thought of thought. It becomes all the more urgent to know how ontology responds to this appeal. At the same time, the encounter, in Aristotle, between an ontological problem of unity coming from a dialogue with sophistry and a theological problem of separation coming from a dialogue with Platonism provides a sort of paradigmatic example of the attraction between different spheres of discourse.[15]

It is therefore of little consequence that Aubenque exaggerates the heterogeneity of theological and ontological discourse and that he overdramatizes the encounter between an 'impossible ontology,' one lacking a conceivable unity among the categories, and a 'useless theology' (331) lacking a fixed relation between the God who reflects upon himself and the world he ignores. On the contrary, by transforming once again into an aporia Aristotle's thesis in *Metaphysics* E 1 that the science of immovable substance is universal because it is primary, Aubenque makes problematical just what is at issue, namely the new semantic aim resulting from the encounter between the two orders of discourse.[16]

A new conceptual problem must be worked out, arising from the very interference between theology – even astral theology – which envisions not a hidden God, but a God presented as far away in astral contemplation, and our human discourse on being in the diversity of its categorial acceptations.[17]

Even if the conciliation proposed in E 1 – theology is 'universal ... because it is first' – is only the hypostasis of a problem in search of a solution, it remains that the denounced heterogeneity of ontological discourse on the multiple meanings of being and theological discourse on 'separate' being must not amount to total incommunicability between spheres of meaning. This would endanger the possibility of conceiving the interference required by the very thesis that aporetic ontology takes its perspective from unitary theology. I should even be tempted to see, in these arguments that tend to make this interference unintelligible at the very moment it is alleged, the profound reason that led Aristotle's successors, and perhaps even Aristotle himself, to appeal to analogy.

Let us consider these arguments. The divine, it is stated, being indivisible, cannot receive attribution and can give rise only to negations. In turn, the diversity of the significations of being can apply only to physical things, in which it is possible to distinguish substance, quality, quantity, etc. In the final analysis, motion is the difference making the unity of being impossible in principle, and is the reason why the division into essence and accident applies to being. In short, it is because of motion that ontology is not a theology but a dialectic of division and finitude (442). Wherever something is in a state of becoming, predication is possible: predication is based on physical dissociation introduced by motion. But if this is the final word, how can one speak of an interference between ontology and theology? One can indeed criticize the failure of this endeavour. But this is not the question here. We have still to think through the very topic that Aristotle assigned himself, that of conceiving the horizontal unity of the meanings of being together with the vertical unity of beings.[18]

Now, Aristotle indicated the point where the two problematics intersect. It is *ousia*, the first category in attributive discourse and the sole sense of divine being.[19] Beyond this point, the two discourses separate, since nothing can be said concerning a being that is *ousia* alone, and since, in regard to beings that are *ousia* and something else also, the unity of meaning is dispersed. In any case, the divergence between the impossible discourse of ontology and the futile discourse of theology, the twinning of tautology and circumlocution, of empty universality and limited generalization – all proceed from a common centre, *ousia*, which, in Aubenque's words, 'will signify nothing other than the act of that which is, the completion of what is given in the fulfilment of presence, or, to use a word we have encountered before, *entelechy*' (406). Ontology may indeed be only the human substitute for a theology that remains impossible for us; *ousia* is still the crossroads where these avenues meet.

If the two discourses thus intersect at a point at once common to both and localizable in each of them, should not the 'sought after' science, drawing upon its own resources, respond to the proposal of unity made by the other discourse? Is it not from this internal necessity that the problem of analogy arises? The textual evidence in this regard is *Metaphysics* Λ 5,

1071 a 33-5. It says first that 'the causes of all [things] are the same or analogous.' Secondly, it states that the primacy of divine *ousia* underlies the categorial unity of being: 'The causes of substances may be treated as causes of all things.' The thesis remains unchanged even if one takes the 'as' (*bôs*) in the weak sense of an *as if.*[20] In its third part, the text specifies (further, *eti*) that it is because the final cause is 'first in respect of complete reality (*entelechy*)' that it is 'the cause of all things.'[21]

It is in this way that an *aporetic* reading of Aristotle highlights by contrast the doctrine of analogy, to the very extent that this reading began by bracketing it. Even if one finds this notion to be nothing but a problem hypostatized into a reply, it nevertheless designates the conceptual labour by which the human, the too human, discourse of ontology attempts to respond to the entreaty of *another* discourse, which is itself perhaps only a non-discourse.

A question is in fact raised by the concept of reference *ad unum.* If there is no generic commonality among the many meanings of being, what can be the nature of the 'common notion' suggested by Aristotle in *Metaphysics* Γ 2, 1003 b 14? Can there exist a non-generic commonality to rescue the discourse on being from its aporetic state?

The concept of analogy, evoked at least once in this context by Aristotle, intervenes at this point. The problem it raises here is the result of a second-order reflection on the *Categories*. It arises from the question of whether, and to what extent, reference to a first term is itself a *conceivable* relation. We have seen how this order of derivation can be produced by reflecting on the conditions of predication. We must now ask what sort of relation is generated in this way. Here the mathematical notion of analogy of proportion provides a means of comparison. Its origin guarantees its scientific status. By the same token, one can understand the approximation of the relation *ad unum* and proportional analogy as an effort to extend to the transcendental relation the benefit of the scientific character that belongs to the analogy of proportion.

I am all the more disposed to recognize the heterogeneous character of this *rapprochement* in that the earlier analysis of the points of interference of theological and ontological discourse has prepared us to pose the problem of analogy in terms of the intersection of discourses. Indeed, application of the concept of analogy to the series of meanings of being is itself also an instance of the intersection of spheres of discourse. And this intersection can be understood without reference to theological discourse, even if theological discourse will employ analogy later on in an effort to annex ontological discourse – at the price, however, of greatly altering this concept.

In Aristotle, certainly, the pure concept of analogy has nothing to do with the question of categories. It is due to a shift in meaning that weakens the original criteria that this concept is joined to the theory of categories and that a tangential relation in Aristotle is turned into a clear intersection in medieval philosophers.

It is this conceptual exercise more than its admittedly disappointing results that is of interest here. Contemporary logicians and philosophers may be justified in claiming that this effort has failed and that the theory of analogy is nothing but a pseudo-science. It can even be stated that this pseudo-scientific character extends to the theological use of analogy as well, and that this in turn reflects upon the initial transcendental structure, enclosing onto-theology in a vicious circle. To my mind, this is not what is important. My express purpose is to show how, by entering the sphere of the problematic of being, analogy at once retains its own conceptual structure and receives a transcendental aspect from the field to which it is applied. Indeed, to the extent that it is marked by the domain in which it intervenes in its own distinct way, the concept of analogy assumes a transcendental function. By the same token, it never returns to poetry, but retains in regard to poetry the mark of the original divergence produced by the question, what is being? In what follows, we shall show that this inclination towards divergence is in no way weakened by the theological use of analogy. The rejection of metaphor as an improper analogy will attest to this.

It is not unimportant that the mathematical notion of analogy – far from being self-evident as a summary definition might lead one to believe (A is to B as C is to D) – crystallizes a prolonged exercise of thought. Its final definition expresses the solution to a paradox, namely how to 'master the "impossible relationships" between certain geometric dimensions and whole numbers, by reducing them indirectly to consideration of relations of wholes alone, or, more precisely, to inequalities of size.'[22]

Could one not say that it is the conceptual labour incorporated in the definition, rather than its result, that was taken as a model for philosophical thought? Here again, extension from a radically non-poetic pole occurs through the weakening of criteria.

The closest application is provided by the definition of distributive justice in the *Nicomachean Ethics* 5:3. The definition rests on the idea that this virtue implies four terms, two persons (equal or unequal) and two shares (advantages and disadvantages in the realms of honour or wealth); and that it establishes proportional equality in distribution between these four terms. But the application here of the idea of number, proposed by Aristotle,[23] concerns extension not of the idea of number to irrationals but of proportion to non-homogeneous terms, provided that they can be said to be equal or unequal in some particular relation.

In biology, the same formal conception of proportion permits not only classification (by saying, for example, that flying is to wings as swimming is to fins), but also demonstration (e.g., if certain animals have lungs and others do not, the latter possess an organ that takes the place of a lung). By lending themselves to proportional relationships such as these, functions and organs provide the outline of a general biology (*De Part. An.* 1:5).

The relation of analogy begins its migration towards the transcendental sphere when it is charged with expressing the identity of principles and elements that cut through the diversity of genera: thus, it is said, 'as sight is in the body, so is reason in the soul, and so on in other cases' (*Nicomachean Ethics* 1:4, 1096 b 28-9). Analogy still remains, formally, an equality of relations among four terms.[24]

The decisive step, the one that concerns us here, is taken in *Metaphysics* Λ 4 and 5, where analogy is applied to the problem of the identity of principles and elements belonging to different categories.[25] Its formulation certainly still allows an equality or similarity of relations to appear; thus, one can write that privation is to form, on the level of elements, as cold is to heat in sensible bodies, as black is to white in qualities, as darkness is to light in relatives. In this respect, the transition from proportional analogy to reference *ad unum* is more than hinted at in a text from the *Metaphysics*,[26] to which medieval philosophers will return relentlessly. 'Healthy,' Aristotle notes, is said analogously of the cause of health, of a sign of health, and of the healthy subject. 'Medical' is said analogously of the doctor, the scalpel, the operation, and the patient. Analogical extension is governed, then, by the order of the categories.

This formulation, however, cannot hide the fact that the analogy here concerns the categories, the very terms in which 'principles' (form, privation, and matter) come together through analogy. Not only is the number of these terms not specified by the relation itself, but the sense of the relation has changed. What is in question is the manner in which the terms themselves relate to one another, whereas the reference *ad unum* is limited to establishing dominance (the first term) and hierarchy (reference to the first term). This final weakening of the criteria results in a displacement from proportional analogy to the analogy of attribution.[27]

Modern logicians will be more sensitive than were medieval philosophers to the logical break that interrupts the extension of analogy as it moves from mathematics to metaphysics. To logicians, the unscientific features of analogy, taken in its final sense, add up to an argument against analogy.[28] The great text of *Metaphysics* A 9, 992 b 18-24 is turned against the philosopher and becomes the ultimate evidence of the unscientific character of metaphysics.[29]

Aristotle's failure, however, can have two meanings, between which a purely logical analysis cannot choose. According to the first, the transcendental project as such is stripped of all meaning; in line with the second, this project must be taken up again on some basis other than analogy and yet still remain faithful to the semantic aim that presided over the search for a *non-generic unity* for the meanings of being. It is this interpretation that we have tried to develop here, by stressing in each instance the conceptual labour crystallized in the logical result. Because the 'search' for a non-generic bond of being remains a task for thought, even after Aristotle's failure, the problem of a 'guide line' has continued to be raised down to modern philosophy. The reason the *Categories* has proved capable of continual consideration and reworking is that *once* the difference between the analogy of being and poetic metaphor was indeed thought.

In this respect, the first paragraph of the *Categories* remains highly significant. To say that there are not two classes of things to name – synonyms and homonyms – but three classes, with the insertion of paronyms, is to open up a new domain for philosophical discourse based on the existence of *non-accidental homonyms*. From this point on, there is a continuous chain formed from the paronyms in paragraph 1 of the *Categories* to the reference *pros hen, ad unum* in *Metaphysics* Γ 2 and E 1. The new possibility of thought opened up in this way was that of a non-metaphorical and properly transcendental resemblance among the primary significations of being. To say that this resemblance is unscientific settles nothing. It is more important to affirm that because it breaks with poetics, this purely transcendental resemblance even today attests, by its very failure, to the search that animated it – namely, the search for a relation that is still to be thought otherwise than by science, if thinking scientifically means thinking in terms of genus. But the primary task remains to master the difference between transcendental analogy and poetic resemblance. Based on this initial difference, the non-generic bond of being can be – and without a doubt must be – thought according to a model that will no longer owe anything to analogy as such. But this step beyond analogy was possible only because analogy itself had been a step beyond metaphor. It will thus have proved decisive for thought that a segment of equivocalness was wrested *once* from poetry and incorporated into philosophical discourse, just at the time when philosophical discourse was forced to disengage itself from the sway of pure univocity.

2 / METAPHOR AND *ANALOGIA ENTIS*: ONTO-THEOLOGY

The second counter-example that can be opposed to the thesis of the discontinuity between speculative discourse and poetic discourse is much more formidable. It is provided by a mode of discourse that itself is already a *composite* of ontology and theology. Following Heidegger, who himself follows Kant here,[30] we can call it simply *onto-theology*. In fact, the doctrine of *analogia entis* reaches its full development within the bounds of this composite discourse. For our own investigation, therefore, it is important to know if the initial split Aristotle established between speculative discourse and poetic discourse was preserved in the composite discourse of onto-theology.

The Thomist doctrine of analogy provides invaluable testimony in this respect.[31] Its express purpose is to establish theological discourse at the level of science and thereby to free it completely from the poetical forms of religious discourse, even at the price of severing the science of God from biblical hermeneutics.

And yet the problem here is singularly more complex than that of the ordered diversity of the categories of being in Aristotle. It concerns the possibility of speaking rationally of the creative God of the Judeo-Christian tradition. At issue, then, is the possibility of extending to the question of divine names the problematic of analogy to which the equivocal nature of the notion of being gives rise.

The new use of the concept of analogy might appear to be justified by the parallelism between the initial discourse situations. The problem in both cases is, in fact, to maintain a middle course between two impossibilities. For Aristotle, confronting the problem of the unity of the categories of being, the difficulty was to escape the dilemma of the generic unity of being and the pure and simple dispersion of its meanings. Reference to a primary term offered itself as a median solution. Now, theological discourse encounters a similar choice: to impute a discourse common to God and to his creatures would be to destroy divine transcendence;[32] on the other hand, assuming total incommunicability of meanings from one level to the other would condemn one to utter agnosticism.[33] It therefore seemed reasonable to extend the concept of analogy to theology by means of the invention (after Aristotle) of a third modality of attribution – analogous attribution – equidistant from univocal and equivocal attribution.[34] The doctrine of the analogy of being was born of this desire to encompass in a single doctrine the horizontal relation of the categories of substance and the vertical relation of created things to the Creator. This project defines onto-theology.

I shall not try to trace the history of the concept of *analogia entis* here. I only want to reappropriate the semantic aim of the conceptual enterprise which crystallized in the Scholastic debate; and I want to show further that, just when this semantic aim seems alligned completely with that of metaphorical statements (mainly because of a return to a Platonic and neo-Platonic type of participation), instead a new split is forged between speculative and poetic discourse.

What remains remarkable indeed, for us who come after the Kantian critique of this type of ontology, is the way in which the thinker deals with the difficulties inherent in his chosen solution. On the one hand, the Aristotelian solution to the categorial problem is retained in its general outline.[35] On the other hand, its application to the theological domain encounters such enormous obstacles that the very concept of analogy must continuously be redeployed and reshaped into new distinctions. The elaboration of these new distinctions is precisely the conceptual labour whose aim is what we are fundamentally interested in.

The main source of all the difficulties is the need to base analogical predication on an ontology of participation.[36] In fact, analogy functions at the level of names and predicates, and it belongs to the conceptual order. But the condition of the possibility of analogy lies elsewhere, in the very communication of being. Participation is the generic name given to the set of solutions tendered to this problem. To participate means, approximately, to have partially what another possesses or is fully. As a result, the struggle for an adequate concept of participation underpins the struggle for an adequate concept of analogy.[37] But then, is not participation evidence that metaphysics has turned to poetry through its lamentable recourse to metaphor, as Aristotle argues against Platonism?

It is significant, then, that Thomas did not stop with the solution closest to Platonic exemplarism, which was adopted in his *Commentary on Book I of the Sentences* when he was still influenced by Albert the Great. Two modalities were distinguished there. In addition to the order of priority (*per prius et posterius*) found in the series 'being, power and act' or in the series 'being, substance and accident,' it is necessary to conceive of an order of descendance (*a primo ente descendit*) and of imitation (*ens primum imitatur*) where 'one receives from the other *esse* and *rationem*' (Prologue, qu. 1, art. 2). *Distinctio* xxxv specifies (qu. 1, art. 4): 'There is a different analogy [than that of the order of priority] when a term imitates another as far as it can, but does not equal it perfectly, and this is the analogy we find between God and his creatures.' Of course, we must understand the reasons for this recourse to exemplary causality. It allows one to do away with a common term that would precede God and creatures: 'Between God and his creatures, there is no similarity by reason of something held in common but by imitation; whence we say the creature resembles God but not the inverse, as Dionysius says.'[38] So participation through deficient resemblance implies no common form that is possessed unequally. It is God himself who communicates his image. The diminished image ensures an imperfect and inadequate representation of the divine exemplar, halfway between fusion in a single form and radical heterogeneity. But the price to be paid is complete disjunction between attribution of divine names and categorial attribution. Theological discourse loses any basis in the categorial discourse on being.

Thomas did not stop at this solution for two opposing reasons that had to be developed in turn. On the one hand, direct resemblance is a relation still too close to univocity; on the other hand, in its formal character, exemplary causality must be subordinated to efficient causality, which alone founds the communication of being that underlies analogical attribution. The discovery of being as act then becomes the ontological keystone of the theory of analogy.

However, at the time of the *De Veritate*, St Thomas had first to test a distinction between two sorts of analogy, both capable of falling within the Aristotelian *analogia*. The distinction, borrowed from the Latin translation of Euclid (book 5, def. 3 and 5), is that between *proportio* and *proportionalitas*.[39] *Proportio* relates two quantities of the same kind in a direct relation of one to the other, where the value of one by itself determines the value of the other (for example, a number and its double). But St Thomas does not limit this first type of analogy to the order of magnitudes, any more than he will so limit *proportionalitas*. He extends *proportio* to any relation involving a 'determinate distance' (*determinata distancia*) and a strict relationship (*determinata habitudo*). This is why he is able to connect to *proportio* the relation of reference to a first term, as in the example of health, and thus the categorial relation of accidents to substance. What is essential is that the relation be direct and definite. *Proportionalitas*, on the other hand, contains no direct relation between two terms. It merely posits *similitudo proportionum*, a resemblance of relations (for example, 6 is to 3 as 4 is to 2). But just as *proportio* is not only mathematical, so *proportionalitas* posits a similarity of relations between any terms whatever; thus, we can say that the intellect is to the soul as sight is to the body. The advantages for theological discourse are evident. Between the created and God, the distance is indeed infinite: *finiti ad infinitum nulla est proportio*.[40] Now proportional resemblance establishes no determinate relation between the finite and the infinite since it is independent of distance. Yet this does not entail an utter absence of relationship. It is still possible to say: what the finite is to the finite, the infinite is to the infinite. In other words, divine science is to God as human science is to the created.[41]

In this way, exemplary causality, to the extent that it falls under the concept of *proportio*, still implied a relation that was too direct, thereby suppressing the infinite distance that separates beings from God. *Proportionalitas*, on the other hand, does not do justice to the communication of being that we conceive in the notion of creative causality. The formalism of *proportionalitas* impoverishes the abundant and complex network formed by participation, causality, and analogy.

The task is therefore immense. The relation of participation must be conceived in such a way as to imply no earlier term, and so no univocal attribution of perfection to God and to creatures. In addition, *proportio creaturae*, which always exists between the effect and its cause, must be given a sense that would make it compatible with the disproportion between the finite and the infinite.[42] Finally, the distance between the finite and the infinite must be conceived as a simple dis-semblance, without confusing this idea – which alone is essential – with that of a spatial exteriority, which is excluded in any case by the immanence of divine causality.[43]

It is to satisfy all these requirements that being is conceived in the works following the *De Veritate*, and particularly in the two *Summae*, less as form than as act, in the sense of *actus essendi*. Causality is then no longer the resemblance of copy to model but the communication of an act, the act being at once what the effect has in common with the cause and that by reason of which the effect is not identical to the cause.[44]

It is creative causality, therefore, that establishes between beings and God the bond of participation that makes the relation by analogy ontologically possible.

But what sort of analogy? The works subsequent to the *De Veritate* propose a new sort of split within the concept of analogy, a split which does not correspond to the distinction that preceded the *De Veritate*. In fact, the new break does not separate horizontal analogy, which governs the sequence of categories, from vertical analogy, which rules the hierarchy of the divine and the created. Instead, two manners of ordering a diversity are set in opposition, two manners that apply to horizontal and vertical analogy alike. The first analogy, we read in the *De Potentia*, qu. 7, art. 6, is that of two things to a third (*duorum ad tertium*); accordingly, quantity and quality relate to one another in relating to substance. This is not the manner in which God and the created relate to being. The second analogy is that of one thing to another (*unius ad alterum*, or again *ipsorum ad unum*). Accidents relate directly in this manner to substance. This is also the manner in which created being relates to the divine. The analogy goes directly from the set of secondary analogues to the principal analogue, without anything preceding God that might be established as a common genus. At the same time, this relation is capable of proceeding from the most eminent to the less excellent, following an asymmetrical order of perfection. Such is the mode of community half-way between the equivocal and the univocal.[45]

So the two uses of analogy are brought together once again, but at the price of a final correction to its definition.[46]

Yet the new price to be paid is higher than ever. To the very extent that thinking is no longer satisfied with the overly formal relation of *propor-*

tionalitas (now rendered problematic by the extrapolation beyond the sphere of mathematics), thinking is forced to base the diversity of names and concepts upon an ordering principle inherent in being itself and to assign the synthesis of unity and diversity required by discourse to efficient causality itself. In short, even causality has to be thought as analogical.[47] If indeed we can name God on the basis of the creature, it is 'accordingly as there is some relation of the creature to God as to its principle and cause, wherein all the perfections of things pre-exist excellently' (*Summa Theologiae* 1 a, qu. 13, art. 5). Here we see the distinction among univocity, equivocalness, and analogy carried from the level of meanings back to that of efficiency. If causality were single and undivided, it would engender only the same; if it were purely equivocal, the effect would cease to be like its agent. The most heterogeneous cause must therefore remain analogous cause. It is this structure of the real that prevents language in the final analysis from being completely dislocated. The likeness of causality resists the dispersal of logical classes that ultimately would force us to silence. In the interplay of Saying and Being, when Saying is at the point of being forced to silence by the force of the heterogeneity of being and beings, Being itself revives Saying by means of underlying continuities that provide an analogical extension of its meanings to Saying. But, at the same time, analogy and participation are placed in a mirror relationship, conceptual unity and the unity of the real corresponding exactly to one another.[48]

This circle of analogy and participation was forced to give way under a barrage of criticism. Not that the semantic intention animating the search for a continually more adequate concept of analogy was ever called into question. It is at the physical level, at the precise point where equivocal cause lends aid to analogical discourse, that the circular relation was broken by the combined blows of Galilean physics and the Humean critique. After this break, the full consequences of which are drawn out by the Kantian dialectic, the conceptual unity capable of encompassing the ordered diversity of the meanings of being remains to be thought.

Still, the battle for an ever more adequate concept of analogy remains telling on one count: the refusal to compromise in any way with poetic discourse. This refusal is expressed in the care always taken to distinguish between analogy and metaphor. I would call such concern the distinctive feature of the semantic aim of speculative discourse.

Does not the recourse to participation, however, imply a return to metaphor? Does not the passage from the *De Potentia* (qu. 7, art. 6, ad. 7) referred to above say that 'even the participatory form in the creature is inferior to its *ratio*, which is God, as the fire's heat is inferior to heat of the sun by which the sun engenders heat'? And does not the *Summa* say (1 a, qu. 13, art. 5): 'For example, the sun by the exercise of its one power produces manifold and various forms in these sublunary things. In the same way ... all perfections existing in creatures divided and multiplied pre-exist in God unitedly.'

Ah, the sun! Oh, the fire! The heliotrope – which heralds every trope of resemblance – cannot be far away![49]

Now it is precisely at the point of greatest proximity that the line between analogy and metaphor is most firmly drawn. When, in fact, is analogy closest to metaphor? When it is defined as proportionality. And this is precisely what, in turn, 'can happen in two ways' (*dupliciter contingit*) (*De Veritate* qu. 2, art. 11). On the one hand, the attribution is only symbolic; on the other, it is truly transcendental. In symbolic attribution (*quae symbolice de Deo dicuntur*), God is called 'lion,' 'sun,' etc.; in these expressions 'the name implies something belonging to the thing primarily designated,' and with it 'matter that cannot be attributed to God.' On the other hand, only the transcendentals such as 'being,' 'good,' 'true' can be attributed to God, because they 'include no defect nor depend on matter for their act of existence.' For this reason, during the Scholastic period of the analogy of proportionality, analogical attribution is not only opposed to univocal – that is, generic – attribution. It also introduces two splits within the sphere of analogy: a split within the relation of proportion, in so far as this relation still retains some common things that could precede and encompass God and creatures; and a split within symbolism, which assigns something belonging to what is principally signified to the name attributed to God. Such is the asceticism of denomination requiring the exclusion of poetry.

This purism in analogy does not waver when the communication of the act of being restores the ontological continuity that the relation of proportionality threatened to destroy. The question of metaphor is confronted head-on in the *Summa Theologiae* (1 a, qu. 13, art. 6) under the question: 'Whether names predicated of God are predicated primarily of creatures?' The answer distinguishes two orders of priority: a priority according to the thing itself, which begins with what is first in itself, that is, God; and a priority according to signification, which begins with what is best known to us, that is, creatures. The first type of priority governs analogy properly speaking, and the second, metaphor: 'All names applied metaphorically to God are applied to creatures primarily rather than to God, because when said of God they mean only similitudes to such creatures.' Metaphor indeed is based upon 'similarity of proportion'; its structure is the same in poetic and in biblical discourse. The examples given prove this: to call a meadow laughing and God a lion is to use the same sort of transposition – the meadow is pleasing when it is in flower, just as a man is when he laughs. By the same token, 'God manifests strength in His works, as a lion in his.' In both cases the meaning of the names issues from the domain from which they are borrowed. On the other hand, the name is said primarily of God, not of the creature, when we are dealing with names that aim at his essence: thus goodness, wisdom. The split, therefore, does not separate poetry from biblical language, but these two modes of discourse taken together from theological discourse. In theological discourse the order of the thing has precedence over the order of signification.[50]

Thus two predicative modalities intersect. Regarding the specific topic of the prescription of divine names, this intersection illustrates the union of Aristotelian reason with the *intellectus fidei* in the doctrine of St Thomas.[51]

This intersection of two kinds of transference, following the descending order of being and the ascending order of significations, explains the creation of *composite* modalities of discourse in which the meaning effects of proportional metaphor and transcendental analogy are added together. By means of this chiasmus, the speculative verticalizes metaphor, while the poetic dresses speculative analogy in iconic garb. This criss-crossing is especially noticeable whenever St Thomas states the relation of eminence that is both thought as analogy and expressed at the same time as metaphor.[52] This exchange constitutes a new case of intersection between various spheres of discourse. It is not surprising that the word and the meaning of words are found at the point of intersection. Just as the metaphorical process 'focuses' on the word to the extent of giving the impression that the transfer of meaning affects only the signification of names, so it is on a certain feature of the meaning of a word that the interplay between analogy and metaphor is focused. Thus the word *wise* can be applied analogously to God, even though it is not said in a univocal fashion of God and of men, because the signification presents different features in the two uses. In man, wisdom is a perfection 'distinct' from every other; it 'circumscribes' (*circumscribit*) and 'comprehends' (*comprehendit*) the thing signified. In God, wisdom is the same thing as his essence, his power, his being; the term therefore circumscribes nothing but leaves the thing signified 'as uncomprehended (*ut incomprehensam*) and as exceeding the signification of the name (*excedentem nominis significationem*).' Through this excess of meaning, the predicates attributed to God retain their power to signify without introducing any distinctions in God. It is therefore the *res significata* that is in excess in relation to the *nominis significatio*.[53] This splintering of the name and its signification corresponds to the extension of meaning by which words, in metaphorical statements, can satisfy unusual attribution. In this sense, one can speak of an effect of metaphorical meaning within analogy. If, however, this effect of meaning really originates in the predicative operation itself, it is at the level of predication that analogy and metaphor separate and intersect. One rests on the predication of trans-cendental terms, the other on the predication of meanings that carry their material content with them.

Such is the magnificent exercise of thought which preserved the differ-ence between speculative discourse and poetic discourse at the very point of their greatest proximity.

3 / META-PHOR AND META-PHYSICS

The dispute over *analogia entis* does not exhaust the possibilities of ex-change between speculative and poetic discourse. Up until now the discus-sion has involved only the semantic intentions of each type of discourse that are capable of being taken up in reflection, as is witnessed by this ter-minology, of intention or semantic aim, borrowed from Husserlian pheno-menology. It is indeed for a consciousness that means 'to justify itself,' 'to found itself completely,' and hence to hold itself to be 'entirely responsi-ble for itself,' that the reasons invoked by self-conscious thought are equi-valent to real motives.[54]

Now, a 'geneological' manner of questioning philosophers has emerged, thanks principally to Nietzsche, which does not limit itself to collecting declared intentions but holds them in suspicion and seeks the motives and self-interests behind their reasons. An entirely different sort of implication between philosophy and metaphor comes to light, which links them at the level of their hidden presuppositions rather than at the level of their stated intentions.[55] It is not only the order of the terms that is inverted, philo-sophy preceding metaphor; but the mode of implication is itself reversed, the 'un-thought' of philosophy anticipating the 'un-said' of metaphor.

In the introduction I mentioned Heidegger's celebrated saying: 'The metaphorical exists only within the metaphysical.' This saying suggests that the trans-gression of meta-phor and that of meta-physics are but one and the same transfer. Several things are implied here: first, that the onto-logy implicit in the entire rhetorical tradition is that of Western 'meta-physics' of the Platonic or neo-Platonic type, where the soul is transported from the visible world to the invisible world; second, that meta-phorical means transfer from the proper sense to the figurative sense; finally, that both transfers constitute one and the same *Über-tragung*.

How are these assertions arrived at?

In Heidegger himself the context considerably limits the import of this attack on metaphor, so that one may come to the conclusion that the con-stant use Heidegger makes of metaphor is finally more important than what he says in passing against metaphor.

In the first text in which metaphor is expressly mentioned, lesson 6 of *Der Satz vom Grund*,[56] the context is two-fold. The first context is formed by the very framework of the discussion, which refers back to an earlier analysis of the 'principle of sufficient reason,' that of *Vom Wesen des Grundes*. Heidegger notes that one can *see* (*sehen*) a situation clearly and yet not *grasp* (*er-blicken*) what is at issue: 'We see much and we grasp little' (85). This is true in the case of the principle 'Nothing is without a reason.' *Seeing* (*Sicht*) is not of the same order of penetration as insight (*Einblick*). Now, drawing nearer to what can be grasped means hearing (*hören*) more distinctly and retaining in the ear (*in Gehör behalten*) a certain determining emphasis (*Betonung*) (86). This emphasis makes us perceive a harmony (*Einklang*) between 'is' and 'reason,' between *est* and *ratio*. This is then the task: 'Our thought must grasp with insight what has been heard ... thinking is a grasping by the ear that grasps by sight' (86). In other words, 'thinking is a hearing and a seeing' (86).

The first context is thus formed by the network of the terms *seeing, hearing, thinking,* and *harmony*, which underlies thought as it meditates on the connection between *ist* and *Grund* in the formulation of the Principle of Sufficient Reason.

A second context is formed by introducing an interpretation in the form of an objection ('But we are called upon quickly to explain ...'). Someone says: 'Hearing and seeing can only (*nur*) be called thinking in a transposed sense (*übertragenen*) ...' (86). Indeed, in the earlier discussion 'sensible hearing and seeing were taken over and transferred (*hinübergenommen*) to the domain of non-sensible perception, that is thought. Such transference is μεταφέρειν in Greek; a transposition like this is called metaphor in scholarly language' (86-7). This, then, is the objection: 'It is only in a metaphorical, transferred sense that thought may (*darf*) be called a hearing and a grasping by the ear, a looking and a grasping by the sight' (87). But, Heidegger asks, who is saying 'may' here? He who asserts that hearing and seeing in the proper (*eigentlich*) sense are of the ear and the eye. To which the philosopher replies that there is not first sensible seeing and hearing, which would then be transposed to the non-sensible level. Our hearing and our seeing are never a simple reception by the senses. As soon as we call thought a listening and a seeing, we do not mean this only as (*nur als*) metaphorical transposition, 'but rather as (*nämlich als*) a transposition of the allegedly (*vermeintlich*) sensible into the non-sensible' (88).

It is in this twofold context that the equivalence of the two transfers is asserted: metaphysical transfer of the sensible to the non-sensible, metaphorical transfer of the literal to the figurative. The first transfer is determinative (*massgebend*) for Western thought, the second 'gives the standard for our representation of the nature of language' (89). Here, a statement is made in passing, but it is one we shall return to later: 'This is why metaphor is often used as an aid in the analysis of works of poetry and, more generally, of artistic creations' (ibid.). Then comes the saying: 'The metaphorical exists only within the bounds of the metaphysical' (ibid.).

The twofold context of the saying is significant. The first not only imposes an allusive and digressive tone, but also gives a type of example that circumscribes the field of discussion from the very outset. What kind of metaphors are these? As concerns their content, there are no poetic metaphors, just philosophical metaphors. Instead of being presented with a discourse other than his own, a discourse functioning in a manner different from his own, the philosopher straightaway confronts metaphors produced by philosophical discourse itself. In this respect, what Heidegger does when he interprets poets as philosophers is infinitely more important than what he says polemically, not against metaphor, but against a manner of casting metaphors as particular philosophical statements.

The second context reduces still more the eventual impact of a declaration that at first glance seemed quite impressive. Let us suppose an objection: metaphor to our objector not only is not a poem in miniature, but remains a mere transposition of meaning involving isolated words – seeing, hearing, etc. In order to interpret these single-word metaphors, our objector also introduces the twofold distinction of the proper and the figurative, the visible and the invisible. Finally, he asserts the equivalence (*nämlich*) of these two pairs of terms. So the metaphorical becomes 'merely' metaphorical; at the same time, the objection becomes a restriction (*darf*). It is therefore really the objector who comes under the aegis of Platonism, which then suffers Heidegger's wholehearted denunciation.

As far as I am concerned, I see no reason to recognize myself in this objector. The distinction between proper and figurative meaning applied to individual words is an obsolete semantic notion that does not have to be tacked onto metaphysics to be taken to pieces. An improved semantics is sufficient to unseat it as a 'determinative' conception of metaphor. As for its use in the analysis of poetry or of works of art, it is less a matter of metaphorical expression itself than of a very particular style of interpretation, an allegorizing interpretation that does go hand in hand with the 'metaphysical' distinction between the sensible and the non-sensible.

Let us now consider the remaining assertion, which holds that the separation of sensible and non-sensible is itself 'at the root of the meaning of the term *metaphysics*, and has become a determining norm for Western thought' (89). I am afraid that only a reading forced beyond any justification can make Western philosophy lie on this Procrustean bed. We have already indicated that an ontology other than a metaphysics of the sensible and the non-sensible can respond to the semantic aim of authentically poetic metaphors. And this is what we shall discuss in greater detail at the end of the present Study.

Moreover, Heidegger himself tells us how these 'remarks' (*Hinweise*) should be taken: 'their purpose is to warn us not to jump to the conclusion that the talk of thinking as (*als*) a hearing and a seeing is a mere metaphor, and thus take it too lightly' (89). Our own entire effort too is turned against this 'mere metaphor.'

Now this explicit warning has its positive counterpart in the non-thematized use of metaphor in the very text we have been analysing. True metaphor is not the 'learned theory' of metaphor; it is rather the very uttering that the objection reduced to mere metaphor, namely that 'thought looks in hearing and hears in looking' (89). By speaking in this way, Heidegger produces a deviation with respect to ordinary language, identified with representative thought. This 'leap,' Jean Greisch says, 'places language under the sign of the gift, connoted in the expression *es gibt*. Between "there is" and *es gibt* no passage is possible.'[57] Is not this divergence that of true metaphor?

Let us now consider what in fact makes this utterance a metaphor. It is, at the level of the utterance as a whole, the harmony (*Einklang*) between *ist* and *Grund* in 'nothing *is* without a *reason*.' This harmony is the very one that is seen-heard-thought. So the harmony belonging to the straightforward utterance – that of the principle of sufficient reason – is also the harmony of the second-level utterance, which understands thought as (*als*) the grasp by hearing and by seeing. As for this harmony, it is not a peaceful consonance; lesson 5 of *Der Satz vom Grund* teaches us instead that it is born of an earlier dissonance.[58] Actually, we find that two statements follow from the principle of sufficient reason. The rationalizing statement of representative thought proclaims: 'Nothing is without a why' (67). The statement borrowed from the spiritual poetry of Angelus Silesius says: 'The rose has no why; it flowers because it flowers, / It shows no self-concern, questions not, whether it is seen' (68). Nothing is without a why. And yet the rose is without a why. Without a why, but not without a because. By making the principle of sufficient reason more impenetrable, this vacillation forces the principle itself to be heard (*hören*): 'We must then be attentive to the tone (*Ton*) of its expression' (75). For now it resonates with 'two different tones (*Tonarten*)' (ibid.), one stressing *nothing* and *without*, the other stressing *is* and *reason*. The second, given priority in lesson 6, which was our starting point, must therefore be contrasted with the first emphasis, which is that of representative thought.

In *Unterwegs zur Sprache*,[59] the same struggle between representative thought and meditative thought produces true metaphor at the very point where metaphor in the metaphysical sense is challenged. Here, too, the context is important. Heidegger is attempting to break away from the concept of language formed by representative thought, when it treats language as *Ausdruck*, 'expression' – that is as the exteriorization of the interior, and hence as the domination of the outside by the inside, instrumental mastery attained by a subjectivity.

To help lead the philosopher's steps beyond this notion of representation, a line from Hölderlin is proposed. Here language is called *die Blume des Mundes*, 'the flower of the mouth' (99). The poet also says *Worte, wie Blumen*, 'words, like flowers' (100). The philosopher can welcome these expressions because he himself has called manners of saying *Mundarten*, 'modes of the mouth,' idioms, in which earth and sky, mortals and gods meet. An entire network is thus set vibrating and made to form intersignifying relations. The condemnation, identical to the one in *Der Satz vom Grund*, is then pronounced: 'It would mean that we stay bogged down in metaphysics if we were to take the name Hölderlin gives here in "words, like flowers" as being a metaphor' (100). What is more, protesting against Gottfried Benn's interpretation that reduces *wie* to the comparative 'like,' Heidegger accuses Benn of relegating this poetic expression to a 'herbarium, a collection of dried-up plants' (ibid.). Poetry indeed seems rather to climb back up the slope that language descends when dead metaphors are laid to rest in herbaria. What then is true poetry? It is, Heidegger says, that which awakens 'the largest view'; here 'the word is brought forth from its inception,' and it 'makes World appear in all things' (100, 101).

Now, is this not what *living* metaphor does?

Applying the 'flower' metaphor to language, however, can take us into an entirely different train of thought, one that Heidegger's remark on the interpretation of Gottfried Benn approaches. The flower that blossoms ends one day in a herbarium, just as 'using' does in 'used-up' [*usage, usure*].

In recognizing this we are led from Heidegger's restrained criticism to Jacques Derrida's unbounded 'deconstruction' in 'White Mythology.' Is not the entropy of language just what a philosophy of living metaphor wants to forget? Would not 'metaphysics' be more akin to a plant in a herbarium than to an allegorizing interpretation of metaphors already given in language? Would not a more subversive thought than Heidegger's be one that would support the universal suspicion of Western metaphysics with a more heightened suspicion directed at what in metaphor itself is left unsaid? Now the non-stated in metaphor is used, worn-out metaphor. Metaphoricity functions here in spite of us, behind our backs so to speak. The claim to keep semantic analysis within a metaphysically neutral area only expresses ignorance of the simultaneous play of unacknowledged metaphysics and worn-out metaphor.

Two assertions can be discerned in the tight fabric of Derrida's demonstration. The first has to do with the efficacy of worn-out metaphor in philosophical discourse, and the second with the deep-seated unity of metaphorical and analogical transfer of visible being to intelligible being.

The first assertion moves counter to our entire effort, which has been directed towards the discovery of living metaphor. The stroke of genius here is to enter the domain of metaphor not by way of its birth but, if we may say so, by way of its death. The concept of wearing away [usure][60] implies something completely different from the concept of abuse that English-language authors oppose (as we have seen) to use. This concept carries its own sort of metaphoricity with it, which is not surprising in a conception that aims precisely at demonstrating the limitless metaphoricity of metaphor. In its overdetermination the concept carries first the geological metaphor of sedimentation, of erosion, of wearing away by friction. To this is added the numismatic metaphor of wearing down the features of a medal or a coin. This metaphor in turn evokes the tie, perceived by de Saussure among others, between linguistic value and monetary value: a comparison that invites the suspicion that the using up or wearing away [usure] of things used and worn is also the usury of usurers. At the same time, the instructive parallelism between linguistic value and economic value can be pushed to the point where the *proper* sense and *property* are suddenly revealed as next of kin within the same semantic network. Following this assonance further, one may suspect that metaphor is a sort of 'linguistic surplus value' (7) functioning unknown to speakers, in the manner in which in the economic field the product of human labour is made at once unrecognizable and transcendent in economic surplus value and the fetishism of merchandise.

As we see, the task of reconstructing this network exceeds the resources provided by historical and diachronic semantics, just as it goes beyond the scope of lexicography and etymology. This work stems from a vaster 'discourse on figure' (14) that would measure economic effects and effects of language. A simple inspection of discourse in its explicit intention, a simple interpretation through the game of question and answer, is no longer sufficient. Heideggerian deconstruction must now take on Nietzschean geneology, Freudian psychoanalysis, the Marxist critique of ideology, that is, the weapons of the hermeneutics of suspicion. Armed in this way, the critique is capable of unmasking the *unthought* conjunction of *hidden* metaphysics and *worn-out* metaphor.

The efficacy of dead metaphor takes on its full meaning, however, only when one establishes the connection between the *wearing away* that affects metaphor and the ascending movement that constitutes the formation of the concept. The wearing away of metaphor is dissimulated in the 'raising' of the concept. (*Relève*, raising, is Derrida's very apt translation of the Hegelian *Aufhebung* [sublation, a transformation that partially cancels, a reinterpretation to a higher level].) Henceforth, to revive metaphor is to unmask the concept.

Derrida bases his work here on a particularly eloquent text in Hegel's *Aesthetics*.[61] It begins by stating that philosophical concepts are initially sensible meanings transposed (*übertragen*) to the spiritual order; and it adds that the establishment of a properly (*eigentlich*) abstract meaning is bound up with the effacement of what is metaphorical in the initial meaning and thus with the disappearance of this meaning, which, once proper, has become improper. Now, Hegel employs the term *Aufhebung* to describe this 'raising' of sensible and worn away meaning into the spiritual meaning, which has become the proper expression. Where Hegel saw an innovation of meaning, Derrida sees only the wearing away of metaphor and a drift towards idealization resulting from the dissimulation of this metaphorical origin: 'The movement of metaphorization (the origin and then the effacing of the metaphor, the passing from a proper sensible meaning to a proper spiritual meaning through a figurative detour) is nothing but a movement of idealization' (25). This movement of idealization, common to Plato and Hegel, brings into play all the oppositions that characterize metaphysics: nature/spirit, nature/history, nature/freedom, as well as sensible/spiritual, sensible/intelligible, sensible/sense or meaning. This system 'describes ... the possibility of metaphysics, and the concept of metaphor so defined belongs to [it]' (ibid.).

We must understand that here it is not a question of the genesis of empirical concepts but of the primary philosophemes, those that define the field of metaphysics: *theoria, eidos, logos,* etc. The thesis can be stated as follows: wherever metaphor fades, there the metaphysical concept rises up. We find a text from Nietzsche here to the effect that 'truths are illusions of which one has forgotten that they *are* illusions; worn-out metaphors which have become powerless to affect the senses, coins which have their obverse effaced and now are no longer of account as coins but merely as metal.'[62] Whence the title of the essay, 'White Mythology': 'It is metaphysics which has effaced in itself that fabulous scene which brought it into being, and which yet remains, active and stirring, inscribed in white ink, an invisible drawing covered over in the palimpsest' (11).

The final product of this effectiveness of worn-out metaphor, which is thus replaced by the production of a concept that erases its trace, is that discourse on metaphor is itself infected by the universal metaphoricity of philosophical discourse. In this regard, one can speak of a paradox of the auto-implication of metaphor.

The paradox is this: there is no discourse on metaphor that is not stated within a metaphorically engendered conceptual network. There is no non-metaphorical standpoint from which to perceive the order and the demarcation of the metaphorical field. Metaphor is metaphorically stated. The word *metaphor* and the word *figure* alike attest to this recurrence of metaphor. The theory of metaphor returns in a circular manner to the metaphor of theory, which determines the truth of being in terms of presence. If this is so, there can then be no principle for delimiting metaphor, no definition in which the defining does not contain the defined; metaphoricity is absolutely uncontrollable. The effort to decipher figures in philosophical texts is self-defeating; one is forced instead to 'recognize the *conditions which make it in principle impossible* to carry out such a project' (18). The layer of the first philosophical elements 'cannot be subsumed' (ibid.) because it is itself metaphorical. This layer, in the author's apt expression, 'is therefore self-eliminating every time one of its products (here the concept of metaphor) vainly attempts to include under its sway the whole of the field to which that product belongs' (ibid.). Were one successfully to establish order amid figures, still one metaphor at least would escape: the metaphor of metaphor, the 'extra metaphor.' And so the conclusion: 'The field is never saturated' (ibid.).

This perplexing tactic has proven to be only one episode in a much vaster strategy of deconstruction that always consists in destroying metaphysical discourse by reduction to aporias. Hence we may credit the 'conclusions' of the essay with being scarcely more than one groundwork for an enterprise that foments a good many other subversive manœuvres. We might attack the self-destruction of metaphor through assumption into the concept, that is, into the self-present idea. The other self-destruction (73) would still remain, that which would occur through the ruin of essential oppositions, first that of semantics and syntax, then that of figurative and proper, then, little by little, those of the sensible and the intelligible, convention and nature: in short, all the oppositions that found metaphysics as such.

We have thus returned, by way of an internal critique of worn-out metaphor, to the level on which Heidegger's declaration was located: 'The metaphorical exists only within the metaphysical.' Indeed, the movement of elevation and absorption or 'raising' by which worn-out metaphor is concealed in the figure of the concept is not just some fact of language. It is the pre-eminent philosophical gesture that, in a 'metaphysical' orientation, sights the invisible beyond the visible, the intelligible beyond the sensible, after having first separated them. There is thus only one such movement: the metaphorical 'raising' is also the metaphysical 'raising.'

According to this second assertion, true metaphor is vertical, ascending, transcendent metaphor. Characterized in this way, 'metaphor seems to bring into play the use of philosophical language in its entirety, nothing less than the use of what is called ordinary language *in* philosophical discourse, that is to say, of ordinary language *as* philosophical language' (6).

To grasp the full force of this assertion, we must go back to our own analyses of the interplay of resemblance. It is not uncommon for this play to be compared to analogy, whether analogy signifies quite specifically proportionality as in Aristotle's *Poetics*, or whether it designates in a less technical manner any recourse to resemblance in 'bringing closer' two 'distant' semantic fields.[63] The thesis we are now considering would allege that any use of analogy, although appearing to be neutral in regard to the 'metaphysical' tradition, rests unwittingly upon a metaphysical concept of analogy that points to the referential movement from the visible to the invisible. Primordial 'iconicity' would be encompassed here: everything visible would thus constitute what basically is capable of giving 'an image.' Its resemblance to the invisible would then constitute it as image. As a result, the very first transposition would be the transfer of meaning from the empirical to the 'intelligible place.' Using a method that in this case has no connection with Max Black's logical grammar, the task is then to unmask the metaphysics of analogy down to the seemingly most innocent uses of metaphor. Classical rhetoric continually gives itself away as well: is it by chance that regularly, in the guise of an example, the transfer of the inanimate to the animate reappears? Just so Fontanier eagerly falls back upon this dialectic of the animate and the inanimate to construct the species of metaphor, thereby re-establishing the parallel with the two other basic tropes (metonymy and synecdoche), whose species issued from the logical analysis of the relations of connection and correlation. With metaphor, the species belong no longer to the logical but to the ontological order.[64]

And so, whether we speak of the metaphorical character of metaphysics or of the metaphysical character of metaphor, what must be grasped is the single movement that carries words and things beyond, *meta*.

This privileged orientation of metaphysical metaphor explains the persistence of a few key metaphors that have a special capacity to receive and to concentrate the movement of the 'metaphysical raising.' In the forefront of these metaphors we find the Sun.

One might think that the Sun is simply an illustrative example. Precisely. It is 'the most illustrious, that which illustrates before all else, the most natural lustre that may be' (43). Already with Aristotle the Sun provided a quite unusual metaphor (*Poetics* 1457 b). The lack of a precise word to express the Sun's power to engender is filled by the metaphor of sowing. For Derrida, this is the symptom of a certain decisive characteristic: by its persistence, 'the movement which turns the sun into metaphor' proves to be that which 'turns philosophical metaphor towards the sun' (51). Why indeed is the heliotropic metaphor unique? Because it speaks of the 'paradigm of what is sensible *and* of what is metaphorical: it regularly turns (itself) and hides (itself)' (52). It follows that 'the orbit of the sun is the trajectory of metaphor' (52).

We can see the fantastic extrapolation involved here: 'With every metaphor, there is no doubt somewhere a sun; but each time that there is the sun, metaphor has begun' (53). Metaphor has begun, for with the sun come the metaphors of light, of looking or glancing, of the eye – pre-eminent figures of idealization, from the Platonic *eidos* to the Hegelian *Idea*. By virtue of this, '"idealizing" metaphor ... is constitutive of any element of philosophy in general' (56). More precisely, as the Cartesian philosophy of *lumen naturale* attests, light aims metaphorically at what is signified in philosophy: 'It is to that main item signified in onto-theology that the tenor of the dominant metaphor will always return: the circle of the heliotrope' (69). To this same network of dominant metaphors belong the metaphor of the ground-foundation and that of the home-return, metaphors *par excellence* of reappropriation. They also signify metaphoricity itself: the metaphor of the home is really 'a metaphor for metaphor: expropriation, being-away-from-home, but still in a home, away from home but in someone's home, a place of self-recovery, self-recognition, self-mustering, self-resemblance: it is outside itself – it is itself. This is philosophical metaphor as a detour in (or in view of) the reappropriation, the second coming, the self-presence of the idea in its light. A metaphorical journey from the Platonic *eidos* to the Hegelian Idea' (55).

And so, by reason of their stability, their perdurance, the dominant metaphors ensure the epochal unity of metaphysics: 'A presence disappearing in its own radiance, a hidden source of light, of truth and of meaning, an obliteration of the face of being – such would be the insistent *return* of that which subjects metaphysics to metaphor' (70).

By the same token, the paradox of metaphor's self-implication ceases to appear as a purely formal paradox. It is expressed materially by the self-implication of the dominant metaphors of light and home, where metaphysics signifies itself in its primordial metaphoricity. By being images for idealization and appropriation, light and sojourn are a figure for the very process of metaphorizing and thereby ground the return of metaphor upon itself.

The critical remarks I offer here cannot of course encompass the entire project of deconstruction and dissemination, but only touch upon the line of argument drawn from the collusion of worn-out metaphor with the metaphysical theme of analogy. Besides, this specifically polemical phase of my own argument is inseparable from the positive clarification of the concept of analogy implied in the theory of metaphor developed in the remainder of the present Study.

I should like to examine in its own right the thesis of an unstated effectiveness of worn-out metaphor and shall, for the moment, lay aside the thesis that identifies metaphorical 'raising' with metaphysical 'raising.' The hypothesis to the effect that worn-out metaphor possesses a specific fecundity is strongly contested by the semantic analysis developed in the preceding Studies. This analysis leans towards the position that dead metaphors are no longer metaphors, but instead are associated with literal meaning, extending its polysemy. The criterion of delimitation is clear: the metaphorical sense of a word presupposes contrast with a literal sense; as predicate, this contrasting sense transgresses semantic pertinence. In this respect, the study of the lexicalization of metaphor – for example in Le Guern[65] – greatly contributes to dispelling the false enigma of worn-out metaphor. Indeed, various traits that sustain the heuristic function of metaphor disappear with lexicalization: forgetting the customary meaning causes us to overlook the deviation in relation to the isotopy of the context. So it is only by knowing the etymology of the word that we can reconstruct the Latin *testa* ('little pot') in the French *tête* [head] and the popular metaphor from which the French word is derived. In current usage the metaphor has been lexicalized to such an extent that it has become the proper word; by this we mean that the expression now brings its lexicalized value into discourse, with neither deviation nor reduction of deviation. The phenomenon is thus less interesting than it seems at first. Le Guern even thinks that lexicalization 'involves only a very small number of metaphors among all those that the language creates' (82).

The effectiveness of dead metaphor can be inflated, it seems to me, only in semiotic conceptions that impose the primacy of denomination, and hence of substitution of meaning. These conceptions thereby condemn the analysis to overlook the real problems of metaphoricity, which, as we know, are related to the play of semantic pertinence and impertinence.

But if the problem of denomination is over-emphasized in this way, it is doubtless because one attaches to the opposition between the figurative and the proper a meaning that is itself metaphysical, one which a more precise semantics dispels. In fact, this shatters the illusion that words possess a proper, i.e. primitive, natural, original (*etumon*) meaning in themselves. Now nothing in the earlier analysis has authorized this interpretation. We did admit of course that the metaphorical use of a word could always be opposed to its literal use; but literal does not mean proper in the sense of originary, but simply current, 'usual.'[66] The literal sense is the one that is lexicalized. There is thus no need for a metaphysics of the proper to justify the difference between literal and figurative. It is use in discourse that specifies the difference between the literal and metaphorical, and not some sort of prestige attributed to the primitive or the original. Moreover, the distinction between literal and metaphorical exists only through the conflict of two interpretations. One interpretation employs only values that are already lexicalized and so succumbs to semantic impertinence; the other, instituting a new semantic pertinence, requires a twist in the word that displaces its own meaning. In this way, a better semantic analysis of the metaphorical process suffices to dispel the mystique of the 'proper,' without any need for metaphoricity to succumb along with it.

It is true that in its work of denomination philosophical language appears to contradict the semanticist's judgment concerning the rarity of lexicalized metaphors. The reason for this is simple. The creation of new meanings, in connection with the advent of a new manner of questioning, places language in a state of semantic deficiency; lexicalized metaphor must intervene to compensate for this lack. But, as Fontanier saw perfectly well, what we then require is a trope 'by necessity and by extension in order to supplement words lacking in language for certain ideas ...' (*Les Figures du discours* 90). In short, *catachresis* is called for; moreover, it can be metonymy or synecdoche as easily as metaphor.[67] Therefore, speaking of metaphor in philosophy, we must draw a line boldly between the relatively banal case of an 'extended' use of the words of ordinary language in response to a deficiency in naming and the case – to my mind singularly more interesting – where philosophical discourse deliberately has recourse to living metaphor in order to draw out new meanings from some semantic impertinence and to bring to light new aspects of reality by means of semantic innovation.

The result of this first discussion is that a reflection on the wearing away of metaphors is more seductive than earth-shaking. Perhaps its real fascination for so many minds is due to the disturbing fecundity of the oblivion that seems to be expressed here, but also to the capacity for revival that seems to persist in the most thoroughly extinguished metaphorical expressions. Here again, the semanticist is of great help. Contrary to what is often stated, Le Guern notes that 'lexicalization brings about the total disappearance of the image only under special conditions' (*Sémantique* 87).[68] In the other cases, the image is attenuated but still perceptible; this is why 'almost all lexicalized metaphors can recover their original brilliance' (88). The reanimation of a dead metaphor, however, is a positive operation of de-lexicalizing that amounts to a new production of metaphor and, therefore, of metaphorical meaning. Writers obtain this effect by various concerted and controlled procedures – substituting a synonym that suggests an image, adding a more recent metaphor, etc.

In philosophical discourse, the rejuvenation of dead metaphors is particularly interesting when these metaphors supply a semantic addition. Reanimated metaphor once again functions as fable and as redescription, which characterize living metaphor, and leaves behind its function of mere addition at the level of denomination. De-lexicalization is therefore in no way symmetrical to the earlier lexicalization. In philosophical discourse, moreover, the renovation of extinguished metaphors involves more complex operations than those evoked above. The most remarkable of these is the awakening of etymological motivations, pushed even to false etymology. This procedure, a favourite of Plato's, is common in Hegel and in Heidegger. When Hegel hears *taking-true* in *Wahrnehmung*, when Heidegger hears *non-dissimulation* in *a-lêtheia*, the philosopher creates meaning and in this way produces something like a living metaphor. The analysis of dead metaphor is thus seen to refer back to an initial foundation which is living metaphor.[69]

The baffling fecundity of dead metaphor is even less awesome when one takes true measure of its contribution to the formation of concepts. To revive dead metaphor is in no way to unmask concepts: first of all because revived metaphor functions differently than dead metaphor, but above all because the full genesis of the concept does not inhere in the process by which metaphor is lexicalized.[70]

In this respect the Hegelian text discussed above does not appear to me to justify the thesis of a collusion between metaphor and *Aufhebung*. This text describes two operations that intersect at one point – dead metaphor – but remain distinct. The first operation, which is purely metaphorical, takes a proper (*eigentlich*) meaning and transports it (*übertragen*) into the spiritual order. Out of this expression – non-proper (*uneigentlich*) because transposed – the other operation makes a proper abstract meaning. It is the second operation that constitutes the 'suppression-preservation' which Hegel calls *Aufhebung*. But the two operations, transfer *and* suppression-preservation, are distinct. The second alone creates a proper sense in the spiritual order out of an improper sense coming from the sensible order. The phenomenon of wearing away (*Abnutzung*) is only a prior condition allowing the second operation to be constituted on the ground of the first.

This pair of operations is not fundamentally different from what Kant considers to be the production of the concept in its schema. Thus, the concept of 'foundation' is symbolized in the schema of the 'earth' and of 'construction'; but the meaning of the concept is in no way reduced to its schema. What must be realized is precisely that giving up sensible meaning does not simply give us an improper expression but rather a proper éxpression on the conceptual level. The conversion of this process of wearing away into thought is not the wearing away itself. If these two operations were not distinct, we could not even speak of the concept of wearing away, nor of the concept of metaphor; in truth, there could be no philosophical terms. That there are philosophical terms is due to the fact that a concept can be active as thought in a metaphor which is itself dead. What Hegel precisely conceived was this life of the concept in the death of the metaphor. 'Comprendre' [comprehend, understand] can have a proper philosophical sense because we no longer hear 'prendre' [take, to take hold of] in it. So only half the work has been done when a dead metaphor beneath a concept is revived; it must still be proved that no abstract meaning was produced as the metaphor wore away. This demonstration belongs not to the metaphorical order but to the order of conceptual analysis. This analysis alone can prove that Hegel's Idea is not Plato's Idea, even though it is true to say with Derrida that its traditional metaphorical burden 'continues Plato's system into Hegel's' (57). But noting this continuation is not the same as determining the sense of Idea in each philosopher. No philosophical discourse would be possible, not even a discourse of deconstruction, if we ceased to assume what Derrida justly holds to be 'the sole thesis of philosophy,' namely, 'that the meaning aimed at through these figures is an essence rigorously independent of that which carries it over' (29).

Applying these remarks on the formation of the concept in its schema to the concept of metaphor is enough to dispel the paradox of the metaphoricity of all definitions of metaphor. Speaking metaphorically of metaphor is not at all circular, since the act of positing the concept proceeds dialectically from metaphor itself. Thus, when Aristotle defines metaphor as the *epiphora* of the word, the expression *epiphora* is qualified conceptually by its insertion in a network of intersignifications, where the notion of *epiphora* is bounded by the primary concepts *phusis, logos, onoma, sēmainein*, etc. *Epiphora* is thus separated from its metaphorical status and constituted as a proper meaning, although 'the whole surface of [this discourse],' as Derrida says, 'is worked by metaphor' (31). The subsequent determination of the concept of metaphor contributes to this conceptual conversion of dead metaphor underlying the expression *epiphora.* It does so either by the method of differentiation, which allows one to distinguish among various strategies of *lexis,* or by exemplification, which provides an inductive basis for the concept of the operation indicated. Let us add that the conceptualization of different metaphors is aided not only by the lexicalization of the metaphors employed, as in the case of the vocable 'transposition,' but also by the rejuvenation of worn-out metaphor, which places the heuristic use of living metaphor in the service of conceptual formation. This is true of other metaphors for metaphor evoked so frequently in the present work: screen, filter, lens, superimposition, overload, stereoscopic vision, tension, interanimation, change of labels, idyll and bigamy, etc. Nothing prevents the fact of language that metaphor constitutes from being itself 'redescribed' with the help of the various 'heuristic fictions' produced sometimes by new living metaphors, sometimes by worn-out metaphors that have been revived. Far from admitting the concept of metaphor to be only the idealization of its own worn-out metaphor, the rejuvenation of all dead metaphors and the invention of new living metaphors that redescribe metaphor allow a new conceptual production to be grafted onto the metaphorical production itself.

So we see that the abyss-like effect produced by 'this implication of what is to be defined in the definition' (55) is dispelled when we discern the proper hierarchy with respect to the concept of *epiphora* and its schema.

We can now consider the theoretical core common to Heidegger and Derrida, namely, the supposed collusion between the metaphorical pair of the proper and figurative and the metaphysical pair of the visible and invisible.

I myself hold this connection not to be necessary. The example of Fontanier, mentioned above, is instructive in this regard. His definition of metaphor – 'presenting an idea under the sign of another idea more striking or better known'[71] – in no way implies the division into species that he subsequently infers from the consideration of objects. Likewise, his initial definition is illustrated by innumerable examples that involve no transfer from the visible to the invisible: 'the *swan* of Cambrai, the brilliant *eagle* of Meaux,' '*consuming* remorse,' 'courage *craving* for peril and praise,' 'what is well conceived is expressed with *clarity*,' etc. These examples can all be interpreted in terms of tenor and vehicle, focus and frame. I should be inclined to think that the shift from a definition of metaphor drawn from the operation to a definition drawn from the kind of objects results in part from studying metaphor within the framework of the word (the kinds of object then serving as guide in identifying kinds of word), and in part from the substitution theory, which continually sacrifices the predicative (hence syntagmatic) aspect to the paradigmatic aspect (and so to classes of objects). This shift can be avoided if we carry the theory of metaphor from the level of the word back to the level of the sentence.

Consequently, if the substitution theory of metaphor presents a certain affinity to the 'raising' of the sensible into the intelligible, the tension theory eliminates every advantage that accrues to this latter notion. The play of semantic impertinence is compatible with all the calculated errors capable of making sense. So it is not metaphor that carries the structure of Platonic metaphysics; metaphysics instead seizes the metaphorical process in order to make it work to the benefit of metaphysics. The metaphors of the sun and the home reign only to the extent that they are selected by philosophical discourse. The metaphorical field in its entirety is open to all the figures that play on the relations between the similar and the dissimilar in any region of the thinkable whatsoever.

As for the position of privilege assigned to metaphysical discourse itself – a privilege that governs the partitioning of the narrow zone of metaphors where this discourse is schematized – this seems indeed to spring from the suspicion governing the strategy of deconstruction. The counter-example proposed in the Aristotelian philosophy of metaphor is valuable here. We shall call upon this counter-example one last time in concluding our inquiry.

4 / THE INTERSECTION OF SPHERES OF DISCOURSE

It is now possible to return to the question raised at the start of this Study: *what* sort of philosophy is *implied* in the movement that carries our inquiry from rhetoric to semantics and from sense towards reference? The earlier discussion has revealed the close connection between the question of the *content* of the implicit ontology and that of the *mode* of implication between poetic discourse and speculative discourse. What has only been suggested in the foregoing critical remarks remains to be stated in positive terms.

I shall therefore be undertaking two tasks at once: to erect a general theory of the intersections between spheres of discourse upon the difference we have recognized between modalities of discourse, *and* to propose an interpretation of the ontology implicit in the postulates of metaphorical reference that will fit this dialectic of modalities of discourse.

The dialectic outlined here considers self-evident the need to abandon the naïve thesis that the semantics of metaphorical utterance contains ready-made an immediate ontology, which philosophy would then have only to elicit and to formulate. From the perspective of this dialectic, it would appear equally disastrous for the dynamism of discourse as a whole if we were to lay down our arms too soon and agree to the thesis suggested by Wittgenstein's *Philosophical Investigations* – a tempting thesis due to its liberalism and its irenicism – to the effect that language games are radically heterogeneous. As Plato remarks in the *Philebus* – it is bad to arrive too quickly at the one or at the many. Philosophy's eminence lies in the art of arranging ordered manifolds. A general theory of interferences based on the phenomenology of the semantic aims of each discourse ought to be elaborated in this spirit. The particular intention that directs the system of language functioning in metaphorical utterances includes a demand for elucidation to which we can respond only by approaching the semantic possibilities of this discourse with a different range of articulation, the range of speculative discourse.

It can be shown that, on the one hand, speculative discourse has its condition of *possibility* in the semantic dynamism of metaphorical utterance, and that, on the other hand, speculative discourse has its *necessity* in itself, in putting the resources of conceptual articulation to work. These are resources that doubtless belong to the mind itself, that are the mind itself reflecting upon itself. In other words, the speculative fulfils the semantic exigencies put to it by the metaphorical only when it establishes a break marking the irreducible difference between the two modes of discourse. Whatever the subsequent relation of the speculative to the poetic may be, the first extends the semantic aim of the second at the cost of a transmutation resulting from its transfer into another zone of meaning.

The reference postulates stated at the beginning and end of Study 7 are truly at issue in this dialectic, which governs the passage to an explicit ontology where the meaning of being implicit in these postulates comes to reflection. Between the implicit and the explicit there is all the difference that separates two modes of discourse, and that cannot be eliminated when the first is taken up into the second.

(a) As could be seen by the end of Study 3, affirming the gain in meaning that results from founding a new semantic pertinence at the level of the metaphorical statement as a whole, the conceptual articulation proper to the speculative mode of discourse finds its condition of *possibility* in the semantic functioning of metaphorical utterance. But this gain in meaning is inseparable from the tension not just between the terms of the statement, but also between two interpretations – a literal interpretation restricted to the established values of words, and a metaphorical interpretation resulting from the 'twist' imposed on these words in order to 'make sense' in terms of the statement as a whole. The resulting gain in meaning is thus not yet a *conceptual* gain, to the extent that the semantic innovation is not separable from the switching back and forth between the two readings, from their tension and from the kind of stereoscopic vision this dynamism produces. We might say then that the semantic shock produces a conceptual need, but not as yet any knowledge by means of concepts.

This thesis is strengthened by our interpretation of the work of resemblance in Study 6. At that point we traced the gain in meaning back to a change in 'distance' between semantic fields, that is, to a predicative assimilation. Now, in saying that this is (like) that – whether the *like* is 'marked' or not – the assimilation does not reach the level of an identity of meaning. The 'similar' is not the 'same.' To see the similar, in Aristotle's words, is to apprehend the 'same' within and in spite of 'difference.' This is why we were able to refer this schematization of a new sense back to productive imagination. The gain in meaning is thus inseparable from the predicative assimilation through which it is schematized. This is another way of saying that the gain in meaning is not carried to the concept, to the extent that it remains caught in the conflict of 'same' and 'different,' although it constitutes the rough outline and the demand for an instruction through the concept.

A third suggestion results from the thesis developed in Study 7 to the effect that the reference of the metaphorical statement could itself be considered a split reference. For a split sense, we might say, a split reference. This is what we meant when we lodged metaphorical tension right within the copula of the utterance. Being as, we said, means being and not being. In this way, the dynamism of meaning allowed access to the dynamic vision of reality which is the implicit ontology of the metaphorical utterance.

The present task is thus made more specific. It will consist in showing that the passage to the explicit ontology called for by the postulate of reference is inseparable from the passage to the concept called for by the structure of meaning found in the metaphorical statement. Therefore, juxtaposing the results of the earlier Studies is no longer enough; instead these results must be linked more closely together by showing that every gain in meaning is at one and the same time a gain in sense and a gain in reference.

In a study on theological discourse and the symbol,[72] Jean Ladrière observes that the semantic functioning of the symbol – in our terms, of metaphor – is an extension of a dynamism of meaning that can be found in even the simplest utterance. The novelty of this analysis in relation to our own consists in its description of this dynamism as a criss-crossing of acts – acts of predication and acts of reference. Ladrière adopts Strawson's analysis of propositional acts, conceived as the combination of a singularizing operation of identification and a universalizing operation of characterization. Then, like John Searle in *Speech Acts*, he places this analysis within the framework of a theory of discourse and is thus able to speak of the relation between sense and reference as a commingling of operations. The dynamism of meaning is shown to be a dual and intersecting dynamism where any progress towards concepts has as its counterpart a more extensive exploration of the referential field.

Indeed, in ordinary language we master the predicative use of abstract meanings only by relating them to objects, which we designate in the referential mode. This is possible because the predicate is such that it performs its characteristic function only in the context of the sentence, when it targets this or that relatively isolable aspect within a determined referent. The lexical term is, in this respect, only a rule for use in a sentence context. So we master meaning by varying the conditions for use in relation to different referents. Conversely, we investigate new referents only by describing them as precisely as possible. Thus the referential field can extend beyond the things we are able to show, and even beyond visible, perceptible things. Language lends itself to this by allowing the construction of complex referential expressions using abstract terms that are already understood, i.e. definite descriptions in Russell's sense. In this way predication and reference lend support to one another, whether we relate new predicates to familiar referents, or whether, in order to explore a referential field that is not directly accessible, we use predicative expressions whose sense has already been mastered. So what Jean Ladrière has termed the power of signifying, in order to stress its operative and dynamic character, is the intersection of two movements. One movement aims at determining more rigorously the conceptual traits of reality, while the other aims at making referents appear (that is, the entities to which the appropriate predicative terms apply). This circularity between the abstractive phase and the concretizing phase makes this power of signifying an unending exercise, a 'continuing Odyssey.'[73]

This semantic dynamism, proper to ordinary language, gives a 'historicity' to the power of signifying. New possibilities of signifying are opened up, supported by meanings that have already been established. This 'historicity' is carried by the attempt at expression made by a speaker who, wanting to formulate a new experience in words, seeks something capable of carrying his intention in the network of meanings he finds already established. Thanks to the very instability of meaning, a semantic aim can find the path of its utterance. Therefore, it is always in a particular utterance – corresponding to what Benveniste calls the instance of discourse – that the sedimented history of assembled meanings can be recovered in a new semantic aim. Placed in the perspective of its use, meaning appears less like a determined content, to take or to leave, than (in Jean Ladrière's words) like an inductive principle capable of guiding semantic innovation. The act of signifying is an 'initiative that, as if for the first time, makes the syntactic elements coming from a syntactical history reappropriated in this effort produce truly new effects of meaning' (133).

This is the synthesis we can now make of the theory of the instance of discourse in Émile Benveniste, the speech act theory in Austin and Searle, and the theory of sense and reference in Strawson (which stems from Frege).

On this groundwork the tension theory we applied to three different levels of metaphorical utterance can then be located: the tension between the terms of the statement, the tension between literal interpretation and metaphorical interpretation, and the tension in the reference between is and is not. If it is true that meaning, even in its simplest form, is in search of itself in the twofold direction of sense and reference, the metaphorical utterance only carries this semantic dynamism to its extreme. As I tried to say earlier drawing upon a poorer semantic theory, and as Jean Ladrière says much better on the basis of the more subtle theory we have just summarized, the metaphorical utterance functions in two referential fields at once. This duality explains how two levels of meaning are linked together in the symbol. The first meaning relates to a known field of reference, that is to the sphere of entities to which the predicates considered in their established meaning can be attached. The second meaning, the one that is to be made apparent, relates to a referential field for which there is no direct characterization, for which we consequently are unable to make identifying descriptions by means of appropriate predicates.

Unable to fall back upon the interplay between reference and predication, the semantic aim has recourse to a network of predicates that already function in a familiar field of reference. This already constituted meaning is raised from its anchorage in an initial field of reference and cast into the new referential field which it will then work to delineate. But this transfer from one referential field to the other supposes that the latter field is already in some way present in a still unarticulated manner, and that it exerts an attraction on the already constituted sense in order to tear it away from its initial haven. It is therefore in the semantic scope of the other field that the energy capable of achieving this uprooting and this transfer resides. But this would not be possible if meaning were a stable form. Its dynamic, directional, vectoral character combines with the semantic aim seeking to fulfil its intention.

Two energies converge here: the gravitational pull exerted by the second referential field on meaning, giving it the force to leave its place of origin; and the dynamism of meaning itself as the inductive principle of sense. The semantic aim that animates the metaphorical utterance places these two energies in relation, in order to inscribe a semantic potential (itself in the process of being superseded) within the sphere of influence of the second referential field to which it relates.

But the metaphorical utterance, even more than plain utterance, provides only a semantic sketch without any conceptual determination. It is doubly sketchy. On the one hand, as regards its sense, the metaphorical utterance reproduces the form of a movement in a portion of the trajectory of meaning that goes beyond the familiar referential field where the meaning is already constituted. On the other hand, it brings an unknown referential field towards language, and within the ambit of this field the semantic aim functions and unfolds. At the origin of this process, therefore, there is what I shall call the ontological vehemence of a semantic aim, hinting at an unknown field that sets it in motion. This ontological vehemence cuts meaning from its initial anchor, frees it as the form of a movement and transposes it to a new field to which the meaning can give form by means of its own figurative property. But in order to declare itself this ontological vehemence makes use of mere hints of meaning, which are in no way determinations of meaning. An experience seeks to be expressed, which is more than something undergone. Its anticipated sense finds in the dynamism of simple meaning, relayed by the dynamism of split meaning, a *sketch* that now must be reconciled with the requirements of the concept.

(b) That speculative discourse finds something like the sketch of a conceptual determination in the dynamism described above does not bar it from beginning in itself and from finding the principle of its articulation within itself. By itself it draws on the resources of a conceptual field, which it offers to the unfolding of a meaning sketched metaphorically. The *necessity* of this discourse is not the extension of its possibility, inscribed in the dynamism of the metaphorical. Its necessity proceeds instead from the very structures of the mind, which it is the task of transcendental philosophy to articulate. One can pass from one discourse to the other only by an *epoché*.

But what are we to understand by speculative discourse? Must we see it as the equivalent of what above we repeatedly termed conceptual determination, in opposition to the semantic sketches of metaphorical utterances? I should reply that speculative discourse is the discourse that establishes the primary notions, the principles, that articulate primordially the space of the concept. Concepts in scientific language as well as in ordinary language can never actually be derived from perception or from images, because the discontinuity of the levels of discourse is founded, at least virtually, by the very structure of the conceptual space in which meanings are inscribed when they draw away from the metaphorical process, which can be said to generate all semantic fields. It is in this sense that the speculative is the condition of the possibility of the conceptual. It expresses the systematic character of the conceptual in a second-order discourse. If, in the order of discovery, the speculative surfaces as a second-level discourse – as meta-language, if one prefers – in relation to the discourse articulated at the conceptual level, it is indeed first discourse in the order of grounding. This discourse is at work in all the speculative attempts to order the 'great genera,' the 'categories of being,' the 'categories of understanding,' 'philosophical logic,' the 'principal elements of representation,' or however one wants to express it.

Even if one does not recognize that it can be articulated in a distinct discourse, this power of the speculative supplies the horizon or, as it has been called, the logical space on the basis of which the clarification of the signifying aim of concepts is distinguished radically from any genetic explanation based on perception or images. In this respect, Husserl's distinction[74] between the *Aufklärung* of 'acts of knowing' and any genetic-style *Erklärung* draws its source from the speculative horizon in which meaning is inscribed when it takes on conceptual status. If a sense that is 'one and the same' can be discerned in a meaning, it is not just because one sees it that way but because one can connect it to a network of meanings of the same order in accordance with the constitutive laws of the logical space itself.

The Husserlian-style critique, which is expressed in the opposition between *Aufklärung* and *Erklärung*, is possible only on the basis of this speculative horizon. The speculative is what allows us to say that 'to understand a (logical) expression' is something other than 'finding images.'[75] It allows us to say, further, that the scope [*visée*] of the universal is something other than the display of the images that accompany it, illustrate it, even coincide with the 'distinction' of speculative features and the 'clarification' of the tenor of meaning. The speculative is the very principle of the disparity [*inadéquation*] between illustration and intellection, between exemplification and conceptual apprehension. If the *imaginatio* is the kingdom of 'the similar,' the *intellectio* is that of 'the same.' In the horizon opened up by the speculative, 'same' grounds 'similar' and not the inverse. In fact 'wherever things are "alike," an identity in the strict and true sense is also present.'[76] What affirms this? Speculative discourse does, by reversing the order of precedence of metaphorical discourse, which attains 'same' only as 'similar.' By reason of the same founding principle, generic apprehension (*Auffassung*)[77] is rendered irreducible to the purely substitutive function of image-representation. Far from the concept's being reduced to an abbreviation, by reason of some principle of thrift and economy, some play of substitution, it is the concept that makes this play of re-presentation possible.[78] Signifying is always something other than representing. The same capacity of inscription in logical space enables the interpretation functioning in perception to become the seat of two distinct aims: one that tends towards individual things, and the other that tends towards logical signification, where interpretation at the perceptual or imaginative level plays nothing more than a 'supportive' role.[79]

The image no doubt introduces a moment of absence and, in this sense, an initial neutralization of the 'positing' inherent in perceptual belief.[80] But apprehending a sense that is one and the same is something else again.

This critique of 'the image' in Husserl is of the highest significance to us. It can be transposed easily into a critique of 'metaphor' in so far as the *imaginatio* includes not only so-called mental images but also, and especially, predicative assimilations and schematizations that underlie metaphorical utterance. *Imaginatio* is a level and an order of discourse. *Intellectio* is another level and another order. Here metaphorical discourse encounters its limit.

This containment of metaphorical discourse by speculative discourse can be restated as follows (the language is borrowed, as above, from Jean Ladrière). The signifying aim of the concept works free of interpretations, schematizations, and imaginative illustrations only if a horizon of constitution is given in advance, the horizon of speculative *logos*. By reason of this opening of horizon, the concept becomes capable of functioning semantically solely in terms of the configurational properties of the space in which it is inscribed. The resources of systematization involved simply in the play of articulation in speculative thought are substituted for the resources of schematization involved in the play of predicative assimilation. Because it forms a system, the conceptual order is able to free itself from the play of double meaning and hence from the semantic dynamism characteristic of the metaphorical order.

(c) But does this discontinuity of semantic modalities imply that the conceptual order abolishes or destroys the metaphorical order? My inclination is to see the universe of discourse as a universe kept in motion by an interplay of attractions and repulsions that ceaselessly promote the interaction and intersection of domains whose organizing nuclei are off-centred in relation to one another; and still this interplay never comes to rest in an absolute knowledge that would subsume the tensions.

The attraction that speculative discourse exerts on metaphorical discourse is expressed in the very process of interpretation. Interpretation is the work of concepts. It cannot help but be a work of elucidation, in the Husserlian sense of the word, and consequently a struggle for univocity. Whereas the metaphorical utterance leaves the second sense in suspension, while its reference continues to have no direct presentation, interpretation is necessarily a rationalization that at its limit eliminates the experience that comes to language through the metaphorical process. Doubtless it is only in reductive interpretation that rationalization culminates in clearing away the symbolic base. These interpretations are readily expressed as follows: such and such a symbol seemed to intend to say something new in regard to a referential field that was only intimated or anticipated; finally, after due consideration, the symbol signifies only this positing of desire, that class membership, such a degree of strength or weakness of fundamental will. In relation to this true discourse, symbolic discourse becomes synonymous with illusory discourse.

It must be granted that these reductive interpretations are consistent with the semantic aim characteristic of the speculative order. Every interpretation aims at relocating the semantic outline sketched by metaphorical utterance inside an available horizon of understanding that can be mastered conceptually. But destruction of the metaphorical by the conceptual in rationalizing interpretations is not the only outcome of the interaction between different modalities of discourse. One can imagine a hermeneutic style where interpretation would conform both to the notion of concept and to that of the constitutive intention of the experience seeking to be expressed in the metaphorical mode.

Interpretation is then a mode of discourse that functions at the intersection of two domains, metaphorical and speculative. It is a composite discourse, therefore, and as such cannot but feel the opposite pull of two rival demands. On one side, interpretation seeks the clarity of the concept; on the other, it hopes to preserve the dynamism of meaning that the concept holds and pins down. This is the situation Kant considers in the celebrated paragraph 49 of the *Critique of the Faculty of Judgment*. He calls 'the spirit (*Geist*) in an aesthetic sense,' 'the life-giving principle of mind (*Gemüt*).' The metaphor of life comes to the fore at this point in the argument because the *game* in which imagination and understanding engage assumes a task assigned by the Ideas of reason, to which no concept is equal. But where the understanding fails, imagination still has the power of 'presenting' (*Darstellung*) the Idea. It is this 'presentation' of the Idea by the imagination that forces conceptual thought to *think more*.[81] Creative imagination is nothing other than this demand put to conceptual thought.[82]

This sheds light on our own notion of living metaphor. Metaphor is living not only to the extent that it vivifies a constituted language. Metaphor is living by virtue of the fact that it introduces the spark of imagination into a 'thinking more' at the conceptual level.[83] This struggle to 'think more,' guided by the 'vivifying principle,' is the 'soul' of interpretation.

5 / ONTOLOGICAL CLARIFICATION OF THE POSTULATE OF REFERENCE

How will speculative discourse reply, given its resources, to the semantic aim of poetic discourse? Through an ontological clarification of the postulate of reference presupposed in the preceding Study.

This clarification is not a linguistic but a philosophical task. The relation of language to its counterpart, reality, concerns the conditions for reference in general, and thus the meaning of language as a whole. Now, semantics can only allege the relation of language to reality but cannot *think* this relation as such.[84] Perhaps it will venture a philosophical conclusion unawares, by positing language as a whole and in itself as mediation between man and the world, between man and man, within the self itself.

Language then appears as that which raises the experience of the world to its articulation in discourse, that which founds communication and brings about the advent of man as speaking subject. By implicitly assuming these postulates, semantics takes as its own a thesis of 'the philosophy of language' inherited from von Humboldt.[85] But what is this philosophy of language if not philosophy itself, to the extent that it thinks the relation between being and being-said?

It will be objected, before proceeding any farther, that it is not possible to speak of a relation like this because there is no standpoint outside language and because it is and has always been *in* language that men claim to speak *about* language.

This is certainly true. Yet speculative discourse is possible, because language possesses the *reflective* capacity to place itself at a distance and to consider itself, as such and in its entirety, as related to the totality of what is. Language designates itself and its other. This reflective character extends what linguistics calls meta-linguistic functioning, but articulates it in another discourse, speculative discourse. It is then no longer a function that can be opposed to other functions, in particular to the referential function;[86] for it is the knowledge that accompanies the referential function itself, *the knowledge of its being-related to being*.

This reflective knowledge allows language to know that it is installed in being. The usual relationship between language and its referent is reversed: language becomes aware of itself in the self-articulation of the being which it is about. Far from locking language up inside itself, this reflective consciousness is the very consciousness of its openness. It implies the possibility of stating propositions regarding what is and of saying that this is brought to language in our saying it. This knowledge articulates the reference postulates in a discourse other than semantics, even when the latter is distinguished from semiotics. When I speak, I know that something is brought to language. This knowledge is no longer intra-linguistic but extra-linguistic; it moves from being to being-said, at the very time that language itself moves from sense to reference. Kant wrote: 'Something must be for something to appear.' We are saying: 'Something must be for something to be said.'

This proposition makes reality the final category upon which the whole of language can be thought, although not known, as the being-said of reality.

We must now attempt an ontological clarification against the background of this general thesis, not only of the postulates of reference in general, but of the postulate of *split* reference in accordance with the semantic aim of poetic discourse.

It is first as a *critical* instance, directed against our conventional concept of reality, that speculative discourse in its own sphere of articulation takes up the notion of split reference. The following question has arisen repeatedly: do we know what is meant by world, truth, reality? At the very heart of semantic analysis, this question anticipated the critical moment of speculative discourse. But the logical space of this question had not yet been opened. For this reason, it had to remain unarticulated, like a doubt infecting the non-critical uses of the concept of reality by many theorists. Consequently, we were suspicious of the distinction, held to be self-evident, between denotation and connotation. To the extent that this distinction amounted to one between cognitive and emotive values of discourse, we could see in it only the projection on the poetic level of a positivist prejudice holding that scientific discourse alone states reality.[87] We were set on the path of a properly critical use of the concept of reality by two more articulated themes. Poetic discourse, we said, is that in which the *epoché* of ordinary reference is the negative condition allowing a second-order reference to unfold. Furthermore, this unfolding is governed by the power of redescription belonging to certain heuristic fictions, in the manner of scientific models.[88]

Our task now is to work out the critical scope of the notions of secondary reference and redescription in order to insert them into speculative discourse.

One might be tempted to turn this critical function into a plea for the irrational. And, indeed, upsetting customary categorizations has the effect of a logical disordering through impertinent comparisons and incongruous encroachments, as if poetic discourse were working for the step by step de-categorization of our entire discourse. As regards second-order reference – the positive counterpart to this disordering – it seems to mark the invasion of language by the ante-predicative and the pre-categorial, and to require a concept of truth other than the concept of truth-verification, the correlative of our ordinary concept of reality.

In this regard, the earlier analysis provides further suggestions. The discussion of the notions of appropriateness and accuracy in Nelson Goodman's nominalism[89] allowed us to see that the appropriate character of certain verbal and non-verbal predicates can be assumed by speculative discourse only at the price of remaking the correlative concepts of truth and reality. The same question persistently returned in connection with what we ventured to call lyrical *mimêsis*, to express the power of redescription involved in the poetic articulation of so-called moods.[90] These poetical textures, we said, are no less heuristic than fictions in narrative form; feeling is no less ontological than representation. Does not this generalized power of 'redescription' explode the initial concept of 'description' to the extent that the latter remains within the limits of representation by objects? By the same count, must we not forgo the opposition between a discourse turned towards the 'outside,' which would be precisely descriptive discourse, and a discourse turned towards the 'inside,' which would portray only a mood and raise it to the hypothetical level? Is it not the very distinction between 'outside' and 'inside' that is shaken along with that between representation and feeling?

Other distinctions are shaken in turn, such as the distinction between discovering and creating and between finding and projecting. Poetic discourse brings to language a pre-objective world in which we find ourselves already rooted, but in which we also project our innermost possibilities. We must thus dismantle the reign of objects in order to let be, and to allow to be uttered, our primordial belonging to a world which we inhabit, that is to say, which at once precedes us and receives the imprint of our works. In short, we must restore to the fine word *invent* its twofold sense of both discovery and creation. It is because analysis had remained imprisoned within these familiar distinctions that the concept of metaphorical truth sketched at the end of Study 7 seemed caught in an insurmountable antinomy. The 'meta-poetics' of a Wheelwright, which we could call naïve, and the critical vigilance of a Turbayne, which did away with the ontological vehemence of poetic utterance through the concerted mastery of 'as if,' continued to oppose one another on the field of a verificationalist concept of truth, itself bound up with a positivist concept of reality.[91]

As we feared, it is here that the critical instance seems to turn into a plea for the irrational. When the reference to objects set over against a *judging* subject is suspended, is not the very structure of utterance shaken? When so many firmly recognized distinctions are erased, does not the notion of speculative discourse itself evaporate, and with this notion the dialectic of speculative and poetic?

This is the moment to recall the central contribution of Study 7: split reference, we said, signifies that the tension characterizing metaphorical utterance is carried ultimately by the copula *is*. Being-as means being *and* not being. Such-and-such was and was not the case. Within the framework of a semantics of reference, the ontological import of this paradox could not be seen; 'to be' operated there only as an affirmative copula, as being/apophansis. The distinction at the very centre of being as copula between the relational sense and the existential sense was at least an indication of a possible recovery by speculative discourse of the dialectic of being, of which the apophantic mark is this paradox of the copula *is*.

By what feature will the speculative discourse on being answer to the paradox of the copula, to the apophantic *is/is not*?

Going further back in our study, the interpretation of being-as reminds us in turn of an enigmatic remark made by Aristotle, a remark that to my knowledge is never taken up again in the body of his works. What does it mean for living metaphor 'to set (something) before the eyes'? Setting before the eyes, *Rhetoric* 3 replies, is to 'represent things as in a state of activity' (1411 b 24-5). And the philosopher specifies: when the poet infuses life into inanimate things, his verse 'represents everything as moving and living; and activity is movement' (1412 a 8).

By referring at this point in his reflection to a category of 'first philosophy,' Aristotle leads us to seek the key to ontological clarification of reference by reconsidering the meanings of being on the level of speculative thought. Yet it is worth noting that he does not refer again to the distinctions between the categorial significations of being but to an even more radical distinction, between being as potentiality and being as actuality.[92]

Extending the field of the polysemy of being in this way is of the greatest importance for our own viewpoint. It signifies, first of all, that the ultimate meaning of the reference of poetic discourse is articulated in speculative discourse: indeed, actuality has meaning only in the discourse on being. This signifies as well that the semantic aim of metaphorical utterance does intersect most decisively with the aim of ontological discourse, not at the point where metaphor by analogy and categorial analogy meet, but at the point where the reference of metaphorical utterance brings being as actuality and as potentiality into play. Finally, it signifies that this intersection of the poetic and the ontological does not concern tragic poetry alone,[93] since the remark in the *Rhetoric* cited above extends to poetry as a whole; it applies to lyrical *mimêsis* as well, what (to use an expression suggested in Study 7) we have termed the power 'to represent things as in a state of activity.'

But what indeed can this be interpreted to mean?

Do not these same difficulties that concern the ontology of power and act arise at the level of poetry as well? For, as we have been taught by Aristotle himself, ontology says hardly more than this: potency and actuality are defined correlatively, that is to say, in a circular fashion;[94] the corresponding discourse is not demonstrative but inductive and analogical.[95] Of course, we established above that analogy is not a lamentable metaphor. But to the difficulties of ontological discourse in general are added the difficulties proper to these two most radical meanings of being: did Aristotle really master the differing degrees of the concept of potency?[96] Did he order convincingly the closely related concepts of actuality, *praxis*, *poiêsis*, motion?[97]

As a result, it can only be in an exploratory and not in a dogmatic fashion, by questioning instead of asserting, that we can attempt to interpret the formula 'signifying things in act.' And this interpretation is inseparable from the ontological clarification of the postulate of metaphorical reference.

What, then, are we to understand by 'signifying things in act'?

This may mean seeing things as *actions*. This is certainly the case in tragedy, which shows men 'as acting, as in act.' And indeed, action has a special place in that the act inheres entirely in the agent, as vision does in the one who sees, life in the soul, and contemplation in the mind. In acting, the act is whole and entire in each of its moments and does not cease when the end is attained: 'At the same time we are living well and have lived well, and are happy and have been happy' (*Metaphysics* Θ 6, 1048 b 25-6). This vision of the world as a grand *gesture* might be that of a Goethe rewriting Saint John's Prologue: 'In the beginning was the Act.' And yet, to see all things as actions, is this not to see them as 'human, all too human,' and so to accord an improper prerogative to man himself?

Is seeing all things in act seeing them in the manner of a work of art, a result of technical production? Would reality then come to be seen in our eyes as some vast artifice engendered by an artist's will, provided 'nothing external hinders,' as it is stated in *Metaphysics* Θ 7? But does this not burden our gaze with an anthropomorphism even heavier than in the preceding interpretation?

Would seeing all things in act then be seeing them as naturally blossoming? This interpretation seems closer to the examples in the *Rhetoric* (seeing inanimate things as animate). Is this not what we ourselves suggested at the end of Study 1 – *lively* expression is that which expresses existence as *alive*? Signifying things in act would be seeing things as not prevented from becoming, seeing them as blossoming forth. But then would not signifying things in act also be signifying potency, in the inclusive sense that stands for every production of motion or of rest? Would the poet then be the one who perceives power as act and act as power? He who sees as whole and complete what is sketchy and in process, who perceives every form attained as a promise of newness? In short, he who reaches this 'source of the movement of natural objects, being present in them somehow, either potentially or in complete reality' (*Metaphysics* Δ 4, 1015 a 18-19), which the Greeks called *phusis*?[98]

For the modern philosopher, coming after the death of Aristotelian physics, this sense of *phusis* is perhaps empty once more, something that poetic language asks speculative discourse to consider. It is then the task of speculative discourse to seek after the place where appearance signifies 'generating what grows.' As this sense is no longer to be sought in the region of objects, that occupied by physical bodies and living organisms, it indeed seems to be at the level of appearance as a whole and as such that the poetic verb 'signifies things in act.' In relation to this open and unlimited acceptation, signifying actions, signifying artifice, and signifying movement are already determinations, that is to say, limitations and restrictions that miss something of what is indicated in the expression 'signifying the blossoming of appearing.' If there is a point in our experience where living expression states living existence, it is where our movement up the entropic slope of language encounters the movement by which we come back this side of the distinctions between actuality, action, production, motion.

So, once more, the task of speculative discourse is to seek after the place where appearing means 'generating what grows.' This project and this program lead us once more across the path of Heidegger. The final stages of his philosophy attempt to make speculative thought resonate with the poet's utterance. It is all the more appropriate to evoke Heidegger here in that, at the heart of his critique of the metaphysical interpretation of metaphor, the metaphor of blossoming forced itself upon him as the metaphor for metaphor. The 'flowers' of our words – *Worte, wie Blumen* – utter existence in its blossoming forth.[99]

In truth, as our investigation enters its next to last stage, Heidegger's philosophy steps forth as intermingled and inescapable attempt and temptation. It is an attempt from which we must draw inspiration whenever it manifestly contributes to clarifying speculative thought in accordance with the semantic aim that animated Aristotle's investigation into the multiple meanings of being; and it is a temptation we must shun when the difference between speculative and poetic threatens once again to disappear.

I agree with the principal commentators on Heidegger[100] that the core of his thought in its last stage is the belonging-together of *Erörterung* and *Ereignis*. The first term designates both the search for the 'place' and also the 'commentary' on this search. The second term designates the 'thing itself' that is to be thought. The belonging-together of *Erörterung* and *Ereignis* as the 'topology of being' is what typifies speculative thought in its 'constitutive gesture.'

That the meaning of *Ereignis* has the same aim as what was formerly thought as actuality/potency is confirmed negatively by the refusal to reduce its scope to event (*Geschehnis*) or to process (*Vorkommnis*). Furthermore, it is confirmed positively by the relation between *Ereignis* and the *es gibt* that announces every blossoming of appearing under the connotation of 'gift.' *Ereignis* and *es gibt* mark the opening and the unfolding by reason of which there are objects for a judging subject. The 'thing' that is given to thought in this way is called, in the vocabulary of topology, 'region,' the capacity for coming to a 'meeting,' the nearness of the 'near.' But have we not been prepared for these variations in distance by the play of resemblance?

That *Erörterung* in its turn marks the difficulty of saying that corresponds to the difficulty of being[101] should not surprise a reader who has already acknowledged the conceptual labour incorporated into the old doctrine of the analogy of being. When the philosopher fights on two fronts, against the seduction of the ineffable and against the power of 'ordinary speech' (*Sprechen*), in order to arrive at a 'saying' (*Sagen*) that would be the triumph neither of inarticulateness nor of the signs available to the speaker and manipulated by him – is he not in a situation comparable to that of the thinker of Antiquity or the Middle Ages, seeking his path between the powerlessness of a discourse given over to the dissemination of meanings and the mastery of univocity through the logic of genera?

By moving towards *Ereignis*, *Erörterung* moves towards a 'same,' an 'identical,' by which it is defined as speculative thinking.[102] And this 'same' is like analogy for the Ancients, to the extent that here, too, resemblance assembles [*ressembler ... c'est rassembler*].

Does this mean that once again speculative discourse threatens to merge with poetry? Not at all. Even if *Ereignis* is called a metaphor,[103] it is a philosopher's metaphor, in the sense in which the analogy of being can, strictly speaking, be termed a metaphor, but one which always remains distinct from a poet's metaphor. The very way in which Heidegger juxtaposes poetic discourse and philosophical discourse without confusing them, as in *Aus der Erfahrung des Denkens*,[104] confirms that the gulf cannot be bridged between the Same that is to be thought and poetic resemblance. What is remarkable, in this short text, is that the poem does not serve as an ornament to the philosophical aphorism, and that the latter does not constitute the poem's translation. Poem and aphorism are in a mutual accord of resonance that respects their difference. To the imaginative power of thought-full poetry, the poet replies with the speculative power of poeticizing thought.

Certainly the difference is infinitesimal when the philosopher approves a thinking poetry – that of poets who themselves write poetically on language, like Hölderlin – and when he responds in a thinking that poeticizes, 'semi-poetic thinking.' But even here, speculative thought employs the metaphorical resources of language in order to create meaning and answers thus to the call of the 'thing' to be said with a semantic innovation. A procedure like this has nothing scandalous about it as long as speculative thought knows itself to be distinct and responsive because it is thinking. Furthermore, the philosopher's metaphors may well resemble those of the poet – like the latter, they diverge from the world of objects and ordinary language – but they do not merge with the poet's metaphors.

The same must be said in regard to the well-known practice of etymologism, a practice already found in Plato and in Hegel. The philosopher has a perfect right to try and say what is strange and distant by rejuvenating some dead metaphor or by restoring some archaic meaning of a word. Our own investigation has prepared us to say that this language ploy involves no mystique of 'primordial meaning.' A buried sense becomes a new meaning in the present instance of discourse. This is all the more true when speculative thought adopts the new meaning in order to blaze a path to the 'thing' itself. The return of ancient metaphors – that of light, the ground, the home, the way or path – must be regarded in the same manner. Their use in a new context is a form of innovation. The same metaphors can contribute to a Platonism of the invisible or glorify the visibility of appearance. This is why if no metaphor is privileged, neither is any forbidden. So it is not surprising that the ancient meditation on the polysemy of being returns and that, in the manner of the theorists of the analogy of being, we meditate on signifying more – on a *Mehrdeutigkeit* – which is distinguished from pure and simple dissemination – from *Vieldeutigkeit*.[105] In confronting this new polysemy of being, philosophy confirms that thinking is not poeticizing.

It will be objected that this way of reading Heidegger takes into account neither his wish to break with metaphysics, nor the 'leap' outside its circle that poeticizing thought demands.

It is here, I admit, that I regret the position assumed by Heidegger.

This inclosure of the previous history of Western thought within the unity of 'the' metaphysical seems to me to express a sort of vengefulness – which this thinking, nevertheless, calls us to renounce – along with a will to power that seems inseparable from it.[106] The unity of 'the' metaphysical is an after-the-fact construction of Heideggerian thought, intended to vindicate his own labour of thinking and to justify the renunciation of any kind of thinking that is not a genuine overcoming of metaphysics. But why should this philosophy claim for itself alone, to the exclusion of all its predecessors, that it breaks through and innovates? It seems to me time to deny oneself the convenience, which has become a laziness in thinking, of lumping the whole of Western thought together under a single word, metaphysics.[107]

If one can say that Heidegger is part of the lineage of speculative philosophy, it is to the extent that he in fact pursues a task analogous to that of his predecessors by means of new thinking and new language, and in the interests of a new experience.

What philosopher worthy of the name prior to Heidegger has not meditated on the metaphor of the way and considered himself to be the first to embark on a path that is language itself addressing him? Who among them has not sought the 'ground' and the 'foundation,' the 'dwelling' and the 'clearing'? Who has not believed that truth was 'near' and yet difficult to perceive and even more difficult to say, that it was hidden and yet manifest, open and yet veiled? Who has not, in one way or another, linked the forward movement of thought to its ability to 'regress,' to take a step 'backward'? Who has not attempted to distinguish the 'beginning of thinking' from any chronological starting point? Who has not conceptualized his own task essentially as a labour of thought directed toward itself and against itself? Who has not believed that to continue one must make a break and 'leap' outside the circle of accepted ideas? Who has not opposed thinking based on a horizon to knowledge based on objects, opposed meditating thought to representative thought? Who has not known that ultimately the 'way' and the 'place' are the same, and 'method' and 'thing' identical? Who has not seen that the relation between thinking and being is not a relation in the logical sense of the word, that this relation presupposes no terms preceding it but, in one way or another, constitutes the belonging-together of thinking and being? Finally, what philosopher before Heidegger has not attempted to think identity other than as tautology, on the basis of this belonging-together of thinking and being?

This is why, in contrast to the interpretation Heidegger gives of his work, the value of his philosophy of *Erörterung-Ereignis* lies in its contribution to the continuous and unceasing problematic of thinking and of being. Let the philosopher write *Sein, Seyn, S̶e̶i̶n̶* one after the other – it is still the question of being that is posed in what is crossed out. Nor is it the first time that being has had to be cancelled out in order to be recognized in its reserve and in its generosity, in its modesty and in its gratuitousness. Like the speculative thinkers who preceded him, Heidegger is seeking the key word, 'the one that decisively carries the whole movement.' For him, *es gibt* is this key word. It carries the mark of a determined ontology, in which the neutral is more expressive than the personal and in which the granting of being at the same time assumes the form of something destined. This ontology proceeds from a listening turned more attentively to the Greeks than to the Hebrews, more to Nietzsche than to Kierkegaard. So be it. It is appropriate that we in turn be attentive to this ontology without soliciting it. As such an ontology, however, it cannot assume the privilege of opposing all other ontologies by confining them inside the bounds of 'the' metaphysical. Its unacceptable claim is that it puts an end to the history of being, as if 'being disappeared in *Ereignis.*'

The price of this claim is the inescapable ambiguity of the later works, divided between the logic of their continuity with speculative thought and the logic of their break with metaphysics. The first logic places *Ereignis* and the *es gibt* in the lineage of a mode of thought that unceasingly rectifies itself, unceasingly searches for a *saying* more appropriate than ordinary *speech*, a *saying* that would be a *showing* and a *letting-be*; a mode of thought, finally, which could never leave discourse behind. The second logic leads to a series of erasures and repeals that cast thought into the void, reducing it to hermeticism and affectedness, carrying etymological games back to the mystification of 'primitive sense.' Above all, this second logic invites us to sever discourse from its propositional character, forgetting Hegel's lesson in regard to speculative propositions, which do not cease to be propositions.[108] This philosophy gives new life in this way to the seductions of the unarticulated and the unexpressed, even to a kind of despair of language resembling that found in the next to last proposition in Wittgenstein's *Tractatus.*

In concluding, I should like to retain only this excellent statement from the later works of Heidegger: 'Between these two [thinking and poetry] there exists a secret kinship because in the service of language both intercede on behalf of language and give lavishly of themselves. Between both there is, however, at the same time an abyss for they "dwell on the most widely separated mountains."'[109]

What is described here is the very dialectic between the modes of discourse in their proximity and in their difference.

On the one hand, poetry, in itself and by itself, sketches a 'tensional' conception of truth for thought. Here are summed up all the forms of 'tensions' brought to light by semantics: tension between subject and predicate, between literal interpretation and metaphorical interpretation, between identity and difference. Then these are gathered together in the theory of split reference. They come to completion finally in the paradox of the copula, where being-as signifies being and not being. By this *turn* of expression, poetry, in combination with other modes of discourse,[110] articulates and preserves the experience of belonging that places man in discourse and discourse in being.

Speculative thought, on the other hand, bases its work upon the dynamism of metaphorical utterance, which it construes according to its own sphere of meaning. Speculative discourse can respond in this way only because the *distanciation,* which constitutes the critical moment, is contemporaneous with the experience of belonging that is opened or recovered by poetic discourse,[111] and because poetic discourse, as text and as work,[112] prefigures the distanciation that speculative thought carries to its highest point of reflection. Finally, the splitting of reference and redescription of reality submitted to the imaginative variations of fiction strike us as specific figures of distanciation, when they are reflected and rearticulated by speculative discourse.

What is given to thought in this way by the 'tensional' truth of poetry is the most primordial, most hidden dialectic – the dialectic that reigns between the experience of belonging as a whole and the power of distanciation that opens up the space of speculative thought.

From existentialism to the
philosophy of language*

Nineteen sixty-one was the year when I published *Fallible Man* and *The Symbolism of Evil*, and at that time a specific problem occupied my mind: how is it possible to introduce within the framework of a philosophy of the will, on which I had written ten years earlier, some fundamental experiences such as guilt, bondage, alienation, or, to speak in religious terms, sin? As such this problem could be expressed in terms of an existential philosophy. All existential philosophies of the forties and fifties had met this problem. We may speak of inauthentic life with Heidegger, or boundary situations (*Grenzsituationen*) with Jaspers, or of Being and Having and of despair with Gabriel Marcel. My problem belonged to the sphere of questions, with a somewhat more specific interest. My problem was to distinguish between finitude and guilt. I had the impression, or even the conviction, that these two terms tended to be identified in classical existentialism at the cost of both experiences, guilt becoming a particular case of finitude and for that reason beyond cure and forgiveness, and finitude, on the other hand, being affected by a kind of diffused sense of sadness and despair through guilt. This is why I chose *Finitude and Guilt* as a general title for the two volumes of which I spoke and the problem was that of their difference and of their connection.

But at the same time, a secondary problem emerged, which tended afterwards to pass to the forefront of my inquiries. This was the problem of language. Why? Because in order to introduce the dimension of evil into the structure of the will, a fundamental change in the method of description itself was required. In my first work I had relied heavily on a reflective method which came from both Husserl and the existentialist pair, Jas-

* Reprinted from *Criterion* 10, 3 (Spring 1971) by permission of the Divinity School, University of Chicago. Originally presented in address form before the Divinity School at a luncheon on 5 May 1971. Translated by David Pellauer.

pers and Marcel, to whom I had devoted two books. I may now call this kind of first description an existential phenomenology, although at the time I did not dare call it phenomenology for I did not wish to cover my own attempt with the authority of Husserl, whom I was translating into French. It was phenomenology, however, in the sense that it tried to extract from lived experience the essential meanings and structures of purpose, project, motive, wanting, trying, and so on.

I note in passing that phenomenology at that time had already attacked problems which now are in the forefront of the school of linguistic analysis with the philosophy of action. But if it was phenomenology, it was existential phenomenology in the sense that these essential structures implied the recognition of the central problem of embodiment, of *le corps propre*. Anyhow, whatever might be the relation between phenomenology and existentialism in this first attempt, this kind of philosophizing did not yet raise any particular problem of language, for a direct language was thought to be available. This direct language was ordinary language in which we find words like purpose, motive, and so on. This is why I now believe that there is an intersection of the philosophy of ordinary language and phenomenology at this first level.

Now the consideration of the problem of evil brought into the field of research new linguistic perplexities which did not occur earlier. These linguistic perplexities were linked to the use of symbolic language as an indirect approach to the problem of guilt. Why an indirect approach? Why symbolic language when we have to pass from a philosophy of finitude to a philosophy of guilt? This was the question that intrigued me. The fact is that we have a direct language to say purpose, motive, and 'I can,' but we speak of evil by means of metaphors such as estrangement, errance, burden, and bondage. Moreover, these primary symbols do not occur unless they are embedded within intricate narratives of myth which tell the story of how evil began: how at the beginning of time the gods quarrelled; how the soul fell into an ugly body; or how a primitive man was tempted, trespassed a prohibition, and became an exiled rebel.

It seemed, therefore, that direct reflection on oneself could not go very far without undertaking a roundabout way, the detour of a hermeneutic of these symbols. I had to introduce a hermeneutical dimension within the structure of reflective thought itself. In other words, I could speak of purposive action without symbolic language, but I could not speak of bad will or of evil without a hermeneutic. This was the first way in which the problem of language appeared in a kind of philosophy which was not at first a philosophy of language, but a philosophy of the will. I had been compelled by my initial subject to inquire into the structure of symbolism and myth, and this inquiry by itself led me to the more general problem of hermeneutics. What is hermeneutics if there is something like an indirect language, a metaphorical language, if there are symbols and myths?

But I must now say that at that time I was not aware of the real dimension of the hermeneutical problem. Perhaps because I did not want to be drawn into the immensity of this problem, I tried to limit the definition of hermeneutics to the specific problem of the interpretation of symbolic language. I still held this position in my book on Freud which I shall come to in a moment. In the last chapter of *The Symbolism of Evil* and in the first part of *Freud and Philosophy*, I defined symbolism and hermeneutics in terms of each other. On the one hand, a symbolism requires an interpretation because it is based upon a specific semantic structure, the structure of double meaning expressions. Reciprocally, there is a hermeneutical problem because there is an indirect language. Therefore I identified hermeneutics with the art of deciphering indirect meanings.

Today I should be less inclined to limit hermeneutics to the discovery of hidden meanings in symbolic language and would prefer to link hermeneutics to the more general problem of written language and texts. (I shall come to this at the end.) Nevertheless, such was the way I was introduced to the hermeneutical problem.

At the same time, or maybe somewhat later, I felt compelled to shift my interest from the original problem of the structure of the will to the problem of language as such, which had remained subsidiary even at the time when I was studying the strange structures of the symbolism of myths. I was compelled to do so for several reasons which I will now try to explain. First, my reflection on the structure of psychoanalytic theory; secondly, the important change in the philosophical scene, at least in France, where structuralism was beginning to replace existentialism and even phenomenology; thirdly, my continuing interest in the problem raised by religious language, and, more specifically, by the so-called theologies of the Word in the post-Bultmannian school; and finally, my increasing interest in the British and American school of ordinary language philosophy, in which I saw a way both of renewing phenomenology and of replying to the excesses of structuralism.

My interest in psychoanalysis was in a sense the result of my interest in the problem of will, bad will, and guilt. I could not go very far indeed in a reflection concerning guilt without encountering the psychoanalytic interpretation of guilt. But psychoanalysis was also directly linked to linguistic perplexities due to its own use of symbolic structures. Not only the problem of guilt, therefore, compelled me to consider the problem of psychoanalysis, but also the general structure of language according to psychoanalysis. Are not dreams and symptoms some kind of indirect language? What is more, psychoanalysis claims to give not only a specific interpretation of dreams and symptoms, but also of the whole fabric of cultural symbols and of religious myths, which I had previously approached with a merely descriptive method similar to that used in comparative history of religions and especially by Mircea Eliade. Therefore, I had to consider something which had escaped my reflections until then, the fact that there was not only one hermeneutic, but two hermeneutics, since psychoanalysis claimed to interpret symbols by reducing them. The idea of a reductive hermeneutic could no longer be overlooked. In fact, I had to understand that Freud was only one of the exponents of the reductive hermeneutic, and that Marx and Nietzsche, and before them Feuerbach, had to be understood as the fathers of this reductive method. The claim of psychoanalysis to explain symbols and myths as fruits of unconscious representations, as distorted expressions of the relation between libidinal impulses and the repressive structure of the super-ego, compelled me to enlarge my first concept of hermeneutics beyond a mere semantic analysis of double meaning expressions.

Hermeneutics appeared henceforth as a battle field traversed by two opposing trends, the first tending toward a reductive explanation, the second tending toward a recollection or a retrieval of the original meaning of the symbol. My problem was to link these two approaches and to understand their relation as dynamic and as moving from first *naïveté* through critique toward what I called at the time a second *naïveté*. Therefore, without giving up my earlier definition of hermeneutics as the general theory of symbolic language, I had to introduce into the theory the polarity between these two hermeneutical requirements and to link philosophical reflection not only to a semantics of indirect language, but to the conflictual structure of the hermeneutical task. In this way a dramatic element was added to the previous recognition of the necessity of the detour through obscure and hidden meaning.

My book on Freud, published in 1965, reflects this double recognition, first of the necessity of the detour through indirect signs, and secondly of the conflictual structure of hermeneutics and thus of self-knowledge. Self-knowledge is a striving for truth by means of this inner contest between reductive and recollective interpretation.

Now a word about the second reason for shifting from existential phenomenology to a more linguistically concerned kind of philosophizing. I spoke of a general change in the philosophical scene in France, chiefly due to the emergence of structuralism as the main trend in philosophy. This new model of philosophizing came from linguistics; more precisely, it was an effort to extend to semantics and to all semiological disciplines the model which had succeeded in phonology. Inasmuch as there are signs in human life, the structural model was to be utilized. As you know, this structural model relies mainly on the affirmation that language, before being a process or an event, is a system, and that this system is not established at the level of the speaker's consciousness, but at a lower level, that of a kind of structural unconscious. Structuralism as a philosophy draws radical consequences from this epistemological model which directly affect the presuppositions of existentialism. First of all, the primacy of subjectivity which was so strongly emphasized by existentialism is overthrown by this displacement of analysis from the level of the subject's intentions to the level of linguistic and semiotic structures.

Hermeneutics is also called into question along with existential phenomenology and existentialism. The idea that language is a closed system of signs, within which each element merely refers to the other elements of the system, excludes the claim of hermeneutics to reach beyond the 'sense' – as the immanent content of the text – to its 'reference,' i.e., to what it says *about* the world. For structuralism, language does not refer to anything outside of itself, it constitutes a world for itself. Not only the reference of the text to an external world, but also its connections to an author who *intended* it and to a reader who *interprets* it are excluded by structuralism. This twofold reference to a subject of the text, whether author or reader, is rejected as psychologism or 'subjectivism.'

Confronted by this situation, I tried to react in the following way. First, I tried to become more competent in linguistic problems. Secondly, I tried to incorporate within hermeneutics as much as I could of this structural approach by means of a better connection between the stage of objective explanation and the stage of subjective appropriation. My discussions about and with Lévi-Strauss reflect this effort.

The kind of hermeneutics which I now favour starts from the recognition of the objective meaning of the text as distinct from the subjective intention of the author. This objective meaning is not something hidden behind the text. Rather it is a requirement addressed to the reader. The interpretation accordingly is a kind of obedience to this injunction starting from the text. The concept of 'hermeneutical circle' is not ruled out by this shift within hermeneutics. Instead it is formulated in new terms. It does not proceed so much from an intersubjective relation linking the subjectivity of the author and the subjectivity of the reader as from a connection between two discourses, the discourse of the text and the discourse of the interpretation. This connection means that what has to be interpreted in a text is what it says and what it speaks about, i.e., the kind of world which it opens up or discloses; and the final act of 'appropriation' is less the projection of one's own prejudices into the text than the 'fusion of horizons' – to speak like Hans-Georg Gadamer – which occurs when the world of the reader and the world of the text merge into one another.

This shift within hermeneutics from a 'romanticist' trend to a more 'objectivist' trend is the result of this long travel through structuralism. At the same time, I had to depart from my previous definition of hermeneutics as the interpretation of symbolic language. Now I should tend to relate hermeneutics to the specific problems raised by the translation of the objective meaning of written language into the personal act of speaking which a moment ago I called appropriation. In that way, the broader question, What is it to interpret a text? tends to replace the initial question, What is it to interpret symbolic language? The connection between my first definition and the new emerging definition remains an unsolved problem for me, which will be the topic of my forthcoming work. The course which I gave at this university last year represented the first attempt to overcome this difficulty.

I want now to say a few words concerning the third field of inquiry in which I found an impulse and a help for my effort to co-ordinate phenomenology and the philosophy of language. The post-Bultmannian schools of theology, especially those of Ebeling and Fuchs, seemed to me to be following a parallel evolution. Bultmann had imposed two fundamental limitations upon the theory of religious language. On the one hand, myth was taken to be the opposite of Kerygma. In that way, demythologization became the central problem and this prevented grasping the question of religious language as a unique problem. On the other hand, understanding had to be opposed to objectification in a manner similar to the opposition between *Verstehen* and *Erklären* inherited from Dilthey. Thus Biblical theology remained trapped in the perplexities of romanticist hermeneutics. The recognition of this led post-Bultmannian exegetes and theologians to subordinate the problem of demythologizing and the problem of existential interpretation to the broader problem of the 'linguisticality' of human experience which makes possible both the emergence of texts and the response of interpretation to this emergence. The polarity between myth and Kerygma, on the one hand, and between interpretation and explanation, on the other hand, appeared to be only partial solutions to the more general question of how religious language functions.

Therefore studies devoted to the word *God* and in general to 'God-talk' appear from this broader standpoint to be more fruitful than the studies of myth and of demythologizing. These inquiries intersect the linguistic and semantic question of how a word functions in different contexts. They also intersect the question of how a form of discourse – such as a narrative, an oracle, a psalm, or a parable – is linked to a specific theological content. This is why I am so interested in what Donald Evans, John Macquarrie, and Langdon Gilkey are doing in the field of the semantics of religious discourse. And I am just as interested in what Gerhard von Rad,

Joachim Jeremias, Daniel Via, and Norman Perrin are saying concerning the relation between the narrative form or the form of the parable and specific kinds of confession of faith.

What we need now is a new framework which would allow us to connect Biblical hermeneutics to general hermeneutics conceived as the question of what is understanding in relation to text-explanation. It is the function of general hermeneutics to answer problems such as: What is a text? i.e., what is the relation between spoken and written language? What is the relation between explanation and understanding within the encompassing act of reading? What is the relation between a structural analysis and an existential appropriation? Such are the general problems of hermeneutics to which a Biblical hermeneutics has to be submitted.

On the other hand, the problem of the specificity of Biblical hermeneutics is perfectly legitimate: but it could only be raised, in a consistent manner, against the background of a general hermeneutics. Questions like these would arise: What do we mean by the Kerygmatic kernel of 'preaching'? What are the connections between faith and Word, between the character of 'disclosure' belonging to all religious texts and even to non-religious texts (tragedy, poetry, novels, etc.) and what is intended by the concept of revelation? What is the contribution of a general theory of discourse and of texts to the traditional notion of inspiration? All these classical problems may be renewed when related in some dialectical way to the topics and methods of a general hermeneutics.

I finish this survey of the problems and methods which contributed to my present concern for a philosophical hermeneutics with a few words concerning the growing influence of the British and American school of ordinary language philosophy on my inquiries. I do not think that this philosophy has the last word, but I do think that it is at least a necessary first stage in philosophical inquiry. To my mind, the contribution of ordinary language philosophy is twofold. First, it has proved that ordinary language does not, cannot, and must not function according to the model of ideal languages constructed by logicians and mathematicians. The variability of semantic values, their sensitivity to contexts, the irreducibly polysemic character of lexical terms in ordinary language, these are not provisory defects or diseases which a reformulation of language could eliminate, rather they are the permanent and fruitful conditions of the functioning of ordinary language. This polysemic feature of our words in ordinary language now appears to me to be the basic condition for symbolic discourse and in that way, the most primitive layer in a theory of metaphor, symbol, parable, etc.

Secondly, ordinary language now appears to me, following the work of Wittgenstein and Austin, to be a kind of conservatory for expressions which have preserved the highest descriptive power as regards human experience, particularly in the realms of action and feelings. This appropriateness of some of the most refined distinctions attached to ordinary words provides all phenomenological analysis with linguistic guidelines. Now the recapturing of the intentions of ordinary language experiences may become the major task of a linguistic phenomenology, a phenomenology which would escape both the futility of mere linguistic distinctions and the unverifiability of all claim to direct intuition of lived experience. Thanks to this grafting of linguistic analysis to phenomenology, the latter may be cured of its illness and find its second wind. (I surmise that the same thing may be said of ordinary language philosophy; that its conjunction with phenomenology could also enhance and renew it.)

Not only phenomenology, but also hermeneutics may draw some benefit from an accurate inquiry into the functioning of ordinary language. I have already alluded to the connection between the functioning of symbolic discourse and the polysemic structure of our ordinary words. We may extend the parallelism further: understanding, in the most ordinary sense of the word – let us say, in conversation – is already an intersubjective process. Inasmuch as ordinary language differs from an ideal language in that it has no fixed expressions independent of their contextual uses, to understand discourse is to interpret the actualizations of its polysemic values according to the permissions and suggestions proposed by the context. What happens in the far more intricate cases of text-interpretation and what constitutes the key problem of hermeneutics is already foreshadowed in the interpretive process as it occurs in ordinary language. Thus the whole problem of text-interpretation could be renewed by the recognition of its roots in the functioning of ordinary language itself.

Such are the problems I am now working and reflecting on.

Notes

Full bibliographical information for publications identified in the notes by author and title may be found in the list of works cited.

TRANSLATOR'S INTRODUCTION

1 Aristotle *Poetics* 1459 a 5-8, Ingram Bywater, trans. in *The Basic Works of Aristotle*
2 For other English-language introductions to Ricoeur's thought, see Don Ihde *Hermeneutic Phenomenology: The Philosophy of Paul Ricoeur.* Northwestern University Press, Evanston, Ill. 1971; David M. Rasmussen *Mythic-Symbolic Language and Philosophical Anthropology: a Constructive Interpretation of the Thought of Paul Ricoeur.* Nijhoff, The Hague 1971; and Patrick Bourgeois *The Extension of Paul Ricoeur's Hermeneutic* Nijhoff, The Hague 1975. Ihde's book contains a selective but extensive Ricoeur bibliography.
3 Translations of many of Ricoeur's important contributions in these areas have appeared in *Political and Social Essays* Joseph Bien and David Stewart, trans., Ohio University Press, Athens, Ohio 1974.

STUDY 1

1 Gérard Genette 'La rhétorique restreinte'
2 Concerning the beginnings of rhetoric, see E.M. Cope *An Introduction to Aristotle's Rhetoric* I: 1-4; A.É. Chaignet *La Rhétorique et son histoire* 1-69; O. Navarre *Essai sur la rhétorique grecque avant Aristote*; R. Barthes 'L'ancienne rhétorique, aide mémoire' 175-6; G.A. Kennedy *The Art of Persuasion in Greece.*
3 Socrates attributes this formula to Gorgias in the course of the dialogue that pits him against the Athenian master of rhetoric (*Gorgias* 453 a). Its germ, however, was discovered by Corax, a student of Empedocles, and the first author (followed then by Tisias of Syracuse) of a didactic treatise (*techné*) on the oratorical arts. The expression itself conveys the idea of a governing and sovereign operation (Chaignet *Rhétorique* 5).
4 Diogenes Laeartius 8: 57; 'in the *Sophist* Aristotle reports that "Empedocles was the first to discover (*eurein*) rhetoric"' (cited in Chaignet *Rhétorique* 3, n.1).
5 The *Protagoras, Gorgias,* and *Phaedrus* lay out Plato's uncompromising condemnation of rhetoric: 'But we won't disturb the rest of Tisias and Gorgias, who realized

that probability deserves more respect than truth, who could make trifles seem important and important points trifles by the force of their language, who dressed up novelties as antiques and vice versa, found out how to argue concisely or at interminable length about anything and everything' (*Phaedrus* 267 a-b, trans. Hackforth; see also *Gorgias* 449 a-458 c). Finally, 'true' rhetoric is dialectic itself, i.e. philosophy (*Phaedrus* 271 c).

6 'To be brief, then, I will express myself in the language of geometricians – for by now perhaps you may follow me. Sophistic is to legislation what beautification is to gymnastics, and rhetoric to justice what cookery is to medicine' (*Gorgias* 465 b-c, trans. W.D. Woodhead). The generic term for these simulations of art – cookery, cosmetics, rhetoric, sophistic – is 'flattery' (*kolakeia*, ibid. 463 b). The underlying argument of which this polemic presents the negative side, is that the mode of being called 'health' in the order of the body has a counterpart in the order of the spirit. This homology of the two 'therapies' regulates that of the two pairs of authentic arts, gymnastics and medicine on the one hand and justice and legislation on the other (*Gorgias* 464 c).

7 '... to discover the means of coming as near such success [in persuading] as the circumstances of each particular case allow' (*Rhetoric* 1, 1355 b 10); '... it is the function of one and the same art [rhetoric] to discern the real and the apparent means of persuasion, just as it is the function of dialectic to discern the real and the apparent syllogism' (1355 b 15); 'Rhetoric may be defined as the faculty of observing in any given case the available means of persuasion' (1355 b 25); 'But rhetoric we look upon as the power of observing the means of persuasion on almost any subject presented to us' (1355 b 32).

8 In book 2, chapter 24 of the *Rhetoric* (1402 a 17-20), Aristotle credits Corax with inventing the rhetoric of the probable: 'It is of this line of argument that Corax's *Art of Rhetoric* is composed. If the accused is not open to the charge – for instance if a weakling be tried for violent assault – the defence is that he was not likely to do such a thing.' Nevertheless, Aristotle cites Corax in the context of 'apparent enthymemes,' or paralogisms. Plato before him had given the honour of fathering probabilistic argumentation to Tisias 'or whoever it really was and whatever he is pleased to be called after [Corax, the crow?]' (*Phaedrus* 273 c). Regarding the use of such *eikota* arguments in Corax and Tisias, see Chaignet *Rhétorique* 6-7, and J.F. Dobson *The Greek Orators* chapter 1, section 5.

9 The enthymeme, the 'rhetorical syllogism' (*Rhetoric* 1356 b 5), and 'the example,' which belongs to the inductive order (1356 b 15), are frameworks for arguments that 'deal with what is in the main contingent' (1357 a 15). Now a contingency or a 'probability is a thing that usually happens; not, however, as some definitions would suggest, anything whatever that usually happens, but only if it belongs to the class of the "contingent" or the "variable." It bears the same relation to that in respect of which it is probable as the universal bears to the particular' (1357 a 34-5).

10 For the various hypotheses concerning the order of composition of the *Rhetoric* and the *Poetics*, see Marsh McCall *Ancient Rhetorical Theories of Simile and Comparison* 29-35.

11 References to the actual wording of the *Poetics* are to be found in *Rhetoric* 3: 2, 1; 3: 2, 5; 3: 2, 7; 3: 10, 7. The development of *eikôn* in the *Rhetoric*, which has no counterpart in the *Poetics*, poses a separate problem; for this, see section 3 of this Study, below.

12 Ingram Bywater, trans. in *The Basic Works of Aristotle*
13 The problem of translating the greek *lexis* has inspired a variety of solutions. Among French translators, Hatzfeld and Dufour (*La Poétique d'Aristote* Lille-Paris 1899) employ 'discours'; J. Hardy says 'élocution'; and Dufour and Wartelle (Éditions Les Belles Lettres 1973) use 'style' for *lexis* in *Rhetoric* 3. Among English translators, W.D. Ross says 'diction,' as does Bywater; E.M. Cope says 'style' and calls the *Aretai Lexeôs* the 'various excellences of style.' D.W. Lucas translates *lexis* by 'style' (*Aristotle's Poetics* 109), and says (ad 1450 b 13): '*lexis* can often be rendered by *style*, but it covers the whole process of combining words into an intelligible sequence.'
14 *On Interpretation* chap. 2: 'By a noun we mean a sound significant by convention, which has no reference to time, and of which no part is significant apart from the rest' (16 a 19-20); chapter 3: 'A verb is that which, in addition to its proper meaning, carries with it the notion of time. No part of it has any independent meaning, and it is a sign of something said of something else' (16 b 6, trans. Edghill).
15 Ross translates *logos* by 'speech' (ad. loc.).
16 *On Interpretation* chapter 4: 'A sentence (*logos*) is a significant portion of speech, some parts of which have an independent meaning, that is to say, as an utterance, though not as the expression of any positive judgment' (16 b 26-8). 'Yet every sentence is not a proposition; only such are propositions as have in them either truth or falsity. Thus a prayer is a sentence, but is neither true nor false' (17 a 1-5). Chapter 5: 'Let us, moreover, consent to call a noun or a verb an expression only (*phasis*), and not a proposition, since it is not possible for a man to speak in this way when he is expressing something, in such a way as to make a statement, whether his utterance is an answer to a question or an act of his own initiation ... of propositions one kind is simple, i.e. that which asserts or denies something of something' (17 a 17-21).
17 The definition is the unity of meaning of a thing: 'Therefore there is an essence only of those things whose formula (*logos*) is a definition (*orismos*). But we have a definition not where we have a word (*onoma*) and a formula (*logos*) identical in meaning (for in that case all formulae or sets of words would be definitions; for there will be some name for any set of words whatever, so that even the *Iliad* will be a definition), but where there is a formula of something primary,' i.e. of a substance as opposed to accidents (*Metaphysics* Z 4, 1030 a 6-11 trans. Ross). See also *Metaphysics* H 6, 1045 a 12-14. A unity of meaning of this sort has absolutely no need for the sentence as its foundation.
18 See below, Study 6, section 1.
19 D.W. Lucas makes the following remark in *Aristotle's Poetics* 204: '*Metaphora*: the word is used in a wider sense than English "metaphor," which is mainly confined to the third and fourth of Aristotle's types.' The generic notion of transposition is assumed by the use of the terms *metaphora* and *metapherein* in diverse contexts in Aristotle's work. For example the *Eudemian Ethics* makes use of species in place of an unnamed genus (1221 b 12-13), transfers a quality of one part of the soul to the entire soul (1224 b 25), and claims that we 'metaphorize' in naming intemperance *akolasia* (1230 b 12-13). Note the parallel text in the *Nicomachean Ethics* 3: 15 (1119 a 36-b 3). Thus, metaphorical transposition serves to fill the gaps in common language.
20 *Physics* 3: 1, 201 a 15; 5: 2, 226 a 32-b 1

21 This paradox is the core of the argument of the article 'La mythologie blanche' by Jacques Derrida: 'In every rhetorical definition of metaphor is implied not just a philosophical position, but a conceptual network within which philosophy as such is constituted. Each thread of the net in addition forms a turn of speech (we might say a metaphor, but that the notion is too derivative in this case). Thus the definiens presupposes the definiendum' ('White Mythology' 30). This recurring theme is particularly striking in Aristotle, whom Derrida explores at length (18 ff.): The theory of metaphor 'seems to belong to the great unmoving chain of Aristotelian ontology, with his theory of the analogy of being, his logic, his epistemology, and more precisely with the basic organisation of his poetics and his rhetoric' (36). A detailed exegesis and a discussion of Derrida's thesis as a whole are to be found in Study 8, section 3 below. I will mention here just some technical points concerning the interpretation of Aristotle: (1) The name is never so tightly bound to the being of things, in Aristotle, that things could not be named differently, or that one could not vary their names in the diverse ways enumerated under the heading of *lexis*. Of course, *Metaphysics* Γ asserts that 'not to have one meaning is to have no meaning' (1006 a 30-b 15). But this univocity does not exclude the possibility of a word having more than one meaning; it prevents only, in Derrida's own words, 'a spread which cannot be controlled' (49). Hence, a limited polysemy is permitted. (2) As for the analogy of being, this is strictly speaking a medieval doctrine, founded moreover on an interpretation of the relationship of the entire series of categories to its first term, substance (*ousia*). There is nothing to justify this short-circuit between proportional metaphor and the analogy of being. (3) As we shall see later, there is no link between the notion of 'current' (*kurion*) meaning and 'proper' meaning, if by the latter one understands a primitive, original, indigenous meaning. (4) The ontology of metaphor which seems to suggest the definition of art in terms of *mimêsis* and its subordination to the concept of *phusis* is not necessarily 'metaphysical,' in the sense that Heidegger has given to this word. At the end of this first Study I will propose an interpretation of the implicit ontology of Aristotle's *Poetics* that in no way employs the transition from the visible to the invisible; see below, 34.

22 Concerning the notion of deviation, see below, Study 5, sections 1 and 3.

23 Rostagni, it is true, translates *kurion* by *proprio* (*Index* 188 *ad proprio*); cf. *ad* 1457 b 3 (125).

24 This point is crucial for Derrida's interpretation. It constitutes one link in the demonstration of the close connection between the theory of metaphor and Aristotelian ontology. Even though the *kurion* of the *Poetics* and *Rhetoric* and the *idion* of the *Topics* do not coincide, Derrida says that 'this whole "metaphorology" seems to be sustained by the notion of the *idion*, though it does not occupy the forefront' ('White Mythology' 48). Now, a study of the *Topics* offers encouragement neither to the assimilation of *kurion* and *idion*, nor especially to the interpretation of *idion* as being original, primitive, indigenous in the 'metaphysical' sense. The manner in which the *Topics* deals with *idion* is based on considerations completely outside the theory of *lexis*, and foreign in particular to the theory of ordinary or unusual denominations. The 'proper' (or 'Property,' trans. Pickard-Cambridge) is one of the four foundational notions that the tradition has called the 'predicables,' to distinguish them from the 'predicaments,' which are the categories (cf. Jacques Brunschwig, introduction to the French translation of the *Topics*). It is with this in mind that the 'proper' ('property') is distinguished from

'accident,' 'genus,' and 'definition.' Now what does this mean, that the 'proper' should be a predicable? It means that every proposition (every concrete focus of reasoning) and every problem (every subject with which discourse is concerned) 'indicates either a genus or a peculiarity or an accident' (101 b 17). In turn the peculiarity, or proper or property, is divided into two parts, one signifying 'the essential of the essence' (Brunschwig's translation of *to ti ên einai*; often called quiddity) and the other not signifying it. Now the first of these parts is called 'definition' in the *Topics*, while the second is the 'proper' ('Property') in its strict sense. Thus we have four predicables, 'property or definition or genus or accident' (101 b 25). From these notions all propositions are formed, because every proposition must assign its predicate in terms of one of these predicables. Accordingly and henceforth, it appears that in setting the 'proper' among the predicables, Aristotle situates it on a level distinct from that of denomination, to which alone belongs the opposition among ordinary words and metaphorical words, lengthened, abbreviated, and coined words, etc. On the other hand, the 'proper' belongs to a logic of predication. This latter builds upon a double polarity: essential and non-essential, coextensive and non-coextensive. Definition is at once both essential and coextensive, while accident is neither essential nor coextensive. The proper is located midway between these two poles, as something which is not essential, but coextensive: 'A "property" is a predicate which does not indicate the essence of a thing, but yet belongs to that thing alone, and is predicated controvertibly of it' (102 a 18-19). Thus, to be capable of reading and writing is a property (is proper) with respect to being human. By contrast, to sleep is not proper to man, since this predicate can be applied to another subject and, conversely, cannot be substituted for the predicate 'man'; although nothing prevents it being implied that a given subject happens to be a man. Thus, the proper is somewhat less than the definition, but much more than an accident which may or may not belong to one and the same subject. Since it does not point to essence, I should say that the criterion retained for the proper is the commutability of subject and predicate, what Aristotle calls convertibility. As we see, no metaphysical abyss reveals itself here. It suffices that the predicate should be coextensive without being essential, according to the 'crossed dichotomy' detailed above in the manner of J. Brunschwig. Furthermore, this criterion of coextensiveness finds its true function within argumentation itself: to show that a predicate is not coextensive is to refute a proposed definition. An appropriate method corresponds to this strategy, the *topic of the proper*, which applies to the good use of non-definitional predicates that are neither generic nor accidental. Finally – and above all – the location of the theory of the proper within the *Topics* is enough to remind us that we are not here in a fundamental, or constitutive, order, but in the order of dialectic. 'The formal objects' of dialectic, points out Brunschwig, are 'the discourses about things and not the things themselves' (introduction 50); like 'games based on a contract ... each predicable corresponds to a particular type of contract' (ibid.). The partial topic of the 'proper' is not exempt in this regard; it regulates the workings of discourse relative to the application of coextensive but non-essential predicates. Aristotle devotes book 5 of the *Topics* to it; there we find the 'proper' defined again, in chapter 2 (129 b 1 ff.) and chapter 4 (132 a 22-6). So Aristotle would only have had to make a 'proper' meaning of this notion, in order to oppose the series of deviations of denomination to it; but he needed the notion of 'current' meaning, which defines its use in denomination.

25 Study 7, section 3

26 See Study 3 on the opposition between interaction theory and substitution theory.

27 Concerning the vocabulary of substitution in Aristotle, see 1458 b 13-26: 'To realize the difference one should take an epic verse and see how it reads when the normal words are introduced [*epithemenôn*].' He proceeds to use verb forms of 'substitution' four times in succession: *metatitheis, metathentos, metathêken, metatitheis* (1458 b 16, 20, 24, 26 respectively). Substitution works in both directions, from the current word to the rare or metaphorical, and from the latter to the former: 'The same should be done with the strange word, the metaphor, and the rest; for one has only to put the ordinary words in their place to see the truth of what we are saying' (1458 b 18). But see the following note for the major exception, which occurs when metaphor names an 'anonymous' genus.

28 We have already pointed to this use of metaphor as the transfer of naming in the case of an 'anonymous' genus, or of a thing that has no name. Examples abound; cf. *Physics* 5, the definition of growth and decay, the definition of *phora*. The problem is dealt with explicitly in the first chapter of *On Sophistical Refutations*, concerning ambiguity: 'For names are finite and so is the sum-total of formulae (*logoi*), while things are infinite in number. Inevitably, then, the same formulae, and a single name, have a number of meanings' (165 a 10-13, trans. Pickard-Cambridge).

29 Concerning the relationship between analogy and resemblance, see Study 6, section 4.

30 Gilbert Ryle *The Concept of Mind* 16 ff., 33, 77-9, 152, 168, 206

31 See below, Study 4, section 5.

32 Max Black *Models and Metaphors*. On model and redescription, see below, Study 7, section 4.

33 H.-G. Gadamer *Wahrheit und Methode*; on *metaphoric*, see 71, 406 ff.

34 E.D. Hirsch *Validity in Interpretation* 169 ff.

35 On the workings of resemblance, see Study 6, *passim*; sections 3 and 4 of this Study take up the interpretation and discussion of the Aristotelian theory once more, this time from a less historical and more systematic point of view.

36 McCall devotes a whole chapter to *eikôn* in Aristotle (*Ancient Rhetorical Theories* 24-53). See also Cope *Introduction* 290-2.

37 On vehicle and tenor in I.A. Richards, see Study 3, section 2.

38 See below, Study 3, note 1.

39 McCall *Ancient Rhetorical Theories* 51, cites 3: 4, 1406 a 20, 1406 b 25-6, 1407 a 14-15; 3: 10, 1410 b 17-18; 3: 11, 1412 b 34-5, 1413 a 15-16.

40 Whereas E.M. Cope saw a perfect correspondence between the definition of simile as an 'extended metaphor' and the definition, coming from Cicero and Quintillian, of metaphor as a 'contracted simile' (*Introduction* 290), McCall insists that the later tradition 'reverses' matters (*Ancient Rhetorical Theories* 51). The case of Quintillian (ibid. 178-239) is particularly striking. He states: *in totum autem metaphora brevior est similitudo* ('on the whole metaphor is a shorter form of *similitudo*') (ibid. 230, from *De Institutione Oratoria Libri Duodecim* 8: 6, 8-9). McCall remarks that Quintillian has put the matter more strongly than if he had just said *brevior est quam similitudo*, or *brevior est similitudine*, expressions 'which would put metaphor and *similitudo* on an equal footing' (230). It is true that Le Guern disputes this interpretation (*Sémantique de la métaphore et de la metonymie* 54, note 1), invoking the Paris edition of 1527, which gives *brevior quam similitudo*. If this were so, 'the classical explanation of metaphor would have its origin in a corruption of the text of Quintillian' (ibid.). The consistency

of the post-Aristotelian tradition lends little credibility to this hypothesis. We will take this discussion up again when we look at the works of Le Guern and examine the fundamental relationships between metaphor and simile or comparison (Study 6, section 1).

41 As we saw earlier (note 9), *paradeigma* is distinct from *enthumêma* as a probable induction is from a probable deduction. There are two kinds of *paradeigma* or example, actual (or historical) parallels and invented parallels. The latter can be either 'illustrations' (*parabolê*) or 'fables' (*logoi*), such as Aesop's fables (*Rhetoric* 2: 20, 1393 a 28-31). Ultimately, the heart of the opposition is between historical example, to which *paradeigma* reduces, and the illustrative parallel, which is the essence of *parabolê*. The unity of historical example and fictive comparison is purely epistemological, in that both are forms of persuasion or proof. On all this, see McCall *Ancient Rhetorical Theories* 24-9.

42 This adjective, *haploun* ('simple'), raises various problems of interpretation and also of translation. To call comparison simple, when one says on the other hand that it 'speaks, or is made, on the basis of two,' seems to be contradictory. Certainly one must agree that comparison, made up of only two terms and one relationship, is 'simple' compared with proportional metaphor, which is composed of four terms and two relationships (see McCall's discussion of Cope's and Roberts' interpretations, ibid. 46-7). For my part, I do not see any contradiction in calling simple the expression 'a shield is a cup,' from which the terms 'Arès' and 'Dionysius' are absent. This does not prevent its being composed of two terms. By contrast, McCall uses the translation 'involves two relations' (45), the reason actually being its closeness to proportional metaphor. He refers to *Rhetoric* 3: 4 (1407 a 15-18), which makes a point of the reversibility of proportional metaphor; if one can give the fourth term the name of the second, one must be able to do the opposite – for example, if the cup is the shield of Dionysius, it is quite appropriate to call the shield the cup of Arès.

43 E.M. Cope (*The Rhetoric of Aristotle with a Commentary*) translates 3: 10, 11 as follows: 'Similes ... are composed of (or expressed in) two terms, just like the proportional metaphors' (137). And he comments: 'The difference between a *simile* and a metaphor is – besides the greater detail of the former, the simile being a metaphor *writ large* – that it always *distinctly expresses* the two terms that are being compared, bringing them into *apparent* contrast; the metaphor, on the other hand, *substituting* by *transfer* the one notion for the other of the two compared, identifies them as it were in one image, and expresses both in a *single* word, leaving the comparison between the object illustrated and the analogous notion which throws a new light upon it, to suggest itself from the manifest correspondence to the hearer' (137-8).

44 It is the same in 3: 10, 7: the example borrowed from Pericles contains the explicit marks of comparison (*houtôs ... hôsper*); on the other hand, that taken from Leptines displays metaphor's brevity – 'he would not have the Athenians let Greece "lose one of her two eyes"' (1411 a 2-5). The examples of 3: 11, 12 and 3: 11, 13 are also to be considered from this point of view (1413 a 2-13). It is true that Aristotle's quotations are generally inexact. Among those that can be verified (*Republic* 5: 469 d-e; 6: 488, a-b 10: 601 b), the first two contain neither the conjunction nor the verb nor the adjective of comparison ('Do you see any difference between ...?' 'Conceive this sort of thing happening ...'); only the third contains a term of comparison ('resemble'). The grammatical mark can vary, however, without affecting the general meaning of the comparison. This is noted by McCall, who speaks of

an 'overall element of comparison' in connection with 'stylistic comparison' (36), as opposed to the illustrative comparison whose purpose is to prove.

45 See below, Study 3, section 4.

46 A similar relationship underlies the suggested affinity between proverbs (*paroimiai*) and metaphors (1413 a 14-16). These are metaphors, it is suggested, that relate species to species. The proverb is, in effect, a comparison pursued between two orders of things (the man abused by the guest whom he has received into his house and the rabbit eating the crop of the peasant who brought him onto his land) (ibid.). The 'like' of comparison can be omitted here just as in metaphor, and with the same result: the relationship is that much more striking to the extent that it is unexpected, even paradoxical and bewildering. This same paradox, which is connected to explicit or implicit comparison, is also the kernel of hyperbole, which is nothing but an exaggerated comparison that is developed in the face of obvious differences. Thus, Aristotle can say, 'Successful hyperboles are also metaphors' (1413 a 19).

47 In this sense, 'new' metaphors (to use a name borrowed from Theodorus), which Aristotle likens to 'paradoxical' metaphors, are not exceptions to a rule, but rather are metaphors *par excellence*.

48 Why does Aristotle say the *eikôn* is 'of the nature of poetry' (1406 b 25) when the *Poetics* ignores it? (The sole mention of the word *eikôn* in the *Poetics* has nothing to do with comparison – 1448 b 10, 15.) Is the opening not provided when the *Poetics* extols 'the art of metaphorizing well' and links it to the ability to perceive similarities (1459 a 5-8)? All we can do is note this strange neglect: 'the odd absence of *eikôn* from the *Poetics* must be left unresolved' (McCall *Ancient Rhetorical Theories* 51).

49 Study 8, section 5

50 'Now since architecture is an art and is essentially a reasoned state of capacity to make, and there is neither any art that is not such a state nor any such state that is not an art, *art* is identical with a state of capacity to make, involving a true course of reasoning. All art is concerned with coming into being, i.e. with contriving and considering how something may come into being which is capable of either being or not being, and whose origin is in the maker and not in the thing made; for art is concerned neither with things that are, or come into being, by necessity, nor with things that do so in accordance with **nature** (since these have their origin in themselves)' (*Nicomachean Ethics* 1140 a 6-16, trans. Ross).

51 It would be impossible to over-emphasize the humbling – the 'loss of prestige,' says Jacques Brunschwig in his introduction to Aristotle's *Topics* – that dialectic suffers in passing from Plato's hands into those of Aristotle. Sovereign and synoptic science in Plato, it is only the theory of probabilistic argumentation with Aristotle (cf. Pierre Aubenque *Le Problème de l'être chez Aristote; Essai sur la problématique aristotélicienne* 251-64; M. Gueroult 'Logique, argumentation et histoire de la philosophie chez Aristote').

52 The *endoxa* of *Rhetoric* 1: 11 (1355 b 17) are defined precisely in *Topics* 1: 10 (104 a 8): 'Now a dialectical proposition consists in asking something that is held [*endoxos*] by all men or by most men or by the philosophers, i.e. either by all, or by most, or by the most notable of these, provided it be not contrary to the general opinion; for a man would probably assent to the view of the philosophers, if it be not contrary to the opinions of most men' (trans. Pickard-Cambridge). The *endoxa* are ideas taken up into the 'inter-play' [*jeu à deux*] that constitutes dialectical discussion (Brunschwig *Topiques* xxiii). This characteristic of propositions

is the signature of dialectical syllogism, whose premises are 'assented to in reality' (ibid. xxiv), as opposed on the one hand to demonstrative syllogism, whose premisses are intrinsically true, and on the other hand to 'apparently endoxal' propositions, which make reasoning materially eristic.

53 Brunschwig relates the question of *topoi* to that of dialectical reasoning in the following way: 'As a first approximation, the *topoi* can be described as rules, or if one prefers, as recipes for argumentation, arranged to supply effective tools to a very precisely laid out activity, that of dialectical discussion' (ibid. ix). The author adds: 'Closely bound up with the activity which they pretend to take from the level of blind practice and advance to that of methodic art, the *Topics*, the *vademecum* of the perfect dialectician, run the risk of appearing to be an art of winning at a game that no one plays any longer' (ix). But then, why speak of *topoi* to designate this 'machinery for constructing premises on the basis of a given conclusion' (xxxix)? One can emphasize the fact that the *topoi* are scattered about, or the fact that each has an assembling function. On the one hand, stress can be put on the 'non-systematic and seemingly headless [character] of logical thought' in the dialectical order (xiv), and on the closed nature of the isolated units located in this fashion. But one can also draw attention to the fact, as does *Rhetoric* 2: 26 (1403 a 17), that each *topos* 'embrac(es) a large number of particular kinds of enthymeme.' This unifying function is exercised in succession by the topics of accident, genus, proper or property (book 5), and definition.

54 I. Düring, in *Aristoteles, Darstellung und Interpretation seines Denkens*, sees grounds in this opposition between prose and poetry for calling *Rhetoric* book 3 'die Schrift "von der Prosa"' (149 ff.). While mindful of the definition in the *Poetics* (1450 b 13), which identifies *lexis* with the verbal expression of thought, Düring notes that in the context of the *Rhetoric*, *lexis* tends to become more and more like 'die literarische Kunstprosa' (150), yet without reducing to a theory of kinds of style (*charaktères* or *genera dicendi*), which is a hellenistic creation.

55 It is interesting to note the reasons for this superiority: 'It was naturally the poets who first set the movement going; for words represent things, and they had also the human voice at their disposal, which of all our organs can best represent other things' (*Rhetoric* 3: 1, 1404 a 20-2).

56 On figure, see Study 5, section 2.

57 On the adherence of meaning to the sensible in poetry, see Study 6, section 2.

58 Cope observes that while the overall outline was already familiar in Aristotle's time, the division into four 'excellences' – purity, perspicuity, ornament, and propriety – 'is not accurately made, nor the order regularly followed' (*Introduction* 279). Moreover, the line is broken frequently, by the study of similitude for instance (see above), or by considerations that do not fit easily into an enumeration of the virtues of *lexis*, like the remarks concerning the 'form' of *lexis* (rythm, free-running and periodic style, 3: 8 and 9).

59 The verb that designates deviation – *exallattô, exallaxai* – comes up twice: 'Such variation from what is usual' (1404 b 8) and 'They depart from what is suitable, in the direction of excess' (1404 b 30). In each instance, an unusual usage is opposed to one that is customary and commonplace (*to de kurion kai to oikeion*, ibid. 32) or suitable (*prepon*, ibid. 30).

60 It is more difficult to relate to the theme of 'clarity' what is said immediately after in regard to the 'beauty' words should have: 'The beauty, like the ugliness, of all words may, as Licymnius says, lie in their sound or in their meaning' (3: 2, 12, 1405 b 6-7). And a bit further on: 'The materials of metaphor must be beautiful

to the ear, to the understanding, to the eye or some other physical sense' (ibid. 1405 b 17-18). It seems that the function of pleasing prevails here over that of indirect signification. The polarity of clarity and beauty might reflect something of the tension at the heart of eloquence or style, which was spoken of earlier.

61 For Cope, this disquisition on errors of style or bad taste does not imply the introduction of a specific excellence or virtue that would be 'warmth' in style (*Introduction* 286-90).

62 The same argument – avoidance of what would be too poetic – is applied to metaphors intended as euphemisms, and in general to circumlocutions (3: 6, 4, 1407 b 32-5).

63 Cope's commentary is particularly brilliant and *asteïon*! (*Introduction* 316-23).

64 See Study 8, section 3.

65 The ontological implications of this claim of Aristotle's will be taken up again below, 42-3, and Study 8, section 5.

66 See below, 40-1.

67 Ross gives the same rendering; Lucas opts for 'communication by means of words.'

68 J. Hardy remarks, 'The text and the meaning of this sentence are very much in doubt.' The French translation – 'car quelle serait l'œuvre propre du personnage parlant, si sa pensée était manifeste et ne résultait pas de son langage' – is less clear than Bywater's, which emphasizes that language in general, like the figure in particular (as mentioned earlier), functions as the manifesting, the 'making-it-appear,' of discourse. Hence, what 'thought' still lacks in order to become *poem* is the 'appearing.' In this regard, Derrida observes: 'If there were no difference between *dianoia* and *lexis* there would be no room for tragedy ... The difference is not restricted to the possibility that a character may think one thing and say another. He exists and acts in the tragedy only on condition that he speak' ('White Mythology' 32).

69 Richard McKeon 'Literary Criticism and the Concept of Imitation in Antiquity,' and 'Imitation and Poetry' 102-223

70 In the second text cited in the preceding note, McKeon points to the *aesthetics of genius* as the source of the pejorative interpretation of *mimēsis*.

71 For our conciliation of *mimēsis* and redescription, see Study 7, section 4.

72 On all this see McKeon, to whom, in large part, the development of what follows is owed. He insists on the necessity of always recreating the philosophical contexts in which a concept acquires meaning, and of relating every definition to the philosopher's own methodology.

73 McKeon writes: 'Imitation functions in that system as the *differentia* by which the arts, useful and fine, are distinguished from nature' (*Critics and Criticism* 131).

74 Leon Golden and O.B. Hardison *Aristotle's Poetics, a Translation and Commentary for Students of Literature* 68-9, 79, 87, 93, 95-6, 115; and the epilogue, 'On Aristotelian Imitation,' 281-96. Similarly, Gerald F. Else (*Aristotle's Poetics: The Argument*) is justified in dwelling on the paradox of defining *poiēsis* as *mimēsis*. He notes, with reference to 1451 b 27-33: 'What the poet "makes," then, is not the actuality of events but their logical structure, their meaning' (321). It is in this manner that creating and imitating can coincide. In this way also, the feeling of terror itself can be caused 'by imitation' (1453 b 8), in that the plot itself *is* the imitation (410-11, 447-50).

75 It constitutes, according to Hardison (*Aristotle's Poetics* 96), the 'first logical unit' of the *Poetics*. At the same time it adds to the significance of Aristotle's introduc-

tory remark, 'Let us follow the natural order and begin with the primary facts'
(1447 a 13).

76 Ibid. 115. Hardison depends here on a Leon Golden article, 'Catharsis.'

77 'Tragic imitation, then, can be understood as a six-part process that begins with
plot' (Hardison *Aristotle's Poetics* 286).

78 Hardison goes so far as to say that the tragic poem 'universalizes' history or
nature (ibid. 291 ff.). History as such proffers nothing but the singular, nothing
but undifferentiated individuals. Now the story is an intelligible interpretation
of history, in a broad sense including or embracing a collection of single things.
An action thus 'universalized' would obviously not be a copy.

79 The interpretation of tragic *katharsis* proposed by Golden acquires a certain
measure of plausibility at this point, to the extent at least that the purification
of pity and terror is mediated by the clarification effected by the intelligibility of
the plot, spectacle, characters, and thought.

80 See Study 7, sections 4 and 5.

81 See the words 'perfection' or 'virtue' (*aretê*, 1458 a 18), 'rule of moderation'
(*metrion*, 1458 b 12), 'improper' (*aprepòs*, ibid. 14), 'proper use' (*to harmottom*,
ibid. 15, and *prepontôs khrêsthai*, 1459 a 4).

82 It is worth noting the occurrences of the word *phusis* in the *Poetics*, as these constitute a network replete with allusion pointing beyond that work. *Mimêsis* is the
first thing to be mentioned if one is to follow 'the natural order' (1447 a 12):
here, 'nature' designates the division of knowledge according to the order of things,
in virtue of which imitation is to be found in the orbit of the sciences of 'making.'
The concept of *telos* occasions an indirect allusion to nature: 'It is the action in it,
i.e. its Fable or Plot, that is the end and purpose of tragedy' (1450 a 22). In a
slightly less allusive fashion it is said that 'the first essential [*arkhê*], the life and
soul [*psukhê*], so to speak, of Tragedy is the Plot' (1450 a 38), whereas thought
and character are the 'natural causes' of the actions (1450 a 1). As for imitation
itself, it is linked to nature in that 'Imitation is natural [*sumphoton*] to man'
(1448 b 5); moreover, man is distinct from the animals in that 'he is the most
imitative of creatures' (ibid. 7). It is nature again that among men distinguishes
the most gifted artists (mastery of metaphor 'is a sign of genius [*euphuias*],'
1459 a 7); indeed, poets take up comedy or tragedy as their own natures dictate
(1449 a 15). Finally, among all the poetic genres, the development of tragedy,
which is born in improvisation and is thus in continuity with nature, culminates
at a certain point when it attains 'its natural form' (1449 a 15). Furthermore, the
characteristics of order, of completeness (*teleion*), of symmetry – in brief, everything that makes of a tragedy a perfect composition, something whole in itself –
at the same time reveal 'the limit ... set by the actual nature of the thing' (1451 a
9). Thus the concept of nature, although not *thematized* as such in the *Poetics*,
returns repeatedly as an *operational* concept (in E. Fink's sense of this opposition).

83 For Derrida ('White Mythology' 36-7), the tightly drawn agreement linking *mimêsis* and *phusis* constitutes one of the most penetrating indices of the dependence
of metaphorology with respect to onto-theology. One could say that this partner-
ship reveals the 'gesture constitutive of metaphysics and of humanity' (37). The
preceding note owes much to Derrida, in both its substance and its tone of analysis.

84 The formula 'art imitates nature' pervades Aristotle's work. Vianney Décarie
(*L'Objet de la métaphysique selon Aristote*) notes it already in the *Protrepticus*,
where it contrasts with a Platonic formulation (*Laws* 10: 888 e-890 d): 'And
nature's product always has an end and it is always constituted in view of a higher

end than that of the product of art; for art imitates nature, not nature art' (23 and note 3). The formula does not serve here to distinguish, nor even to co-ordinate; it seeks to subordinate. But the context shows us why: the exhortation to philosophize, which is the object of the treatise, is based upon 'the will of nature' (ibid.). It is necessary, therefore, to move from the teleology of art to an even *higher* teleology. In a different way, Aristotle's *Physics* (2: 2. 194 a 21-7) argues from what is seen in art to what must be demonstrated in the case of nature, namely, composition of form and of matter, and teleology. The argument reads as follows (trans. Hardie and Gaye): '*If* ... art imitates nature ... it would be the part of physics also to know nature in both its senses [form and matter].' And the text continues, 'nature is the end or "that for the sake of which"' (194 a 28). The same formula evidently could be read in the opposite sense and would thus distinguish art from nature on the grounds that art receives the characteristic of having an end from nature. This is the very source of the autonomy of art: for it is not the things produced, there to be copied, which are imitable in nature, but production itself and its teleological order, which remains to be understood and which the plot may reconstruct. On imitation in Aristotle, see Aubenque *Le problème de l'être chez Aristote* 487-508. (Study 8, section 1 contains a detailed discussion of this work.)

85 This interpretation will be taken up again and extended at the end of Study 8.

STUDY 2

1 Gérard Genette 'La rhétorique restreinte' 158-71
2 See Study 1, section 1.
3 Certain neo-rhetoricians contrast the rhetoric of style with the rhetoric of the invention of proofs and arguments and with that of composition (following Aristotle's tripartite plan in his *Rhetoric*), and they treat this as a contrast between the paradigmatic and the syntagmatic (Roland Barthes 'L'ancienne rhétorique, aide-mémoire' 175-6). A properly discursive theory of metaphor, like the interaction or the controversion theory, will deprive this distinction of much of its force.
4 Rhetoric implies even a theology: 'But it is given only to God to be able to embrace, in one single view, all individuals, whatever kind they may be, and to see them all together and singly at the same time' (*Les Figures du discours* 42).
5 Fontanier's 'Forewords,' 'Prefaces,' and 'Preambles' (21-30) (271-81) are of great interest in this connection. There he praises his 'system,' 'undeniably the most reasoned-out and the most philosophical, as well as the most complete, yet to appear in our language, and perhaps in any other' (23), 'a rational and philosophical system, all of whose details have been sorted out and interconnected in such a way that, in their collectivity, they form an absolutely coherent whole' (28).
6 Aristotle *Rhetoric* 3: 1, 2; cf. above, Study 1, 31 and 37.
7 Fontanier simply observes that 'this metaphor ought not be looked upon as a true figure, because we have no other word in the language for the same idea' (63).
8 I cannot resist quoting these wonderful lines by Gérard Genette: 'To identify a unit of discourse is quite necessarily to compare and oppose it implicitly to what could be, in such a situation and in its stead, another "equivalent" unit, that is, something at once similar and different ... To perceive a language is, quite necessarily, to imagine a silence or another language in the same place or at the same

point in time ... Where keeping silent or saying something else are impossible, there the fullness of speech is lacking: this is what Fontanier's monumental argument with catachresis symbolizes and brings out ... Speaking that is obligated does not oblige; speech that was not chosen from among other possible ways of speaking says nothing – it is not speech. If there were no figure, would there even be language?' ('Introduction' 12-13).

9 *Les Figures du discours* 66-7; 221-31; 279-81; 451-9
10 281, 451 ff., 461 ff., and passim. The ascendancy of the word can still be seen even in the definition of these figures (283, 323). Only the figures of style and of thought are less subservient to the word: the former because they are obviously features of discourse; the latter because they are 'independent of words, of expression, and of style' (403), although this puts them in danger of not being figures at all ('Perhaps it is unfortunate that these are called figures in this way, when they have to do only with thought alone, with thought considered abstractly and without regard for the form that it can borrow from language – they consist in nothing, so to speak, but a certain twist of spirit and imagination ... [403]).
11 How different the figures of signification are from all the others, exclaims Fontanier, 'for, unlike these last, they consist not in several words but in a single word; and what they present through an unaccustomed image is not a whole thought, a collection of ideas, but a single and unique idea, a simple element of thought!' (453).
12 With respect to the nomenclature, consult Henri Morier *Dictionnaire de poétique et de rhétorique.*
13 I.A. Richards *The Philosophy of Rhetoric* 96 ff.; see below, Study 3, section 2.
14 Jacques Derrida 'White Mythology'
15 Nelson Goodman *Languages of Art*
16 It seems that, for Fontanier, the possibility of double meaning gives the advantage to allegory: 'Instead of transforming the object and modifying it to a greater or lesser extent, as metaphors do, allegories leave the object in its natural state and only reflect it, like some kinds of transparent mirrors' (205).
17 Marcus B. Hester *The Meaning of Poetic Metaphor*
18 Émile Benveniste *Problems in General Linguistics*

STUDY 3

1 Émile Benveniste *Problems in General Linguistics*
2 Émile Benveniste 'La forme et le sens dans le langage'
3 *Problems in General Linguistics* 217-22
4 Paul Grice 'Meaning,' 'Utterer's Meaning, Sentence-Meaning and Word-Meaning,' and 'Utterer's Meaning and Intentions'
5 Plato *Cratylus* 425 a, 431 b-c ('the statement is a synthesis of name and verb,' trans. Jowett); *Theaetetus* 206 d; *Sophist* 261 d-262 d
6 '... there could not be a statement that was a statement about nothing' (*Sophist* 263 c, trans. Cornford).
7 Strawson *Individuals* part 2
8 Bertrand Russell 'On Denoting.' Cf. L. Linsky *Referring.*
9 On the ontological postulate connected to the identifying function, cf. John Searle *Speech Acts.* The axiom of existence is formulated thus: 'Whatever is referred to must exist' (77).

10 P.F. Strawson 'On Referring.' See also Linsky *Referring*.

11 J.L. Austin *How to Do Things With Words*

12 Aristotle *On Interpretation* paragraph 1

13 Austin *How to Do Things* lecture 1

14 Peter Geach *Mental Acts*. On the 'commitment' proper to every act of discourse and on the psychological factor of 'desire' and 'belief' implied by this 'commitment,' cf. Searle *Speech Acts* 64-71; Paul Ricoeur 'Discours et Communication.'

15 Benveniste *Problems in General Linguistics* chapters 13 and 14

16 Gottlob Frege 'On Sense and Reference'

17 Edmund Husserl *Logical Investigations* Investigation 1, Investigation 5

18 Benveniste *Problems in General Linguistics* part 5 'Man and Language'

19 Roman Jakobson 'Linguistics'

20 It is not without interest to note that of three studies brought together in this chapter, one is put under the aegis of 'rhetoric,' the second under that of 'logical grammar,' and the third under 'literary criticism.' There could be no more striking sign of the uncertain character of the boundaries of these disciplines. This makes the attempt to root all three in a single semantics all the more significant.

21 Study 2, section 2

22 Ludwig Wittgenstein *Philosophical Investigations* §23 'But how many kinds of sentence are there? Say assertion, question, and command? – There are *countless* kinds ...'

23 Study 1, 32

24 The expression *command* (which inspires the title of the sixth lecture, 'The Command of Metaphor' *Philosophy of Rhetoric* 115 ff.) is suggested by Aristotle's famous statement in the *Poetics* (1459 a 8), which Richards translates as follows: 'The greatest thing by far is to have a command of metaphor. This alone cannot be imparted to another: it is the mark of genius, for to make good metaphor implies an eye for resemblances' (ibid. 89).

25 'Language is vitally metaphorical, that is, it marks the before unapprehended relations of things and perpetuates their apprehension, until words, which represent them, become, through time, signs for portions or classes of thought instead of pictures of integral thoughts: and then, if no new poets should arise to create afresh the associations which have been thus disorganized, language will be dead to all the nobler purposes of human intercourse' (quoted in ibid. 90-1).

26 Study 2, 57

27 Richards *Philosophy of Rhetoric* 96. The fundamental meaning of the term *tenor* is captured in the following passage by Berkeley, quoted by Richards (4-5): 'I do ... once for all desire whoever shall think it worth his while to understand ... that he would not stick on this or that phrase, or manner of expression, but candidly collect my meaning from the whole sum and tenor of my discourse, and laying aside the words as much as possible, consider the base notions themselves ...' In *The New Rhetoric: A Treatise on Argumentation*, Ch. Perelman and L.O. Olbrechts-Tyteca introduce the two expressions *thème* and *phore*, which might be good translations for tenor and vehicle. However, the authors limit the application of their pair of terms to analogy, that is, to the relationship of proportionality: 'We propose that *thème* refer to the terms A and B taken together, on which the conclusion bears ... and that *phore* refer to the terms C and D taken together, which provide the basis for the reasoning ...' (501).

28 In this text borrowed from appendix C of the *Statesman's Manual*, Coleridge compares the growth of the imaginary to vegetal growth. Or, more precisely, it is in

meditating on the changes between individu~¹ and cosmic life, through which the part becomes the 'visible organism' of the whole, that at the same time the meaning of every symbol is, metaphorically, produced. Indeed, a symbol, 'while it enunciates the whole, abides itself as a living part of that unity of which it is the representative' (Richards *Philosophy of Rhetoric* 109). On metaphor according to Coleridge, see I.A. Richards *Coleridge on Imagination.*

29 Richards (*Philosophy of Rhetoric* 116) cites Johnson's statement that every word that 'gives us two ideas for one' is a metaphor.

30 A. Breton *Les Vases communicants* (cited in ibid. 123)

31 The problem of resemblance is discussed below, in Study 6.

32 Study 7

33 Chapter 3. See also chapter 13 of *Models and Metaphors* entitled 'Metaphor and Archetypes.'

34 'Metaphor and Archetypes,' ibid.

35 Colin M. Turbayne *The Myth of Metaphor.* Cf. below, Study 7.

36 'All literary works fall into three main classes: poems, essays, and prose fiction' (126).

37 See Study 1, section 5.

38 Cf. especially chapters 4 and 5.

39 Beardsley adds an important argument to the present critique of the theory of metaphor in 'The Metaphorical Twist.' There he states that comparison takes place between objects whereas opposition exists between words. The 'twist' is brought about by tensions within discourse itself. Consequently, a theory of verbal opposition is distinct from object comparison theory as the order of words is distinct from the order of things. The connotations to which a purely semantic theory has recourse are to be found in the realm not so much of objects as of everyday beliefs concerning these objects. A second argument is that looking for a motif of comparison leads almost inevitably to the imagination as a matter of individual psychology. In effect, one must interpolate not only the term that completes the comparison but also the meaning it carries; in conjuring an absent term, explication is at the mercy of the reader's idiosyncratic imagery as much as that of the poet. Beardsley's final argument is that to invoke a comparison is also to ask whether it is appropriate or too far-fetched. As the 'controversion' theory abundantly proves, there is practically no limit to the 'fit' between a metaphorical attribute and a given subject.

40 In 'The Metaphorical Twist,' directed as much against psychologism as against realism, Beardsley strongly emphasizes that 'the opposition that renders an expression metaphorical is ... within the meaning-structure itself' (299). The logical opposition that compels the reader to pass from central to marginal meanings can be defined independently of any intentionality. The distinction between two levels of meaning (primary and secondary) as well as logical opposition within a single level (that of attribution) are semantic and not psychological facts. The passage from designation to connotation can be described entirely with the resources of a semantic analysis of the sentence and the word.

41 Jeremy Taylor *Of Holy Living* London 1847; see ibid. 302, note 20.

42 *Collected Poems of Wallace Stevens* 286 (cited in ibid. 304, note 22)

STUDY 4

1 Robert Godel *Les Sources manuscrites du Cours de linguistique générale de Ferdinand de Saussure* 189 ff.

2 In an 1883 article, 'Les lois intellectuelles du langage' (*Annuaire de l'Association pour l'encouragement des études grecques en France*), Michel Bréal confers the name of semantics on the 'science of meanings [*significations*]'; he pledges to turn his wits no longer 'to the flesh and form of words' but to 'the laws that preside over the transformation of meanings, the choice of new expressions, the birth and death of expressions.' Accordingly, changes in the meanings of words are inserted at the first level of this new science. This fundamental orientation is confirmed in Arsène Darmesteter's work *La vie des mots étudiée dans leurs significations* and later in that of Bréal *Essai de sémantique: Science des significations.*

3 Josef Trier *Der deutsche Wortschatz im Sinnbezirk des Verstandes*

4 The proper level of the sentence seems about to be recognized when the distinction is made between associative and syntagmatic relations, whose interplay constitutes the 'mechanism of language' (*Course in General Linguistics* part 2, chapters 5 and 6). In fact it is 'outside discourse' (123) that words associate *in absentia*, and it is 'in discourse' (ibid.) that words combine *in presentia* in a syntagmatic relation. It seems, then, that the theory of relations between signs would find reference to discourse essential. Even more than the associative relation, the syntagmatic relation appears bound to appeal to a theory of the discourse-sentence: is it not said that 'the sentence is the ideal type of syntagma' (124)? There is no hint, nevertheless, of anything of this sort. Syntagmas do not depend on speech but on language, for they are 'pat phrases in which any change is prohibited by usage' (ibid.). It is clear that de Saussure recognizes only a psychological difference (constraint versus freedom) between language and speech, itself founded on a sociological difference (speech is individual, language is social) (14). As a 'part of the inner storehouse that makes up the language of each speaker' (123), the syntagma depends thus on language and not on speech. Hence, the *Course* ignores entirely the properly logical difference between discourse and language, that is to say, the difference between the predicative relation in discourse and the opposition-relation between signs in the language system. In this fashion one can say that de Saussure has a theory of speech in the individual and psychological sense, but not a theory of discourse in the properly semantic sense defined at the beginning of the third Study. He also never gives the sentence a status comparable to that of the entities about which the essence of the *Course* is organized.

5 Reference is made here to the schema proposed by Stephen Ullmann in *The Principles of Semantics* 31-42. A good deal of time will be spent on this in the second section of this Study.

6 Michel Le Guern *Sémantique de la métaphor et de la métonymie* 121

7 Hedwig Konrad *Etude sur la métaphore*

8 The discussion of the work of Michel Le Guern (Study 6, section 1) will occasion a return to Hedwig Konrad's treatment of synecdoche (113), simile (150), symbol (151), and ellipsis (116). Further, examination of the 'metaphysical implications' of metaphor in Derrida (Study 8, section 3) will provide the opportunity to speak of the notes on personifications (139). And the notion of semantic impertinence in Jean Cohen (Study 5, section 3) will remind us of what is said here about enigma (148).

9 The *Rhétorique générale* of the Groupe de Liège in Study 5, and the *Sémantique de la métaphore et de la métonymie* by Le Guern in Study 6

10 'Hence, the role of the concept of a substantive is to symbolize a unique and individual structure, and to determine in our minds the special place that each of

the object's representations should have in relationship to the others. Those among the ensemble of attributes that are possessed *par excellence* and in a unique way play a special demarcative role. We call this specific interrelation of attributes the fundamental order of the concept' (66). The author refers specifically (51) to the notion of *Gegenstandsbezug* in the second *Logical Investigation* of Edmund Husserl. And it is not overdone to draw a parallel as well between this analysis and what P.F. Strawson says in *Individuals: An Essay in Descriptive Metaphysics* about the identifying function of logical subjects. But Strawson shows that the concept cannot fulfil the function of identifying singular things without the addition of demonstratives and of indicators of place and time. In this sense, it is doubtful whether the concept, if completely unaided, would be able to enframe an individual.

11 'The word that serves to designate concrete objects must itself in every instance evoke a single and unique structure. The word *rose* evokes the particular structure of the rose; the word *tree*, that of a tree. In order to designate several objects, a word would have to evoke an amorphous sum of general attributes. But then the word would no longer be the symbol of precise objects and would not produce the borrowed effect immediately upon being transposed from its standard use ... Thus, in its normal use, the *meaning* is a concept' (72). And further on: 'The word does not change meaning with a partial change in the partial representation of an object. The word does not change meaning as long as it applies to one of the logical species' (79).

12 Geoffroy de Vinsauf *Poetria Nova*

13 This was also seen by Geoffroy de Vinsauf: according to him, metaphor is based on a privileged analogy. One can take as the transposed term the thing that stands forth as *the most obvious representative of the attribute* – milk and snow for whiteness, honey for sweetness, etc. (cited by Konrad *Étude sur la métaphore* 18).

14 Aristotle was aware of this, for he defined three of the classes of metaphor in terms of a relation that brings genus and species into play. The author endeavours to show that in reality the four classes are defined in relation to the transposition from species to species (ibid. 100 ff.).

15 For the same reason the author stays clear of assimilations between myth and metaphor, which are found in Cassirer among others (ibid. 154-62).

16 Of special note is the study of *celestial metaphors* in Victor Hugo (131-6). The author concludes her discussion in the following fashion: 'All his comparisons have the effect of taking us into an atmosphere of illusion and of dreams; for Victor Hugo develops and justifies his analogies as much as possible, so that he gives the impression of having discovered a new truth, of having perceived more profound relationships existing in reality between beings and things' (136).

17 Discussing the concept of *ascription* in a context different from our own (to ascribe the act X to A), Peter Geach notes that the question of opposing *ascription* and *description* would not be posed, were it not for the fact that 'what is regularly ignored is the distinction between calling a thing "P" and predicating "P" of a thing' ('Ascriptivism' *Phil. Review* 69, 2 [1960] reprinted in Geach *Logic Matters*).

18 Recognizing that naming is not the function of simile, the author rather curiously sets simile on the side of the aesthetic (149), encouraged in this view, it seems, by the hyperbolistic character, the intentional exaggeration of literary comparisons. The argument is not incisive.

19 In appearance only, as the difficulties of the componential analysis will show (Study 5, section 4).

20 Perhaps in its turn this second divorce will call for a revision, in particular in the domain of metaphor, which offers especially strong justifications from the *psycholinguistic* point of view; see below, Study 6, section 6.

21 Stephen Ullmann *The Principles of Semantics, Précis de Sémantique française, Semantics: An Introduction to the Science of Meaning*

22 Gustaf Stern *Meaning and Change of Meaning*

23 K. Nyrop *Grammaire historique de la langue française*

24 L. Bloomfield *Language*, Z.S. Harris *Methods in Structural Linguistics*, C.E. Osgood 'The Nature and Measurement of Meaning'

25 A. Meillet *Linguistique Historique* 1: 30, cited in Ullmann *Principles of Semantics* 54. The old definitions, from an era when anti-psychologism was not so marked, did not hesitate to make the word correspond to a mental entity, the identity of the same notion in the spirit. Thus Meillet writes: 'To each notion there is attached a phonic compound called *word*, giving body to this notion in the subject's thought and raising the same notion or a similar notion in his interlocutor' (*Linguistique historique* 2: 1 and 71, quoted in Ullmann 51). Similarly L.H. Gray, 'the smallest thought-unit vocally expressible' (*Foundations of Language* [New York 1939] 146, quoted in Ullmann 51).

26 Let us recall here the definition of L. Bloomfield, 'minimum free-form' (*Language* 178; Ullmann *Principles of Semantics* 51). Similar is J.R. Firth's definition of the word as 'lexical substitution-counter,' which in addition brings in the test of communication, transposed from phonology to lexicology ('The Technique of Semantics' cited in Ullmann 56).

27 Here Ullmann cites the works of G. Matoré (*Le Vocabulaire et la société sous Louis-Philippe* and *La Méthode en lexicologie*), which he compares to Trier's research on semantic fields (see Ullmann *Semantics* 252).

28 André Martinet 'Le mot.' We will retain his definition: 'Segment of the spoken chain or of the written text, such that one can separate it from its context by saying it by itself or by separating it with a white space from the other elements of the text and attribute a meaning or a specific function to it' (40). See also *Eléments de linguistique générale* and *A Functional View of Language*.

29 C.K. Ogden and I.A. Richards *The Meaning of Meaning* 11

30 Z. Gombocz *Jelentéstan*

31 On polysemy see *Principles of Semantics* 114-25, *Précis* 199-218, *Semantics* 159-75.

32 L. Wittgenstein *Philosophical Investigations* par. 67

33 Cf. Roman Jakobson 'Linguistics.' We will refer especially to 453 ff. concerning the 'Essentials and goals of contemporary linguistics.'

34 *Principles of Semantics* part 4, 'Historical Semantics' 171-258, *Précis* chapter 10 'Why Words Change Meaning' (236-69), chapter 11 'How Words Change Meaning' (270-98)

35 Ullmann (*Principles of Semantics* 117) approvingly quotes the following words of W.M. Urban: 'The fact that a sign can intend one thing without ceasing to intend another, that, indeed, the very condition of its being an *expressive* sign for the second is that it is also a sign for the first, is precisely what makes language an instrument of knowing. This "accumulated intension" of words is the fruitful source of ambiguity, but it is also the source of that analogous predication, through which alone the symbolic power of language comes into being' (*Language and Reality* 112). It will be noted that this cumulative character is described in the framework of descriptive semantics, in the section on polysemy.

36 *Principles of Semantics* 220 ff. *Précis* 270 ff.
37 On the signifier as acoustic image, see the *Course in General Linguistics* 12, 15, 66. On the signified as concept, see ibid. 12, 66, 103, 114.
38 W. Wundt *Völkerpsychologie*, 'die Sprache'
39 It is true that only the second sort of relation is called 'associative relation' by de Saussure (*Course in General Linguistics* 123 ff.). The syntagmatic relation is simply grafted on to the linear character of language, that is, the aspect of temporal succession; in no way is the syntagmatic solidarity called association by contiguity. Jakobson's interpretation thus constitutes an innovation: 'The constituents of a context are in a state of contiguity, while in a substitution set signs are linked by various degrees of similarity which fluctuate between the equivalence of synonyms and the common core of antonyms' ('Two Aspects of Language and Two Types of Aphasic Disorders' 243-4).
40 Léonce Roudet 'Sur la classification psychologique des changements sémantiques'
41 Z. Gombocz *Jelentéstan*
42 Henri Bergson 'L'effort intellectuel' in *L'Energie spirituelle*, *OEuvres* 930-59
43 G. Esnault *L'Imagination populaire: métaphores occidentales*. Cf. below, note 92.
44 Cf. above, Study 1, 33.
45 I have already alluded (Study 1, section 1) to Gérard Genette's denunciation of rhetoric restricted to two figures, or even to one alone, that being metaphor.
46 The quotation from Wordsworth should be noted (*Semantics* 213): 'The song would speak / Of that interminable building reared / By observation of affinities / In objects where no brotherhood exists / To passive minds.'
47 *Course in General Linguistics* 9, Robert Godel *Les Sources manuscrites* 42 ff.
48 Roman Jakobson 'Linguistics' 458
49 *Course in General Linguistics* 79 ff.
50 Ullmann takes this up: 'A purely synchronistic notion, polysemy bears important consequences of a diachronic order: words can acquire new acceptations without losing their primitive meaning. The result of this faculty is an elasticity of semantic relations that is without parallel in the domain of sounds' (*Précis* 199).
51 Ullmann *Principles of Semantics* 40. This panchronistic perspective imposes itself equally on historical semantics (ibid. 231, 255-7).
52 Ullmann *Précis* 200-7
53 Ibid. 242: 'Vocabulary is not rigidly systematized, as are phonemes and grammatical forms: at any moment one can add to it an unlimited number of elements that are new in every case, comprising words as well as meanings.'
54 Ibid. 215-16
55 Ibid. 243
56 *Course in General Linguistics* 66
57 We have grafted this distinction between the signified and the denoted onto the fundamental dichotomy of the sign and the sentence, that is, in the terminology of Émile Benveniste, the opposition of the semiotic plane and the semantic plane; cf. above, Study 3, section 1.
58 On this equivocity in the word *meaning*, see my article 'Sens et signe.'
59 The distinction that Gottlob Frege makes between meaning (or sense) and denotation (*nominatum*, reference) is established first at the level of the proper name, then extended to the whole proposition: 'A proper name (word, sign, sign-compound, expression) expresses its sense, and designates or signifies its nominatum. We let a *sign express* its sense and *designate* its nominatum' ('On Sense and Reference' *Readings in Philosophical Analysis* 89).

60 Ullmann *Précis* 243
61 Groupe μ *Rhétorique générale* 97 ff.; see below, Study 5, section 4.
62 'It is in speech, the concrete realization of language, that changes present them-selves' (*Précis* 237).
63 Study 7, section 4
64 Ullmann *Semantics* 195
65 Ibid. 248
66 *Course in General Linguistics* 126
67 Ullmann *Semantics* 195
68 Ibid. 193
69 'Linguistics'
70 This absence of grammatical autonomy reminds us that the word is the product of the analysis of a statement. Edward Sapir defines the word as 'one of the smallest, completely satisfying bits of isolated "meaning" into which the sentence resolves itself' (*Language: An Introduction into the Study of Speech* 35). Meillet's definition of the word, which incorporates grammatical use into the semantic function, was cited earlier (note 25). This is why the word has no semantic iden-tity that can be separated from its syntactic role: it has meaning only when in-vested with a grammatical role corresponding to a type of employment in dis-course.
71 Ullmann *Semantics* 55, 64-7
72 Wittgenstein *Philosophical Investigations* par. 43
73 Ibid. par. 11
74 Ibid. par. 31. For the same concept in de Saussure, see the *Course in General Linguistics* 22, 88, 110.
75 Gilbert Ryle 'Ordinary Language' 120-1
76 Wittgenstein *Philosophical Investigations* par. 7 ff.
77 Ullmann *Semantics* 67
78 Émile Benveniste 'La forme' 37
79 Wittgenstein *Tractatus Logico-Philosophicus* 2.01, 2.011, 2.02
80 Edmund Husserl *Ideas I* par. 94
81 Benveniste 'La forme et le sens'
82 Ibid. 38
83 Ibid.
84 Ibid.
85 Jakobson 'Linguistics' 422: 'The variability of meanings, particularly their mani-fold and far-reaching figurative shifts, and an incalculable aptitude for multiple paraphrases are just those properties of natural language which induce its creati-vity and endow not only poetic but even scientific activities with a continuously inventive sweep. Here, indefiniteness and creative power appear to be wholly interrelated.'
86 Ullmann *Semantics* 52
87 Strawson *Individuals* 20-1
88 Cited in Ullmann *Précis* 207
89 Study 5, section 3
90 Study 7, section 3
91 Esnault notes that metaphor appears to follow the order of things: 'It respects the pathways, the constant order of natural phenomena' (quoted in Ullmann *Précis* 285).

STUDY 5

1 One must add the important work by Michel Le Guern *Sémantique de la méta-phore et de la métonymie*, which also represents the most recent state of research in the French language. However, only brief references will be made to this work in the present Study, because of its strong ties with the theses of Roman Jakobson, which will be discussed only in Study 6, and because of the role given to 'the associated image,' a role that cannot be appreciated without the framework of the next Study.

2 L. Prieto and Ch. Muller *Statistique et Analyse linguistique*

3 A.-J. Greimas *Sémantique structurale, Recherche de méthode, Du sens: Essais sémiotiques*

4 G. Genette 'La Rhétorique restreinte'

5 G. Genette 'La rhétorique des figures.' See above, Study 2, 52.

6 Tzvetan Todorov *Littérature et Signification* appendix: 'Tropes et Figures'

7 See above, Study 3, 84.

8 Ibid. 90-9

9 It is enough to compare the two definitions: rhetoric is 'the knowledge of the different meanings with which a single word is used in a single language' (C. Dumarsais *Des tropes* v, quoted in Todorov *Littérature et Signification* 94); and on the other side, 'It is in the province of grammar to tell us the true sig-nification of words, and their meaning when used in discourse' (*Des tropes* 22).

10 G. Genette 'Figures' in *Figures I* 205-21

11 The following remark by Gérard Genette brings together all the traits discussed here (hiatus and consciousness of hiatus, virtuality of unmarked language, trans-latability in principle of figures): 'The spirit of rhetoric is wholly contained in this consciousness of a hiatus between real language (that of the poet) and a virtual language (the one that would have used the simple and common expres-sion) that needs only to be re-established in thought in order to delimit a space of figures' (*Figures I* 207). Again: 'The rhetorical fact begins at the point where I can compare the form of this word or of this sentence with that of another word or another sentence that could have been used in their place and in whose stead, one may speculate, they appear.' And again: 'Every figure is translatable, and carries its translation visible in transparency, like a filigree or a palimpsest, beneath its apparent text. Rhetoric is linked to this duplicity of language' (211). It is in this sense that Genette accepts the aphorism of Pascal inscribed as exergue to *Figures I*: 'Figure carries absence and presence.' This is also the source of the justification for Fontanier's opposition between catachresis, whose use is forced, and figure, which combines things freely.

12 Cf. above, Study 3, 95.

13 Jean Cohen *Structure* 22

14 The relative degree zero is attained by a series of successive approximations: (1) prose, (2) written prose, (3) written scientific prose. (1) 'We wish to compare poetry to prose, and by prose we provisionally understand usage, that is the assemblage of the statistically most prevalent forms in the language of a single linguistic community' (ibid. 21). (2) 'The principle of homogeneity demands that poetry that is written be compared to written prose' (ibid. 22). (3) 'Which among all the types of written prose is to be chosen as norm? From all the evi-dence, one must turn towards the writer who is least oriented to aesthetic goals, that is, towards the scientist' (ibid.).

15 Remarking that statistics is the general science of deviations and stylistics the science of linguistic deviations, Jean Cohen proposes 'to apply the results of the second to the first: the poetic fact then becomes measurable, and expresses itself as the average frequency of deviations presented by poetic language in relation to prose' (ibid. 15). Accordingly, the enterprise enters into an aesthetic-scientific project. Poetics must establish itself as a quantitative science: 'Poetic style will be the average deviation of the collection of poems, on the basis of which it would be theoretically possible to measure the "poetic degree" of a given poem' (ibid.).

16 Genette *Figures I* 211

17 Ibid

18 *Rhétorique générale* 30-44

19 Greimas *Sémantique structurale* 69 ff.

20 Cf. above, Study 1, 17-20.

21 Ibid. 34

22 Ibid. 31-2 and 37

23 P. Fontanier *Les Figures du discours* 63

24 Ibid. 64

25 Roman Jakobson 'Closing Statements: Linguistics and Poetics'

26 For his part, Jakobson assigns these two arrangements to the principle of similarity (choice among similar terms) and to the principle of contiguity (linear construction of the sequence). We will discuss this particular aspect of the Jakobson definition of metaphorical process in Study 6, which is devoted to the operation of resemblance.

27 Cf. Study 7, section 2

28 Todorov *Littérature et Signification* 102

29 The preceding section already quoted this text of Genette: 'The spirit of rhetoric is wholly contained in this consciousness of a hiatus between real language (that of the poet) and a virtual language (the one which would have used the simple and common expression) that needs only to be re-established in thought in order to delimit a space of figures' (*Figures I* 207).

30 Quoted in ibid. 220

31 'Espace et Langage' in ibid. 103

32 Northrop Frye *Anatomy of Criticism*

33 Todorov *Littérature et Signification* 99

34 Versification aims only at 'weakening the structuring of the message' (96), at 'jumbling the message' (99). 'The history of versification, followed through two centuries, exhibits the progressive increase of de-differentiation' (101).

35 Plato *Sophist* 251 d, 253 c

36 Noam Chomsky *Aspects of the Theory of Syntax*. On generative semantics, which has separated gradually from the generative and transformational grammar set out in this work by Chomsky, cf. Françoise Dubois-Charlier and Michel Galmiche 'La Sémantique générative.'

37 I leave aside the case of lack of determination (personal pronouns, proper names, demonstratives, adverbs of time and of place, tenses of verbs, which are without determination in context: 155-63), which poses another problem, that of the absence of contextual referent, and introduces another type of interpretation at the properly referential level. For this reason, this analysis is not exactly in the right place in a chapter on 'determination.' One does not determine the meaning of a link by determining the extension (of the chain involved); 'I' has no extension. Besides, these connectives are not in the position of epithets.

38 Cohen notes: 'If one extends the process on the diachronistic plane, one has the "metaphor in common use"; if one concentrates it into synchrony, one has the "newly-invented metaphor." This is the only one to be studied here; as we saw, by definition the metaphor in common use is not a poetic deviation' (*Structure* 114, note 1).

39 Perhaps Cohen over-extends the 'genus' a bit, by calling all figures metaphor, including rhyme and inversion. But, in order to speak of rhyme-metaphor, one would have had to demonstrate the phenomenon of reduction of deviation on the plane of versification, which was not done and which perhaps may be beyond doing. Indeed, in the final analysis it definitely seems that every reduction of deviation will be semantic.

40 Cf. above, Study 4, 131-2.

41 Le Guern's *Sémantique* and the *Rhétorique générale* have in common the hypothesis of componential analysis of the signified, taken over from Greimas, in virtue of which metaphor is to be treated as an alteration of the semic organization of a lexeme. But this thesis from structural semantics is transferred into the framework of an opposition borrowed from Jakobson, that of metaphorical and metonymic processes. For this reason I will postpone its examination until after discussion of Jakobson's thesis. Furthermore, the latter is reinterpreted so as to have the sense of an opposition between intralinguistic relation and extra-linguistic or referential relation: 'In transferring this distinction from Jakobson's analysis, one must take care that the metaphorical process concerns the semic organization, while the metonymic process modifies only the referential relation' (Le Guern 14). As observed subsequently (15, note 17), a serious split results with the analyses of the *Rhétorique générale*. In fact, since the notion of semic organization is opposed to that of a switching of reference, it takes on a quite different meaning through the contrast. When the time comes, other important differences between Le Guern and the Groupe de Liège will be underlined. An analysis of the whole of Le Guern's work is to be found in Study 6, section 5.

42 Cf. Study 3, section 1; Study 4, sections 1 and 5.

43 The semantics of Le Guern and of the Groupe de Liège are entirely at one on the precise point of the definition of metaphor in terms of alteration of semic composition. Both of them confer the same primacy on the lexeme, that is, on the word ultimately and not on the sentence. Both of them suppose a semic composition prior to the lexeme, on the basis of which metaphor is explained 'through the suppression or more exactly by the bracketing of one portion of the constitutive semes of the lexeme used' (Le Guern *Sémantique* 15).

44 Greimas *Sémantique structurale* 42 ff.

45 Cf. below, Study 6, section 1.

46 Can the question of semantic segmentation be resolved without recourse to the structure of the referent? This is what Le Guern must presuppose, in order to reserve modifications of the referential relation for the operation of metonymy. The opposition between semic reorganization and reference switching supposes that semic analysis and conceptual or objective analysis are entirely dissociated. In his chapter 'Towards Semic Analysis' (*Sémantique* 114 ff.), Le Guern reproaches most attempts at analysing the lexeme in terms of semes of sliding 'towards a structuring of the universe' (114), something that forces an encyclopaedic and therefore impossible responsibility on semic analysis (ibid.). This reproach is connected to the author's more general concern to dissociate semantics from logic, some important consequences of which – the role of the associated image, the difference between metaphor, symbol, similarity, comparison,

and so on – will be seen in the next Study. According to him, the metaphorical uses of a word mark precisely the difference between semic analysis and referential knowledge of the object. The difficulty with this criterion is that it involves only lexicalized metaphors, which, by the author's own admission, are but very few in number (82). Our constant theme, that the dictionary contains no living metaphors, says the same thing. Moreover, the argument runs the risk of circularity, if metaphor reveals semantics as such, an abstraction from metaphor, and if semic analysis is to explain metaphorical usage.

47 The authors use the name 'mode Σ' for the mode that breaks a class down into species, because the class is the sum (Σ) of its species; they call the mode of decomposition into disjunctive trees 'mode π,' because the object is the logical product (π) that results from the distributive decomposition.

48 The semantics of Le Guern resists this reduction of metaphor to a double synecdoche, not only in virtue of the polarity (borrowed from Jakobson) of metaphorical process and metonymic process, but for a reason derived from its own analysis of synecdoche (*Sémantique* 29-39). Synecdoche does not constitute a homogeneous category. One of its species – the synecdoche of the part and the whole – is similar to metonymy; like metonymy, it is defined as a switching of reference between two objects connected by an extra-linguistic relationship, and is explained by restitution of the entire reference that undergoes only an ellipsis in the figurative statement. Synecdoche of the part and the whole is just a somewhat special metonymy, in which switching of reference prevails over the ellipsis procedure. On the other hand, synecdoche of species and genus brings nothing into play but the procedure of abstraction which is at the base of all denomination. Here too, I would observe that the figure does not consist in the passage from species to genus, but in the misapprehension through which the one is designated in the terms of the other. But I agree completely that metonymy and synecdoche belong on the same side, in that they can be defined and explained as accidents of denomination.

49 Léon Cellier 'D'une rhétorique profonde: Baudelaire et l'oxymoron.' For the authors of the *Rhétorique générale*, the difference proposed by Cellier between antithesis and oxymoron ('contradiction tragically proclaimed for antithesis, paradisaically assumed for oxymoron') concerns only the *ethos* of figures, not their analysis on the formal level (120).

50 Jean Cohen 126

51 Jean Cohen writes: 'So we have the right to analyse "fox" as a "more cunning animal," the second trait alone being retained in metaphorical usage' (ibid. 127).

52 For this discussion, cf. Study 3, section 3.

53 Le Guern (*Sémantique* 39-65) offers a palpably different analysis of the family of language facts arising from the relation of similarity. We shall reserve its discussion for the next Study, section 5.

54 The negation of the referential function of metaphorical discourse by the new rhetoric will be examined in Study 7; let us here just underline the solidarity of this thesis with the postulates of the theory. Only the theory of the statement-metaphor, by reinserting figure into the framework of the theory of discourse, can reopen the problematic of meaning and reference that the reduction to the word closed off. The semantics of Le Guern poses an analogous problem, but for different reasons. The counterpart of the close link instituted between metonymy and reference is the exclusion of all problems of reference from the semic analysis of metaphor. Consequently, the denotative deficiency (in the sense of cognitive

information) can be made up only by an excess of connotation (in the sense of associated affective value); hence, an investigation of motivations (to teach, to please, to persuade) takes the place of an inquiry into the referential import of the metaphorical statement.

STUDY 6

1 The history of this reversal of priority between metaphor and simile after Aristotle is to be found in Marsh McCall *Ancient Rhetorical Theories of Simile and Comparison.*
2 *Course in General Linguistics* part 2, chapters 5 and 6
3 Roman Jakobson 'Results of the Conference of Anthropologists and Linguists' 567, 565
4 Nicolas Ruwet, the translator of 'Two Aspects of Language and Two Types of Aphasic Disturbances' into French, did not fail to expose the divergence between Jakobson's classification and that suggested by Freud in *The Interpretation of Dreams* (*Essais de linguistique générale* 66, note 1). Is it enough to claim, with Jakobson himself, 'the imprecision of the concept of condensation, which in Freud seems at the same time to cover cases of metaphor and cases of synecdoche'? Or must it rather be admitted that the phenomena that Freud placed under the general title of *Entstellung* escape language? My view on this topic can be found in *Freud and Philosophy: An Essay on Interpretation* 88 ff. and 134 ff.
5 The following table presents the succession of viewpoints under which the polarity of the two processes is effected:

process	operation	relationship	axis	domain	linguistic factor
metaphor	selection	similarity	substitution	semantics	code (signification in the code)
metonymy	combination	contiguity	concatenation	syntax	message (contextual signification)

6 'Two Aspects' 258
7 Pierre Fontanier *Les Figures du discours* 79
8 Jakobson 'Results of the Conference' 566
9 Michel Le Guern *Sémantique de la métaphore et de la métonymie*
10 A.J. Greimas *Sémantique structurale, Recherche de Méthode*
11 Le Guern speaks readily of the 'kinship,' the 'close connection' (24) of the two functions. These are, he states, two 'complementary aspects of the same mechanism' (*Sémantique* 28).
12 Cf. above, Study 5, section 4. We will return to the problem of reference in Study 7; but then reference will not be understood only as a correspondence at the level of denomination or naming, but as a capacity for describing reality that proceeds from the statement in its entirety. Cf. above also the discussion of metaphor *in praesentia* and of simile in the *Rhétorique générale* (Study 5, 166).

13 We will discuss this claim in Study 7, where the distinction between denotation and connotation will come under scrutiny again from the point of view of the referential function of the statement. The properly 'image-ing' function of metaphor will be discussed at the end of the present Study. What interests us here is the way in which denotation and connotation function together.

14 Le Guern's extremely rich and insightful work interests us on other counts as well. After outlining the facts of language under the jurisdiction of rhetoric and locating metaphor in relation to other expressions of analogy, the author introduces the analysis of motivations. This explanation is imposed within a theory that denies metaphor the referential thrust which it accords to metonymy, at least in the order of naming. It is established also by virtue of the relationship between denotation and connotation. Psychological connotation itself calls for an explication in terms of motifs. This will be taken up again in Study 7, where it will be asked whether the investigation of motivations must replace that of reference. But before that, reference must have been given another sense than the simple reference of naming, so that the reference of attribution might be considered. Finally, the valuable observations on the lexicalization of metaphor will be recalled when another debate takes place, on the role of 'dead' metaphor in philosophy (Study 8, section 3).

15 Paul Henle 'Metaphor' (this essay develops in modified form the 'Presidential Address' opening the *Proceedings of the Western Division of the American Philosophical Association*, 1953-4). The theory of M.B. Hester, which will be discussed later (section 6), belongs to the same network of problems.

16 Henle quotes the following statement of Kenneth Burke: 'Metaphor is a device for seeing something *in terms* of something else ... A metaphor tells us something about one character considered from the point of view of another character. And to consider A from the point of view of B is, of course, to use B as *a perspective* on A' (*Grammar* 503-4; 'Metaphor' 192).

17 Keats 'To Hope' in *Poems* (1807), quoted in Henle 'Metaphor' 176

18 In Study 7 I will propose an ontological, not just a psychological, interpretation of the 'transference of feeling' characteristic of the poetic function of metaphor.

19 On the relationship between metaphor and symbol (in the sense in which I have used this term since *The Symbolism of Evil*), see my article 'Parole et symbole.'

20 Cf. above, Study 3, section 2.

21 Max Black *Models and Metaphors* 43. Cf. above, Study 3, section 3.

22 Cf. above, Study 3, section 4.

23 The following references to Aristotle may be reinserted into the framework of the Aristotelian theory of metaphor set out in Study 1. In particular, see section 3 on simile,' and pages 34-5 on 'set before the eyes' and 'pronouncing the inanimate animate.'

24 Concerning 'making appear,' cf. Study 5, section 2 (on *figure*).

25 We are brought to the end of our discussion of Le Guern's *Sémantique* by this difficulty, namely, in what sense is the associated image a linguistic entity?

26 In an article in the *Nouvelle Révue Française* on 1 January 1935, Paul Valéry called figures 'these calculated errors' (*Œuvres* [La Pléiade] 1: 1289-90, quoted in Albert Henry *Métonymie et Métaphore* 8). The same author (to whom more space will be given in section 5) quotes this surprisingly apt observation from the poet Reverdy: 'The image is a pure creation of the spirit. It cannot be born from a comparison, but from the meeting of two distant realities. The more the relationships between the two proximate realities are remote and accurate, the stronger

will be the image – the more emotive power and poetic reality it will have' (ibid. 57). Claudel (*Journal* [La Pléiade] 1: 42) concurs: 'Metaphor, like reasoning, resembles, but from farther off' (quoted in ibid. 69, note 26).

27 This power of metaphor to reduce a 'distance' between logical genera comes up again in other contexts in Aristotle himself; in this vein the rapprochement of metaphor and enigma: 'For all metaphors imply an enigma; plainly, therefore, a metaphor (so borrowed) must be itself well converted' (*Rhetoric* 3, 1405 b 4-5); so too with the rapprochement of metaphor and antithesis, where antithesis and resemblance seek to be understood together (ibid., 1410 b 35, 1411 b 2).

28 The theory of substitution overlooks this mechanism because its point of departure is metaphor *in absentia*, which is restricted formally to substituting the present term for an absent term that must be interpolated (thus Henle thought it necessary to interpolate a 'cloak' in Keats' verse that speaks of a soul 'enwrapped' in 'gloom'). But the dynamics of metaphor *in absentia* are revealed only by metaphor *in praesentia*, where it is the interaction among all the terms of the statement that instigates the substitution of a present term for an absent term.

29 Philip Wheelwright *Metaphor and Reality* 72 ff.

30 Gaston Esnault sees in metaphor 'a self-transferring intuition' [... *qui se transporte*]' (quoted in Henry *Métonymie* 55). It is 'direct intuition [... *en ligne droite*]'; thanks to it, 'the mind affirms an intuitive and concrete identity' (ibid. 57). We will use this affirmation in our own way, giving as the primary meaning of 'image' this same movement in its intuitive moment. Taking up the intuitionist tradition, Henry aptly says: 'Born of a sensible reaction, [metaphor] is a new intuition that departs from and attains imagination. The felicitous contemplation of the perceived brings about a rich moment in which a living synthesis, actualizing the interaction of two factors, is created' (ibid. 59).

31 Nelson Goodman *Languages of Art, An Approach to a Theory of Symbols* 69

32 On the Same and the Similar, see Aristotle *Metaphysics* Δ, chapter 9: 'Those things are called "like" which have the same attributes in every respect, and those which have more attributes the same than different, and those whose quality is one; and that which shares with another thing the greater number or the more important of the attributes (each of them one of two contraries) in respect of which things are capable of altering, is like that other thing' (1018 a 15-18). The second acceptation of the word *similar* or *like* would seem to be particularly appropriate to the case of metaphor.

33 Thus R. Herrschberger, in 'The Structure of Metaphor,' holds that metaphor 'refers to the likeness of otherwise unlike things' (434). The 'tension' consists in this, that the interpreter is invited by the poem to take account of the dissimilarities as well as the resemblances among its multiple referents: 'Perceiving the likeness between the multiple referents of a metaphor, a person thirsty for an aesthetic experience, and the poem permitting, *makes an effort* to include as many seeming-unlikenesses as possible' (ibid.). The reconciliation of opposites and the maintenance of their tension are equally necessary to the constitution of poetic experience. In the same sense, Douglas Berggren declares that metaphor 'constitutes the indispensable principle for integrating diverse phenomena and perspectives without sacrificing their diversity' ('The Use and Abuse of Metaphor' 237).

34 C.M. Turbayne *The Myth of Metaphor* 12

35 Gilbert Ryle *The Concept of Mind* 10

36 I concur entirely with Michel Le Guern on this point (*Sémantique* 52-65).

'Similitude' comparison rests on a logical usage of analogy; it is an implicit reasoning. Metaphor properly speaking rests on a purely semantic usage of analogy; it is a direct transference, expressed well by the unusual attribution in metaphor *in praesentia*. My only reservation concerns the use of the word *analogy* to cover these diverse uses. I prefer 'resemblance, similarity [*ressemblance*],' which is the substantive formed from 'similar [*semblable*].' The word *analogy* should be reserved either for Aristotelian analogy, i.e. proportional relationship of four terms (on which metaphor by analogy is constructed, a transference crossing over between the second and the fourth terms of the proportional relationship), or for the *analogia entis* of mediaeval metaphysics. (Analogy in this last acceptation will be discussed in section 2 of the last Study.)

37 Hans-Georg Gadamer *Wahrheit und Methode* part 3, 406 ff.

38 Stanislas Breton, reflecting on the work of Rubina Giorgi, works in a similar fashion with a view to ordering imagination, schema, and image. He subordinates these three terms to the symbol; and the symbol, itself issuing from the problem of the interval between 'limit' and the 'unlimited,' sets an interpretative activity in motion and opens a path. It is this path that is articulated in the triad named above: *imagination becomes image through the schema* (S. Breton, 'Symbole, schème, imagination: Essai sur l'œuvre de R. Giorgi'). Breton's reflections are not unrelated to my attempt at anchoring the image in semantic innovation. The notion of interval, however, presupposed by that of symbol, activates an inquiry into difference that exceeds the limits of this Study and relates more to the ontology articulated in Study 8.

39 Gaston Esnault *L'Imagination populaire, métaphores occidentales*

40 Bernard Pottier 'Vers une sémantique moderne' and *Présentation de la linguistique. Fondements d'une théorie*

41 A.J. Greimas *Sémantique structurale*

42 I am leaving aside the distinction between metonymy and synecdoche, which Henry connects to the quite subtle distinction between semic field and semantic or associative field (25-6): 'Metonymy and synecdoche are modalities of a single fundamental figure: a figure of focalization and of contiguity. They do not differ in their logic, but in their fields of application' (*Métonymie* 26).

43 This is how one might challenge the opinion of Charles Bally, who prefers to see nothing in figures but 'laziness of thought' and 'laziness of expression' (*Traité de Stylistique française* § 197).

44 The important stylistic developments established on this psycholinguistic foundation are bracketed here. I note only that the study of series (in Saint-John Perse, for example), the determination of dominant figures, and finally the interest shown in 'tonal adequacy' – that is, to appropriateness to context – enjoin consideration no longer of a word, nor even a sentence, but an entire *work* (49). We will encounter these problems again, raised by the link between style and work, in Study 7.

45 This is anticipated even more by Cl.-L. Estève than by Esnault: 'To metonymy or synecdoche, we see, metaphor always adds transference from one object to another, thanks to a feature that is common in some way to both of them' (*Études philosophiques sur l'expression littéraire* quoted in Henry *Métonymie* 65).

46 William Bedell Stanford *Greek Metaphor: Studies in Theory and Practice*

47 Deviation of language in Jean Cohen should rather be assimilated to change of denomination, which results, as Albert Henry and Hedwig Konrad have shown,

from perception of an identity between two foci with two semic fields superimposed on them.

48 Marcus B. Hester *The Meaning of Poetic Metaphor*
49 Susanne Langer *Philosophy in a New Key*
50 Northrop Frye *Anatomy of Criticism*
51 R. Wellek and A. Warren *Theory of Literature*
52 On sense and reference, see Study 3, 73-4, and Study 7.
53 John Hospers *Meaning and Truth in the Arts*
54 Hester *Poetic Metaphor* 160-9
55 Similarly, Michel Le Guern emphasizes that the 'associated image' is not a free
    connotation, but 'bound' (*Sémantique* 21).
56 Ludwig Wittgenstein *Philosophical Investigations* II, xi
57 Again we encounter Le Guern's distinction between logical comparison and
    semantic analogy.
58 Virgil C. Aldrich 'Image-Mongering and Image-Management,' and 'Pictorial
    Meaning, Picture-Thinking and Wittgenstein's Theory of Aspects' 75-6
59 Owen Barfield *Poetic Diction: A Study in Meaning* 81, quoted in Hester *Poetic
    Metaphor* 27
60 Gaston Bachelard *The Poetics of Space* introduction xi-xxxv; *The Poetics of
    Reverie* introduction 1-26
61 *The Poetics of Space* xix
62 Ibid. And further: 'The essential newness of the poetic image poses the problem
    of the speaking being's creativeness. Through this creativeness the imagining
    consciousness proves to be, very simply but very purely, an origin. In a study
    of the imagination, a phenomenology of the poetic imagination must concen-
    trate on bringing out this quality of origin in various poetic images' (xx).
63 The term and theme are taken from Eugène Minkowski *Vers une Cosmologie*
    chapter 9.
64 Bachelard *Poetics of Reverie* 3-6
65 Ibid. 18

STUDY 7

1   Émile Benveniste 'La forme et le sens dans le langage' 35
2   Gottlob Frege 'On Sense and Reference'
3   Benveniste 'La forme et le sens' 37
4   P.F. Strawson *Individuals: An Essay in Descriptive Metaphysics*
5   Part 1, chapter 4, section 2, 'Axioms of Reference'
6   G.G. Granger *Essai d'une philosophie du style*
7   As an epigraph to his work the author uses this text, taken from the *Metaphysics*
    of Aristotle (A 981 a 15): 'Actions and productions are all concerned with the
    individual; for the physician does not cure *man*, except in an incidental way, but
    Callias or Socrates or some other called by some such individual name, who hap-
    pens to be a man.'
8   Monroe C. Beardsley *Aesthetics* 134
9   Jakobson 'Closing Statements: Linguistics and Poetics' 353 ff.
10 Study 6, section 1
11 Suzanne Langer *Philosophy in a New Key*
12 W.K. Wimsatt *The Verbal Icon* 231

13 Marcus B. Hester *The Meaning of Poetic Metaphor.* Cf. above, Study 6, section 6
14 Suzanne Langer *Feeling and Form: A Theory of Art* 212, cited in Hester *Poetic Metaphor* 70
15 T. Todorov *Littérature et Signification* 102
16 Jean Cohen *Structure du langage poétique* 199-225
17 Mikel Dufrenne *The Phenomenology of Aesthetic Experience* 442
18 R. Ruyer 'L'expressivité'
19 *Rhétorique générale* 24
20 Michel Le Guern *Sémantique de la métaphore et de la métonymie* 20-1. See Study 6, section 1.
21 *Anatomy of Criticism* 80
22 Martin Heidegger *Being and Time* paragraph 29
23 *Languages of Art* 6, 3: 241-6
24 See the left side of the table opposite. The table does not originate with Goodman. Rather, I have drawn it up for myself as a guide through the distinctions and terminology of this difficult work, particularly its first two chapters.
25 *Languages of Art* 10-19
26 Ibid. 241-4
27 Ibid. 52-7
28 Ibid. 74-81
29 Ibid. 81-5
30 Ibid. 70
31 Ibid. 71-4
32 Ibid. 77
33 Max Black *Models and Metaphors* 37
34 Goodman *Languages of Art* 73, 80
35 Ibid. 85
36 Black *Models and Metaphors* 219-43
37 Mary B. Hesse 'The Explanatory Function of Metaphor'
38 Stephen Toulmin *The Philosophy of Science: An Introduction* 38-9 cited in Goodman *Languages of Art* 239
39 C.G. Hempel and P. Oppenheim 'The Logic of Explanation'
40 Stephen C. Pepper *World Hypotheses* 91-2 cited in Black *Models and Metaphors* 239-40
41 One can find in the work of Philip Wheelwright (*Metaphor and Reality*) an attempt to establish a hierarchy of metaphors according to their degree of stability, their 'comprehensiveness or breadth of appeal' (98 ff). For Wheelwright, metaphors endowed with integrative power are called symbols. At the lowest level he finds the dominant images of a particular poem; then the symbols that have 'personal' significance and permeate an entire work; next, the symbols shared by an entire cultural tradition; then those that link the members of a vast secular or religious community; and finally, at the fifth level, the archetypes that hold meaning for all of humanity, or at least a major part of it – for example, the symbolism of the moon and of shadows, or that of lordship. This idea of an organization into levels is taken up again by Berggren ('The Use and Abuse of Metaphor' 248-9). From a completely different point of view, that of stylistics, Albert Henry (*Métonymie et Métaphore* 116 ff.) shows that it is combinations of metaphors as second-level figures (which he details with extraordinary subtlety) that integrate the rhetorical procedures of an entire work whose task it is to promote the poet's singular vision. When referring earlier to the analysis of Albert Henry (see above, 203), I empha-

	LITERAL APPLICATION OF A SYMBOL				METAPHORICAL APPLICATION OF A SYMBOL
	orientation of reference	category of symbols	logical extension	domain of application	
R E F E R	*to denote* ... (from symbol towards thing) →	verbal = description; non-verbal = representation ≠ imitation	multiple; singular; null (painting [of a] unicorn)	objects and events	
				transference	
R E N C E	*to exemplify* ... = to be denoted = to possess = relationship of a label ↑ sample	verbal = exemplified predicate; non-verbal = colour sample		feelings	→ metaphysical denotation 'expression' figurative possession or metaphorical exemplification (*sad* colours in a painting)

· sized that reference to a world and return-reference to an author go hand in hand with this intertwining that raises discourse to the level of a work.
42 Study 1, section 5
43 Paul Ricoeur *Fallible Man* part 4 'Affective Fragility'
44 Berggren 'The Use and Abuse of Metaphor'
45 Ibid. 1: 249
46 Ibid. 1: 253
47 Ernst Cassirer *The Philosophy of Symbolic Forms* volume 1 *Language* chapter 5 'Language and the Expression of the Forms of Pure Relation: The Sphere of Judgment and the Concepts of Relation'
48 *Rhétorique générale* 114-15
49 Coleridge, appendix C to *The Statesman's Manual* quoted in I.A. Richards *The Philosophy of Rhetoric* 109
50 Owen Barfield *Poetic Diction: A Study in Meaning*
51 Wheelwright *Metaphor and Reality* 17
52 Philip Wheelwright *The Burning Fountain* 25-9, 55-9
53 Wheelwright *Metaphor and Reality* 38-9
54 Ibid. 19, 30, 130, and *passim*
55 Bacon *Novum Organum* 1: 44, quoted in Turbayne *Myth of Metaphor* 29
56 The expression belongs to William Bedell Stanford in *Greek Metaphor: Studies in Theory and Practice* 105. It has been taken up by numerous English-language writers.
57 *Closing Statements* 371

STUDY 8

1 É. Benveniste 'Catégories de pensée et catégories de langue' *Études philoso-phiques* (December 1958) 419-29, published also in *Problems in General Linguistics* 55-64
2 The first six categories refer to *nominal* forms: that is, the linguistic class of nouns; then, in the general class of adjectives, two types of adjectives designating quantity and quality; then the comparative, which is the 'relative' form by reason of its function; then the denominations of place and time. The next four are all *verbal* categories: the active voice and the passive voice; then the category of *mediative* verbs (as distinct from active verbs); then that of the *perfect* as 'being a certain state.' (It should be noted that Émile Benveniste's linguistic genius succeeds in interpreting these last two categories, which have embarrassed countless interpreters.) In this way, Aristotle 'thought he was defining the attributes of objects but he was really setting up linguistic entities' (60).
3 The second study bears the very direct title 'The System of Aristotle's *Categories* and its Logical and Metaphysical Signification' (44-125). I shall invert the order followed by Jules Vuillemin in his work because my purpose is different from his: Vuillemin wants to show that analogy comes from a pseudo-science which links up with theology. This is why he moves directly to a discussion of analogy and its logical deficiency in the first study of his book. Since I want to show the split between philosophical and poetic discourse at the point where they appear to be closest, I go directly to the point where the split is widest: this is the point where Jules Vuillemin does justice to the systematic construction of the Aristotelian treatise on the *Categories*.

4 Vuillemin *De la logique* 110
5 'In the same way, Aristotle assumes the theory of analogy in the *Categories*:
   being is said in different ways, but these different acceptations are ordered in
   that they all derive, more or less directly, from a fundamental acceptation that
   is the attribution of a secondary substance to a primary substance' (ibid. 226).
6 'For it must be either by an equivocation that we say [things] *are*, or by adding
   to and taking from the meaning of "are" (in the way in which that which is not
   known may be said to be known) – the truth being that we use the word neither
   ambiguously nor in the same sense, but just as we apply the word *medical* by
   virtue of a *reference* to one and the same thing, not *meaning* one and the same
   thing, nor yet speaking ambiguously; for a patient and an operation and an instrument are called medical neither by an ambiguity nor with a single meaning,
   but with reference to a common end' (*Metaphysics* Z 4, 1030 a 31 – b 4). In
   L'Objet de la métaphysique selon Aristote, Vianney Décarie exhibits the connection between book Z and the outline of the multiple meanings of being in
   book Δ; he underlines that 'the other categories derive their meaning from this
   primary being' (138). This pivotal semantic and ontological function of *ousia* is
   lost from sight somewhat in an aporetic interpretation of Aristotelian ontology.
7 Vuillemin *De la logique* 229. For Vuillemin, the 'pseudo-science' into which
   Western philosophy has strayed begins here. According to him, analogy was
   erased from modern philosophy only when, in Russell, Wittgenstein, and Carnap, a single, fundamental signification was attributed to the copula, namely,
   that an element belongs to a class. 'At that moment, the notion of analogy
   disappeared and Metaphysics as a science was made possible' (228). This, of
   course, assumes that the meaning of the word *to be* is exhausted in this logical
   reduction – precisely what we deny in the present work.
8 'It is indeed this ontological description, superimposed on logical description,
   that can properly be considered the guiding thread of the deduction' (ibid.
   78). 'Philosophical analysis must continually correct grammatical appearances
   and reverse the order of subordination that grammar implies. At the same time,
   it makes the guiding thread of the deduction apparent' (ibid. 86).
9 This is what Jules Vuillemin does: 'So, if there is no quiddity, in the primordial
   sense, with respect to a composite such as *white man*, there will be quiddity in
   a derivative sense. There will be predications by analogy, not in a synonymous
   but in a paronymous fashion; the predication is thus "transcendental"' (ibid. 63).
10 Vuillemin restores the fundamental breakdown by subdividing each of the two
   classes of essential and accidental predication into primordial and derivative,
   then each of the four classes obtained in this way in terms of the difference
   between primary substance and secondary substance. The table of *a priori*
   possibilities of predication is found in ibid. 66-75.
11 Vuillemin recognizes this: 'The theory of analogy, implicit in the theory of
   paronyms, allows us to consider under the same principle – although, we might
   say, in a progressively diminishing relation – the signification of the copula, the
   relation of subordination between secondary substances, and the relations of
   subordination between abstract particulars and abstract generalities on the one
   hand and between abstract generalities on the other' (ibid. 111). We shall say
   nothing here regarding the fourth part of the *Categories* (paragraphs 10-15):
   Enumerating post-predicaments, Jules Vuillemin observes, allows the series of
   categories to be placed within Aristotle's metaphysics; by introducing the rudi-

ments of a theory of motion, the treatise sets out the distinction between three kinds of substance and the subordination of the universe to the third substance (God), and sketches 'the unity of logic, physics and theology' (ibid.).

12 'So, too, there are many senses in which a thing is said to be, but all refer to one starting-point: some things are said to be because they are substances, others because they are affections of substance, others because they are a process towards substance, or destructions or privations or qualities of substance, or productive or generative of substance, or of things which are relative to substance, or negations of one of these things or of substance itself' (*Metaphysics* Γ 2, 1003 b 6-10). On this point, we refer to V. Décarie's excellent commentary, which stresses again the 'common notion' role of *ousia*, thanks to which 'a single science is entrusted with studying all beings as beings' (*L'Objet de la métaphysique* 102).

13 Pierre Aubenque *Le problème de l'être chez Aristote: Essai sur la problématique aristotélicienne*

14 Aubenque goes so far as to see in Aristotle a tragic character comparable to that of Pascal, who upheld 'the impossibility of the necessary' (ibid. 219, note 2).

15 The text in question here is *Metaphysics* E 1, where Aristotle applies his notion of reference to a first term no longer to the sequence of meanings of being but to the very hierarchy of beings. Therefore, *ousia* is no longer the first of the categories; rather, divine *ousia* is supreme being. This reference to a first term, no longer on the level of meanings but on the level of beings, is supposed to serve as the basis for the very discourse on being. 'For one might raise the question,' Aristotle says, 'whether first philosophy is universal, or deals with one genus, i.e. some one kind of being; for not even the mathematical sciences are all alike in this respect – geometry and astronomy deal with a certain particular kind of thing, while universal mathematics applies alike to all. We answer that if there is no substance other than those which are formed by nature, natural science will be the first science; but if there is an immovable substance, the science of this must be prior and must be first philosophy, and universal in this way, because it is first' (*Metaphysics* E 1, 1026 a 23-30). V. Décarie's enquiry into 'the object of metaphysics according to Aristotle' attests to the continuity of the link between ontology and theology throughout the entire Aristotelian corpus (concerning this passage from the *Metaphysics*, see Décarie *L'Objet de la métaphysique* 111-24).

16 Aubenque readily grants this: 'The reality of *khôrismos* can be experienced less as an irremediable separation than as the invitation to overcome it. In short, between ontological investigation and contemplation of the divine, relations can and must exist that the word *separation* is not sufficient to express fully' (335).

17 Cf. Aubenque's analysis of theological appendices in various places in *Metaphysics* Γ and of the physical preparation in Λ 1-5 of the theological exposition in Λ 6-10 (*Le problème de l'être chez Aristote* 393 ff.)

18 'The impossible ideal of a world whose unity would be restored ... must remain, at the very heart of irremediable dispersion, the guiding principle of human investigation and action' (402). And a little further on: 'The unity of discourse could never be given in itself; nor could it ever be "sought," moreover, if discourse were not directed by the ideal of a subsisting unity' (403). Again: 'If the divine does not exhibit the unity ontology seeks, it nonetheless guides ontology in its search' (404). And finally: 'It is the necessity of motion that, through the mediation of philosophical discourse, divides being against itself according to a plurality of meanings, the unity of which is still indefinitely "sought after"' (438).

19 'Ousia,' Aubenque says, 'is one of the rare words that Aristotle employs to speak both of sub-lunary realities and of divine reality, without any indication that this common denomination is merely metaphorical or analogical' (*Le Problème de l'être chez Aristote* 405). This remark should be followed by a more decisive recognition of the unitive function that falls to the category of *ousia*.

20 Aristotle 'can only have meant the following: human discourse must proceed *as if* the causes of essences were the causes of all things, as if the world were a well ordered whole and not a rhapsodic series, as if all things could be traced back to the first among them, that is to essences, and to the first of the essences, as to their Principle' (ibid. 407).

21 David Ross understands this in the following way: 'Except as regards the first cause, things in different genera have only analogically the same causes' (*Aristotle* 175).

22 Jules Vuillemin *De la logique* 14. The author shows that the mathematical notion of analogy stems from the modification by Theaetetus of an earlier definition that applied only to rational numbers. It is through the operation of *alternating diminution* – which 'implies development *ad infinitum*' (ibid. 13) – that the idea of number could be extended to irrationals by Greek mathematicians.

23 '... (proportion being not a property only of the kind of number which consists of abstract units, but of number in general [*holòs arithmou*]). For proportion is equality of ratios, and involves four terms at least ...' (*Nichomachean Ethics* 1131 a 30-2).

24 It is at this point in the continuous extension of mathematical analogy and in the weakening of its criteria that the relation of proportionality rejoins the theory of metaphor, or at least its most 'logical' aspect, proportional metaphor (cf. Study 1). But poetic discourse merely utilizes it, whereas philosophical discourse sets out its theory, placing it on a trajectory of meaning somewhere between mathematical proportion and reference *ad unum*.

25 'The causes and the principles of different things are in a sense different, but in a sense, if one speaks universally and analogically, they are the same for all' (*Metaphysics* Λ 4, 1070 a 31-3). See also Λ 5, 1071 a 4 and 27, and, of course, the passage cited above (Λ 5, 1071 a 33-7).

26 *Metaphysics* Γ 2, 1003 a 34-b 4; Z 4, 1030 a 35-b 3

27 On this point, cf. Vuillemin *De la logique* 22.

28 Considering the terms of analogy themselves, he will observe that the common attribution of being to substance and to accident implicitly reduces judgments of relation to judgments of predication. Now, the true judgment of predication (if one puts aside essential definition) does not allow reciprocation. But above all, by placing substance at the head of metaphysics, philosophy designates a term for which no science exists, since substance is in every case a determined individual and science deals only with genera and species. For this reason, the order of things escapes the scientific order, which is abstract and does not treat substances in the primary sense. Considering in addition the relation of the other categories to substance, the logician can only repeat Aristotle's own admission: if science is generic and if the bond of being is not generic, then the analogical bond of being is not scientific. We must then recognize 'the lack of scientific communicability among the genera of being' (ibid. 41).

29 'In general, if we search for the elements of existing things without distinguishing the many senses in which things are said to exist, we cannot find them, especially

if the search for the elements of which things are made is conducted in this manner. For it is surely impossible to discover what "acting" or "being acted on," or the "straight" is made of, but if elements can be discovered at all, it is only the elements of substances; therefore either to seek the elements of all existing things or to think one has them is incorrect' (*Metaphysics* Λ 9, 992 b 18-25).

30 Immanuel Kant *Critique of Pure Reason* book 3, chapter 3, section 7, A 632: 525. Martin Heidegger *Was ist Metaphysik?* 19-20 (the English translation in Werner Brock, ed. *Existence and Being* lacks this introduction).

31 Among the most recent works we must cite Bernard Montagnes *La Doctrine de l'analogie de l'être d'après saint Thomas d'Aquin*. The author lays before us the series of solutions attempted by Aquinas (65-114) in response to the excessive role accorded by Cajetan to analogy of proportionality. According to G.P. Klubertanz in *St Thomas Aquinas on Analogy: A Textual Analysis and Systematic Synthesis*, proportional analogy appeared at a particular point in Aquinas' career and then disappeared. Book 4 of the *Commentaire au Livre I des Sentences* and the *De Veritate* are held to provide evidence for this stage in the doctrine.

32 On the reasons for rejecting univocal attribution, see the *Commentaire au Livre I des Sentences Dist.* xxxv, qu. 1, art. 3, ad. 5: 'Nothing is common to the eternal and to the corruptible as both the commentator and the philosopher himself assert. The science of God is eternal, ours is corruptible, a science we manage to lose through forgetfulness and acquire through instruction or attention. Science, therefore, is applied to God and to us in different ways.' And later (ibid. art. 4): 'His being (*esse*) is his nature, because of what certain philosophers say: namely, that he is a being (*ens*) not in an essence (*essentia*) which he knows not by a science, and so on, until we understand that his essence is nothing other than his being (*esse*) and that it is the same for all other properties; as a result, nothing can be said univocally of God and of creatures.' The *De Veritate* says in the same sense that *esse* is proper to each being; that with respect to God, his nature is his *esse*; and that the term *ens*, therefore, cannot be univocally held in common. The *De Potentia* insists upon the diversity and the non-uniformity of being.

33 On the reasons for avoiding equivocal attribution Aquinas writes: 'Because if that were so, it follows that from creatures nothing at all could be known or demonstrated about God; for the reasoning would always be exposed to the fallacy of equivocation (*fallacia aequivocationis*). Such a view is against the Philosopher, who proves many things about God, and also against what the Apostle says: "*The invisible things of* GOD *are clearly seen being understood by the things that are made*" (Rom. 1: 20)' (*Summa Theologiae* I a, qu. 13, art. 5 in *Basic Writings of Saint Thomas Aquinas.*) The reconciling of St Paul and Aristotle is itself significant for its combination of two traditions and two cultures.

34 The division of predicates into univocal, equivocal, and analogous comes not from Aristotle but from Arab Aristotelianism, which itself inherits the class of ambiguous terms (*amphibola*) invented by Alexander of Aphrodisa in his commentary on Aristotle. Cf. H.A. Wolfson 'The Amphibolous Terms in Aristotle, Arabic Philosophy and Maimonides.'

35 That Aristotle provided the basic thread of the solution by analogy is confirmed by the several properly philosophical passages on analogy that do not deal with divine names. Such is the case with the *De Principiis Naturae* and the *Commentary* to Γ 2 of Aristotle's *Metaphysics*. The *De Principiis* introduces the question of analogy through that of the identity of principles (matter and form) within the diversity of beings. Analogy is an identity distinct from generic identity; it

is based on a type of *attributio* (a term borrowed from Averroes' commentary
on the *Metaphysics*), analogical *attributio*, which is based on *rationes* that are not
totally different, as is the case in equivocal *attributio* (when a single *nomen* –
dog – corresponds to different *rationes* – the animal and the constellation). *Attributio* in turn is ordered according to degrees of unity in beings. There follows
the well known example of the predicate *sanum*, which is said analogously of
the subject (man), of the sign (urine), and of the means (medicine), by reason
of a fundamental signification, which in this case is the aim (health). But this
basic meaning can refer to the efficient cause, as in the example of the predicate *medicus*, which is said first of the agent (doctor), then of the effects and
of the means. It is therefore the unity in the order of the being that governs
the unified diversity of the modes of attribution: being is said first (*per prius*)
of the substance, then by derivation (*per posterius*) of the other situations. The
analogical link among principles thus reflects that among beings. The agreement
here is called *secumdum analogiam, sive secumdum proportionem.* Analogy is
inserted between the identical and the heterogeneous. The commentary on
Aristotle's *Metaphysics* (*In XII Libros Metaphysicorum expositio Liber IV*)
follows the same line. The theme *ens* is said in various ways (*dicitur multipli-
citer*). But if the same notion (*ratio eadem*) does not govern the series of the
acceptations of being, 'then it is said "to be predicated analogously," i.e.,
proportionally (*illud dicitur 'analogice praedicare,' idest proportionaliter*),
according as each one by its own relationship is referred to that one same
thing (*per respectum ad unum*).' Then the examples of *sanus* and *medicus*
are brought up again. And St Thomas says: 'And just as the above-mentioned
terms have many senses, so also does the term being (*ens*). Yet every being is
called such in relation to one first thing (*per respectum ad unum primum*)'
(*Commentary on the Metaphysics of Aristotle* John P. Rowan, trans., 218).
The *Summa Theologiae* attests to the longevity (and the stability) of the
properly transcendental theory stemming from Aristotle: 'In names predicated of many in an analogical sense, all are predicated through a relation to
some one thing; and this one thing must be placed in the definition of them
all. And since *the essence expressed by the name is the definition*, as the Philosopher says, such a name must be applied primarily to that which is put in the
definition of the other things, and secondarily to these others according as they
approach more or less to the first' (I a, qu. 13, art. 6).

36 See H. Lyttkens *The Analogy Between God and the World.* The first 150 pages
    of this work are devoted to the history of analogy from the pre-Socratics to
    Albert the Great; the author demonstrates the genuinely neo-Platonic ancestry
    of the theme of participation underlying the Aristotelian vocabulary of analogy
    by reference to a first term. More recently, C. Fabro in *Participation et causalité
    selon S. Thomas d'Aquin* shows that analogy constitutes only the semantics of
    participation, which, in conjunction with causality, concerns the very reality of
    being underlying the concepts by which being is represented. In the same way,
    Montagnes writes: 'The doctrine of analogy is composed of the synthesis of two
    themes: one of Aristotelian origin, that of unity by reference to a first term; the
    other of Platonic origin, that of participation' (*La Doctrine de l'analogie de l'être*
    23).

37 The great work in this domain remains that of L.B. Geiger, *La Participation dans
    la philosophie de S. Thomas d'Aquin*: 'Analogy is the logic – more precisely, part
    of the logic – of participation' (78).

38 On analogy in Pseudo-Dionysius, cf. V. Lossky 'Le rôle des analogies chez Denys le Pseudo-Aréopagyte.' M.D. Chenu remarks: 'The slow maturation of the doctrine of the analogy of being can be taken as a criterion here. It is one of the points where the curious and fruitful meeting of Aristotle and Dionysius can be noted; this will be one of the first observations of the young Thomas Aquinas. Aristotle, so inexplicit concerning the exigencies of the transcendent, will soon supply the logical and metaphysical co-ordinates allowing the establishment of its conceptual status (potency and act); but it is Dionysius who will henceforth set out its being so strikingly' (*La Théologie au XIIe siècle* 313).

39 The scholasticism that comes down to us from John of St Thomas and Cajetan has identified the Thomist doctrine of analogy purely and simply with analogy of proportionality; cf., in particular, M.T.L. Penido *Le Rôle de l'analogie en théologie dogmatique*. In Montagnes' judgment, the chapter devoted to 'Preliminary Philosophical Questions' is merely 'an exposition of Cajetan's thought and not that of Saint Thomas' (*La Doctrine de l'analogie de l'être* 11, note 12).

40 This saying comes from Aristotle himself (text in Montagnes *La Doctrine de l'analogie de l'être* 84, note 34). Theology thereby recreates a certain incommensurability which could be compared to the situation the geometry of the Ancients had to confront. Like Greek *analogia*, the Scholastic *proportionalitas* turns terms that are not directly *proportionata* into *proportionabilia* (*De Veritate* qu. 23, art. 7 ad. 9; quoted in ibid. 85, note 36).

41 'But in the other type of analogy, no definite relation is involved between the things which have something in common analogously, so there is no reason why some name cannot be predicated analogously of God and creature in this manner' (*De Veritate* qu. 2, art. 11; in *Truth* 1: 113).

42 Cf. text in Montagnes *La Doctrine de l'analogie de l'être* 88-9

43 'By his creative presence, [God] is not distant but very close: *est in omnibus per essentiam, inquantum adest omnibus ut causa essendi* (I a, qu. 8, art. 3)' (ibid. 89).

44 L. de Raeymaeker ('L'Analogie de l'être dans la perspective d'une philosophie thomiste') stresses the subordination of the formal theory of analogy to the realist theory of causality and participation: 'It is through concrete participation and according to an individual mode that each particular being possesses its *esse* and takes part in the perfection of perfections. We must conclude from this that the principle of unity of the totality of concrete and individual beings cannot itself be anything but real as well. Located at the point where the lines of participation converge, it is the real source from which spring particular beings, and upon which, by virtue of their participation, these beings never cease to be entirely dependent' (105). No one has contributed more than Étienne Gilson to the recognition of the central position of the doctrine of being as act in the thought of St Thomas: see *The Christian Philosophy of St Thomas Aquinas*, and *Being and Some Philosophers* 74-107.

45 'Whatever is said of God and creatures is said according as there is some relation of the creature to God as to its principle and cause, wherein all the perfections of things pre-exist excellently. Now this mode of community is a mean between pure equivocation and simple univocation. For in analogy the idea is not, as it is in univocals, one and the same; yet it is not totally diverse as in equivocals; but the name which is thus used in a multiple sense signifies various proportions to some one thing ...' (*Summa Theologiae* I a, qu. 13, art. 5).

46 Vuillemin devotes a section of his first study on analogy to 'certain developments in the notion of analogy in St Thomas' (*De la logique* 22-33). He attempts to arrange within a single table distinctions that (according to the authors cited

above) were really substitutions for one another: namely, the distinction in the *Sentences* between analogy according to *intentio* by itself, according to *esse*, and according to *intentio et esse*; then the distinction in the *De Veritate*, where analogy of proportionality is opposed to analogy of proportion; and finally the distinction in the *Summa Contra Gentiles*, where the extrinsic relation of two terms to a third is contrasted with the internal relation of subordination of one term to another. The advantage of this systematization is that it accounts for all the distinctions synchronically. Its major drawback is that it displaces analogy of proportionality – which becomes just the 'element of rhetoric and of poetry' (33), to the extent that it 'is in fact metaphor and equivocal' (32) – in order to reserve for analogy of one term to another the domain of general metaphysics and special metaphysics or theology (33). But this is to forget that analogy of proportionality, besides its kinship with proportional metaphor, was called upon in its time to occupy the same place and to play the same role as the intimate and direct subordination of one term to another, when it functions between the finite and the infinite.

47 On *agens univocum* and *agens aequivocum*, cf. *De Potentia* qu. 7, art. 6 ad. 7. The *Summa Theologica* I a, qu. 13, art. 5 ad. 1, also proclaims the anteriority of the equivocal agent in relation to the univocal agent: '... unde oportet primum agens esse aequivocum.'

48 'Henceforth the structure of analogy and that of participation are strictly parallel and correspond to one another as the conceptual aspect and the real aspect of the unity of being' (Montagnes *La Doctrine de l'analogie de l'être* 114).

49 On the persistence of the solar metaphor and the heliotrope according to J. Derrida, cf. the following section.

50 'Hence as regards what the name signifies, these names are applied primarily to God rather than to creatures, because these perfections flow from God to creatures; but as regards the imposition of the names, they are primarily applied by us to creatures which we know first. Hence they have a mode of significa-tion which belongs to creatures, as was said above' (I a, qu. 13, art 6, conclu-sion).

51 M.-D. Chenu *La Théologie comme science au XIIIe siècle*. The author shows how the conflict of exegesis (the art of *lectio*) and theology (aspiring to the rank of a science governed by the order of the *quaestiones*) is moderated by St Thomas into a superior harmony without juxtaposition or confusion, but through quasi-subalternation (67-92). The *Commentary on the Sentences* still leaves the *modus symbolicus* of exegesis and the *modus argumentativus* of theology unconnected. As Chenu notes, 'the method named by three synonyms – *meta-phorica, symbolica, parabolica* – covers the very extensive content in Scripture of non-conceptual forms of expression ... St Thomas founds such a method upon the principle of the accommodation of the word of God to the rational nature of man to whom this word was addressed: man knows intelligible truth only through sensible realities' (43). Even when the understanding had by faith and knowledge founded on principles are better integrated in 'theological rea-son' (8), forming an organic continuity, a split will remain between hermeneu-tics and theological science. The place of metaphor in hermeneutics attests to this. Not only does metaphor belong to hermeneutics by reason of the place it occupies in the theory of the four meanings of Scripture, but, along with par-ables and various figurative expressions, it is also part of the literal or historical meaning, which is distinguished as a whole from the three-fold spiritual meaning (7th *Quodlibet*, qu. 6, *Summa Theologiae* I a, qu. 10). The literal meaning per-

tains to things signified by the words employed, whereas in the spiritual meaning things signified on the initial level become in turn signs of other things (in this way, the Law of the Old Testament is the figure of that of the New). On this point cf. H. de Lubac *Exégèse médiévale* part 2, 2: 285-302. It is true that the literal meaning has a wide range, even multiple acceptations, as primary significa-tion in contrast to a second signification and as the meaning intended by the author. For this reason, the expression *hand of God* still carries a literal meaning; but it attributes to God not bodily limbs but 'what is signified by bodily limbs, that is the operative quality' (1 a 2 ae, qu. 102, art. 2 ad 1; quoted in ibid. 277, note 7). De Lubac concedes, 'Ordinary language, however, even in the Church, has not always heeded the Angelic Doctor's suggestion, since today, quite to the contrary, we constantly speak of allegory in connection with what, in contrast to allegory, he termed parabolical or metaphorical meaning' (ibid. 278).

52 'Univocal predication is impossible between God and creatures. The reason of this is that every effect which is not a proportioned result of the power of the efficient cause receives the similitude of the agent not in its full degree, but in a measure that falls short; so that what is divided and multiplied in the effects re-sides in the agent simply, and in an unvaried manner. For example, the sun by the exercise of its one power produces manifold and various forms in these sub-lunary things. In the same way, as was said above, all perfections existing in creatures divided and multiplied pre-exist in God unitedly' (I a, qu. 13, art. 5, conclusion).

53 St Thomas ibid.

54 E. Husserl 'Author's Preface to the English Edition' *Ideas* 5-22

55 F. Nietzsche *Rhétorique et Langage* and S. Kofman *Nietzsche et la métaphore*

56 M. Heidegger *Der Satz vom Grund* 77-90

57 J. Greisch 'Les mots et les roses. La métaphore chez Martin Heidegger' 473

58 Heidegger *Der Satz vom Grund* 63-75

59 M. Heidegger *On the Way to Language*. For a general discussion of Heidegger's notion of metaphor, see below, section 5.

60 'And first of all we shall direct interest upon a certain wearing away of meta-phorical force in philosophical intercourse. It will become clear that this wearing away is not a supervenient factor modifying a kind of trope-energy which would otherwise remain intact; on the contrary, it constitutes the very history and struc-ture of philosophical metaphor' ('White Mythology' 6). 'It was also necessary to subject this notion of *wearing away* to scrutiny, for it seems to be systematically connected with the metaphorical perspective. It is to be found wherever the theme of metaphor has a special place' (13). And a bit later: 'This feature, the notion of wearing away, belongs without doubt not to a narrow historical and theoretical configuration, but more certainly to the notion of metaphor itself, and to the long metaphysical sequence which it determines, or which is deter-mined by it' (14) (Moore's translation slightly altered).

61 Hegel *The Philosophy of Fine Arts* 2: 139-40 quoted in ibid. 24-5

62 Nietzsche 'On Truth and Falsity in their Ultramoral Sense (1873)' *Works* 2: 180 quoted in ibid. 15

63 Cf. above, Study 6, section 4.

64 Cf. Study 2, sections 4 and 5.

65 Michel Le Guern *Sémantique de la métaphore et de la métonymie* 44-5, 82-9

66 'By the ordinary (*kurion*) word I mean,' Aristotle writes, 'that in general use in a country' (*Poetics* 1457 b). As regards the 'proper' (*idion*) sense in Aristotle, we

have shown that it has nothing to do with some sort of primitive sense (*etumon*), cf. Study 1, note 24. See also the discussion of Derrida's interpretation of the Aristotelian theory of metaphor in Study 1, note 21.

67 On newly-invented and forced metaphor in Fontanier, cf. Study 2, section 6.

68 For example when the thing named by the proper sense is found much more rarely than that designated by the metaphorical sense (for instance, the latin *testa*); or when one of two terms for the same thing takes over the non-figurative acceptation (for instance, the French noun *aveuglement*, deprived by *cécité* of the non-figurative sense of 'blindness,' now usually means the state of being confounded or incapacitated as by a passion).

69 The theory of living metaphor governs the intentional genesis not only of the *wearing away*, which gives rise to dead metaphor, but also of *abuse* in the sense of Turbayne and Berggren (cf. Study 7, section 5).

70 A. Henry 'La reviviscence des métaphores' *Métonymie et Métaphore* 143-53

71 P. Fontanier *Les Figures du discours* 95

72 Jean Ladrière 'Discours théologique et symbole'

73 Ibid. 131

74 Edmund Husserl *Logical Investigations* volume 1: 348

75 Ibid. 299-300

76 Ibid. 342-3. H.H. Price's important work *Thinking and Experience* begins with a discussion of the fundamental choice implied in the problem of recognition: do things resemble one another because they are examples of the *same* which is universal, or do we find rather that they are 'the same again' because they evince a resemblance?

77 *Logical Investigations* 1: 309-11

78 Ibid. 1: 393-8. In this context, *Repräsentation* signifies to stand for, to take the place of, to be substitutable for (*vertreten*).

79 Ibid. 339

80 Husserl *Ideas I* §99 and §111. Despite the first two *Logical Investigations*, Husserl has written that 'the element which makes up the life of phenomenology, as of all the eidetic sciences, is fiction' (*Ideas* 184).

81 'By an aesthetic idea I mean that representation of the imagination which induces much thought (*viel zu denken*), yet without the possibility of any definite thought whatever, i.e. *concept*, being adequate to it, and which language, consequently, can never get quite on level terms with or render completely intelligible' (A 190; *Critique of the Faculty of Judgment* 175-6).

82 'If now, we attach to a concept a representation of imagination belonging to its presentation, but inducing solely on its own account such a wealth of thought as (*so viel ... als*) would never admit of comprehension in a definite concept, and, as a consequence, giving aesthetically an unbounded expansion to the concept itself, then the imagination here displays a creative activity, and it puts the faculty of critical ideas (reason) into motion – a motion, at the instance of a representation, towards an extension of thought, that, while germane, no doubt, to the concept of the object, exceeds (*mehr ... als*) what can be laid hold of in that representation or clearly expressed' (A 192, ibid. 177).

83 Like poetry and eloquence, which Kant will evoke a bit later, it 'gives the imagination an impetus (*Schwung*) to bring more thought into play in the matter, though in an undeveloped manner, than (*mehr ... als*) allows of being brought within the embrace of a concept, or, therefore, of being definitely formulated in language' (A 193, ibid. 178).

84 Frege states axiomatically that it is the search and the desire for truth that makes us pass from sense to denotation, in accordance with a 'design implied in speech and thought' (see above, Study 7, 218). Reality figures in Benveniste's semantics as a 'discourse situation,' as 'a series of circumstances unique in each case,' and finally as a 'particular object to which the word corresponds in concrete circumstances or in usage' ('La forme et le sens' 36-7). In the case of John Searle, it is the function of singularizing identification belonging to propositions that postulates the existence of something (above, Study 7, section 1, 219).

85 This thesis should not be confused with Whorf's interpretation: to say that language gives form simultaneously to the world, to the interchange between men and to man himself does not attribute this formative power to the lexical or grammatical structure of language; it says, rather, that man and the world are fashioned by the totality of the *things said* in a language, by poetry as well as by ordinary language and by science.

86 For Jakobson, the meta-linguistic function is one of the dimensions of the communicative relation, together with the other five – emotive, conative, phatic, referential poetic. The meta-linguistic function consists in the relation not to a referent, but to the codes immanent to the structure of a language; it is expressed, for example, in the definitions in the form of equations by which one element of a code is related to other elements of the same code (cf. above, Study 7, section 2).

87 Cf. above, Study 7, section 2.

88 Ibid., section 4

89 Cf. ibid., section 3.

90 Ibid., section 2

91 The Heideggerian tone of these remarks is undeniable; the opposition between truth-as-manifestation and truth-as-agreement, familiar to us since the exposition in *Sein und Zeit*, is easily recognized here. Nevertheless, I am postponing taking a firm position in regard to Heideggerian thought as a whole until such time as my own analysis has reached a more advanced critical state, namely, when it is no longer possible to evoke the 'early' Heidegger without forming an opinion in regard to 'late' Heidegger.

92 Concerning the word *being*, *Metaphysics* Δ 7 (1017 a 35-b 9) stresses that the distinction between potency and actuality holds throughout the series of categories (not only substance can be actually and potentially, but also quality, state, and so on). The distinction is thus a second-order ontological-transcendental distinction since it duplicates categorial analysis. In *Die Entelechie* 141-70 Uwe Arnold strongly emphasizes the very radical nature of the theory of entelechy as it relates to categorial analysis: 'The enunciative sense (*Aussagensinn*) of being, *ousia*, is implied in the determinations of possibility, energy, and entelechy, even before it is directly determined by the categories. Existence, possibility, energy, and entelechy are concepts that necessarily apply to everything that is categorially real, yet can add nothing at all to the empirical concept; they are transcendentally presupposed concepts; they mediate the actualizability of every natural potentiality, to the extent that they do not concern objects immediately, but, in a mediate fashion, concern the sense of immediateness that belongs to objects. It is this presuppositional meaning (*Voraussetzungssinn*) that forms the basis for the systematic character of Aristotelian philosophy' (142-3).

93 As quoted already from the *Poetics*, tragedy imitates life in that the tragedians 'present their personages as acting (*hôs prattontas*) and doing (*energountas*)' (*Poetics* 1448 a 28). In Aristotle, the transition between *praxis* and *energeia* is

made possible by a hinge-concept – *ergon* – with a dual function: in ethics, it designates the unique 'function' of man as such underlying the diversity of his acquired knowledge and abilities (*Nichomachean Ethics* 1: 6); in ontology, it is taken to be synonymous with entelechy. *Metaphysics* Θ 1 says: 'And since "being" is in one way divided into individual thing, quality and quantity, and is in another way distinguished in respect of potency and complete reality, and of function ...' (1045 b 33). And further on (Θ 8): 'For the action is the end, and the actuality is the action. And so even the *word* "actuality" is derived from "action" and points to the complete reality (*entelechy*)' (1050 a 22).

94 *Metaphysics* Δ 12 and Θ 1-5 define 'potency' in the strict sense of the word, that is as potency 'in relation to movement': it is a principle of change that is in something other than the thing changed or in that same thing *qua* other. But potency in the broad sense of being able to be (Θ 6-8) is simply a correlative: potency refers to actuality as the power to be refers to being; actuality is even said to be 'prior to potency' (Θ 8). What we think, then, is simply the difference between actuality and potency: 'Actuality, then, is the existence of a thing, not in the way which we express by "potentially" ... The thing that stands in contrast to each of these exists actually' (Θ 6, 1048 a 31-5).

95 The definition is inductive; it is based on particular examples ('We say that potentially, for example, a statue of Hermes is in the block of wood ...'). It is analogical; here we cannot define by genus and specific difference: 'But be content to grasp the analogy: that it is as that which is building is to that which is capable of building, and the waking to the sleeping, and that which is seeing to that which has its eyes shut but has sight' (Θ 6, 1048 a 37-b 3).

96 In the first section of *Metaphysics* Θ (§1-5), potency 'strictly speaking' is defined 'in relation to movement'; the question then has to do with how it becomes actual, according to whether it concerns an artificial, natural or rational being (Θ 2 and 5). In the second section (§6-7), potency is taken in a broader sense, corresponding to the scope of the concept of actuality which itself is defined, as we have seen, by induction and by analogy: 'And I mean by potency not only that definite kind which is said to be a principle of change in another thing or in the thing itself regarded as other, but in general every principle of movement or of rest' (1049 b 7-9). Actuality is the correlative of this sort of potency; it is in relation to this potency that actuality is prior with respect to definition, time, and substantiality (Θ 8). On this discussion, cf. V. Décarie *L'Objet de la métaphysique selon Aristote* 157-61.

97 In this sense movement is actuality – 'actuality of what is potentially' the *Physics* states; and the text quoted above from the *Rhetoric* (1412 a 10) calls this to mind. In *Metaphysics* Θ, movement and actuality are also related notions: 'for actuality in the strict sense is thought to be identical with movement' (Θ 3, 1047 a 32-3). The distinction between *praxis* and *poiēsis* tends, however, to separate them: immanent action (*praxis*) which has its own exercise for end, is alone truly actuality; transitive action (*poiēsis*), which reaches its end in the thing produced externally, is only movement (Θ 6).

98 In *Metaphysics* Δ 4, at the term *phusis*, we read: '"Nature" means: (1) the genesis of growing things ... (2) that immanent part of a growing thing, from which its growth first proceeds, (3) the source from which the primary movement in each natural object is present in it in virtue of its own essence ... From what has been said, then, it is plain that nature in the primary and strict sense is the essence of things which have in themselves, as such, a source of movement' (Δ 4, 1014 b 16-1015 a 15).

99 Heidegger *On the Way to Language* 99-100; cf. above, section 3.
100 O. Pöggeler *Der Denkweg Martin Heideggers*, O. Laffoucrière *Le Destin de la pensée et la 'mort de Dieu' selon Heidegger* 1-40, L.B. Puntel *Analogie und Geschichtlichkeit*
101 These expressions are taken from S. Breton *Du Principe* 137.
102 'Every thinker thinks one only thought ... The thinker needs one thought only. And for the thinker the difficulty is to hold fast to this one only thought as the one and only thing he must think; to think this One as the Same; and to tell of this Same in the fitting manner' (*What is Called Thinking?* 50). J. Greisch, who quotes this text, makes the following comment: 'To question Heidegger's thought in a thoughtful manner is to question oneself first in regard to this "Same" which keeps it going' ('Identité et différence dans la pensée de Martin Heidegger. Le chemin de l'*Ereignis*' 73).
103 Greisch 'Les mots et les roses': '*Ereignis* would be the ultimate recourse guaranteeing thought of metaphor in Heidegger, and consequently the survival of philosophical discourse itself' (449).
104 Heidegger 'The Thinker as Poet' in *Poetry, Language, Thought*. We shall pause at these aphorisms: 'The poetic character of thinking is still veiled over. – Where it shows itself, it is for a long time like the utopism of a half-poetic intellect. – But poetry that thinks is in truth the topology of Being. – This topology tells Being the whereabouts of its actual presence (*die Ortschaft seines Wesen*)' (12).
105 Heidegger *What is Called Thinking?* 71, *On the Way to Language* 192
106 Greisch 'Identité et différence' 83
107 The current tendency to include all of Western thought inside the great catch-all of 'representation' invites the same criticism. Those who do so forget that in philosophy the same words continually reappear with a new meaning formed by the constellation of other senses in a given context. On this point, I cannot agree with Jean Greisch when he sees in 'representative thought' 'the single look cast at being.' This is, he holds, 'the basic determination underlying all the historical realizations of this thought' (ibid. 84). Yet the same author writes: 'The *Ereignis* confronts us immediately with the perpetual torment of thought, which is the problem of its relation to being' (77). Does not Heidegger himself say with respect to *Ereignis* that, if it is what is Unheard in thought, it is also 'the oldest of the old in Western thought' (*On Time and Being* 24)?
108 G.W.H. Hegel *The Phenomenology of Mind* preface iv. Must we hold Hegel to task for having exalted the subject by writing 'truth is the subject'? This subject is not the pretentious and solitary self that Heidegger justly attacks. What applies to representation applies to the subject: there is no single philosophy of the subject, immobile and fixed behind us.
109 Martin Heidegger *What is Philosophy?* 95
110 The experience of belonging gives sustenance to modes of discourse other than poetic discourse. It precedes not only aesthetic consciousness and its judgment of taste, but historical consciousness and its critique of prejudices as well, along with all consciousness of language and its claim to master and manipulate signs. In this threefold division, we can see the three 'regions' of H.-G. Gadamer's hermeneutical philosophy in *Wahrheit und Methode*.
111 In 'The Task of Hermeneutics' and 'The Hermeneutical Function of Distanciation' I develop this dialectic of belonging and distanciation within the framework of German-language hermeneutics from Schleiermacher to Gadamer and in relation to the debate found in the latter, first with the abstract sciences and then

with the critical social sciences, mainly with ideology-critique. This last aspect
is the central concern of my essay 'Herméneutique et critique des idéologies.'
112 In 'What is a Text?' I show in what way the notion of 'text' includes the multiple modes of distanciation associated not only with writing, but with the
production of discourse as a work.

Works cited*

Aldrich, Virgil C. 'Pictorial Meaning, Picture-Thinking, and Wittgenstein's Theory of Aspects' *Mind* 67 (January 1958)
- 'Image-Mongering and Image-Management' *Philosophy and Phenomenological Research* 23 (September 1962)
Aristotle *The Basic Works of Aristotle* ed. and intro. Richard McKeon. New York, Random House 1941
- *The Rhetoric and the Poetics of Aristotle* intro. and notes Friedrich Solmsen. New York, Random House Modern Library 1954
- *Rhétorique* trans. J. Hardy. Paris, Editions des Belles Lettres 1932, 5th edition 1969
Arnold, Uwe *Die Entelechie* Vienna and Munich, Oldenbourg 1965
Aubenque, Pierre *Le Problème de l'être chez Aristote: Essai sur la problématique aristotélicienne* Paris, PUF 1962
Austin, John Langshaw *How to Do Things with Words* ed. J.O. Urmson. Oxford, Clarendon Press 1962
Bachelard, Gaston *The Poetics of Reverie* trans. Daniel Russell. New York, Orion 1969 (*La Poétique de la rêverie* Paris, PUF 1960)
- *The Poetics of Space* trans. Maria Jolas. Boston, Beacon 1969 (*La Poétique de l'espace* Paris, PUF 1957)
Bacon, Francis *Novum Organum* (1626) London, Routledge and Sons 1905
Bally, Charles *Traité de Stylistique française* Geneva-Paris, Georg et Klincksieck, 3rd edition 1951
- *Linguistique générale et linguistique française* Berne, A. Francke 1932, 4th edition 1965

* An extensive annotated bibliography of works on the subject of metaphor may be consulted in Warren A. Shibles *Metaphor: an Annotated Bibliography and History* Whitewater, Wisconsin, Language Press 1971

Barfield, Owen *Poetic Diction: A Study in Meaning* New York, McGraw-Hill 1928, 2nd edition 1964

Barthes, Roland 'L'ancienne rhétorique, aide-mémoire' *Communications* 16 (Paris, Éditions du Seuil 1970): 172-229

Beardsley, Monroe C. *Aesthetics* New York, Harcourt, Brace and World 1958

- 'Metaphor' in *Encyclopaedia of Philosophy* ed. Paul Edwards. New York, Macmillan 1967. 5: 284-9

- 'The Metaphorical Twist' *Philosophy and Phenomenological Research* 22 (March 1962): 293-307

Benveniste, Émile 'La forme et le sens dans le langage' *Le Langage: Actes du XIIIᵉ congrès des sociétés de philosophie de langue française* Neuchâtel, La Baconnière 1967, 27-40

- *Problems in General Linguistics* trans. Mary Elizabeth Meek. Coral Gables, Florida, University of Miami Press 1971 (*Problèmes de linguistique générale* Paris, Gallimard 1966)

Berggren, Douglas 'The Use and Abuse of Metaphor' *Review of Metaphysics* 16 2 (December 1962): 237-58; 3 (March 1963): 450-72

Bergson, Henri *Œuvres* Édition du centenaire. Paris, PUF 1970, 930-59

Black, Max *Models and Metaphors* Ithaca, Cornell University Press 1962

Bloomfield, Leonard *Language* New York, Holt, Rinehart and Winston 1933, 2nd edition 1964

Bréal, Michel *Essai de sémantique: Science des significations* Paris, Hachette 1897, 5th edition 1911

- 'Les lois intellectuelles du langage' *Annuaire de l'Association pour l'encouragement des études grecques en France* 1883

Breton, Stanislas *Du Principe* Paris, Bibl. des Sc. Rel. 1971

- 'Symbole, schéme, imagination: Essai sur l'œuvre de R. Giorgi' *Revue philosophique de Louvain* February 1972

Brunschwig, Jacques Introduction in Aristotle *Topiques, livres I à IV* Paris, Éditions des Belles Lettres 1967

Bruneau, Charles and Ferdinand Brunot *Précis de grammaire historique de la langue française* Paris, Masson 1937

Bühler, Karl *Sprachtheorie: die Darstellungsfunktion der Sprache* Jena, Gustav Fischer 1934

Burke, Kenneth *A Grammar of Motives* New Jersey, Prentice Hall 1945

Cassirer, Ernst *The Philosophy of Symbolic Forms* trans. R. Mannheim. New Haven and London, Yale University Press 1953 (*Philosophie der Symbolischen Formen* 3 vols. Darmstadt, Wissenschaftliche Buchgesellschaft 1924)

Cellier, Léon 'D'une rhétorique profonde: Baudelaire et l'oxymoron' *Cahiers internationaux de symbolisme* no. 8, 1965: 3-14

Chaignet, Anthelme Édouard *La Rhétorique et son histoire* Paris, E. Bouillon et E. Vieweg 1888

Chenu, Marie-Dominique *La Théologie au XIIe siècle* Paris, Vrin 1957

- *La Théologie comme science au XIIIe siècle* Paris, Vrin 1957

Chomsky, Noam *Syntactic Structures* The Hague, Mouton 1957

- *Aspects of the Theory of Syntax* Cambridge, MIT Press 1965

Cohen, Jean *Structure du langage poétique* Paris, Flammarion 1966

Cope, Edward Meredith *An Introduction to Aristotle's Rhetoric* London and Cambridge, Macmillan 1867

Cope, Edward Meredith and John Edwin Sandys *The Rhetoric of Aristotle with a Commentary* 3 vols. Cambridge, Cambridge University Press 1877; Hildesheim and New York, Georg Olms Verlag 1970

Crane, Ronald Salmon, ed. *Critics and Criticism: Essays in Method by a Group of the Chicago Critics* Chicago, University of Chicago Press 1952, 1970

Darmesteter, Arsène *La Vie des mots étudiés dans leurs significations* Paris, Delagrave 1887

Décarie, Vianney *L'Objet de la métaphysique selon Aristote* Montreal-Paris, Vrin 1961

De Lubac, Henri *Exégèse médiévale* Paris, Aubier 1964

De Raeymaeker, Louis 'L'analogie de l'être dans la perspective d'une philosophie thomiste' *L'Analogie, Revue internationale de philosophie* 87 (1969) 1: 89-106

Derrida, Jacques 'White Mythology' trans. F.C.T. Moore *New Literary History* 6 (1974) 1: 5-74 ('La mythologie blanche' in *Rhétorique et philosophie, Poétique* 5. Paris, Éditions du Seuil 1971)

Dilthey, Wilhelm 'Die Enstehung der Hermeneutik' (1900) *Gesammelte Schriften* Leipzig-Berlin, Teubner 1921-58, vol. 5

Dobson, John Frederic *The Greek Orators* New York, Freeport 1919, 1967

Dubois-Charlier, Françoise and Michel Galmiche 'La Sémantique générative' in *Langages* 27 (Paris, Didier-Larousse, September 1972)

Dufrenne, Mikel *The Phenomenology of Aesthetic Experience* trans. E.S. Carey *et al.* Evanston, Ill., Northwestern University Press 1973 (*Phénoménologie de l'expérience esthétique* Paris, PUF 1953)

Dumarsais, César *Des tropes ou des differents sens dans lesquels on peut prendre un même mot dans une même langue* Paris, Dabo-Butschert 1730, 1825

Düring, Ingemar *Aristoteles, Darstellung und Interpretation seines Denkens* Heidelberg, Carl Winter 1966

Durkheim, Émil and M. Mauss *Primitive Classification* trans. R. Needham. London, Cohen and West 1963 ('De quelques formes primitives de la classification: Contribution à l'étude des representations collectives' in *Année sociologique* Paris 1901-2)

Eberle, Rolf 'Models, Metaphors, and Formal Interpretations' appendix to Colin M. Turbayne *The Myth of Metaphor* University of South Carolina Press 1970

Else, Gerald F. *Aristotle's Poetics: The Argument* Cambridge, Mass., Harvard University Press 1963

Esnault, Gaston *L'Imagination populaire: métaphores occidentales* Paris, PUF 1925

Estève, Cl.-L. *Études philosophiques sur l'expression littéraire* Paris, Vrin 1938

Fabro, Cornelio *Participation et causalité selon S. Thomas d'Aquin* Louvain, Publications universitaires de Louvain 1961

Firth, John Rupert 'The Technique of Semantics' *Papers in Linguistics* (1934-51). Oxford University Press 1957 (originally in *Transactions of the Philological Society* 1935)

Fontanier, Pierre *Les Figures du discours* (1830) Paris, Flammarion 1968 (introduction by Gérard Genette 'La rhétorique des figures')

Frazer, Sir James *The Golden Bough* New York, Macmillan 1923

Frege, Gottlob 'On Sense and Reference' in *Philosophical Writings of Gottlob Frege* trans. Max Black and Peter Geach. Oxford, Blackwell 1952; also in *Readings in Philosophical Analysis* ed. H. Feigl and W. Sellars. New York, Appleton-Century-Crofts 1949 ('Über Sinn und Bedeutung' *Zeitschrift für Philosophie und philosophische Kritik* 100, 1892)

Freud, Sigmund *The Interpretation of Dreams* trans. James Strachey *Standard Edition* London, 1953 forward: vol. 4 and 5 (*Die Traumdeutung. Gesammelte Werke* Frankfurt, S. Fischer 1961, vol. 2 and 3)

Frye, Northrop *Anatomy of Criticism* Princeton University Press 1957

Gadamer, Hans-Georg *Truth and Method* translation ed. Garrett Barden and John Cumming. New York, Seabury Press 1975 (*Wahrheit und Methode* Tübingen, J.C.B. Mohr 1960, 3rd edition 1973)

Geach, Peter *Mental Acts* London, Routledge and Kegan Paul 1957

– *Logic Matters* Berkeley, University of California Press 1972

Geiger, Louis-Bertrand *La Participation dans la philosophie de S. Thomas d'Aquin* Paris, Vrin 1942, 2nd edition 1953

Genette, Gérard *Figures I* Paris, Éditions du Seuil 1966

– 'La rhétorique des figures' introduction to Pierre Fontanier *Les Figures du discours* Paris, Flammarion 1968

– 'La rhétorique restreinte' *Communications* 16. Paris, Éditions du Seuil 1970

Gilson, Étienne *The Christian Philosophy of St. Thomas Aquinas* trans.

L.K. Shook, CSB. New York, Random House 1956 (*Le Thomisme* Paris, Vrin, 6th edition 1965)

- *Being and Some Philosophers* Toronto, Pontifical Institute of Medieval Studies 1952 (*L'Être et l'Essence* Paris, Vrin 1948)

Godel, Robert *Les Sources manuscrites du Cours de linguistique générale de Ferdinand de Saussure* Geneva, Droz; Paris, Minard 1957

Golden, Leon 'Catharsis' *Transactions of the American Philosophical Association* 42 (1962): 51-60

Golden, Leon and O.B. Hardison *Aristotle's Poetics, a Translation and Commentary for Students of Literature* Englewood Cliffs, Prentice-Hall 1958

Gombocz, Zoltàn *Jelentéstan* Pécs 1926

Goodman, Nelson *Languages of Art, An Approach to a Theory of Symbols* Indianapolis, Bobbs-Merrill 1968

Granger, Gilles-Gaston *Essai d'une philosophie du style* Paris, A. Colin 1968

Greimas, Algirdas Julien *Sémantique structurale, Recherche de méthode* Paris, Larousse 1966

- *Du Sens. Essais sémiotiques* Paris, Éditions du Seuil 1970

Greisch, Jean 'Identité et différence dans la pensée de Martin Heidegger. Le chemin de l'*Ereignis*' in *Revue des sciences philosophiques et théologiques* 57: 1 (Paris, Vrin, January 1973): 71-111

- 'Les mots et les roses. La métaphore chez Martin Heidegger' in *Revue des sciences philosophiques et théologiques* 57: 3 (Paris, Vrin, July 1973): 443-56

Grice, Paul 'Meaning' *Philosophical Review* 1957

- 'Utterer's Meaning, Sentence-Meaning, and Word-Meaning' *Foundations of Language* August 1968

- 'Utterer's Meaning and Intentions' *Philosophical Review* 1969

Groupe μ (J. Dubois, F. Edeline, J.M. Klinkenberg, P. Minguet, F. Pire, H. Trinon, Centre d'études poétiques, Université de Liège) *Rhétorique générale* Paris, Larousse 1970

Gueroult, Martial 'Logique, argumentation et histoire de la philosophie chez Aristote' in *La Théorie de l'argumentation. Perspectives et applications* (essays in honour of Ch. Perelman) Louvain-Paris, Nauwelaerts 1963

Hardison, O.B. *See* Leon Golden

Hardy, J. notes in Aristotle *Rhetoric* trans. J. Hardy. Paris, Éditions des Belles Lettres 1932, 5th edition 1969

Harris, Zellig Sabbettai *Methods in Structural Linguistics* Chicago, University of Chicago Press 1951

Hegel, Georg Wilhelm Friedrich *The Phenomenology of Mind* trans. J.B. Baillie. New York, Macmillan, 2nd edition 1931

Heidegger, Martin *What is Philosophy?* trans. W. Kluback and J.T. Wilde. New Haven, College and University Press 1956 (*Was ist das – die Philosophie?* Pfullingen, Neske 1956, 3rd edition 1963)
- *Der Satz vom Grund* Pfullingen, Neske 1957
- *Being and Time* trans. John Macquarrie and Edward Robinson. New York and Evanston, Harper and Row 1962 (*Sein und Zeit* Tübingen, Niemeyer 1927, 10th edition 1963)
- *Was ist Metaphysik?* with 1949 introduction. Frankfurt, Klostermann, 9th edition 1965
- *What is Called Thinking?* trans. F.D. Wieck and J.G. Grey. New York, Harper and Row 1968 (*Was heisst Denken?* Tübingen, Niemeyer 1954, 3rd edition 1971)
- *On the Way to Language* trans. Peter D. Hertz. New York, Harper and Row 1971 (*Unterwegs zur Sprache* Pfullingen, Neske 1959)
- *Poetry, Language, Thought* trans. Albert Hofstader. New York, Harper and Row 1971 (*Aus der Erfahrung des Denkens* Pfullingen, Neske 1954)
- *On Time and Being* trans. Joan Stambaugh. New York, Harper and Row 1972 (*Zur Sache des Denkens* Tübingen, Niemeyer 1969)
Hempel, C.G. and P. Oppenheim 'The Logic of Explanation' in *Readings in the Philosophy of Science* ed. H. Feigl and M. Brodbeck. New York, Appleton-Century-Crofts 1953
Henle, Paul 'Metaphor' in *Language, Thought, and Culture* ed. Paul Henle. Ann Arbor, University of Michigan Press 1958
Henry, Albert *Métonymie et Métaphore* Paris, Klincksieck 1971
Herschberger, Ruth 'The Structure of Metaphor' *Kenyon Review* 5 (1943)
Hesse, Mary B. 'The Explanatory Function of Metaphor' appendix to *Models and Analogies in Science* University of Notre Dame Press 1966, 1970; originally in *Logic, Methodology and Philosophy of Science* ed. Y. Bar-Hillel. Amsterdam, North-Holland 1965
Hester, Marcus B. *The Meaning of Poetic Metaphor* The Hague, Mouton 1967
Hirsch, Eric Donald *Validity in Interpretation* New Haven and London, Yale University Press 1967, 1969
Hjelmslev, Louis *Prolegomena to a Theory of Language* 1943; English trans. University of Wisconsin Press 1961
- *Essais linguistiques* (*Travaux du Cercle linguistique de Copenhague, XII*) Copenhagen, Nordisk Sprog-og Kulturforlag 1959
Hospers, John *Meaning and Truth in the Arts* Chapel Hill, University of North Carolina Press 1948
Humboldt, Wilhelm von *Über die Verschiedenheit des menschlichen Sprachbaues und ihren Einfluss auf die geistige Entwicklung des Menschengeschlechts* 1836. Bonn. Dümmler 1960

Husserl, Edmund *Ideas I* trans. W.R. Boyce Gibson. London, Collier-Macmillan 1962 (*Ideen I* in *Husserliana III* The Hague, Nijhoff 1950, 'Nachwort zu den *Ideen I*' in *Husserliana V* 1952)
- *Logical Investigations* trans. J.N. Findlay. London, Routledge and Kegan Paul 1970 (*Logische Untersuchungen* Halle, Niemeyer 1913)
Jakobson, Roman 'Results of the Conference of Anthropologists and Linguists' in *Selected Writings. II: Word and Language* Paris-The Hague, Mouton 1971; originally in *Supplement to International Journal of American Linguists* 19/2 (1953)
- 'Closing Statements: Linguistics and Poetics' in *Style in Language* ed. T.A. Sebeok. Cambridge, MIT Press 1960
- 'Linguistics' in *Main Trends of Research in the Social and Human Sciences. I: The Social Sciences* The Hague-Paris, Mouton-UNESCO 1970
- 'Two Aspects of Language and Two Types of Aphasic Disorders' in *Selected Writings. II: Word and Language.* Paris-The Hague, Mouton 1971; originally in Jakobson and M. Halle *The Fundamentals of Language* The Hague, Mouton 1956
Kant, Immanuel *Critique of the Faculty of Judgment* trans. James Creed Meredith. Oxford, Clarendon Press 1952
- *Critique of Pure Reason* trans. Norman Kemp Smith. New York, St Martin's 1965
Kennedy, George Alexander *The Art of Persuasion in Greece* Princeton University Press 1963
Klubertanz, George Peter *St Thomas Aquinas on Analogy: A Textual Analysis and Systematic Synthesis* Chicago, Loyola University Press 1960
Kofman, Sarah *Nietszche et la métaphore* Paris, Payot 1972
Konrad, Hedwig *Etude sur la métaphore* Paris, Lavergne 1939; Vrin 1959
Ladrière, Jean 'Discours théologique et symbole' *Revue des sciences religieuses* 49, 1-2 (Strasbourg 1975): 116-41
Laffoucrière, Odette *Le Destin de la pensée et la 'Mort de Dieu' selon Heidegger* The Hague, Nijhoff 1967
Langer, Susanne K. *Philosophy in a New Key* New York, New American Library 1951
- *Feeling and Form: A Theory of Art* New York, Scribner's 1953
Le Guern, Michel *Sémantique de la métaphore et de la métonymie* Paris, Larousse 1973
Linsky, Leonard *Referring* London, Routledge and Kegan Paul 1967
Lossky, Vladimir 'Le rôle des analogies chez Denys le pseudo-Aréopagite' *Archives d'histoire doctrinale et littéraire du Moyen-Age* 1930, 279-309
Lucas, Donald William *Aristotle's Poetics* Greek text, introduction, commentary and appendices. Oxford, Clarendon Press 1968
Lyttkens, H. *The Analogy between God and the World. An Investigation*

of its Background and Interpretation of its Use by Thomas of Aquino
Uppsala, Almqvist and Wiksells 1952

Martinet, André *Éléments de linguistique générale* Paris, A. Colin 1961

– *A Functional View of Language* Oxford, Clarendon Press 1962

– 'Le mot' *Diogène* 51, Paris, Gallimard 1965

Marty, Anton *Untersuchungen zur Grundlegung der allgemeinen Grammatik und Sprachphilosophie* Halle, Niemeyer 1908

Matoré, Georges *La Méthode en lexicologie. Domaine française* Paris, Didier 1953

– *Le Vocabulaire et la société sous Louis-Philippe* 2nd ed. Geneva, Slatkine Reprints 1967

McCall, Marsh *Ancient Rhetorical Theories of Simile and Comparison* Cambridge, Mass., Harvard University Press 1969

McKeon, Richard 'Literary Criticism and the Concept of Imitation in Antiquity' *Modern Philology* August 1936; reprinted in *Critics and Criticism* (*see* R.S. Crane)

– 'Imitation and Poetry' in *Thought, Action and Passion* Chicago, University of Chicago Press 1954, 1968

Meillet, Antoine 'Comment les mots changent de sens' *Année Sociologique* 1905-1906; reprinted in *Linguistique historique et Linguistique générale* 2 vols. Paris, Champion 1921 and 1938

Minkowski, Eugène *Vers une cosmologie: Fragments philosophiques.* Paris, Aubier 1936

Montagnes, Bernard *La Doctrine de l'analogie de l'être d'après St Thomas d'Aquin* Louvain-Paris, Nauwelaerts 1963

Morier, Henri *Dictionnaire de poétique et de rhétorique* Paris, PUF 1961

Navarre, Octave *Essai sur la rhétorique grecque avant Aristote* Paris, Hachette 1900

Nietzsche, Friedrich 'Rhétorique et Langage' texts translated, edited and annotated by P. Lacoue-Labarthe and J.-L. Nancy *Poétique* 5, Éditions du Seuil 1971, 99-142

Nyrop, Kristoffer *Grammaire historique de la langue française* vol. 4: *Sémantique* Copenhagen, E. Bojeson 1913

Ogden, Charles Kay and Ivor Armstrong Richards *The Meaning of Meaning* London, Routledge and Kegan Paul 1923, 8th edition 1946

Osgood, Charles Egerton 'The Nature and Measurement of Meaning' *Psycholinguistic Bulletin* 49 (1952): 197-237

Osgood, Charles Egerton and Thomas A. Sebeok *Psycholinguistics: A Survey of Theory and Research Problems* Bloomington, Indiana University Press 1965

Peirce, Charles Sanders *Collected Papers* Cambridge, Mass., Harvard University Press 1931-58, vol. 2: *Elements of Logic*

Penido, M.T.L. *Le Rôle de l'analogie en théologie dogmatique* Paris, Vrin 1931

Pepper, Stephen C. *World Hypotheses* Berkeley, University of California Press 1942

Perelman, Ch. and L. Olbrechts-Tyteca *The New Rhetoric: A Treatise on Argumentation* trans. J. Wilkinson and P. Weaver. University of Notre Dame Press 1969 (*La Nouvelle Rhétorique: Traité de l'Argumentation* 2 vols. Paris, PUF 1958)

Plato *Collected Dialogues* ed. Edith Hamilton and Huntington Cairns. New York, Pantheon Books 1961

Pöggeler, Otto *Der Denkweg Martin Heideggers* Pfullingen, Neske 1963

Pottier, Bernard 'Vers une sémantique moderne' in *Travaux de linguistique et de littérature* Strasbourg, Centre de Philologie et de Littératures romanes de l'Université de Strasbourg 1964, 2, 1

– *Présentation de la linguistique: Fondements d'une théorie* Paris, Klincksieck 1967

Price, Henry Habberly *Thinking and Experience* London-New York, Hutchinson's University Library 1953, 2nd edition 1969

Prieto, L. and Ch. Muller *Statistique et Analyse linguistique* Strasbourg, Faculté des lettres et sciences humaines de Strasbourg 1966

Puntel, L.B. *Analogie und Geschichtlichkeit* vol. 1. Freiburg i. B., Herder 1969

Quintilian *De Institutione Oratoria Libri Duodecim* Leipzig 1798-1834

Richards, Ivor Armstrong *Principles of Literary Criticism* New York, Harcourt, Brace 1925

– *Coleridge on Imagination* London, Routledge and Kegan Paul 1934, 3rd edition 1962

– *The Philosophy of Rhetoric* Oxford University Press 1936, 1971

Ricoeur, Paul *Fallible Man* trans. Charles Kelbley. Chicago, Henry Regnery 1965 (*L'Homme faillible* Paris, Aubier 1960)

– 'Sens et signe' in *Encyclopaedia Universalis* Paris 1968

– *Freud and Philosophy: An Essay on Interpretation* trans. Denis Savage. New Haven and London, Yale University Press 1970 (*De L'interprétation: Essai sur Freud* Paris, Éditions du Seuil 1965)

– 'What is a Text? Explanation and Interpretation' in David Rasmussen *Mythic-Symbolic Language and Philosophical Anthropology* The Hague, Nijhoff 1971 ('Qu'est-ce qu'un texte?' in *Hermeneutik und Dialektik, Festschrift* in honour of H.-G. Gadamer. Tübingen, Mohr 1970, vol. 2, 181-200)

– 'Discours et Communication' in *La Communication, Actes du XVème Congrès des Sociétés de philosophie de langue française* Montreal, Éditions Montmorency 1973

- 'Herméneutique et critique des idéologies' in *Démythologisation et Idéologie* ed. Castelli. Paris, Aubier 1973
- 'The Task of Hermeneutics' and 'The Hermeneutical Function of Distanciation' trans. David Pellauer *Philosophy Today* 17 2/4 (1973): 112-41
- 'Parole et symbole' *Revue des sciences religieuses* 49, 1-2 (Strasbourg 1975): 142-61

Ross, William David *Aristotle* London, Methuen 1923, 1949

Roudet, Léonce 'Sur la classification psychologique des changements sémantiques' *Journal de psychologie* 18 (1921)

Russell, Bertrand 'On Denoting' (1905) in *Logic and Knowledge: Essays (1901-1950)* London, Allen and Unwin 1956

Ruwet, Nicolas 'Préface' to Roman Jakobson *Essais de linguistique générale* Paris, Éditions de Minuit 1963

Ruyer, Raymond 'L'expressivité' *Revue de métaphysique et de morale* 1954

Ryle, Gilbert *The Concept of Mind* London, Hutchinson 1949; Harmondsworth, Penguin 1963
- 'Ordinary Language' *The Philosophical Review* 62 (1953) also in *Philosophy and Ordinary Language* ed. C. Caton. Urbana, Ill., University of Illinois Press 1963

Sapir, Edward *Language: An Introduction into the Study of Speech* London 1921

Saussure, Ferdinand de *Course in General Linguistics* trans. Wade Baskin. New York Philosophical Library 1959; New York, McGraw-Hill 1966 (*Cours de linguistique générale* critical edition ed. Tullio de Mauro. Paris, Payot 1972)

Searle, John *Speech Acts* Cambridge University Press 1969

Shelley, Percy Bysshe 'Defence of Poetry' *The Complete Works of Percy B. Shelley* 10 vols. New York, Gordian Press 1965, vol. 7

Shibles, Warren A. *An Analysis of Metaphor* The Hague, Mouton 1971
- *Metaphor: an Annotated Bibliography and History* Whitewater, Wisconsin Language Press 1971

Stanford, William Bedell *Greek Metaphor: Studies in Theory and Practice* Oxford, Blackwell 1936

Stern, Gustaf *Meaning and Change of Meaning, with Special Reference to the English Language* Göteborgs Högskolas Årsskrift 1931, Indiana University Press 1968

Stevens, Wallace *The Collected Poems of Wallace Stevens* New York, Knopf 1955

Strawson, Peter Frederick 'On Referring' *Mind* 59 (1950)
- *Individuals: An Essay in Descriptive Metaphysics* London, Methuen 1959

- 'Intention and Convention in Speech Acts' *The Philosophical Review* 63 (1964)

Thomas Aquinas (Saint) *Commentaire au Livre des Sentences* Rome, Piana 1570

- *Summa Theologiae* in *Basic Writings of Saint Thomas Aquinas* ed. Anton C. Pegis, revised trans. New York, Random House 1945 (*Summa theologica* Rome Léonine

- *Lexicon of Saint Thomas Aquinas* R.J. Deferrari and McGuiness. Washington, Catholic University of America Press 1948

- *De Potentia (Quaestiones disputatae)* Turin, Pession 1949

- *De Principiis Naturae* Fribourg, Pauson 1950

- *Truth* trans. R.W. Mulligan, SJ. Chicago, Henry Regnery 1952 (*De Veritate* [*Quaestiones disputatae*] Turin, Spiazzi 1949)

- *Commentary on the Metaphysics of Aristotle* trans. John P. Rowan. Chicago, Henry Regnery 1961 (*In XII Libros Metaphysicorum expositio Liber IV* Turin, Cathala-Spiazzi 1950)

Todorov, Tzvetan *Littérature et Signification* Paris, Larousse 1967

Toulmin, Stephen Edelston *The Philosophy of Science: An Introduction* London-New York, Hutchinson's University Library 1953

Trier, Joseph *Der deutsche Wortschatz im Sinnbezirk des Verstandes: Die Geschichte eines sprachlichen Feldes, I: Von den Anfängen bis zum Beginn des 13 Jh.* Heidelberg 1931

- 'Deutsche Bedeutungsforschung' *Germanische Philologie: Ergebnisse und Aufgaben: Festschrift für O. Behaghel* Heidelberg 1934

- 'Das sprachliche Feld. Eine Auseinandersetzung' *Neue Jahrbücher für Wissenschaft und Jugendbildung* 10 (1934)

Turbayne, Colin Murray *The Myth of Metaphor* Yale University Press 1962; revised edition with appendix by R. Eberle, 'Models, Metaphors, and Formal Interpretations,' University of South Carolina Press 1970

Ullmann, Stephen *The Principles of Semantics* Glasgow, University Publications; Oxford, Blackwell 1951

- *Précis de Sémantique française* Berne, A. Francke 1952, 3rd edition 1965

- *Semantics: An Introduction to the Science of Meaning* Oxford, Blackwell 1962, 1967

Urban, Wilbur Marshall *Language and Reality* London, Allen and Unwin, New York, Macmillan 1931, 3rd edition 1961

Vinsauf, Geoffroy de *Poetria Nova* ed. E. Faral in *Les Arts poétiques des XIIe et XIIIe siècles* Paris, Champion 1958

Vuillemin, Jules *De la logique à la théologie: Cinq études sur Aristote* Paris, Flammarion 1967

Wellek, René and Austin Warren *Theory of Literature* New York, Harcourt, Brace and World 1949, 3rd edition 1956

Wheelwright, Philip *The Burning Fountain* revised edition Indiana Universit
Press 1968

– *Metaphor and Reality* Indiana University Press 1962, 1968

Whorf, Benjamin Lee *Collected Papers on Metalinguistics* Washington,
Foreign Service Institute, Dept. of State 1952

Wimsatt, W.K. with M. Beardsley *The Verbal Icon* University of Kentucky
Press 1954

Wittgenstein, Ludwig *Philosophical Investigations* trans. G.E.M. Anscombe.
Oxford, Blackwell 1953, 3rd edition 1968 (*Philosophische Untersuchunge*
Oxford, Blackwell 1953, 3rd edition 1968)

– *The Blue and Brown Books* New York, Harper 1958

– *Tractatus Logico-Philosophicus* trans. D.F. Pears and B.F. McGuiness.
London, Routledge and Kegan Paul 1961 (*Logisch-philosophische
Abhandlung* 1922)

Wolfson, Harry Austryn 'The Amphibolous Terms in Aristotle, Arabic
Philosophy and Maimonides' *Harvard Theological Review* 31 (1938):
151-73

Wundt, Wilhelm *Völkerpsychologie: Eine Untersuchung der Entwickelungs*
gesetze von Sprache, Mythos und Sitte 2 vols. Leipzig 1922

Index of authors

Aesop 329
Albert the Great 274, 359
Aldrich 212, 329
Alexander of Aphrodisias 358
Angelus Silesius 283
Archytas 27, 192
Aristotle 3, 6, 7, 9-43, 47-8, 52-3, 55-6,
  65-6, 77, 79, 86, 89, 92, 104, 119, 136,
  154, 174, 185, 188, 191-9, 202, 217,
  219, 226, 230, 237, 244-5, 248, 258,
  259-75, 288, 293, 295, 297, 307-9,
  323-34, 336, 339, 348-51, 354-7,
  359-60, 362, 364-5
Arnold 364
Aubenque 265-8, 330, 334, 356-7
Austin 14, 73, 90, 298, 321, 336
Averroes 359

Bachelard 214-15, 351
Bacon 253, 354
Bally 350
Balzac 9
Bar-Hillel 159
Barfield 214, 351, 354
Barthes 147, 323, 334
Baudelaire 120
Beardsley 4, 26, 90-9, 137, 139, 154,
  191, 194, 197, 208, 222, 235, 243,
  351
Benn 284
Benveniste 4, 62-76, 79, 92, 102, 129-30,
  157-8, 175-6, 180, 198, 217, 261-2,
  298, 335-6, 341-2, 351, 354, 364
Berggren 246, 254-5, 349, 352, 354, 363
Bergson 117, 147, 250, 341

Berkeley 336
Black 4, 6, 22, 66, 81, 83-90, 94-9, 131,
  133, 137, 168-9, 190-1, 193, 195, 197,
  208, 236, 240-4, 288, 328, 348, 352
Bloomfield 117, 127, 340
Boileau 63
Bourgeois 323
Bréal 103, 111, 114, 131, 338
Breton, André 82, 337
Breton, Stanislas 350, 366
Bruneau 136
Brunschwig 326-7, 330-1
Bühler 105-6
Bultmann 320
Burke, Edmund 167
Burke, Kenneth 348
Bywater 325

Cajetan 358, 360
Carnap 124, 159, 227, 355
Cassirer 105-7, 214, 231-2, 248, 339,
  354
Cellier 167, 346
Chaignet 323-4
Chaplin 178
Chenu 360-1
Chomsky 152, 344
Cicero 328
Claudel 349
Cohen 131, 136, 139-41, 149-57, 162,
  164, 166, 168-9, 183, 194, 204-5,
  227-8, 237, 338, 343, 346, 350, 352
Cope 323, 325, 328-9, 331-2
Corax 323-4
Corneille 63

Darmesteter 103, 338
Décarie 333, 355-6, 365
De Lubac 362
De Raeymaeker 360
Derrida 34, 259, 284-9, 293-4, 326, 332-3, 335, 338, 361, 363
Descartes 252-3, 289
Dilthey 220, 320
Diogenes Laeartius 323
Dionysius the Areopagite 274, 360
Dobson 324
Dubois-Charlier 344
Dufour 325
Dufrenne 227, 352
Duhem 241
Dumarsais 52, 63, 118, 137, 178, 343
Düring 331
Durkheim 107

Ebeling 320
Eliade 318
Else 332
Empedocles 10, 323
Entwistle 126
Esnault 118, 200-2, 341-2, 349-50
Estève 350
Euclid 242, 275
Evans 320

Fabro 359
Feuerbach 318
Fink 333
Firth 130, 340
Fontanier 4, 44, 48-65, 78, 80, 86, 88, 118, 120, 136, 138, 143, 145, 166-7, 174, 179-80, 199, 207, 288, 291, 294, 343-4, 347, 363
Frazer 178
Frege 73-4, 90, 92, 181-2, 217-20, 298, 336, 341, 351, 364
Freud 178, 285, 317-18, 347
Frye 148, 209-10, 225-7, 229, 245-6, 344, 351
Fuchs 320

Gadamer 22, 198, 319, 328, 350, 366
Galilei 277
Galmiche 344
Geach 336, 339
Geiger 359

Genette 9, 52-4, 136, 138-9, 141-2, 146-9, 155, 170, 323, 334, 341, 343-4
Geoffroy de Vinsauf 106, 108, 204, 339
Gilson 360
Giorgi 350
Godel 102, 337, 341
Goethe 308
Golden 37, 332-3
Gombocz 112, 117, 340-1
Goodman 6, 19, 59, 132, 196, 231-9, 244-5, 305, 335, 349, 352-3
Gorgias 33, 323
Granger 219, 351
Gray 340
Greimas 105, 135, 142, 161, 181-2, 185, 201, 343-5, 347, 350
Greisch 283, 362, 366
Grice 70, 335
Griffith 178
Groupe μ (Groupe de Liège) 134, 141-3, 157-72, 182, 228, 248, 338, 342, 345
Guéroult 330

Hamelin 260
Hardison 37, 332-3
Hardy 325, 332
Harris 111, 340
Hatzfeld 325
Hegel 260, 286, 289, 292-3, 310, 313, 362, 366
Heidegger 7, 34, 229, 259, 273, 280-5, 292, 294, 309-13, 315, 352, 358, 362, 364, 366
Hempel 242, 352
Henle 188-91, 193, 199, 207, 209, 348
Henry 201-6, 348-50, 352, 363
Heraclitus 251
Herrschberger 349
Hesse 240, 242, 245, 352
Hester 61, 207-14, 225, 231, 254, 335, 348, 351-2
Hilbert 242
Hirsch 94, 328
Hjelmslev 112, 158
Hölderlin 246, 284, 310
Homer 19, 25-6, 34-5
Hopkins 214
Hospers 211, 351
Hugo 153, 202, 339
Humboldt, von 63, 304

Hume 189, 277
Husserl 74, 105, 129, 209, 225, 280, 301-2, 315-16, 336, 339, 342, 362-3

Ihde 323

Jaeger 267
Jakobson 5-6, 17, 76, 117, 121, 130, 144-6, 161, 164, 174-85, 191, 198, 209, 222-4, 226, 228-9, 256, 336, 340-5, 347, 351, 364
James 81
Jaspers 315-16
Jeremias 321
John, Saint 308
John of St Thomas 360
Johnson 338
Jung 244

Kafka 84
Kant 30, 189, 199, 208, 211, 258, 260, 262, 266, 273, 277, 292, 303-4, 358, 363
Keats 189, 348-9
Kelvin 241
Kennedy 323
Kierkegaard 312
Klubertanz 358
Kofman 362
Konrad 104-10, 201-2, 204, 338, 350

Lacoue-Labarthe 362
Ladrière 292-9, 302, 363
Laffoucrière 366
Langer 209, 227, 351-2
Le Guern 104, 157, 180-7, 199, 202, 207, 228, 290-1, 328, 338, 343, 345-9, 351-2, 362
Leibniz 65
Leptines 329
Levi-Strauss 319
Lewin 244
Licymnius 331
Linsky 335-6
Lossky 360
Lucas 325, 332
Lyttkens 359

McCall 324, 328-30, 347
Macquarrie 320

McKeon 37, 332
Mallarmé 149, 152-3, 169
Marcel 315-16
Marmontel 60
Martinet 340
Marty 111-12
Marx 285, 318
Matore 340
Mauss 107
Maxwell 241
Meillet 108, 111, 340, 342
Minkowski 351
Montagnes 358-61
Morier 335
Muller 343

Nancy 362
Navarre 323
Newton 253
Nietzsche 10, 280, 285-6, 312, 318, 362
Nyrop 111, 340

Parmenides 262
Pascal 343, 356
Paul, Saint 358
Péguy 114, 185
Peirce 34, 180, 189-90, 225, 231, 240
Penides 360
Pepper 244, 352
Perelman 336
Pericles 329
Perrin 321
Plato 11, 34, 37, 42, 45, 70, 152, 253, 261, 267, 286, 289, 292-3, 310, 323-4, 331, 333, 335, 344
Pöggeler 366
Pope 224
Pottier 201, 350
Price 363
Prieto 135, 343
Protagoras 73
Pseudo-Dionysius see Dionysius the Areopagite
Puntel 366

Quintilian 25, 328

Racine 60
Rad 320
Rasmussen 323

Renouvier 260
Reverdy 348
Richards 4, 24, 44, 57, 76-87, 93, 95, 99, 112, 119, 188, 193, 207-8, 211, 235, 249, 298, 328, 335-7, 340, 354
Ricoeur 220, 323, 336, 347, 354
Riffaterre 203
Rimbaud 171, 185
Roberts 329
Ross 325, 332, 357
Rostagni 326
Roudet 117, 341
Russell 71-2, 235, 335, 355
Ruwet 347
Ruyer 228, 352
Ryle 21, 89, 128, 170, 197, 235, 252, 328, 342, 349

Saint-John Perse 203, 350
Sapir 342
de Saussure 69-70, 102-4, 110-12, 115-18, 120-32, 134-5, 144, 175-6, 178, 185, 285, 338, 341-2
Schelling 249-50
Schleiermacher 220, 366
Searle 219, 297-8, 335-6, 364
Shakespeare 211
Shelley 80
Shibles 369
Sidney 226
Socrates 323
Spinoza 252
Stanford 203, 352
Stern 103, 111, 340
Stevens 99
Strawson 70-2, 130, 218, 297-8, 335-6, 339, 342, 351

Taylor 337

Theodorus 330
Thomas Aquinas, Saint 258, 273-80, 358-62
Tisias 323-4
Todorov 140, 145, 149, 227-8, 343-4, 352
Toulmin 241, 243, 352
Trier 103, 126, 135, 338, 340
Troubetzkoy 112, 135
Turbayne 89, 171, 197, 235, 251-4, 306, 337, 349, 363

Ullmann 5, 111-32, 338, 340
Urban 340
Uspenski 178

Valéry 136, 150, 224, 348
Verlaine 153
Vigny 153
Vuillemin 262, 265, 354-5, 357, 360

Warren 210, 351
Wartelle 325
Wellek 210, 351
Whateley 76
Wheelwright 83, 195, 251, 254-5, 306, 349, 352, 354
Whitehead 78
Whorf 364
Wimsatt 209-10, 351
Winckler 106
Wittgenstein 6, 61, 79, 113, 124, 128-9, 209-12, 218, 235, 258, 295, 313, 321, 336, 340, 342, 351, 355
Wolfson 358
Wordsworth 341
Wundt 106, 111, 117, 341

Via 321